# THE SUBJECT
## IN QUESTION

# THE SUBJECT IN QUESTION

## THE LANGUAGES OF THEORY AND THE STRATEGIES OF FICTION

# DAVID CARROLL

THE UNIVERSITY OF CHICAGO PRESS

CHICAGO AND LONDON

David Carroll is associate professor in the Department of French and Italian at the University of California, Irvine.

The University of Chicago Press, Chicago 60637
The University of Chicago Press, Ltd., London
© 1982 by The University of Chicago
All rights reserved. Published 1982
Printed in the United States of America
89 88 87 86 85 84 83 82    5 4 3 2 1

Library of Congress Cataloging in Publication Data

Carroll, David, 1944–
    The subject in question.

    Includes bibliographical references and index.
    1. Fiction.    2. Criticism.    3. Simon, Claude—
Criticism and interpretation.    I. Title.
PN3335.C3        801'.953        82-1995
ISBN 0-226-09493-6            AACR2

# CONTENTS

# ACKNOWLEDGMENTS

I want to thank Richard Regosin, Frank Lentricchia, and Suzanne Gearhart for their careful readings of this manuscript; and I am especially grateful for their critical comments which enabled me to question, rethink, and eventually rewrite various parts of the text.

Parts of the book have previously appeared in print: chapter 2 appeared in a slightly shorter form, under the title "For Example: Psychoanalysis and Fiction or the Conflict of Generation(s)," in *Sub-Stance*, no 21 (1978); a shorter version of the first two sections of chapter 4 was published in *Yale French Studies*, no. 59 (1980); and chapter 6 was first published in a slightly different form, under the title "Diachrony and Synchrony in *Histoire*," in *MLN* 92, no. 4 (1977).

I have used English editions of all the texts cited whenever possible. When the reference is to a French edition, the translation is my own. I have also found it necessary, however, to modify many of the published translations used; but it is only in those cases when I felt that the changes I introduced have substantially transformed the translations that I have indicated that the translation has been modified; i.e. when I had to add key concepts or even whole phrases that the translator had distorted beyond recognition or simply suppressed, or when a serious mistake in translation had been made. For the many translations that have only been slightly modified, no indication is given.

# INTRODUCTION
# Between
# Theory and
# Fiction

Critical theory has probably never been as alive as it is in the United States today. Programs in theory are being organized at American universities at an ever increasing rate, and colloquia devoted to theoretical issues are more and more frequent. Few major programs in literature would dare to be without at least some courses in theory, and only the rare candidate for a position in literature at a major university would want to admit to being ignorant of the major currents of contemporary critical theory—even if being "too theoretical" could harm the candidate's chances at many institutions still resisting the "invasion" of theory. But can such a phenomenon be rightly described as an invasion? Is theory an alien outsider threatening the integrity of literature? Does literature constitute a distinct, autonomous field? This book answers such questions in the negative and analyzes why the differences between theory and fiction are poorly accounted for when they are formulated in terms of a simple opposition between two distinct entities.

Even when the purpose of courses in literature or theory is to protect literature from such an invasion and to propose an authentic theory of literature originating from within literature itself—as is still very often the case—it is necessary to move outside of literature or at least away from the strict reading of literary texts themselves and into philosophy, history, psychoanalysis, linguistics, and other fields in order to undermine the pertinency of these fields and get back to literature and "true textual analysis." This detour is highly significant and reveals at the very least the inevitability of theory, the way in which the concept of "literature in itself" is itself theoretical in at least two senses: (1) it is a position of long standing within the history of theory; and (2) in defining itself or even in producing "literary" figures of itself, literature is performing a theoretical function. There is no textual reading, no matter how close to the text it stays, which is not implicated in problems of theory. The age of innocence of literature is (once again) past—the resistance to theory indicates that another such age may be on its way in or, at the very least, that the return of such an age is desired.

Whatever the dangers of abstract theorizing may be, should we really bemoan the loss of such innocence or nostalgically long for the mythical time before theory, when the reading of literary texts was supposedly purer, more literary, free of philosophical argumentation and theoretical jargon? Innocence may simply be a form of theoretical naiveté—the desire for which, even when resisted, is probably never completely overcome—but it is not in this instance at least (and most likely never) a disinterested naiveté, one which is truly innocent. The refusal—or inability—to question the interests implied in a position cannot represent a defense of the position. In the case of formalism, the implication of the forces, arguments, and "jargon" which constitute a so-called strictly literary position or reading of a text is that literature constitutes a closed field, that literary discourse is unique and therefore privileged, that it possesses a truth or complexity other discourses lack. Moreover, the argument for the specificity of literature is far from being empirical, for it depends on a specific theoretical tradition for support and borrows its categories and strategies from aesthetics, rhetoric, linguistics—i.e. philosophy—as it denounces the invasion of theory into literary studies. The formalist or aestheticist argument against theory is thus a theoretical argument—it is not just one theory of literature among others but the dominant literary ideology.

And yet the resistance to theory is not always naive, not completely nostalgic, misguided, or simply reactive. Theory presents some dangers; it too encourages a form of motivated naiveté concerning its interests and limitations. Were theory to become totally imperialistic and to dominate the study of literature, were departments of literature to become departments of theory which simply used literature to provide theory with its examples—as some fear is already happening—or, just as bad, were programs in theory to split off from programs in literature and function in isolation from (or even opposition to) them, then theory should be resisted, its abstract, speculative tendencies challenged not in the name of some literary ideality but in terms of the historical implications of its own terminology, rhetoric, and logic. For what would it mean "to do theory" or "to do literature" by itself? Is either ever a pure activity even in the most extreme cases when the autonomy of either field is assumed or proclaimed, when the "doing" explicitly attempts to be singular and to have a precise object on which to operate? Does theory ever really separate itself from the examples which form it as much as they are formed by it? Does literature ever really exist as an autonomous object in itself outside of theory, before theory, or at the origin of theory? The position *between theory and fiction* I am attempting to articulate here results from the impossibility of answering these questions affirmatively.

Rather than place theory and literature (in this case theory and fiction) against each other in a sterile opposition, in this book I use fiction strategically to indicate the limitations of theory and theory to indicate the limitations of fiction—each revealing the premises, interests, and implications of the other. Each is not so much opposed to the other as always-already implicated in the other. For to raise the question of the conflictual relationship between theory and fiction only in the form of a simple opposition is already to limit the question seriously and reduce the impact and force of each of its terms. As a starting point, I would claim only that we do not know exactly what theory is or what fiction is and that theories that take either as a given, that posit the field either constitutes as self-evident, closed or already defined, are limited by such assumptions. The conflict between theory and fiction is also within each. Each is itself divided, plural, conflictual; each is from the beginning penetrated by discourses, languages (jargons), oppositions, premises, and strategies which are not strictly speaking original to it and whose history and implications it cannot totally make its own. The *between* of "between theory and fiction," then, is as much inside theory as outside, as much inside fiction as outside. This book attempts to give neither a theoretical account of fiction nor a fictional account of theory (to make theory into a particular form of fiction); rather it analyzes the limitations of each strategy and suggests ways of exceeding these limitations.

The space between theory and fiction is not a space of compromise, synthesis, or transcendence; it is a space of conflict and contradiction. Neither is it the space where the common interests of theory and fiction can be isolated, a space where theory and fiction say the same thing about themselves and each other; nor is it a space which transcends the conflicts of interests and specificity of each in the name of a new theory or a new concept or practice of fiction. To master, encompass, and make sense of fiction has perhaps always been the goal of theory; but fiction, insomuch as it claims to be fundamentally literary, has a parallel goal: to resist theory, to inscribe theory within itself, to produce its own theory of itself and thus reduce the impact of all forms of speculative thought on it. One of my purposes is to analyze the contradictory premises governing theoretical, speculative strategies on the one hand and literary, poetic, figurative strategies on the other, as well as the effects of each on both theory and fiction.

Because the subject(s) in question in this book is/are dual and conflictual, the subject(s) of theory and fiction, each of the following chapters in its form and argumentation is also at least double. Each consists of a critical analysis of a different theoretical position which holds an important place in contemporary critical theory (structuralism, linguistics, Marxism, contemporary historiography, formalism, etc.) and a reading of one or more of the novels of the contemporary French novelist, Claude Simon. Even though there is a heavy emphasis on theoretical questions in each chapter, I have not written a book whose unique subject is critical theory, a book which would treat theory as a separate entity, a discipline unto itself. Rather than accept the limitations theory imposes on itself when it defines itself as an area cut off from all others, as an autonomous, self-sufficient, and self-generating discourse dominating from above its "objects" which it constitutes, situates, and defines, I have attempted in this book to situate my analyses *between* theory and one of these "objects"—fiction—and *in* neither one. This book is not, then, simply a reading of the novels of Claude Simon either, for the same things could be said about the limitations of fiction as were just said about theory, when fiction in its turn proposes itself as an autonomous, self-engendered artifact or object for which any "alien" theoretical discourse is by definition reductive, unable to capture its essence, the singularity of its discourse, the originality of its form. The subjects of theory and fiction are thus doubly in question, each in terms of itself and the other.

Concerning the choice of particular theoretical texts and of the novels of Claude Simon, it would be legitimate to ask why, in chapter 2, in order to pursue the question of the relationship between psychoanalysis and fiction, texts of

Sigmund Freud and Jacques Lacan were chosen rather than those of the other contending schools or readings of psychoanalysis; why, in chapter 4, to analyze the problem of representation within a certain Marxist-Hegelian tradition, texts of George Lukács were used and not those of some other Marxist theoretician. The same kind of question could be asked of my choice of Henry James or Claude Lévi-Strauss. There obviously would have been other ways to raise the question of representation and dialectics than through Lukács, other ways to challenge traditional Freudian readings of fiction than through Lacan; and these paths into the questions, I would insist, should also be followed. At the same time, my choice of these and the other theoretical texts treated was motivated by certain historical considerations concerning the place held by the particular text chosen in the tradition each represents: the role Lukács's work has played in determining the nature of dialectical approaches to fiction within the Marxist-Hegelian tradition; the importance of Lacan's radical reading of Freud in terms of any rethinking of psychoanalysis; Henry James's place in a certain formalist tradition emphasizing point of view, etc. In this sense, *being between* also means being between the specific texts chosen and the general tradition carried on and at the same time transformed by these texts. My analyses attempt to deal as much as possible with both aspects of each text treated.

To state the problem in a slightly different way and to choose a specific example, it would be fair to say that my analysis of Lukács treats only one current within the Marxist tradition, no matter how important this current has proved to be. I do not want in any way to give the impression that Marxism is itself closed and unified and that Lukács is representative of the whole tradition (even though Lukács's work often implies that this is so). On the contrary, Marxism is as divided by internal and external conflicts and contradictions as any other tradition, and it is precisely these contradictions that my analysis of Lukács emphasizes against his attempt to resolve them through a concept of representation conceived in dialectical terms. His assumption of a unique origin and his projection of a unified end onto history seriously limit his theory of history and the role of fiction in that history. I have expressly focused on the effects of these assumptions and projections in my reading, implying that other approaches to Marx are both possible and necessary. At the same time, my analysis of Lukács extends beyond him to the tradition of which his work is a part. Thus, at least some of the limitations of Lukács's works are those of the Marxist-Hegelian tradition in general, not present in all dialectical thinkers in the same way but, though most often unquestioned, present in some form nevertheless. I would make the same kind of argument for the other chapters as well—or rather I would hope that the chapters themselves all make this argument and indicate the relationship between the particular theoretical texts analyzed and the general theoretical problematic in question. The success of my analyses rests, I would think, at least in part on how convincingly this relationship is argued.

Why the novels of Claude Simon? By having chosen to focus my reading of fiction on his novels alone, have I not privileged his work and thus a certain form of fiction at the expense of all others? Here too there is no simple response, and I leave it to each chapter to justify the reading given to the particular novel or novels at issue and to articulate the relation of the novels (a relation which is in each case as much internal as external) to the theoretical problems raised. In the sense that the general problems of the relation of fiction to theory is one which I feel should be raised for all fiction and for all theory, Simon's novels hold no special privilege. But this is not to say that the particular form in which theoretical questions are raised in his fictions did not influence the way I came to analyze the various theoretical positions with which they are confronted. A book analyzing the novels of some other twentieth-century novelist (Joyce, Proust, Faulkner, or Beckett, for example) in connection with these same theoretical questions would be a very different book than the one I have written because the form of the analyses would be different and the form of the confrontation between the theories and fictions analyzed also different. It is important, therefore, that in each chapter the form and force of Simon's fictions be felt as well as the form and force of the theories with which they are brought in contact, or with which they bring themselves in contact—for neither fiction nor theory completely dominates or forms the other, neither is simply an example of the other. My claim for Simon's importance at the present historical conjuncture is simply this: his fictions are especially rich because of the intricate ways they raise, formulate, and confront questions of theory as part of their thematics and form. They are one of the places, though not the only one, where such a forceful confrontation occurs.

What stands out as a dominant motif in this book is the way in which the problem of history (the theory, writing, or "practice" of history) is raised in Simon's various novels in different forms. Chapters 4, 5, and 6 are directly concerned with the status of history in these novels, but this question can be found underlying all of my readings of his novels as well as my analyses of the various theoretical positions treated. My interest in Simon is largely due to the fact that in his novels he continually confronts and questions the problem of history (even in the novels' most "formalist" moments) in contrast to so many contemporary novelists and theoreticians who have ignored it. And need I add that history is ignored either when it is taken as a given, the simple, unquestioned ground for everything else, or when it is simply opposed, suppressed, or considered irrelevant? The rethinking and reformulation of history and historical discourse and methodology is one of the most pressing of contemporary theoretical problems, and I shall argue that one of the most powerful aspects of Simon's novels is the critical rethinking and reformulation of history they propose.

The first chapter of this book is the only one which does not include as part of its investigation of a theoretical problem an analysis of Simon's novels. It serves as a kind of "Theoretical Introduction" not because it describes and defends a particular theory which will be used in the course of the book to situate all other theories—this book proposes no metatheory—but rather because it introduces the problem to which I will repeatedly return throughout the book: the problem of the subject in its theoretical and fictional forms. The conflicts between theory and fiction are fundamentally conflicts among various concepts and figures of the subject—the subjects that various theories assume, construct, formulate, and/or defend (the philosophical, historical, psychoanalytical, linguistic subjects) and the subjects assumed and/or figured by fiction. To resolve once and for all the question of the subject would also be to resolve definitively the problem of the relationship between theory and fiction. It would be to decide in terms of what subject, what transcendent or empirical principle, such a resolution could or should be made. All theories and all fictions are tempted by such a resolution in terms of the subject they defend or even strive to be. By analyzing the status of the subject in the various theories and fictions treated in this book and confronting the various subjects with the contradictions, conflicts, or differences constituting them, it becomes apparent how such resolutions are strictly speaking impossible. Whether in a theory of the subject such as phenomenology, which seems to be secure in its knowledge of the subject and its ability to manipulate it, or in a theory situating, dismantling or even proclaiming the absence of the subject such as structuralism, the subject is in question. My analyses situate the different formulations or figures of the subject in critical theory, question them, and reveal the limitations inherent in each formulation. The question of the subject, I argue, is never resolved—it is never absent from the conflicts of theory and fiction.

Different chapters of this book analyze the theoretical positions of Henry James, Claude Lévi-Strauss, Georg Lukács, Emile Benveniste, Jacques Lacan, Michel Foucault, Roland Barthes, Gérard Genette, Jean Ricardou, and Fernand Braudel—in other words many of the major theoreticians who have influenced the way we deal today with problems of language, discourse, narration, textuality, and history, and thus the relationship between theory and fiction. And yet someone is missing from the above list whose work was especially influential in determining the critical strategy I use in the book and the kinds of questions I ask of theory and fiction: Jacques Derrida. Not that Derrida is missing from the book—if anything his work is in question in each chapter and not in one alone, present not as a metatheory, as a response to questions, but rather as a radical way of raising questions, a means of analyzing, displacing, and undermining the assumptions and limitations restricting the relationship between theory and fiction and determining the subject of each. This book, however, is not an attempt to imitate either the style or the content of the analyses Derrida has given to various literary and philosophical texts and to those falling between the two (perhaps in some way all texts); the critical dimension of his questioning would be lost in any such mimicry. Rather I have attempted in my own way in this book, starting from certain problems which Derrida's work has shown to be fundamental, and none more fundamental than that of the status of the subject, to pursue questions which his work has made it possible to pursue in a more radical way than before.

In spite of what is implied by the formation of a school of so-called deconstructive criticism, I would argue that Derrida's work offers no model for deconstructive criticism (if there is any clear sense of what that means) that can be

followed by disciples and applied to various texts in various traditions; if anything, it makes such models appear for what they are: products of a desire for mastery rooted in a conception of literature as an ideal form of discourse. This book is not "Derridean" in any simple sense (and certainly not in the above sense) and should not be read as such, even though it owes much to his work and stresses the importance of his readings of philosophy and literature for any critical strategy. In fact, one of the explicit purposes I had in writing this book in its present form was not only to confront and undermine the restrictions of the various theories of fiction which the following chapters discuss, but also to confront "Derrideanism" (especially in the form it has taken in the United States), to indicate that, in terms of the questions Derrida raises, other forms of analysis are possible than those claiming to be "deconstructive." Deconstructive criticism in the United States has usually meant an aestheticism, formalism, or "ultratextualism" (as I call it in chapter 7) that takes the literary text as having its end in itself, as having already deconstructed all theories attempting to invade its territory and account for it in terms other than its own. I indicate in the last chapter of the book that the various forms of ultratextualism—namely mechanistic, poststructuralist linguistic analysis, and deconstruction taken entirely as textual criticism in a very narrow sense—have the same limitations as other types of formalism and constitute forms of "textual dogmatism."

In intervening in the conflicts surrounding Derrida's work (as well as in the conflicts surrounding Lukács's, Lacan's, etc.) and in insisting on certain aspects of his readings which have been largely neglected or simply rejected—the historical implications of his analyses being for me the most important—I do not claim that mine is the one true reading of Derrida (or of the other theories or fictions analyzed), nor that I possess the true legacy of Derrida's teaching and thus have the legitimate right to use it against the illegitimate Derridean impostures. On the contrary, such problems of truth, legacy, legitimacy, and the schools of theory or criticism derived from them, even though all too common in all areas of theory (and nowhere more common than in the areas of psychoanalysis and Marxism), are not very interesting; except that is, for the political effects (effects of power) resulting from the desire to institutionalize the thought of some figure or other. These effects, no matter the figure being idealized or idolized, should of course be analyzed and combated. Schools tend to limit the possibilities even a radical critical strategy or position has opened up rather than pursue them; they establish an orthodoxy even when the concept of orthodoxy is argued against. That there are now many and conflicting readings of Derrida is not only an inevitable result of the fact that he is being read from many different perspectives, but a hopeful sign that perhaps some aspects of his work which were passed over too quickly in the first and largely literary reading of his texts will be brought to the surface, worked on, and debated. This book is a contribution to such a debate.

Differences of interpretation and position do not have to be repressed in the name of some sort of unanimity (fidelity to an ideal reading) for there to be serious and productive work done—nor do they necessarily have to lead to sterile and fruitless wars among schools or clans, each of which claims to possess the truth of the master. The differences of interpretation and perspective can (and should) themselves be productive. This does not mean, however, that the differences between positions are inconsequential and that all positions are equal and produce the same effects or that pluralism or undecidability can be taken as a solution to all theoretical differences (undecidability which in the uses it is put to by some "Derrideans" ends up being the same thing as pluralism, one of the terms to which it is opposed in Derrida's work). On the contrary, these differences produce different theoretical, ideological, and practical effects—they are not all of the same critical force. I hope that the readings I have given to different theoretical texts and to the novels of Claude Simon will be judged by their own effectiveness and critical force, but if a side effect of this book were to show that a critical strategy not connected to any school of deconstructive criticism could emerge from a reading of Derrida to challenge the premises, strategies, and effects of such a school, then this book will have served another important purpose.

*The Subject in Question* proposes different critical strategies for dealing with the various theoretical and fictional texts treated. It insistently questions and puts into question the subject(s) of theory and fiction in order to argue that neither theory nor fiction is an integral, self-sufficient, that is, ahistorical entity. In questioning the subject in this manner I attempt to take a critical position on the conflicts surrounding its place, status, and figure in theory and fiction, but I do not claim to have resolved any of these conflicts. Such a proposed resolution of conflict could only mean the end of critical investigation of the issues at stake in the conflicts—my purpose in this book is the opposite.

# O N E

## The Subject in Question: Phenomenology, Structuralism, and the New Novel

And even today the notion of a structure lacking any center represents the unthinkable itself.

Jacques Derrida, "Structure, Sign, and Play in the Discourse of the Human Sciences"

### Phenomenology and Fiction: The Subject as Origin

The novel is a burning, lyrical, embarked form of phenomenology!

Michél Deguy, "Claude Simon et la Représentation"

Robbe-Grillet's objects, they too are constructed simply to *be there*.

Roland Barthes, "Objective Literature"

One of the most basic and yet most difficult problems facing any form of history is the determination of its object, the delimitation of the field or space in which it operates. This is especially true of any history of literature, given the problematical nature of the "object," literature, and thus the arbitrary nature of any delimitation. Can any history of a literary genre, in this case, the novel, really limit itself to the analysis of only those texts that call themselves novels, or is it not inevitably obliged (perhaps in spite of its intentions) to confront those critical and theoretical texts intersecting with, generated out of, or even pretending to dominate from the outside the space of the novel? The limits or borders of texts, in spite of what most critics argue or assume, are hardly self-evident. Nor, for that matter, is the division of literary texts into different genres a neutral activity without historical and theoretical implications. If literature is not first postulated as being self-sufficient and autonomous, that is, if its specificity is not simply assumed, then the distinction often proposed between the "inside" constituted by the text (literature, fiction, poetry, etc.) and the "outside" constituted by theory (history, philosophy, sociology, etc.) can hardly be maintained as an absolute—in either direction, for the benefit of either literature or theory.

Were one to write a history of the New Novel, for instance, this history would not consist only of the explanation of the evolution of this particular form of the novel, or of a chronology of the novels themselves taken on their own terms. For the history of the New Novel is also the history of the various theories used to analyze and explain both the form and sense of the various New Novels—the theories which were applied to the New Novel, helped form it, and, in some sense, were transformed by it. In critically analyzing in this chapter first phenomenological and then structuralist approaches to the New Novel—the two approaches that have dominated the theory and criticism of the New Novel—my goal is to understand the implications of the transformation of both the novel and the theory of the novel in recent times. These implications are not only theoretical and determine how fiction is defined and read in general, but also formal, having to do with the way the novel is constructed or produced. For in spite of what is often argued, the question of form is always also a theoretical question; form is never totally "present" in itself without the intervention of some theory to make it "present."

When one studies the "evolution" (transformation) of the theory of the New Novel, two distinct and seemingly totally opposed phases become apparent. The first phase is that of a critical discourse dominated by phenomenological concerns: the novel is defined as the *expression* of an individual subject's total consciousness—and especially of his relation to a world of objects. Dreams, illusions, fantasies, and "true perception" are all considered to be elements of consciousness whose unique origin is a subject defined primarily as a viewer. The New Novel in this phase and according to these concerns can logically be considered to constitute a "new, subjective realism," that of an "école du regard." The second phase, which I will call structuralist, reacts violently against the first, denying the dominance of the subject and replacing perception and consciousness as constituting elements of the novel with language games, rhetorical devices, and logical functions. The concepts *récit* (narrative), fiction, discourse, text, etc., displace and replace the concept "subject" in the various approaches to the novel, and the slogan "antirepresentation" replaces the slogan "realism." A substantial evolution or, as many have argued, a revolution seems to have taken place in the theory of the novel. But rather than study only the nature of the differences between the two theoretical positions, as many others have already done, and thus support the thesis of a radical theoretical change, I intend to analyze the more obscure but more fundamental relationship between these seemingly diametrically opposed positions, and, more precisely, to examine their relation to the "object" (fiction) they pretend to talk about and to the concept of the "subject" they either affirm or negate as the center or origin of the novel. The structuralist transformation of the theory of the New Novel will in fact turn out to be much less radical in terms of the question of the subject than is usually assumed or argued.

Alain Robbe-Grillet quickly becomes the focal point of critical investigation of the novel in the late fifties and early sixties because of his defense and illustration of the New Novel, collected in *Pour un nouveau roman* (1963),[1] and his efforts to associate himself with others whose main theoretical purpose was to offer an alternative to the so-called "classical" or Balzacian novel. The terms of this defense, the concepts put into play by it, and the theoretical area his work delineates dominate, form, and limit the critical-theoretical discourse on the novel in the first phase. Certainly the essays of Roland Barthes from roughly the mid- to late fifties, but extending also into the sixties, should be placed within the same theoretical area: that formulated by a generalized and simplified phenomenology of perception. The dominance of phenomenology should hardly surprise anyone (even though it is often conveniently forgotten by structuralist critics today), given the importance of Sartre and Merleau-Ponty in French thought at the time. It is even less surprising when one considers that the most vital literary theory of that time doing critical battle with traditional historicist theory was centered around Poulet and what came to be known as the Geneva school: a school of consciousness. The first phase, however, is more than simply historical, for, as I will show, its premises and effects, as they are repeated and at work after the fact, are as much structural as historical.

Phenomenological theory defines the New Novel primarily as a *reduction* of the world to its supposedly basic, immediate, "material" existence: "But the world is neither significant nor absurd. It *is*, quite simply... Around us,... things *are there*" (*For a New Novel*, p. 19). Put between brackets and thus supposedly neutralized are all preexisting and thus "metaphysical" significations, whether they be psychological, historical, social, or political. These are to be replaced by a world which is "both more solid and more immediate... Gestures and objects will be *there* before being something" (p. 21). The novel is characterized as accomplishing a fundamental phenomenological goal: a neutral description of the world free of all presuppositions in order to guarantee the immediacy of the relationship between subject and object, self and other, consciousness and reality.

This explains the importance given to *description* in the New Novel and especially to the description of objects. Roland Barthes, in his essay on Robbe-Grillet entitled "Littérature objective"—published first in 1954 and republished in *Essais critiques* (*Critical Essays*, translated by Richard Howard; Evanston: Northwestern University Press, 1972)—emphasizes the fundamental role played by perception in the novels of Robbe-Grillet, the reduction of the world to the visual. He reverses the traditional sense of "objective," which implies a neutral, scientific perspective on the real, by making it refer only to a subjective relation to *objects* in preception: "Robbe-Grillet imposes a unique order of apprehension: the sense of sight. The object is no longer a center of correspondences, a welter of sensations and symbols: it is an optical resistance... Here the object does not exist beyond its phenomenon" (pp. 14–15). Barthes even assigns the novel a didactic role: "It teaches us to look at the world no longer with the eyes of a confessor, a physician, or of God... but with the eyes of a man walking in his city with no other horizon but the spectacle before him, no other power than that of his own eyes" (p. 24). Perception is valorized because it supposedly captures the outside world for a particular subject without transforming its "presence" or assigning to it an ideal, objective essence. The perceiving subject is one with the "presence" of the world in the present through perception, and the world is left intact, exactly as it was before it was perceived: "Let it be first of all by their *presence* that objects and gestures establish themselves, and let this presence continue to prevail over whatever explanatory theory that may try to enclose them in a system of references...and they will be there after-wards, hard, unalterable, eternally present, mocking their own 'meaning'" (*For a New Novel*, p. 21).

The "art" of the New Novelist, says Barthes, pushing Robbe-Grillet's state-ments even further, is not to signify, not to add anything to a world already too full of signification and whose history is a series of philosophical-ideological battles between different systems of signification, but rather to undo significa-tion—to designify we might say. "The author's entire art is to give the object a *Dasein*, a 'being there,' and to strip it of a 'being-something'" (p. 15). *To describe* is quite simply to see. It is not to impose another (metaphysical) sense on the world, but rather to be at one with the real sense of the world, its being-there. This theoretical position criticizes traditional approaches to the novel and their dependence on preexisting systems of sense, whether they be philosophical, historical, or political (viz. Robbe-Grillet's tirade against Sartre's concept of *engagement* and his attempt to neutralize all direct political implications of the novel), in order to attempt to replace them with a "true," subjective approach free of all presuppositions and thus, in its turn, neutral and truly "objective."

The "new" theory of the New Novel, however, rather than constituting a radical departure from the partisan, ideological nature of previous theories and a break with the "classical," metaphysical tradition supporting them, appears to most critics today to resemble the old in many ways, to reconstitute its meta-physics, and to participate in its ideology. A New New Novel and theory of the novel have even been proposed to replace the New Novel, which is no longer considered to be new enough. The theory of perception put forth in the first phase of the New Novel is certainly not without relation to the classical theory of perception underlying all realisms; but it is important also to remember that phenomenology and, insomuch as it attempts to locate itself within this theo-retical space, the New Novel both see themselves as constituting a critical, non-metaphysical approach to the world, one that undermines and pluralizes its preestablished Sense.

The problem of language is never posed by Barthes or Robbe-Grillet, nor, it would be safe to say, by any of the other critics of the New Novel at this time. Language, as such, is quite simply not a problem because it is modeled after perception and thus an effective means, when successfully manipulated—the "art" of the novelist is to teach us to see—of capturing the immediacy and presence of the world. Language *serves* perception by describing neutrally what is; it is the expression of the consciousness of a perceiving subject. When there is opposition between language and perception, as there is in the later work of Merleau-Ponty, who was one of the few major phenomenologists at this time to read seriously Saussure and Lévi-Strauss, perception is chosen over language as the authentic means of being in relation with the world. In other words, language must be equal to or an expression of perception or it cannot participate fully in the "authentic" realm of interpersonal communication and being-in-the-world.[2]

It is not surprising, therefore, that the defense of the New Novel formulated by Robbe-Grillet and supported by Barthes is made in the name of realism. Made not in the name of a universal (idealist) realism which takes the perspective of god or some other universal and assumes that the nature of man (and thus, the nature of the real) is given before the fact, but rather in the name of a *new* realism associated with a *new* concept of man ("New Novel, New Man," writes Robbe-Grillet). Robbe-Grillet formulates the simple, historicist argument that the novel must be of "its own time" and thus must break with the nineteenth-century concept of the novel. The times have changed (Robbe-Grillet leaves the analysis of these changes for the most part to others), and the novel must change with them in order to remain "realistic." This, Robbe-Grillet still claims, is its essence. The nineteenth-century novel (Balzac) is criticized not because it pretends to be realistic, but rather because that kind of realism is no longer adequate today. Objective realism must be replaced by "subjective" realism, says Robbe-Grillet: "The New Novel aims only at a total subjectivity" (*For a New Novel*, p. 138).

The "new realism" is subjective in that it is totally dependent on a subject—a subject who is the unique origin of the novel, origin of his perceptions, experiences, desires, and dreams, and ultimately origin of his own language—a man who narrates himself: "*a man* who sees, who feels, who imagines, a man located in space and time, conditioned by his passions, a man like you and me. And the book reports nothing but his experience, limited and uncertain as it is. He is a man of the here and now who is even his own narrator" (p. 139, translation modified). Robbe-Grillet's answer to those critics who denounced in his work the absence of "man" is to affirm his total presence. Objects exist and are presented in the novel totally in function with this subject-man: "Man is present on every page, in every line, in every word. Even if many objects are presented and are described with great care, there is always and especially the eye which sees them, the thought which reexamines them, the passion which distorts them. The objects in our novels never have a presence outside human perception, real or imaginary" (p. 137). For Robbe-Grillet there are no longer any grounds for deciding what is "objectively real" and what is not; in fact this question even seems without interest, an ideological remnant from another time. The differences between past and present, hallucination and perception, fact and fiction, the visual and the written, etc., are transcended in the consciousness of a living subject (a man of the "here and now") present to himself at all times. The present and presence of the subject are all-inclusive and original; his world organized around his perception of it is autonomous and closed. The novel, like the movie *Last Year at Marienbad*, constructs a "perpetual present... a world without a past, a world which is self-sufficient at every moment" (p. 152).

Structuralist critics today tend to look back at this period and the theory associated with it as a theoretical dark ages in comparison with our present "enlightenment"—our structuralist "science" as compared to their phenomenological "ideology." We supposedly know better than to argue on behalf of the subject today. And yet this attitude itself is no more than a valorization of the theoretical positions dominant today by a simple rejection of those of the past, especially the near past. The *positing* of the subject as center and origin of the novel did not necessarily and in all cases lead to a completely simplified reading of the novel (nor, certainly, to the production of simple, transparent novels), at least no more simple or complex in principle than other readings based on seemingly opposite premises. The concept of the subject does control, limit, and reduce the complex relations between theory and fiction and between history and the text by imposing an *origin* and *sense* on fiction. But the "instance of" or "insistence on" the subject can also produce a reformulation and re-thinking of this concept, and the theory associated with the first phase of the New Novel in some ways did bring about a "questioning of the subject"—at least up to a certain point. The phenomenological enclosure, if I can call it that, is a space, an economy, with specific limitations, like all theoretical spaces. It is nonetheless possible for a reading situated "within" it to do more than naively affirm its premises, apply its arguments, and accept the limitations which govern and close off the space. The "phenomenological phase" of the New Novel should in no way be seen as completely negative or completely reductionary in terms of the question of the subject. No theoretical problematic is ever as simple as that; no theory ever simply "left behind," negated or transcended by another. The "new" never leaves totally behind the "old," nor does it assume it entirely into itself—the movement from one theoretical position to another is at the same time one of conflict, omission, and retention, never the total opposition of one to the other nor the synthesis of one into the other.

### Structuralism and Fiction: the Negation, Displacement, and Return of the Subject

And so it is literally true that the basis of subjectivity is the exercise of language.
I am approaching this subject [subjectivity] evidently as a linguist and not as a philosopher.

Emile Benveniste,
*Problems in General Linguistics*

Chase away subjectivity, it returns at a gallop.

Georges Poulet, "Roland Barthes,"
*La Conscience critique*

Somewhere (in many places, here and there) within and/or between fiction and theory a problem emerged which appeared to put the phenomenological theoretical position entirely into question. A "theoretical break" occurred or rather recurred in many places and many times; and thus a *new* theoretical space was formed—an opening which resulted in a reformulation of the theoretical field and, of course, in new limitations. This theoretical "event," which is more than an event and which touches all the "human sciences," is usually called structuralism.[3] The problem structuralism raises, insists on, and in terms of which the various disciplines are now analyzed and reformulated is of course the problem of language. This interest in language as the fundamental element of all theory and as *the matter* of all texts has had various effects, but the one which interests me the most in this chapter is that which tends to situate the subject and thus undermine its originality and dominance.[4] The subject finds itself now within, not at the source of, language, a function determined by language and not an origin "outside" the textual-linguistic systems surrounding it. In Saussurian terms, the subject's discourse (*parole*) is only possible because of the preexistence of the code (*langue*) within which the subject must situate itself in order to speak or write. For Claude Lévi-Strauss in anthropology, Jacques Lacan in psychoanalysis, and Roland Barthes, Gérard Genette, and others in literary theory, the study of the code (signifier) now becomes the necessary task. Structuralism, or the "instance" or "insistence of the letter" in Lacan's phrase, will constitute the second theoretical phase of the New Novel.[5]

With structuralism, philosophy as such is no longer the explicit model for critical theory, for linguistics replaces it—at least on the surface. Finding his conceptions and his strategy in the work of Saussure, Jakobson, Benveniste, and Greimas, the structuralist critic will push the antimetaphysical stance of phenomenology one step further and reject philosophy itself for a discipline which studies *the matter* of literature: its language. The structuralist critic in his effort to be *for* language, *for* the "text," will be for the most part militantly anti-subject.[6] In fact the problem of the subject soon passes into obscurity, into a space radically outside that is no longer analyzed, no longer pertinent. The insistence on the subject and the whole problem of consciousness associated with it is considered by structuralists to have obscured, if not negated, the problem of language (the work of the signifier); and so now, through a reversal of the problematic, language negates, displaces, and replaces the subject as origin. The subject remains only as a skeleton of its former self, as a function of language.

The advantages of the Saussurian-Jakobsonian model are well known today and evident in such works as Barthes's *S/Z*, Gérard Genette's *Figures (I, II, III)*, and Jean Ricardou's various essays on the New Novel (*Problèmes du Nouveau Roman, Pour une théorie du Nouveau Roman, Le Nouveau Roman*).[7] Rarely, however, are the premises of the structuralist position studied in terms of their theoretical implications for the study of literature. This seems to be a necessary task in order to understand not only the positive aspects of structuralist theory but also its limitations, the theoretical enclosure it too has established. What a theory proscribes is just as important as what it effectively treats, especially in terms of the delimitation of the space it occupies and its relation to other theories and, of course, to fiction.

It is almost impossible to read any essay on the New Novel today without finding references to the work of Jean Ricardou. Of all the structuralist critics he has the most often and vehemently stated his opposition to any theory of the New Novel that is realistic or representational in nature, any theory based on mimetic premises that sees literature as an expression of an individual or collective subject. His objection is first of all theoretical, for he considers the concept of the subject and the theory of representation associated with it to obscure the "true nature" of the literary text and mask its complexity. But it is also political, for he claims that all representational theories of art serve the "ruling ideology" and thus the interests of the ruling class and the state apparatus. Many forms of traditional literary criticism are proscribed, for even the study of such themes and topics as Time (history), Space, and Character is suspect because it tends to reinforce the "realistic illusion" and thus be a product of "referential ideology" (*Le Nouveau Roman*, p. 138). Léon Roudiez, in fact, claims in a matter-of-fact way that Ricardou's concept of the text is completely "different from that of the ruling ideology," that it alone is the "true text" (Claude Simon: *Colloque de Cerisy*, p. 56). As opposed to the "ideological approaches" of others we have the "science of the true text" of Ricardou. The truth of philosophy, of representation, is chased away only to be replaced by the concept of the "true text," the text as a "formal truth." Ricardou and those who take his position are arguing that their theory bears no relation to traditional representational theories of the novel, that it is absolutely and essentially *new* and therefore, one has to conclude, a kind of "epistemological break" (in the Bachelardian sense), a new science.

Ricardou has at times more modestly acknowledged that no one, not even himself, escapes completely from the "ruling ideology" and that the real task is to attempt to undermine it from within (*Claude Simon*, p. 61); but for the most part he acts (by accusing others and quoting himself) as if he were *outside*, as if the concepts and strategy he uses are radically other, untouched by ideology. When he treats the New Novelists as a group rather than as a school, this is to "oppose the concept of expression of the ruling ideology" (*Le Nouveau Roman*, p. 136); and when accused at the Simon colloquium of trying to impose his version of ideology on those present, he answers: "In any case, what one could say in regard to this problem is that the propositions I have made are entirely allergic to what is still taught in general in the State Apparatus. Consequently, and until I am informed otherwise, I am obliged to say that I reject entirely the qualification imposed on my intervention" (*Claude Simon*, p. 32). Besides having a very simplistic view of ideology, Ricardou is blind to what is carried over from previous theories in his own approach: the dependence of his theoretical position on premises to which it is supposed to be "allergic." If this were Ricardou's problem alone, it would be of limited interest; but I would argue that Genette, Todorov, and other formalist-structuralist critics, though less inclined toward overt polemics than Ricardou, work according to similar assumptions: that a formalist-linguistic approach to literature avoids the philosophical and ideological implications of other approaches. The methodology and strategy of these structuralist critics are certainly different from those of phenomenological critics, and this is important, but what is at least of equal importance is that certain basic premises and concepts remain constant. The "revolutionary" aspects of structuralism become more and more problematical as they are analyzed more closely.

Ricardou attacks the "subject" of the "ruling ideology," "the subject, origin, and proprietor of a sense his text is supposed to express" (*Le Nouveau Roman*, p. 15)—i.e. the phenomenological subject. He objects to the question put to the author of a text in a traditional interview, "What do you mean (intend)?" because this gives the author-subject the right if not the obligation to "determine the meaning of his work." For Ricardou the writer-subject is expropriated by his writing, eccentric to himself: "deprived of self and meaning ... he is not at the center but at the borders of his text." He can read his "own" text only from a position of exteriority, from the position of the Other, as if it were written by another. "His text appears to him as something bizarre: something other" (p. 15). This doesn't tell us, however, how the text should be read, just that the author doesn't have the final word, doesn't possess its meaning as an extension of his own subjectivity. Its meaning lies elsewhere.

The "position of the Other" in the structuralist-formalist position refers to the code or signifying *system* preexisting any use of language. One is supposed to read according to certain formal rules of language, according to a certain strategy or logic even, to be determined from the place of the Other, and the study of rhetorical figures, puns, rhymes, and anagrams makes up the major part of Ricardou's version of structuralist-formalism. The place of the Other, this non-subject or antisubject (implicitly the "true" subject of science), consists of *the rules of the game*, the laws which govern the "generation" of a text and its "anti-representative operations." If fiction is "a machine which suppresses the guarantees of established meaning" (*Claude Simon*, p. 38), as Ricardou claims, not only does this general definition of fiction resemble curiously the phenomenological definition given by Robbe-Grillet, but it brings into the theoretical field the problem of how "the machine" is constructed. To analyze the construction of "the machine" and *how it produces*, not the sense of what it produces, is the task the structuralist critics give themselves.

"How did you work?" (*Le Nouveau Roman*, p. 9), is the question Ricardou opposes to the "ideological" question concerning sense. The question of how an author worked seems to remain for him a legitimate question, which might explain why he so frequently uses his own novels as examples of his theory, as examples of how *Fiction* in general is supposedly generated. But does not this question too imply a possible relationship between form and subjectivity—and, therefore, form and meaning—and reveal that by emphasizing the "originality" of language (form) one might not totally negate the subject (or by its negation not more strongly affirm it), that the rules of construction might not be without relation to the subject of meaning? What the subject knows here is the "truth" of form.[8] Is not Ricardou still relying on the subject's authority—whether the author-subject is same or other is not significant for the moment—as a way of fixing not the meaning of the work (its *vouloir-dire*) but its formal sense, the logic or schema of its construction? The subject is considered by Ricardou to be producer rather than original consciousness (in Poulet's sense, for example), but it still seems to be dominant, even if its dominance is not necessarily conscious or immediate but comes by way of the position of the Other and is situated in form. In spite of how hideous he finds this doctrine—the subject as source and ultimate sense of the text—Ricardou hasn't completely avoided reinforcing it.

Ricardou would answer that his analyses have only to do with the texts he studies, that he derives their form from them, not from their author. This, of course, is largely true, but the problem I am raising here has little to do with the conscious author-subject; even though it is implied in the question, "how did you work?" that this subject has some, if not all, of the answers to questions concerning form. The subject Ricardou reinforces is the "formal subject" of the text, the subject who is its center or organizing principle. The *locus* of this subject, for this subject is a locus, dominates Ricardou's (and other structuralists') analyses of fiction. This is the place where the subject who generates or produces form (the author or scriptor, as Ricardou calls him) and the subject who sees the "true form" and the way it functions (the formalist critic) meet and become one. There is no "science" no "true text" without this dual subject identical to itself: subject of production (writer or scriptor) and subject of consumption (reader). This identity is necessary to form insomuch as form is one. That each text has only one logic or principle of construction, as Ricardou's analyses seem to imply, is, however, highly problematical. In any case, the formal "sense" of a text is as dependent on a center or origin (i.e. on a subject) as meaning (in the phenomenological sense) is, if form and meaning are considered to be singular entities. Any formalization of literature assumes this singularity of form and thus centers and gives a sense to the texts it studies. The signifier simply becomes the signified, *the sense* of the text.[9]

It is true that Ricardou also argues that on all levels of the text there is conflict rather than unity or harmony: "The *récit* can no more claim to be rooted in solid ground than can fiction. It is the space of permanent conflict" (*Le Nouveau Roman*, p. 30). The conflict or instability at the heart of the text results from its being torn in two directions at once: toward a referential pole where its "materiality" as text would be negated and toward a pure "literality" where it would signify, represent, and say nothing. Even though he admits that it is illusory to reduce the text to either one of these poles ("referential illusion," "literal illusion"), Ricardou proceeds as if the first "illusion" were the only significant one. Thus, he tends to reduce the complexity of the text by transcending the "conflict" at its heart (its irreducibility to any "present," formal or otherwise) in the name of a coherent logic or formal schema. To chase away the "ideology of representation" only to replace it with what could be called an idealism of the signifier is in fact to remain within the same metaphysical enclosure. Representation, the text as the expression of a subject's relation to the real, and formalism, the text as an autonomous, closed, centered system, are two sides of the same coin.

I would argue that all formalisms, all structuralisms, that simply proscribe the question of the subject are still under its dominance; they still adhere to the premises and concepts associated with the subject. To bar the subject is to have it return in its most simple, and therefore dominant, form there where it is supposed to be absent or irrelevant. There is in fact still a subject in question in structuralism (in question but not questioned), and therefore it will be necessary to locate this subject and analyze its particular characteristics and the premises which support it. To do this it will be necessary to pass by way of Gérard Genette and then Emile Benveniste. Ricardou himself sends us to Genette's "Discours du Récit," in *Figures III* (Paris: Seuil, 1972)—translated by Jane E. Lewin as *Narrative Discourse* (Ithaca: Cornell University Press, 1980)—for the concepts and categories necessary for what is claimed to be a "nonideological," strictly formalist analysis of fiction, a starting point for any analysis which plans to treat the "signifier itself" and hopes to avoid reinforcing the "ideology of representation." Before Genette's analysis is followed, a general comment is needed. In both Genette and Ricardou (to mention the most obvious cases) a technical vocabulary is present which with every publication becomes more and more extensive and complex and in which the categories of analysis multiply at an amazing speed, as if sheer number alone would guarantee that all aspects of texts would be covered (in the figurative and literal sense). This "technicity" I shall study for itself as a general problem in chapter 7, but here I propose only to analyze what I would argue is the basis of their technical languages, the fundamental opposition out of which the other formalist oppositions and categories grow and on which they depend. This opposition is used not only by Genette and Ricardou but also by Barthes, Metz, Todorov, etc.[10]—one could say without exaggeration, by all contemporary structuralist critics of fiction—and therefore it can be considered basic to structuralism itself.

Genette begins by making a distinction between three different senses of the word *récit* (narrative):

> 1) the narrative statement (*énoncé*), the oral or written discourse that undertakes to tell of an event or a series of events...
> 2) the succession of real or fictitious events that constitutes the object of these discourses... "Analysis of the *récit*" in this sense means the study of a totality of actions and situations taken in themselves, without regard for the medium through which knowledge of that totality comes to us...
> 3) an event: not, however, the event that is recounted but that which consists of someone recounting something: the act of narration taken in itself.
> (*Narrative Discourse*, pp. 25–26, translation modified)

To avoid confusion he renames them in the following way. He retains the name *récit* (narrative) for the first, "the signifier, statement (*énoncé*), discourse or narrative text itself"; he calls the second *histoire* (story/history), "the signified or narrative content"; and he names the third *narration*, "the narrative, productive act and, by extension, the entire real or fictive situation in which it takes place" (p. 27, translation modified). Hidden, however, in this triparite division is a dualistic opposition which is its basis and on which Genette's analysis of the *récit* (the narrative-signifier) will depend. Todorov acknowledges this dual aspect, "the work has two aspects rather than only one" (*Communications*, no. 8, p. 127) as does Ricardou in his brief survey of contemporary theories of the *récit*: "What strikes one immediately, beyond the apparent differences of lexicon, is an agreement on the dual aspect of the *récit*" (*Le Nouveau Roman*, p. 27). In Genette's division, the third definition is already implicit in the second; for what ultimately distinguishes *histoire* from *récit*, the signified from the signifier (Saussure's definition of the sign is at work here, displaced, transformed, and active on another level), is the function that calls attention to the act of narration itself. *Histoire* is always in principle a pure abstraction, the referent or "events in themselves," while *récit* marks *the place* and *the time* of the narrator. Structuralist critics will posit *histoire* (the signified) as a simple chronology, an "illusion" against which the complexity of the *récit*-signifier will be highlighted. *Histoire* is the straw man of the opposition, and this is not without consequence for understanding the premises at work within the opposition and its limitations.

Theorists consistently have difficulty in keeping the two terms apart, for one is always sliding into the other: "It is true that it is not always easy to distinguish them ... *Histoire* is an abstraction because it is always perceived and recounted by someone; it does not exist 'in itself'" (Todorov, *Communications*, no. 8, p. 127). "They are almost never found in a pure state in any text" (Genette, *Communications*, no. 8, p. 161). Since both Genette and Todorov admit that there is always a little bit of *récit* in *histoire* and vice versa, one must wonder why these critics at this moment do not put into question the opposition itself rather than continue to apply it as if this "sliding" were inconsequential. Genette does indicate the limitations of this dualistic opposition and other categories derived from it when it comes to the contemporary novel and certain "limit-works" where "the temporal reference is *deliberately* sabotaged" (*Narrative Discourse*, p. 35, my emphasis). Here too, with a gesture which I would say is typical of formalist critics, Genette indicates the limitations of his categories and oppositions and continues to use them as if they had none, as if they were substantial.

In a seemingly modest statement in his Afterword to *Narrative Discourse*, Genette even expresses the wish that his terminology will quickly become outdated, because this would mean that it had been taken seriously, reworked, and revised: "One of the characteristics of what we can call scientific effort is that it knows itself to be essentially depleted and doomed to die out." All he wants for his "technology" is that before joining "other packings lost in the refuse of Poetics" it at least have had "some transitory usefulness" (p. 263, translation modified). What is apparent immediately beneath the modesty, however, is the pretension toward scientific status for his methodology. He feels his categories should be revised and reformed but never (so that they won't be) put into question at their foundation for they *are* "scientific." Genette tries to flee the implications of his categories by implying that they have no philosophical-ideological sense; they are for him *only* rhetorical, linguistic categories. They have no foundation except in *Science* (i.e. in *Truth*). The analysis of the opposition at the basis of structural studies of the *récit* which follows will not have as its purpose the updating of structuralist terminology, as Genette wishes, but rather will study the presuppositions at work in the opposition and their implications—the "nonscientific," partisan nature of structuralist studies of the novel.

The opposition in question here is of course that formulated by Emile Benveniste between *histoire* and *discours* in his article "The Correlations of Tense in the French Verb," in *Problems in General Linguistics* ([vol. 1 only], translated by Mary E. Meek, Coral Gables: University of Miami Press, 1971). (Unlike the translator, I have kept the terms *histoire* and *discours* in French.) Generalizing the observation that there is an unnecessary redundancy in the verb forms for expressing the past in French, Benveniste distinguishes two different but complementary systems of classifications of verbs: "two different levels of utterance, which we shall distinguish as that of *histoire* and that of *discours*" (p. 206). The distinguishing characteristic is the absence or presence of any reference to the moment of narration, and more specifically, the absence or presence of a shifter. The *récit historique* (historical narrative) "excludes every 'autobiographical' linguistic form. The historian never says *je* (I) or *tu* (you) or *maintenant* (now)" (p. 206). The function of the narrator, of the "person" who announces the narration, is proscribed: "As a matter of fact, there is then no longer even a narrator. The events are set forth chronologically as they occurred. No one speaks here; the events seem to narrate themselves" (p. 208). *Discours*, on the other hand, is "every utterance assuming a speaker and a hearer, and in the speaker the intention of influencing the other in some way ... in short, all the genres in which someone organizes what he says in the category of person" (p. 209). Following Jakobson's reformulation of Jespersen's term, Benveniste and those who use the concept of the shifter and the opposition dependent on it will insist that the "person" in question here is a linguistic entity, not at all the same as a living, breathing existential subject in the world or a phenomenological consciousness totally present to itself; i.e. the subject of the utterance (*énoncé*) is not the same as the subject who performs the linguistic act of utterance (of *énonciation*).[11] As Genette says, "All these differences clearly lead to an opposition between the objectivity of the *récit* [here Genette calls *histoire récit*] and the subjectivity of discourse, but it is necessary to specify that it is a question here of an objectivity and a subjectivity defined by criteria of a purely linguistic order" (*Figures II*; Paris: Seuil, 1969, p. 63).

How "purely linguistic" are the linguistic code (its concepts and categories) and the oppositions which differentiate it from other codes?—and specifically, how "purely linguistic" are the shifter and the premises which support it? What separates and differentiates linguistics from its other, philosophy? Benveniste himself, in another essay from this same collection, fears the consequences of the narrow, formalist argument that linguistics constitutes a realm radically opposed to meaning; he regrets that "linguistic analysis, in order to be scientific, should ignore meaning and apply itself solely to the definition and distribution of elements. The conditions of rigor imposed on the procedure require that that elusive, subjective, and unclassifiable element which is meaning or sense be eliminated ... It is to be feared that if this method becomes general, linguistics may never be able to join any of the other sciences of man or culture" (*Problems*, p. 10). And yet, since Saussure, structural linguistics has for the most part defined itself as having the opposite point of view from the speaking subject (the subject of meaning, the intentional subject); its status as a "science" depends on how radically it is able to separate itself from the realm dominated by this subject and "its" sense. According to this argument, linguistics will be a formalism or it will not be. Benveniste, in spite of his awareness of the limitations of formalism, in attempting to give a "linguistic view" of subjectivity *in language* perpetuates the very formalist tradition he criticizes here. The foundation for his theory depends on the very formalism he fears in others.

Let us look again, then, at the opposition *histoire/discours* and at the concept of the shifter on which it depends to see exactly how far from the "speaking subject" linguistics and structuralist theory have separated themselves, how far away from philosophy linguistics has ventured. The "redundancy" in the language on which the opposition depends seems to be at first "historical" in nature; it exists because of a difference in usage (at least "today") between written and spoken language: "the historical utterance (énonciation), today reserved for written language" (*Problems*, p. 206). But the real basis for this opposition is in fact the "essential" difference assumed between written and oral forms of language, no matter the usage "today." In *histoire, no one speaks—* the events present themselves, represent themselves, without the intervention of a speaker. The place of the narrator-speaker is totally absent. Is this not a certain concept of "the written"—writing defined in essentially negative terms—in which language signifies in the total absence of any speaker but where there is a "loss" of force, intelligibility, and even complexity as a result of this absence? "The written" here is a kind of "zero degree" of language, serving only as a support for *discours*. The model for *histoire* (not just its usage today) is a concept of "the written" dictated by a theory of language which sees language primarily as oral discourse and sees "the written" as an inferior mode of *énonciation*.

Fixed and without "life," events are presented simply "as past" in *histoire*; no temporal or spatial complexity is possible. Events are simply there, recorded in a simple series, one after the other, always in their place. *Histoire* ("the written") is a one-dimensional space in which a simple chronology is traced, without any "scriptor" or scriptional function. The only advantage to "historical time" for Benveniste is that it is a guarantee of our sanity, our "rationality," a solid monument to support us: "If it were not fixed, we would be lost in an erratic time and our entire mental universe would be adrift. If it weren't immutable, if years could be exchanged with days or if everyone counted them in his own way, no sensible discourse could any longer be delivered on anything and all history would speak the language of madness" (*Problèmes de linguistique générale II*; Paris: Gallimard, 1974, p. 72). The model for what Barthes calls the "referential illusion of real time," Ricardou the "quotidien," and others simply "the historical," is rooted here in Benveniste's concept of *histoire*. What is not usually seen is that this "illusion," which is a functioning, necessary "illusion," is equivalent to and modeled after a reductionist version of "the written." The complexity of *discours* will be argued *against* the historical, but also *against* "the written;" and one has to wonder if a reductionist theory of the historical always goes hand in hand with a reductionist theory of "the written" as it does here.[12]

*Discours*, on the other hand, can be either written or spoken and thus covers a must larger area than *histoire*: "It is primarily every variety of oral discourse of every nature ... But it is also the mass of writing that *reproduces oral discourse* or that borrows its manner of expression and its purposes" (*Problems*, p. 209; my emphasis). Written *discours* (*discours écrit*) is not really written at all, therefore, but simply a reproduction or copy of (i.e. reduction of) oral discourse, one which has its ends and form. In other words, all *discours* is modeled after oral speech and essentially oral in nature—its origin is in the spoken word. It is essentially oral because it has to do with a speech act in or referring to the present. When past events are narrated in *discours* the perfect tense is used, which "establishes a living connection between the past event and the present in which its evocation takes place" (p. 210). In *discours* everything is brought back to, has its origin in, *the present* or, to be more exact, *a very particular present*.

The present in question we are reminded in essay after essay (for it is easy to forget) is "solely a reality of discourse" (*Problems*, p. 218) and not a "real" present, a present in reality. Curiously enough, as we have already seen, the reality constituted by *discours* retains the essential characteristics traditionally applied to "reality itself." Its origin is in the living and unique present, "an instance which is by definition unique and only valid in its oneness," a present which is also the unique origin of the time associated with *discours*: "This time has its center, a center which is both generative and axial—in the present instance of speech (parole)" (*Problèmes II*, p. 73). The *act* of utterance (*énonciation*), the *speech act* itself, is the essence of this present, the origin from which everything else proceeds.

> Out of the act of utterance (*énonciation*) proceeds the institution of the category of the present, and from the category of the present is born the category of time. The present is, strictly speaking, the source of time... From this continuous present which is coextensive with our own presence, the feeling of continuity we call time is inscribed in consciousness; continuity and temporality engendering themselves in the incessant present of the act of utterance which is the present of being itself. (*Problèmes II*, p. 83)

A reversal has taken place. The philosophical concept of being and the concept of the subject associated with it have been banished only to be reactivated within *discours*, as attributes of a present of *discours* which is dependent on a speech act. The truth of *discours* is that *discours* is the truth, the source and context of "human time" (*Problèmes II*, p. 73) and of *being*, the context of all "human experience." It would not be an exaggeration, then, to say that for Benveniste and the theoretical position he presents *discours* is the realm where the (linguistic) experience of being is possible; *histoire* (the "outside" in general) is defined as the absence of this "experience." More, therefore, is being claimed than is usually admitted—sense has reasserted itself as the true "human experience" of being in the realm which supposedly excluded it. The present of *énonciation*, of *discours*, is also the present of being.

The "experience" of language, any utterance or speech act, is also by nature intersubjective. For *discours* implies communication and is thus never the "experience" of a solitary, solipsistic subject, never "my" words, "my" thoughts, "my" experience alone. Every "I" implies immediately a "you"—real, fictive, or even ideal—to whom the speech act is directed. For every emitter there is a receiver. A unique source, a unique destination, and a unique chain between them are all basic to the communications model on which *discours* is based. *Discours* is always a dialogue: "as a form of discourse, utterance demands two necessary figures, the one source, the other the destination of the utterance. It has the structure of dialogue." A monologue is strictly impossible, for even when I speak to myself I am split into two selves and thus there is an emitter and a receiver: "Monologue is an internalized dialogue which is formulated in an interior language between a speaker-self and a listener-self. Sometimes the speaker-self is the only one to speak; the listener-self remains nevertheless present; his presence is necessary and sufficient for the utterance of the speaker-self to have meaning (*Problèmes II*, pp. 85–86). *Discours* can signify (in spite of what is claimed by others, all forms of structural linguistics, even the most formalist, are concerned with signification; they do constitute a semantics) only if self and other, "I" and "you," are both *present*. *Discours* is threatened by the absence of either figure—threatened by the non-sense, noise, and plurality of senses which result from the absence of either, threatened by the possibility that *the present* of *énonciation* will not be or cannot be assumed. This "threat" to *discours* indicates the possibility of another concept of "the written" (*écriture*), which would be different from *discours* but also different from the concept to which *discours* opposes itself; a concept of *écriture* which is complex and nonreducible to *any* present, to any one signifying chain or logic.[13] *Discours* always tries to dominate and reappropriate this "threat" to itself—its status as a complex entity depends on the simplicity of the "written." Without the illusion of *histoire, discours* becomes illusory.

The other (the receiver) is always-already implied in the act of speech that (the) "I" utter(s), and "he" is or must be able to become one with (be present in) "my" time (the present of *énonciation*) for there to be *discours*, i.e. communication. The other must become one with "my" place and become an "I" also. In this sense the other is not really other but dependent, like (the) "I" am (is), on the code itself, on the present it constitutes and which (the) "I" utter(s). Language is intelligible only when this condition is met: "Such is the condition of intelligibility of language which is revealed by language: it consists in the fact that the temporality of the speaker, although literally foreign and inaccessible to the receiver, is identified by the latter with the temporality which informs his own speech when he becomes in his turn speaker (*Problèmes II*, p. 76). The place (the) "I" hold(s) is still the key, however, the place and time to which the other must come, which he must be able in his turn to assume. The message may come back to the "I" by way of the other, but it does come back. It is the place of the "I"-utterer that dominates. Many "I's" may assume this place, but the place remains in its place. The speaking subject is displaced, placed in the context of the code, but nonetheless reinserted in a position of dominance. Here the potentially irrecuperable splittling or doubling of the subject into emitter and receiver, or subject of *énonciation* and subject of the *énoncé*, is recuperated and transcended. The subject is anchored in its "true" place, in the closed, communication system language is assumed to constitute.

Benveniste does not in fact want to do away with subjectivity; he simply wants to resituate the problematic, reinscribe it in language. With a proposition that has become classic since Saussure, rather than situate the subject in the world, in reality, in history, etc., he places the subject as well as these other contexts within language itself, within language modeled after *discours*. "It is in and through language that man constitutes himself as a *subject*, because language alone establishes the concept of 'ego' in reality, in *its* reality which is that of *being* (*Problems*, p. 224). The "error" of phenomenology and other theories of the subject according to Benveniste was to neglect, even obscure, the true ground of being: language. "Now we hold that this 'subjectivity,' whether it is posited by either phenomenology or psychology, is only the emergence in being of a fundamental property of language. Is 'ego" who says "ego'" (ibid., p. 224, translation modified and completed to conform to the French text). Given this reversal of (retention of) phenomenology, would it be an exaggeration now to say that linguistics is the metaphysics of our time?

This is not to say that nothing changes when language becomes the context and object—can we now say the "subject"?—of critical theory and fiction. The displacement and reinscription of the subject opens up levels of analysis which were not possible before—at the same time as it closes off others. As for the subject, we have seen that the issue is far from resolved. Those structuralist literary critics who, in their haste to show their mastery of formalist, technical categories, proceed as if the matter were settled and the subject and all problems of subjectivity relegated to the ash can of history where only those supporters of the "ruling ideology" still toil in vain, are in fact simply naive or intentionally unconcerned about the principles at the basis of their own theoretical position. The structuralists who assume the absence of any influence of the subject (and thus of philosophy-ideology) on their theory and practice misunderstand the fundamental oppositions at work within their own position and, what is more serious, ultimately reinforce in a simplistic way the very concept of the subject they hoped to have eliminated from or situated in their theory.

As it is for the subject so it is for the problem of representation in general. The use of a theory of "antirepresentation" to characterize the New Novel or the New New Novel is nothing more than a slogan with little theoretical validity. One can never be formalist enough (either in criticism or in fiction) to leave representation and sense completely behind. That doesn't mean, however, that writing is only representation and sense. The alternative is the problem; the necessity to choose between representation and antirepresentation, sense and form, the subject and the code, the signified and the signifier. This is not to say that everything in the structuralist position is determined irrevocably by the subject, or by its place, or by the effects of its "presence." Of course not—how could it be unless we accept uncritically the subject's postulates? But it is important to emphasize that the structuralist position is not simply opposed to the subject, radically other from the space the subject occupies and delineates.

The definition of the *récit* formulated by Genette (and used by others) specifies the level of the text to which the analytical-logical tools of structuralist criticism will be directed, that is, the signifier in the text (the text as signifier);

and it thus supposedly distinguishes the signifier-text from the antithetical concept of the subject and the theories of representation and expression associated with it. Curiously enough, however, the definition of the *récit* itself depends on premises that resemble those explicitly opposed: a concept of the subject which is indeed situated in language but also anchored in its place and time; a concept of the present of discourse that is related to the metaphysical concept of presence and being; and a definition of the text as fundamentally discourse (i.e. oral), making it an attribute of the speaking subject. Some form of the phenomenological subject seems to have survived the "epistemological break" and the "structuralist revolution" so frequently acclaimed.

The point of this chapter, then, has not been to defend phenomenology at the expense of structuralism or vice versa, but rather to analyze the position and function of the subject in both theories and the way and extent to which structuralism perpetuates the premises of phenomenology. The subject, its attributes, and the limitations it imposes on theory are not easily done away with, as all our history (the history of philosophy, of ideas, of literature, of events, and even political and social history) attests. If this history and the limitations it imposes on thought and practice can be challenged, it is not through a simple rejection of the subject, which I would agree is *the problem* of this history, because this can only result in its return and continuation in its most simplified and dominant form. A truly radical questioning of the subject, and the resulting emergence of processes, areas of theory and practice, and strategies not totally dependent on the subject can only be realized by a repeated *working through* and undermining of the premises on which the subject depends and which depend on it. Structuralism, in spite of an initial, critical effect and the potential advantages it produced in paying close attention to the language (and context) of theory and fiction, has had in the last analysis the effect of reinforcing the very concept of the subject it wanted to undermine.

It would be a mistake, therefore, to attempt to read fiction strictly in terms of either of the theoretical positions I have analyzed here or of the others which will be treated in the course of this book, as many have done and continue to do—that is, strictly as *an example* of a theoretical position, an illustration of it. Interacting with and transforming the theories in question, fiction (the "New," "Old" or any other form of the novel) should be read in terms of the limitations of these two positions (and others), not totally inside the area delineated by them, but not totally outside either. If the tendency in recent fiction is for the novels themselves to expose and even assert the linguistic-rhetorical properties around which they are supposedly constructed, this in no way means that these novels must be read only in terms of their "form," of their "linguistic generators," or that the "pure play" of the signifier has effectively eliminated all problems of subjectivity. The subject "haunts" the signifier too, which means that the subject is still in question in fiction as well as theory. If, as I have argued, the subject of phenomenology and the subject of structuralism are indeed ultimately grounded in the same premises, what about the subject of fiction? This subject of fiction, is it a theoretical or fictional subject anyway? And which theory for that matter can decide? Which fiction?

# T W O

## For Example: Psychoanalysis and Fiction or the Conflict of Generation(s)

The whole progress of society rests upon the opposition between successive generations.

Sigmund Freud, "Family Romances"

And it is certainly the confusion of generations which, in the Bible as in all traditional laws, is condemned as the abomination of the word and the desolation of the sinner.

Jacques Lacan, "The Function and Field of Speech and Language in Psychoanalysis"

### The Oedipal Conflicts of Oedipus

Confronted with a power that is law, the subject who is constituted as subject—who is 'subjected'—is the one who obeys."

Michael Foucault, *History of Sexuality*

The generation of a text, its origin, is a problem all theories of literature must face, especially those which apply psychoanalysis or speak in its name. Is this origin simple, with the author seen as the father of a text which expresses *his* unconscious and which continues to speak in *his* absence and after his death in *his* name and with *his* words as one generation of Freudians would claim? Or does the text perhaps not obey this father but another one, not express the interiority of a subject but rather obey and illustrate a law conceived in his name, as another generation now claims? The history of the relationship between psychoanalysis and literature is in fact not unilinear or monolithic but (at least) dual and thus conflictual—a conflict between two fathers or, more precisely, between two concepts of the father and, therefore, between two concepts of the literary text.[1] The conflict is one of generations and between generations (for example, between traditional Freudians and Lacanians), one already evident in the work of Freud himself, and one which continues to determine a large portion of the theoretical field both inside and outside the boundaries of psychoanalysis. What remains constant, however, in spite of the differences between positions, is the privileging of a concept of the father either as simple generator or as occupying the position of a law: a formal, linguistic (symbolic in Lacan's terms) law which acts in its turn and in his place (or he in its place) as generator. In both positions the text is the obedient and servile offspring, the father in one way or another its truth.[2]

The criticism usually made of psychoanalytical interpretations of literature is that they neglect the literariness of a text, its form, for some underlying content and that they impose on literature an "alien" theoretical approach. The most obvious problem with this kind of criticism is both that it speaks in the name of an assumed "literary identity" as well as assumes that "non-alien" approaches to literature exist as alternatives to "alien" theories. Because psychoanalysis is treated as a threatening, "alien" theory and *rejected*, the specific characteristics of applied psychoanalysis are never analyzed in themselves. What is also not recognized is that on a basic, thematic level, some literary texts seem to cry out for a psychoanalytical reading, and, in these cases at least, psychoanalysis can in no sense be considered "alien" to the text. This should not be surprising, however, since literature played an important role in the formation of many of the major Freudian concepts, and thus psychoanalysis was never really an "outside" threatening the "specificity of literature" (assuming this concept has meaning) because it was from the start "literary" in many ways, "inside" as much as "outside." Freud's formulation of the Oedipus complex depended as much on his reading of classical and Shakespearean tragedy as on his analysis of hysteria and his own self-analysis, confirming what analysis had suggested: the existence of Oedipus. Sophocles' drama already does more than give a name to this complex—it is itself a model for psychoanalysis: "The action of the play consists in nothing more than the process of revealing, with cunning delays and ever-mounting excitement—a process that can be likened to the work of psychoanalysis—that Oedipus himself is the murderer of Laius, but further that he is the son of the murdered man and of Jocasta."[3]

In fact, the "truth" which psychoanalysis finds in literature and all cultural formations has always been Oedipus: the process of interpretation in most cases ends here, with the unveiling of this "universal" structure. In *The Interpretation of Dreams* and elsewhere Freud does argue for the necessity of the "over-interpretation" of literary texts, but in each case with the "discovery" of Oedipus he claims that he has attained the most profound level of analysis. Thus he actually grounds his interpretation, and all possible interpretations, in this "deep level": "But just as all neurotic symptoms, and, for that matter, dreams, are capable of being 'over-interpreted' and indeed need to be, if they are to be fully understood, so all genuinely creative writings are the product of more than a single motive and more than a single impulse in the poet's mind, and are open to more than a single interpretation. In what I have written I have only attempted to interpret the deepest layer of impulses in the mind of the creative writer" (*SE* 4: 266). The interpretations of a text may indeed be plural for Freud, but this plurality itself is contained within a space or "economy" which limits and controls it: the triangular structure established by Oedipus. For Freud and his disciples, the principal role of literature was to prove the universality of Oedipus; and literature continues to have the same function for another generation of Freudians (Lacanians), though the implications are different and Oedipus itself is displaced and made to serve different interests. The triangle has been passed from generation to generation: Lacan and more traditional Freudians differ over the place and sense of the triangle, not over the triangular structure itself.

Oedipus is for Freud the history of repression, but it is also the history of a certain literature—the movement from Oedipus present in itself to Oedipus "present" only in a disguised form, that is, repressed, in Hamlet: "Another of the great creations of tragic poetry, Shakespeare's *Hamlet*, has its roots in the same soil as *Oedipus Rex*. But the changed treatment of the same material reveals the whole difference in the mental life of these two widely separated epochs of civilization: the secular advance of repression in the emotional life of mankind. In the *Oedipus* the child's wishful phantasy that underlies it is brought into the open and realized as it would be in a dream. In *Hamlet* it remains repressed; and—just as in the case of a neurosis—we only learn of its existence from its inhibiting consequences" (*SE* 4: 264). Literature and psycho-analysis thus seem inextricably linked for Freud in their generation and history. Lacan will continue this history, postulating an Oedipus even less "visible" than either Sophocles' or Shakespeare's, an Oedipus which is no longer a complex but an example[4] of a symbolic law—but which is still best illustrated (most visible) in a literary text.

Freud privileges literature and conceives of it as an ally of psychoanalysis, one of its sources: "Creative writers are valuable allies and their evidence is to be prized highly, for they are apt to know a whole host of things between heaven and earth of which our philosophy has not yet let us dream. In their knowledge they are far in advance of us everyday people, for they draw upon sources which have not yet opened up for science" ("Delusion and Dream in Jensen's *Gradiva*," *SE* 9: 8). If psychoanalysis, then, is often accused of simply reducing literature to an example of its own theory, this accusation is only partially correct, for in many ways psychoanalysis, as Freud indicates, is also an example, a product, of literature. The question of generation here is complex, even at times "confused," for each term is in some sense generated out of the other, each is an example of the other. This "inter-mixing" is not without consequence for any law (biblical, traditional, linguistic, or symbolic) which attempts to limit, define, and govern either or both of them. As Freud was to discover, his case studies, which he hoped would serve as a defense and proof of the truth of his developing "science," read like fictions rather than scientific treatises. Furthermore, in "Leonardo da Vinci and a Memory of his Childhood" he acknowledges that he may indeed have "merely written a psychoanalytical novel" (*SE* 11: 134). It seems that it is impossible to eliminate "fiction" from the presentation, delimitation, and defense of psychoanalysis, for fiction "invades" its theory and examples at each step along the way.

In most of his writings on art, Freud treats art with great respect, claiming modestly to be able to do no more than analyze a very small portion of the work of art and positing an aesthetic realm which is the essence of art and which resists any "scientific" form of interpretation. He repeatedly claims that he limits himself, and that psychoanalysis should limit itself, to the "non-aesthetic," to what in aesthetic terms is the nonessential. In his "Leonardo," for example, he says: "We must admit that the nature of the artistic function is also inaccessible to us along psycho-analytical lines" (*SE* 2: 136). Freud seems here to be modestly indicating the limits of psychoanalysis when it analyzes art and literature. Elsewhere he places a further limitation on his developing science —psychoanalysis should also not attempt to explain the "genius" of the writer (i.e. his "originality" or "creativity"). In praising Marie Bonaparte in his preface to her *Edgar Poe, étude psychoanalytique*, Freud says: "Investigations of this kind are not intended to explain another author's genius, but they show what motive forces aroused it and what material was offered to him by destiny. There is a particular fascination in studying *the laws of the human mind* as exemplified in outstanding individuals" (*SE* 22: 254, my emphasis). On the one hand, Freud replaces an explanation of "genius" with an analysis of "the motive forces (which) aroused it," thus situating and relativizing the importance of "genius." On the other hand, and perhaps more importantly, he leaves to aesthetics the study of the laws governing its own limited area while giving to psychoanalysis the task of discovering in literature and other cultural products the "laws of the human mind." Psychoanalysis is for Freud limited, that is certain, but it is limited to the universal, that which situates and explains all other areas.

In fact, Freud's modesty in dealing with art and literature is feigned: for in leaving the "essential problems" of art for others more skilled than himself in aesthetic matters, he is not really leaving much. Freud reveals in "Civilization and Its Discontents" that he doesn't think much of aesthetics or aestheticians: "The science of aesthetics investigates the conditions under which things are felt as beautiful, but it has been unable to give any explanation of the nature and origin of beauty, and, as usually happens, lack of success is concealed beneath a flood of resounding and empty words. Psychoanalysis, unfortunately, has scarcely anything to say about beauty either" (*SE* 21: 823). Aesthetics leaves empty the space it is supposed to fill and psychoanalysis is of no direct help here either. But the silence of psychoanalysis is at least in this instance better than the "flood of resounding and empty words" of aesthetics. For beneath the modesty and silence of psychoanalysis, one finds a whole set of programmatic statements concerning art and literature which, although they do not speak directly about "beauty," do delimit and situate the "aesthetic realm"—and in Lacan's case at least, define how to distinguish between "empty" and "full" words. That art has an essence, that it constitutes or contains a truth—whether specific to itself (aesthetic), universal, or both—is a postulate as old as all theories of art, that is to say, as old as the history of philosophy. Psychoanalysis is a moment in this long history, a complex, contradictory moment which points to the conflicts within that history itself.

The relationship between psychoanalysis and art can be seen, therefore, as a conflict between two "truths," with each trying to dominate and situate the other, forcing the analyst and the "aesthetician" to choose one side or the other. The analyst-connaisseur who does not want to reduce art to being *only* an example of psychoanalytic truth must attempt to affirm the two "truths" simultaneously; but his position is difficult if not impossible to maintain—especially given the "empty words" of aesthetics. Psychoanalysis obviously encompasses art for Freud, and its truth ultimately is for him *the truth*; but at various moments in his work the relationship between psychoanalysis and art is not one of domination (of the example by the truth) but one of an irresolvable conflict between theories and "truths." To be between two "truths," as Freud is at these moments (especially in "The Uncanny," 17: 219-52), and as Lacan is up to a point, can be thought of, however, in other terms than those of neutrality or transcendence; for the "in-between" can also be the point where the truth(s) break(s) down, where it can no longer be a question of simply choosing, where the limitations of psychoanalytical truth and literary truth are made evident in terms of each other. Here truth is not the solution but precisely the problem.

Lacan's approach to literature seems initially to be more "literary" than Freud's, more concerned with the "letter" of literature, its form. But for Lacan, Oedipus still determines the truth which informs literature—one which is the ground for differentiating between the Imaginary and the Symbolic, between the sterile, dualistic relation of the ego with its mirror image in the Imaginary, and the "true" and overdetermined relation with a third term (with the place of the father as the law, with the Other or, basically, with language) in the Symbolic. Oedipus makes evident the opening or lack in existence, where desire, the unconscious, and the "true, full word" are found, a lack which structures language and determines the place and function of the signifier. To isolate the signifying chain and the place of the "subject" on this chain as he claims to do in his analysis of Poe's "Purloined Letter"[5] is for him, as it was for Freud, "to interpret the deepest layer" of the text, its origin and truth. But Lacan's "deepest layer" is not located in the "impulses in the mind of the creative writer," as it was for Freud, but in a radical exteriority, in the Other (the Symbolic), which defines both the truth and the letter, the truth in the form of the circulation of the letter. Lacan's version of the truth is complex and even contradictory, "originating" in a lack rather than a plenitude, but it continues to govern Lacan's system nonetheless and be exemplified in literature. For without the "truth of the letter" and the possibility of locating its place, the distinctions between the Symbolic and the Imaginary become blurred ("confused" to use Lacan's words), Oedipus as a closed triangular structure is opened up, and the signifying chain and the circuit it forms are interrupted and short-circuited. Lacan must argue against and attempt to suppress these disturbances in the system at all costs in order that the system and its truth not be threatened, in order that psychoanalytical theory continue to dominate fiction. Literature, then, remains for Lacan as for Freud an example of the truth. What has changed is the nature of the truth itself.

"The Seminar on 'The Purloined Letter'" gives a reading of a literary text which is radically different from and even directly opposed to Freud's own readings of literature and to those of traditional Freudians. It has nothing to do with the biography of the writer, for Edgar Allen Poe, the author-subject, his "lived experiences," and his "individual unconscious" have no place in Lacan's analysis. For Lacan, the subject is never original and at the source of discourse, but a function or place within a symbolic-linguistic system. When Lacan asks who the subject of discourse is, he is asking where the subject is situated along the signifying chain and not what his "real identity" is. As a form of discourse, and thus on its "deepest level" radically other from the speaking or writing subject, "The Purloined Letter" is treated as though it has little if anything to do with Poe; rather it is made to serve as a *parable* for the unconscious in general, as a mise-en-scène, representation, or *example* of the Symbolic at work. "Insisting" on the theme of the "letter" (the letter purloined in the story as a metaphor for the letter as signifier) and the circuit which is supposedly established by its theft-exchange, Lacan's analysis does have to do with the unconscious in (of) the text, not Poe's but *the unconscious* in general: "The unconscious was discovered to be in discourse; it is always there that one finds it in psychoanalysis" (*Ecrits* ["Points"] 1: 10). In this way it avoids the principal limitations of previous psychoanalytical readings of literature and even from a formalist standpoint could be said to stay (for the most part) "within" the text. It does not simply apply theories originating totally "outside" literature to the text, but rather attempts to locate metaphors for language and the function of language "within" the text. If the unconscious is in "discourse" as Lacan claims, Lacan will attempt to remain "inside," on the "deepest level" of the text, to meet and analyze it. Here discourse seems to generate its own theory of itself.

"The Purloined Letter" at the same time, however, still has the status of an example for Lacan, for its chief function is to illustrate, represent, and contain *the truth* of Freud's analytical experience, at least the truth on which Lacan's reading of Freud insists. In this sense it is like traditional applications of psychoanalysis to literature; but I should qualify this immediately by saying that the truth of this example, and all examples, is for Lacan the truth of the letter or signifier and thus a "literary" truth, the truth of literariness. The example, in this sense, is an example of itself, an example of the example, a signifier of the signifier. The signifier for Lacan is constitutive and absolute; all truth and all examples are grounded in it. Its truth is that it alone is supreme: "the supremacy of the signifier in the subject" ("The Seminar," p. 50). All subjects (and therefore all "knowledge" and "science") are totally determined by it:

> If what Freud discovered and rediscovers with a perpetually increasing sense of shock has a meaning, it is that the displacement of the signifier determines the subjects in their acts, in their destiny, in their refusals, in their blindness, in their end and in their fate, their innate gifts and social acquisitions not withstanding, without regard for character or sex, and that willingly or not, everything that might be considered the stuff of psychology, kit and caboodle, will follow the path of the signifier. (P. 60)

"The Purloined Letter" is a very good, one is tempted even to say a perfect, example of the truth. Like Sophocles' *Oedipus* and its "repetition" and transformation in *Hamlet* for Freud, Poe's text holds a privileged place in Lacan's (re)discovery and presentation of the truth; for not only does it *present the truth for all to see* in the form of the dominance of the letter, but like *Oedipus* it also figures the search for the truth on the part of the psychoanalyst. However, Lacan does not want to privilege literature in any way; and so in order to keep fiction *merely as an example* of the truth, he declares at the very beginning of "The Seminar" that it is *truth* which determines and makes possible fiction, never really entertaining for a moment the inverse—that fiction situates, conditions, and even determines the truth—which in fact seems to be an equally plausible position given his presentation.

> Which is why we have decided to illustrate for you today the truth which may be drawn from that moment in Freud's thought under study—namely, that it is the symbolic order which is constitutive for the subject—by demonstrating in a story the decisive orientation which the subject receives from the itinerary of a signifier. It is that truth, let us note, which makes the very existence of fiction possible. (P. 40)

Fiction for Lacan does have a relative advantage in its presentation of the truth that other examples do not have, for the truth which determines it and even makes it possible is present in a "purer" form, seeming to be there arbitrarily: "a fictive tale even has the advantage of manifesting symbolic necessity more purely to the extent that one might believe it to be governed by the arbitrary" (p. 40, translation modified). Lacan would in fact agree with Freud's doubts about the existence of the arbitrary in the *Gradiva*: "There is far less freedom and arbitrariness in mental life, however, than we are inclined to assume—there may be none at all. What we call chance in the world outside can, as is well known, be resolved into laws, which we are only now beginning dimly to suspect" (*SE* 9: 9). The arbitrary is in fact only an appearance, a fiction of fiction ("one might believe it to be governed by the arbitrary"), for the truth governs it also. But through this fiction the truth contained in a fiction *appears* to be arbitrary and thus "pure" (i.e. disinterested). In spite of Lacan's argument on behalf of the "originality" and priority of truth, another fiction is always needed to serve as the context of the truth which is supposed to contain it. The process is potentially and structurally endless.

The moment of undecidability, of contradiction with no simple solution possible, is quickly passed over by Lacan and the contradiction or conflict between truth and fiction resolved. The Freudian-Lacanian truth must dominate its relation to fiction (to any text and any context) and be declared *the origin* of fiction, for the "loss" of the concept of the truth and its "purity" will undermine the whole series of oppositions based on it, especially the one between the Symbolic and the Imaginary. But we have already seen that even as it is declared, the domination of truth is problematical, given its context, and the origin of both terms, truth and fiction, hardly simple. In fact, with Lacan, the problem of justifying the hierarchy becomes even more complicated since the truth is always rooted in the letter-signifier and therefore in this sense "literary." One would not be wrong to say, therefore, that for Lacan the origin and context of the truth is the letter, and at the same time that the letter is determined by the truth. What is the example of what anyway? The question, we can already see, has no simple answer.[6]

Even though Lacan's defense and illustration of the truth reduces the complexity of the relationship between truth and fiction, it does contain an analysis of the illusory nature of any attempt to be master of the signifier and to possess its truth. "The Purloined Letter" illustrates this point well in Lacan's reading

("What Poe's story reveals by my efforts"—*Ecrits* ["Points"] 1: 7), for at the very moment when first the Queen and then the Minister act as if they do possess the letter and that their possession is absolute, they have it stolen from them. One is never master of the letter, for the letter is the only master ("the only master is the signifier"—ibid.). Mastery is equally a temptation for Dupin, who returns the letter to its "rightful place," and for all psychoanalysts, as Lacan asserts (a group to which we can add all linguists and all literary critics), all those who through their "success" in detaining the letter and putting it on its "rightful course"—that is, in determining its "true place" on its circuit and the way it truly functions—act as if they have transcended the realm of the letter and possess its truth. To know the true place of the letter is to know that it determines all subjects, especially and most evidently those who pretend to master it. The problem is, however, how to know its place, without being its dupe.

In general, Lacan's reading of Freud and his "insistence on the letter" should interest all literary critics regardless of their approach and concern with psychoanalysis per se; for the questions Lacan raises about the signifier, are, by and large, the same as those raised by a majority of literary critics today. Contemporary literary theorists especially seem to be in general agreement that their goal is to analyze the signifier, the formal functioning of the text, rather than the signified, its sense; but there is no agreement as to how to go about doing this. Lacan more than most literary theorists puts forth a strategy for defining and determining the signifier and in doing so avoids many of the pitfalls of classical and contemporary formalisms—at least initially.

The chief problem in any theory of form is to define form, which is to say, to locate it. Lacan states that, for him, the letter is not simply functional: "If we could admit that a letter has completed its destiny after fulfilling its function, the ceremony of returning letters would be a less common close to the extinction of the fires of love's feasts. The signifier is not functional" ("The Seminar," p. 56). The signifier does not simply disappear once it has fulfilled its "function," which is normally assumed to be the communication of a message. No hermeneutical approach intent on capturing its sense, no matter how complex, can ever account for the true function of the letter, which is outside of, or rather to the side of (*à côté de*), communication. Nor is the letter, however, ever in full view, at least not for a subject-viewer—nor is the circuit it makes visible in any simple, empirical sense. The visible for Lacan is the realm of the Imaginary, the dualistic relationship between self and other described in the mirror stage which is the basis of narcissism. The police (and with them a certain group of psychoanalysts and literary critics) cannot find the letter even though they look everywhere in the minister's room, even though they exhaust what constitutes for them the empirical, visible space: "the police have looked everywhere ... in terms of a (no doubt theoretical) exhaustion of space" (p. 52). Their blindness and "imbecility" have for Lacan "a subjective source" (p. 55); they look everywhere *they* would have hidden it. The space "they exhaust" is a space determined and constructed around their sense of self; and thus they do not see the letter which is "a little *too* self evident" (Lacan's emphasis), for they misunderstand its nature and the space which contains it. Lacan claims that the *true nature* of the letter is the *true subject* of Poe's story (p. 59) and what he, Lacan, will teach us to recognize, to see. We could ask for no better teaching than this, assuming such truths exist and that it is possible to teach them in an objective, disinterested way as Lacan seems to claim.

The Symbolic, the register determining and determined by the signifier, always escapes the individual subject's perception and consciousness. To move from the Imaginary to the Symbolic is to move from subjective distortion to objective truth; it is to discover the true location of the letter, that is, to discover the truth itself: "Which is to say that a transition is made from the domain of exactitude to the registry of truth. Now this registry ... is situated entirely elsewhere, strictly speaking, at the very foundation of intersubjectivity. It is located there where the subject can grasp nothing but the very subjectivity which constitutes an Other as absolute" (p. 49). Locating the letter is only possible if subjectivity (one's imaginary and alienating sense of self) has been transcended, if the absolute state of the Other has been acknowledged—the Other in this case being the rules governing the formulation, elaboration, and closing off of this linguistic, symbolic space. It is not that the letter is absent from the Imaginary but rather that it will not be recognized there for what it is until one has access to the Symbolic which underlies it. In fact, the Symbolic in each case is determined by the negation of some form of the Imaginary; it emerges there where illusory, subjectivist (or "objectivist") approaches fall short and the complex "intersubjective" code is shown to determine the subject who thought itself to be its own origin. To find the Symbolic one simply has to look beneath, beyond, or to the side of the Imaginary; but it is, I would argue, still a question *of looking*.

Lacan's analysis of the two scenes in which the letter is stolen, first from the queen by the minister and then from the minister by Dupin, constitutes the core of his reading of "The Purloined Letter." Characters occupy different positions on the triangles that structure the two scenes, but what remains constant is the triangular structure (Oedipus) itself. The drama is played out in terms of what is seen and what is not seen, in the "time of a look ... This look presupposes two others ... Thus three moments structuring three looks borne by three subjects, incarnated each time by different characters" (p. 44). The third position on the triangle is privileged for it *sees* everything, what the second position sees, the blindness of the first position, and what it doesn't see, its own blindness in fixing its look on the other and not on the context of the dual relationship it has with the other. The imaginary relationship first the queen and then the minister have with the king and the police respectively constitutes a form of blindness, and what is left exposed and not seen by them, that they are being seen, is the insight of the third position, of the Symbolic. The minister falls from the privileged third position back into the second by not seeing he is being seen:

> And we may properly doubt that he knows what he is thus doing, when we
> see him immediately captivated by a dual relationship in which we find all

the traits of a mimetic lure or of an animal feigning death, and, trapped in the typically imaginary situation of seeing that he is not seen, misconstrue the real situation in which he is seen not seeing. And what does he fail to see? Precisely the symbolic situation which he himself was so well able to see, and in which he is now seen seeing himself not being seen. (P. 61)

The Symbolic participates, then, in a long philosophical history constituted by the difference between what is seen and what is not seen, between truth and error, the visible and the invisible, blindness and insight. What is seen from the position of the Symbolic is not a simple empirical reality but a less visible, more profound (and therefore in reality more visible) triangular structure which underlies and makes possible perception, or should I say vision in general, both its blindspots (the Imaginary) and its insights (the Symbolic).

The third position on the triangle is that of the analyst (and for my purposes here, that of the literary critic) who has learned to recognize the true nature of the signifier, to discover it in its true place, and to acknowledge it as master. A danger still exists for this analyst, however; for, like the minister, his position of insight is easily lost as the temptation to consider himself master of the situation and of the signifier becomes more difficult to resist and he finds himself caught in the second position, not that of total mastery but rather of total weakness: "for she [the queen] believes him capable of anything... having conferred upon him the position that no one is in fact capable of assuming, since it is imaginary, that of absolute master. But in truth it is a position of absolute weakness" (p. 64). The opposition between the Symbolic and the Imaginary, so crucial for Lacan's reading, rests on the assumption that a third position exists and that it can be assumed by the analyst-critic, a neutral position which transcends the narcissistic, dualistic, aggressive conflicts of the Imaginary but at the same time does not pretend to master the ground itself of the opposition: the signifier and the circuit it forms. Lacan asks whether Dupin, in revealing himself to be "above" the median, imaginary position, reveals the author's intentions (p. 69); but even if Dupin (or Poe) himself might fail to maintain the third position on the triangle, the possibility of assuming a neutral position—I would even say the necessity to assume this position—structures and limits Lacan's reading. If the neutrality of the third position and of the Symbolic itself can be shown to be questionable, then Lacan's position on the signifier can hardly be accepted as is—nor can the truth, which makes possible and generates fiction. Perhaps what is not seen even in the Symbolic is that seeing (even seeing that one is being seen) is not enough.

### Unending Conflicts of Generation(s): Castration, Transcendence, and Rivalry

On the subject put into question, didactic psychoanalysis will be our point of departure.
Jacques Lacan, "Du Sujet enfin en question"

To think at the same time sex without the law and power without the king.
Michael Foucault, *History of Sexuality*

The central problem in the relationship between psychoanalysis and literature is that literature is usually treated as derivative—put in the position of an example of a truth that it contains and that at the same time transcends it. But the problem of the example, of the dominance of theory over fiction, is never as simple as is usually thought and not one that concerns only psychoanalytic approaches to literature. It is, in fact, impossible to avoid completely the problem of the example, for in the relationship between any theory and literature, no matter how close to the "nature" of literature this theory might claim to be, no matter how much it might claim to have its origin in literature itself, literature will still be treated in some way as an example. Even in so called textual or "close-reading" approaches whose assumptions about literature and whose theory are at work in their readings without ever being declared or questioned, literature functions as an example of itself or of its "own" laws. The problem, then, is to work through and undermine the hierarchical dominance of theory over text (and the reverse dominance of text over theory) without falling back into a valorization of one over the other, which simply repeats the opposition by reversing it.

Freud uses a certain classical literature as one source of his theory in order to prove that the truth of psychoanalysis is eternal; he claims simply to have rediscovered what poets already knew. But literature after Freud cannot prove this truth in the same way; it can only illustrate this truth or attempt to undermine it. Any novel with Freudian themes today would simply be seen as the work of a "Freudian"; the analytical statement of the truth seems to have made the possibility of being an example of the truth much less desirable, much less forceful. The example predating the theory seems to retain a certain "originality" and dominance over theory as it is being mastered by it—the one following is *only an example.*

The choice of any example is always both arbitrary and calculated at the same time: arbitrary inasmuch as there are, at least in principle, a multitude of possible examples for any law and calculated inasmuch as the choice of a particular example is already an interpretation (even a formulation) of the law it is meant to illustrate. The "example" of Oedipus I have chosen to analyze in this chapter, Claude Simon's *Le Sacre du printemps* (Paris: Calmann-Lévy, 1954), does not escape this dual necessity. It is first of all one of a multitude of contemporary literary examples of Oedipus, since it is constructed in terms of a conflict of generations between stepfather and son; and it illustrates perfectly, therefore, a traditional (Lacan would claim reductionary) version of Oedipus which psychoanalytical critics have been eager to uncover in literature from the time of Freud on. At the same time the choice is calculated; for *Le Sacre,* in spite of or even because of its "simplistic" rendering of Oedipus, stands in opposition to the more sophisticated, the more "advanced" reading and example of Oedipus which Lacan has proposed in his "return to Freud." What is at stake in this conflict between examples is the status of the Law (the Symbolic) itself; what must be analyzed are the assumptions which underlie the opposition between the Imaginary and the Symbolic and the choice of examples.

It is true that Lacan has chosen his example well and in a certain sense *Le Sacre* cannot compete with "The Purloined Letter" in the struggle for psychoanalytical "truth," for it contains within itself neither the scene of its own deciphering and the analytical process which constitutes it nor the problematic of the signifier-letter. If I posit as many have done, at least for the sake of argument, Lacan's "return to Freud" as an advance over previous readings, *Le Sacre* is then in many ways a "bad example," for it tends to "illustrate" Oedipus as a "real experience" rather than the basis of a law which governs the Symbolic. It supports an Oedipus continually attacked by Lacan, that of his principal enemies, the Oedipus of American ego psychology: "This results, we would say, from a prejudice, the same one which distorts from the beginning the concept of the Oedipus complex in making it treat as natural rather than normative the prevalance of the paternal figure" ("Du Sujet enfin en question," *Écrits*, p. 233). But even with a "bad example" of Oedipus which illustrates a simplistic or even "false" version of the truth, we learn something about the truth—at the very least to distinguish between the good and bad form of it, between Lacan's "French Freud" and previous Freuds.[7] More importantly, an analysis of even a "bad example" can show the possibility of (the necessity for) other readings of Freud neither completely "French" nor "German" nor "American"; and given the (at least) *double* relationship between psychoanalytical truth (Freud's? Lacan's?) and literature (Poe's? Simon's?) in general, a thorough analysis of any example should reveal the inability of any theory to encompass its examples totally, of any example to produce complete its own theory of itself.

*Le Sacre*, like "The Purloined Letter," has to do with repetition,[8] in this case recounting two "comings of age" in two separate historical periods: Bernard's and his stepfather's, sixteen years before. Bernard's is a "sentimental education," seemingly removed from historical-political events of any note in a France dormant and cynical. The stepfather's, on the contrary, takes place during the Spanish Civil War while he is attempting to smuggle guns into Spain for the Republican forces; his is a political "coming of age." The two historical periods are clearly indicated, and, unlike later novels of Simon, *Le Sacre* presents no temporal overlapping or intermixing ("confusion") of generations; the historical experiences of a father and son are radically different. And yet in spite of the differences of historical content the two scenes possess a structural similarity; history "repeats itself" as one generation repeats the process of "coming of age" through its conflict with the preceding one. The novel moves from the naive, mystified position of the son, who understands and sees nothing, to the position of knowledge of the father who has gone through a similar experience and has supposedly transcended (understood) the conflict between generations and its truth (Oedipus). The position of the father is privileged for he possesses the knowledge which comes with age; he sees what the others (those in the position of the son or the mother) do not. Whether the father will be able to maintain his precarious position and dominate the scene(s) of conflict remains problematical; equally so whether this transcendent position ever really exists as such.

*Le Sacre*, as well as Simon's other novels (especially *The Palace, Histoire*), insists on the crucial role played by the Spanish Civil War for a whole generation of Europeans. On the global level, Spain marks a failure: a failure in terms of historical and social "progress" as the Republican forces are defeated by the fascists, but a failure also in terms of the ideals and ideology of the progressive forces themselves. The reasons for the defeat in Spain, as Jacques Leenhardt has argued, are for Simon as much internal as external: "The Spanish Civil War... is a very particular moment in the problematic of history: one in which the contradictions of revolutionary ideology are manifested in... a revolution assassinated by itself."[9] But contrary to what Leenhardt implies is his desire to ground Simon's novels in *one* historical event and give them a unique origin, the moment and problematic in question here are not unique; for Spain is a repetition of other such moments in history and is in its turn repeated—i.e. the aftermath of 1789, the defeat in Flanders in World War II in *The Flanders Road*, and the battle of Pharsalus in the novel by that name, to name only the most obvious references. Simon's novels are particularly concerned with those moments in history when "progress" seems to have stopped, when the present is experienced neither as the culmination or fulfillment of the past nor as the potentiality of the future, but rather as an interruption or lack in this process. In fact, in all his novels Simon insists on the failure of history to institute itself as an entirely progressive, continuous process and on the dissemination of this failure or lack throughout history. This lack in (of) history, the negativity which is at the origin of history and repeated in each present, continually conflicts with the positivity of the present, so that the movement from present to present is continually being amputated, each present itself divided, differed, and problematized.

Lack, amputation, division, and negativity are all associated with the concept of castration in psychoanalysis; and it would be tempting in the present context to situate and define metaphorically Simon's "vision" of history in terms of castration. But a problem arises immediately: how is castration to be defined? Within the novel itself castration is defined in terms of the tragic, romantic perspective of Bernard, the son, and thus the novel will disassociate itself from this position by situating and undermining it. Bernard is obsessed with lack: with what history lacks to make it truly progressive, what experience lacks to make it a plenitude, what he (the subject) lacks to be autonomous and complete, and, at the basis of all of these, in *his* view in any case, what women lack to make them men. In all cases, the lack threatens an ideal male potency, and here, as in traditional Freudian theory, castration is a "complex" to be assumed and "overcome." Bernard's "complex" is complicated by a crisis in his life which he projects onto all experience, and all history: the death of his father. The true, authentic, benevolent, and wise father is dead—his replacement is an imposture. Even though Bernard accuses his stepfather of not even trying to replace his father as another might have (p. 69), no one ever really could occupy this place. The ideal is irreplaceable, all replacements by definition inferior copies, impostures.

With the loss of the ideal father, or the ideal of the father (read also here the ego ideal), Bernard's life becomes one of resentment. He will never be himself because the true father is not there to guarantee the authenticity of the son's origin and to establish and pass on his law, that is to say, his power and dominance. All codes, laws, political positions, and ideologies are in conflict and less than ideal (universal) when there is no Ideal to separate the positive from the negative, the authentic from the inauthentic—and, as we shall see as a consequence, nothing to separate the Symbolic from the Imaginary. What Bernard really resents is the loss of the ideal of the self, which follows from the absence of the ideal father. The crisis is of generation and between generations; castration, as it stands for the loss of the ideal—of any totality or plenitude—is complicit with a whole series of romantic, idealistic, and tragic implications. It constitutes a stage to be transcended in the process of "coming of age." If we accept the characterization of castration given by *Le Sacre*—as a complex associated with a stage of development of the child—then the novel as a whole must be situated on the other side of castration. *Le Sacre* has transcended castration insomuch as it has transcended the illusions of Bernard in general and situated him in terms of a position on the Oedipal triangle which it delineates and dominates.

There are, however, other theories of castration. The place of castration in Simon's novel and in traditional Freudian theory, on the one hand, and its place in "The Purloined Letter" and in Lacan's theory in general, on the other, seem to be the most obvious points of difference between "examples," ones which separate Lacan from previous generations of Freudians. For Lacan the signifier and the circuit it constitutes can be located—their place is centered on the lack, absence, or nonplace determined by castration. This is the law established in the "name of the father," by the symbolic father rather than the "real" one. Castration for Lacan applies "equally" to both sexes—"Freud revealed this imaginary functioning of the phallus, then, to be the pivot of the symbolic process that completes *in both sexes*, the putting into question of the sex, by the castration complex" (*Ecrits*, p. 198)—but it is evident, even visible in its veiled-unveiled state in the woman, more precisely between her legs. Here is where Dupin-psychoanalyst knows where to locate the letter,[10] for here is the place from which the letter emerges, to which it returns, and around which it forms a circuit:

> Just so does the purloined letter, like an immense female body, stretch out across the Minister's office when Dupin enters. But just so does he already expect to find it, and has only, with his eyes veiled by green lenses, to undress that huge body. And that is why without needing any more than being able to listen in at the door of Professor Freud, he will go straight to the spot in which lies and lives what the body is designed to hide ... Look! between the cheeks of the fireplace, there's the object already in reach of a hand the ravisher has but to extend. ("The Seminar," pp. 66–67)

The significance of castration for Lacan is ultimately not to constitute a "real" threat to something the male supposedly possesses, even though the mystified child (Bernard, for example) may experience it this way, but rather to be constitutive of the Symbolic in general; just as the signifier of signifiers in the Symbolic, the Phallus, is differentiated from its image and any real, biological organ (either penis or clitoris) with which it might be confused. Castration situates and explains what was traditionally called the "castration complex": it is not equivalent to it, for it is not found on the same level. For Lacan, castration can never be transcended or overcome, for assumption of castration (castration itself), is equivalent to transcendance—it is the truth of the Symbolic, the truth of the truth, the signifier of signifiers.

Lacan's theory is helpful in situating all "idealisms," all positions caught in the Imaginary, especially positions resembling Bernard's. As a resentful son, as Hamlet ("you take yourself for Hamlet?" cynically asks his uncle), Bernard is hostile to everyone: to his stepfather certainly, but even more so to women. Women for him are missing something that men are supposed to possess; as inferior versions of men they threaten and attract them with this "nothing to see" which supposedly constitutes them and their sexuality. Bernard is obsessed with this "lack" in women and *sees* nothing else: "On their back...that's their favorite position" (*Le Sacre*, p. 47); "It's only that they get on their back a little too easily...that's in a sense their function, their functional position" (p. 47); "hypocritical women...their bellies open" (p. 70). The ultimate source and location of the lack threatening Bernard is the woman; her presence (nonpresence) continually reminds him of it.[11]

This obsession with what Bernard sees (does not see) as a lack in the woman (of the woman) assigns to her a nature logically consistent with this lack: "The only thing to do is to consider them once and for all as creatures, if not from another world or inferior, in any case one could say absolutely, resolutely foreign to what constitutes the very essence of life" (*Le Sacre*, p. 74). Not quite human (that is masculine), "like cats, like animals" (p. 87), they possess certain instincts, certain innate gifts: "thanks to that flair, that sixth sense, that special instinct that they must possess for these kinds of things, that is for everything that glitters, everything whose price has nothing to do with its intrinsic value... but on the contrary with its scarcity, its uselessness" (p. 106). Other and inferior, inviting and threatening, the woman embodies absolute positivity and absolute negativity at the same time; the ideal and the abyss man desires or fears.

This, however, is not the perspective of the novel, but of Bernard, a naive, virginal adolescent whose perspective on women as well as his view of history will be treated as violently and destructively idealistic and discredited. But Bernard alone is not in question here, for it is his position that is undermined by the novel, the position from which he *sees*: that is, all romantic idealisms which speak in and through him, all ideologies deceived with the world and centered on the subject. The hostility he feels toward women is simply the other side of idealization, a consequence of *them* not remaining faithful to *his* ideal. When they fall from their ideal status, as they must, women are despised and feared, made responsible for Bernard's own shortcomings. The lack which he, the naive, masculine subject, locates in women is from its "source" multiplied, repeated, and refracted everywhere: in experience, in history, and within the subject itself. When the problem is presented in these terms, it is clearly a problem only for the masculine subject (a redundancy because the concept of the subject has always been conceived as masculine), a speculative problem determined by the position he occupies.[12]

The position Bernard occupies is formulated as a reaction to the crisis resulting from the absence of any substantial origin, from this absence seen as a crisis. Bernard's desire is to be a "pure spirit" (he is a perfect Hegelian-Lacanian "beautiful soul"), to be situated nowhere, to be totally autonomous historically, socially, and even biologically: "If only we had neither a mother nor a father, and because we never get anywhere anyway, why not come from nowhere and especially from no one: to be born the same way we die, from nothing, from chance, and especially not from a man and a woman" (*Le Sacre*, p. 15).[13] The ideal birth for the subject can only be an immaculate one, having no relation to any sexual act, and in particular to any woman, depending only on itself or on chance seen as a pure origin. What keeps Bernard from "seeing clearly" is his obsession with (denial of) feminine sexuality, and in particular that of his mother or any other woman he idealizes in a similar way: "Yes, on her back, what do you expect, that's undoubtedly what keeps me from seeing things sanely as Uncle Georges wants, to be able to imagine sanely one's own mother on her back" (p. 47).

In classical Freudian terms this scene which haunts Bernard (his mother or other women on their back) and which he cannot accept, is the scene of desire for the mother. Bernard's consequent guilt and resentment constitute his Oedipal crisis—all that is left to complete the scene in its classical thematic form is for castration to be introduced directly into the scene. In fact, Bernard even expresses a desire to be castrated in order to put an end to desire: "If one could only get rid of them, cut them off, go to a doctor and say get rid of all that for me, like an appendix, a rotten tooth, a parasite that has no function but to bother me, to get in my way ... Cut that off and the rest at the same time, I no longer have any desire to make use of this pair of monkey's glands" (p. 60). This example, which fits perfectly into the traditional Freudian problematic, is now complete when the final element, castration as punishment for sexual desire (castration here desired rather than inflicted), is introduced to situate and explain Bernard's aggressivity, his rivalry with his stepfather, and his general attitude toward the world. Bernard is a degraded version of Hamlet, a Hamlet whose "tragic" existence is entirely dependent on his inflated sense of self, on the narcissism Lacan equates with the Imaginary. As his uncle accuses him, "You don't give a damn about anything outside of your own little self, to which you think everything is due" (p. 19). "His majesty the ego" reigns.

Bernard's position is discredited by the novel, just as in Lacanian theory. But a position can be discredited in many ways; what now must be investigated is the position from which the discrediting takes place. Is there in fact a perspective in which the limitations of Bernard's youthful resentment can be *seen* for what they are and analyzed "objectively"? Is there a perspective which shares none of the assumptions of Bernard's position and is in no way implicated by it, even by opposition? *Le Sacre* answers in the following terms: one acquires such a perspective from a position of maturity after having gone through the same process oneself, for all generations pass through this "rite of passage." The step-father who was naive and idealistic as Bernard, "something of the nature of a boy scout...one of those disgusting young men of good will" (p. 188), went through a structurally homologous experience. His naïveté was historical-political rather than sentimental-psychological, optimistic in form rather than pessimistic. He was a political idealist who believed as many others did in the rightness of the revolution in Spain, and therefore in the inevitability of its total success, certain that the "positive" moments of July could be continued, that a total break with the past could be accomplished because it was "right and just:" "the July days, the enthusiasm...the assaults on the barracks, the triumphs, that explosion of a dream which was idiotic perhaps, a hope and an illusion, which were insane perhaps, but true for at least several days...during which all constraints, all natural or human laws, the narrow, shameful, derisory barriers within which men place themselves, all these were carried off like so many fetuses, like so much ridiculous and disgusting debris" (pp. 141–42). The novel, however, does not recount these positive moments, for they are long past when the events of December are narrated: "So it was nothing more than a radiant memory of the dusty light of summer, and many had already died, and many more, even though continuing to march and fight, were also dead because they no longer believed in what they were doing...They remained there, not so much in the hope of winning but in order not to be defeated" (p. 142). One always arrives on the scene too late in Simon's Spain, when all hope of plenitude and even the illusion of a positive resolution of conflict have already been lost, when these ideals continue to haunt the political-historical scene but are no longer truly believed in, ideals whose status has been degraded by political necessity.

In the context of this "degraded" situation (all situations are in some sense "degraded" because not full), the stepfather "comes of age," that is, changes positions on the Oedipal triangle, moving from naive idealism to knowledge and understanding. In *Le Sacre*, to come of age is to go beyond narcissism in all its idealistic forms, beyond the space governed by the ego, and to accede to and be situated in terms of other laws: those determined by absence, lack, and nega-tivity rather than presence, plenitude, positivity, and disinterested altruism. It is to replace mystified ideals with realistic goals, false models with true ones, *bad examples with good ones*. In this sense, *Le Sacre* is not as opposed to Lacanian theory and its example of the truth as it first appeared.

There are two forms of political narcissism, if I can call it that, presented in the novel: (1) that of the "boy scout" (the stepfather as a young man) who "sacrifices himself" for the sake of justice and follows principles learned in books; and (2) that of the missionary, bureaucratic party-hack (Suñer) for whom ideological purity is the major concern, the path toward realizing the desired political results being clearly established by tradition and party dogmatism with no compromises or changes possible. In contrast to the two of them is Ceccaldi, the only effective political figure in the novel, a mercenary who demands pay-ment for everything he does and who seems to have no ideals of any sort. Paradoxically, Ceccaldi is the only one to serve the Republican forces effectively; he succeeds in having the guns loaded onto a ship and sent to Spain. In fact, he occupies a privileged position in the novel; he alone is not blinded by the false sense of self implicit in a rigid and absolute identification with an ideal that defines the other two positions, which, rather than being a "sacrificing of the self," is actually another means of inflating the importance of the ego.

The ideological purity of Suñer and the naiveté of the "boy scout" conceal the fact that they, like Ceccaldi, are being paid: "But Suñer too was looking for a currency, a compensation, something that would pay him ... The trick was to know in what currency? And if that way was better than to ask for or simply take money?" (pp. 186-87). No one is really disinterested, no matter what role (fiction) they might play; "and perhaps the boy scout's way is in reality neither altruistic, nor good, nor generous but hypocritically and immeasurably ambitious ... I never allowed myself the luxury of a car, but I did allow myself to be a revolutionary de luxe" (pp. 264-65). To move from the position of blindness, misunderstanding, and idealism, then, to that of insight, comprehension and "political realism," the stepfather *must* move beyond his narcissistic sense of self implicit in the ideals he learned in books and with which he identifies.

The central problematic of this novel, "coming of age," is presented in terms of authenticity and inauthenticity—concepts fundamental to existentialsim, a philosophy of the subject. *Le Sacre*'s version of existentialism is simply non-heroic as opposed to existentialism's many heroic versions.[14] The infantile and mystified narcissism which characterizes both Bernard and his stepfather as a young man defines them as inauthentic because they take their own ideals as absolute and deny that they are motivated by any self-interest or that they receive any payment in return for their "good actions." The fundamental law governing existence is that existence is basically inauthentic and that the path toward authenticity begins with an acknowledgment of this truth. True authenticity is grounded in inauthenticity, in negativity.[15] What the stepfather learns through his experiences in the Spanish Civil War and what he tries to pass on to Bernard is that no one is pure or disinterested, everyone is a dupe to his ideals and sense of self:

> And still others, other traffics even more shameful ... of ideas, words, feelings. Because a man can traffic in everything, I ended up taking account of that too, even to the point of selling himself, lacking other dupes, or rather as a prize customer, the one for whom the best merchandise is reserved, his own ideas, his own feelings, no matter how used, adulterated, faked, falsified. (*Le Sacre*, p. 260)

Authenticity is the transcendance of inauthenticity and must pass by way of it—the truly inauthentic figure is the dupe who takes himself to be authentic and to be totally outside these fundamental laws. The process of maturing, of moving beyond idealism and narcissism, is one of the demystification of this illusion of the subject—a recognition of the subject's place in a conflictual structure of partisan interests which ultimately determines the individual subject in both its authentic and inauthentic forms: "there was more authenticity, truth, force for the salvation of the world to be found in a docker working at four times the normal salary, or in an authentic arms dealer, or in an authentic bordello whore than..." (p. 266). To situate the subject in a system more fundamental than itself, however, is not necessarily to move beyond the subject or to do away with it. In *Le Sacre*, individual subjects are situated, determined by their partisan self-interest; yet the concept of the subject, rather than being undermined, is in fact strengthened by being situated. The question remains: can this also be said for other strategies of situating the subject? The one, for example, that situates it in terms of the letter, that insists on the "insistence of the letter"?[16]

Is it really that easy to move beyond narcissism, beyond the rivalry and aggressivity characterizing the relationship of the subject with itself and with others? To recognize the laws governing history and desire as the stepfather does (in *imitation* of Ceccaldi) is not to dominate them, for it seems impossible to withdraw totally from the circuit, from the conflict of generations. The rivalry between the stepfather and the son is not and cannot be completely transcended, not just in terms of the mother and Bernard's infantile narcissism, but also in terms of Edith and the stepfather's continuing, repeated, adult narcissism, the romantic illusions the stepfather holds onto (as an adult, as the father) concerning women in spite of his "knowledge," in spite of his position on the Oedipal triangle: "no, it wasn't her fault if I had suffered and made others suffer, if I continued desperately to desire something that she had lost a long time before, something that she never even possessed, that she only passed through: a charm, a myth, a clearing between two summer rains... no, not her fault but mine, and it was at myself that I felt like laughing" (pp. 271-72).

The privileged position given to Ceccaldi, therefore, should be scrutinized more closely. His position is privileged because it is one of lucidity; Ceccaldi demands payment directly rather than indirectly, and payment is an acceptance of the nontranscendence of any position, the implication of any position in the network of self-interestedness and rivalry. He makes no attempt to avoid conflict with Suñer—if anything, he looks for it, provokes it, and it eventually causes his death. Withdrawal from the scene of conflict is ultimately impossible except through death, which, however, does not guarantee the "authenticity" of the position. The dead hero ("father") is easier to mystify than any other model, that is all. The stepfather's mystification of Ceccaldi is, however, no less problematical than Bernard's idealization of his dead father. The fact that the stepfather privileges him absolutely is an indication of his own desire for a way out, for transcendence, rather than a statement of the actual existence of such a position. Beneath the apparent opposition between father and son lies a similarity of purpose and a similar desire for transcendence.

The conflict between generations in the novel, between stepfather and stepson, is also a conflict between models (examples), between Ceccaldi and Bernard's own father as absolutes of one sort or another. Idealization always leads to further conflict rather than to its resolution. To occupy Ceccaldi's position is never, then, to dominate the historical scene and the lack or negativity which divides it—it is rather to question any and all idealizations, especially those governing one's own position. In other words, Ceccaldi's position cannot be occupied as such. It too is open to mystification when taken out of context and treated as an absolute. The position of the father (the model) and any law associated with it, whether it is that of the mystified father (Bernard's), the demystified one (Ceccaldi), or some other father (even a symbolic one), is implicated within the scene of conflict and does not transcend it. Mystification and demystification ultimately serve the same ends: each assumes, the first naively and directly, the second from a position of insight, having situated the naiveté of the first, that an authentic existence is possible to attain—that is to say, that the subject can overcome the inauthenticity, the lack, at the heart of existence and realize itself as true and authentic, or in Lacanian terms, that the subject can speak, or be spoken by, a "true," "full" word.

If my analysis of the "bad example" seems inextricably linked to Lacan's analysis of the "good example," if the problematic of the first appears to be carried over into the second, it is not without cause. The replacement of the Imaginary by the Symbolic, the undermining of the first in terms of the second, is in fact a process of demystification. The Lacanian subject may be characterized as eccentric, exterior to or separated from itself (Lacan's use of the "shifter"), but in its "true form" and in its "true place" it nevertheless continues to play an important, even dominant, role in his theory. One theory of the subject has replaced another while carrying on many of its assumptions. As Philippe Lacoue-Labarthe and Jean-Luc Nancy have argued, the displacement of the subject substitutes one subject for another; the subject (in language) still dominates: "One can see that in such formulas that it is a question of utterances (*énoncés*) which displace or dislodge the subject but which are nonetheless enunciations (*énonciations*) of the I, and by which this 'I' conserves for itself the mastery of a certainty which, in spite of its content, concedes nothing to that of the 'I think' (of Descartes). The divergence of the *shifter* even plays the role ultimately of a sort of confirmation of the subject, adhering to its own certitude through the certitude of its divergence from itself" (*Le Titre de la lettre*, p. 124).

To speak in terms of the law is to identify with the law, with the Other, that is with the rules governing language conceived as a closed, circular structure. In terms of what—the truth?—can this be considered to be any less "imaginary" than identifying with an image of oneself, with the other as subject?[17] The position of the analyst (intermittently Dupin in Lacan's reading of "The Purloined Letter") and thus of Lacan is certainly not the same as that of Bernard, who is fascinated and threatened by what he *sees* as a lack in women, a lack which threatens his own assumed potency, mastery, and self-possession. But can it still be argued that the Symbolic is not implicated in this imaginary and narcissistic relationship Bernard has with his own image and his ego ideal (his dead father) in the same way that the authentic alternative to Bernard—the stepfather's model, Ceccaldi—is? In other words, has the complex system Lacan builds from the "fact of castration" situated, enclosed, and completely transcended the Imaginary and all other dualisms? Has it really recuperated and situated all fictions and all other truths as Lacan would lead us to believe? Is it too not haunted by a desire for totality in so much as the Symbolic is postulated as a closed, totalized system?

Lacan accords to the Symbolic an absolute, transcendent status, for it ultimately determines everything else—all subjects, actions, desires, etc.—but he cannot defend its status except in terms of its opposition to the Imaginary. In comparing the "good example" of the truth with the "bad example," we have been led to question the very foundation of the system which makes possible such a distinction. The "good example" and the theory which uses it actually depend on the "bad example" and its system in order to establish themselves as alternatives—the truth taking the place of untruth, the Symbolic replacing the Imaginary, through a process of demystification.

The plot of *Le Sacre*, the "bad example," is even constructed in terms of a purloined object, a ring (a signifier in a system of payment) which, like the "lettre volée," is passed from hand to hand and is not in its proper place at all times: "This ring had already been stolen a first time...Or if you wish, we shall say: misplaced, forgotten, left behind" (*Le Sacre*, p. 276). Following Lacan's definition, it is a purloined "object": "To purloin, says the Oxford dictionary...is a question then of *putting aside*, or, to invoke a similar expression which plays on the two meanings: *mettre à gauche* (to put to the left; to put amiss)...For we are quite simply dealing with a *diverted letter*, one whose course has been prolonged...a *letter in sufferance*" ("The Seminar," p. 59). The ring, like the letter, has a strange or "singular" materiality: "a pebble, a piece of glass, a drop of water, an illusion" (p. 276). Its value comes not from the use to which it can be put (in the letter's case, not from its sense or any function it might serve) but from its very uselessness (p. 106). Stolen by Edith from her mother to pay for an abortion, it is stolen in turn by her brother to give to Bernard, who thinks it has been stolen from him by the young woman with whom he slept. When it finally returns to Bernard (for it was never really stolen from him but was in his pocket), its exchange, actual and imagined, has provoked the "coming of age" of Bernard, led to Edith's accidental abortion, and confirmed the law governing all actions and desires: their ultimate lack of fulfillment—"while it seemed to be fleeing before them, to be hiding, carried off at top speed, impossible to achieve, like the symbol itself, the tarnished and inanimate object of impossible hopes and impossible desires" (p. 237). The circuit the ring has taken from hand to hand, even when Bernard only imagines it to be stolen from him, determines the relationship between the characters of the novel. The return of the ring does not, however, close the circuit, for the ring has from the start been part of a system based on exchange (thievery or gift, it is the same thing)—it has always-already been stolen and therefore can never really return to "its proper place."[18]

To occupy a transcendent position in terms of such conflictual system is an impossible task. All characters in *Le Sacre* (even Ceccaldi ultimately) occupy median positions, positions of rivalry with other positions and characters. No one and no position really transcends the conflict of generation(s) and sexes which constitutes the novel; all presumed positions of neutrality and all attempts to transcend the conflictual structure of the novel are explicitly undermined from within or at least potentially underminable. In terms of the problem of transcendence, the simplicity of the "bad example" is more complex than Lacan's analysis of the "good example"; for Lacan does argue that Dupin (the "good analyst") can and even must withdraw from the political and sexual conflict surrounding the queen and thus retain his transcendent position: "But if he is truly the gambler we are told he is, he will consult his cards a final time before laying them down and, upon reading his hand, will leave the table in time to avoid disgrace" (p. 72). Since Lacan has argued from the beginning that the message of Poe's story is that it reveals the truth without distortion, that the signifier is primary and dominates or determines the subject, it is by means of a signifier that Dupin-analyst is able to withdraw from the circuit and "dominate" it. This signifier has the strange characteristic, unique among all other signifiers, of being neutral, the most destructive of signification: "Do we not in fact feel concerned with good reason when for Dupin what is perhaps at stake is his withdrawal from the symbolic circuit of the letter...And is it not the responsibility their transference entails which we neutralize by equating it with the signifier most destructive of all signification, namely money?" (p. 68). The third position Dupin occupies, the privileged position that the minister before him also occupied but lost in his desire for mastery (lost also was his ability to *see*), is maintained by a sleight of hand, a trick worthy of a master magician, by a supreme fiction, we might say: that is, that being paid neutralizes one's interests in the conflict. Ceccaldi's position in *Le Sacre* indicates in fact the opposite: the fact that everyone is paid makes all neutralization, all transcendence, illusory. The "purity" of the signifier and the truth of the Symbolic are maintained by Lacan—but at what costs? we might ask, continuing the metaphor.[19]

As Jacques Derrida has argued, in "The Purloined Letter" the third position of neutrality is always, from the very start, sliding into the median, second position of rivalry (the Imaginary); and this occurs because of the highly significant, highly conflictual so-called "annihilating signifier." The enemy-brother's conflict between Dupin and the minister began long before the incidents related in "The Purloined Letter," and it seems highly arbitrary to postulate a resolution of the conflict with the letter being returned to its "rightful place." The "rightful place" of the letter in any literary text, even one which overtly indicates such a place, remains a problem—not a solution—if no unique law is assumed to govern its displacement. Add to this the interests of the narrator, another double for Dupin, and the position of transcendence of the Symbolic seems even more questionable. Neutrality is always suspect, whether it be that of science, linguistics, politics, psychoanalysis, or economics—in all its forms it is equal to a desire for mastery. All these theories are "restrained economies" in this sense, relegated to a particular space with specific limitations. No one theory has the last word; no one "economy" dominates in the last instance.

In fact, the Imaginary underlies the Symbolic as much as the Symbolic the Imaginary. The unconscious may be structured like a language, and there may be advantages to situating the subject in terms of the signifier, but the closing off of the language / unconscious structure, its organization around a fixed center or origin (even one which is missing rather than present, a lack rather than a plenitude), is highly problematical when other structuring possibilities are seriously entertained, when the position from which the enclosure is posited (always a position of supposed neutrality) is analyzed and undermined.

In comparing *Le Sacre* to "The Purloined Letter" and reading the first in terms of a model which emphasizes conflict between positions rather than its resolution and thus contrasts with the linguistic-formalist reading proposed by Lacan for the latter, I am making no claims as to the neutrality of any position, my own included, or to the completeness or truth of any reading. For as I have attempted to analyze the arbitrary nature of Lacan's argument on behalf of the signifier-letter, I have at the same time attempted to raise a more general question—the limited, restrained, and therefore partisan nature of any reading, even one which in the name of economics, whether in terms of ideology, politics, or even desire (*économie libidinale*), might propose (either implicitly or explicitly) to explain everything, to dominate or transcend the conflicts and contradictions of theory and fiction, to put forth its own truth as the origin of fiction, or its fiction as the origin of truth. As my reading of *Le Sacre* has argued, with money in all its forms—materialistic and idealistic—taken as a nonneutralizable factor, the partisan conflict between positions within each model and the eventual conflict between possible models must be considered as fundamental and ultimately irresolvable—at least in any permanent or transcendent sense.[20]

Psychoanalysis does, then, make literature into an example of the truth (in all the senses of "example"), as do all other approaches, no matter how formal, no matter how "textual." A psychoanalysis like Lacan's, which is interested in the signifier, in structure and form, offers certain advantages over traditional psychoanalytical approaches; but it, too, fails to investigate the relationship between the truth and its examples (its illustrations and models) or the implications of its own premises which allow it to locate and describe the truth (the circuit of the signifier in this case) and "to leave the table in time to avoid disgrace." What is repressed by Lacan as it is for the most part repressed by Freud, though it is indicated in "Das Unheimliche" ("The Uncanny," *SE*, vol. 17), is that the act of making literature into an example of truth is dual, and that psychoanalysis has always-already been made into an example of fiction by the very process of making literature into an example.

Situated within literature as much as it situates literature, psychoanalysis's claim to the truth—any truth—is specious, as questionable as literature's claim to have no relation to anything outside of itself, to be pure fiction or pure text. Neither truth nor fiction effectively and completely situates the other without being situated in turn. The conflict between theory and fiction, between their respective "truths" and "examples," is potentially endless. What can now be seen also is that the "bad example" is as "good," or as "bad" (ultimately the terms good and bad are not pertinent) as the "good example"—no example is, therefore, completely "good" or "bad" in the complex, conflictual, and open relationship between theory and fiction and their examples.

# T H R E E

# The (Dis)Placement of the Eye ("I"): Point of View, Voice, and the Forms of Fiction

I like to think I occupy the centre, but nothing is less certain. In a sense I would be better off at the circumference ... From centre to circumference in any case it is a far cry and I may well be situated somewhere between the two.

This voice that speaks, knowing that it lies, indifferent to what it says ... knowing itself useless and its uselessness in vain, not listening to itself but to the silence that it breaks ... is it one? ... It issues from me, it fills me, it clamours against my walls, it is not mine, I can't stop it, I can't prevent it, from tearing me, racking me, assailing me. It is not mine.

Samuel Beckett, *The Unnamable*

## The Forms of Consciousness

Form is presence itself. Formality is what is presented, visible, and conceivable of the thing in general. Metaphysical thought—and consequently phenomenology—is the thought of being as form.

Jacques Derrida,
"Form and Meaning: A Note on the
Phenomenology of Language"

Any study of the novel must confront the problem of point of view, for it is indeed a *problem*. Unlike studies of earlier forms of the novel that seem to have no trouble identifying the narrative point of view from which a story is told, criticism of contemporary fiction has found such identification more difficult. Contemporary novelists (especially the French New Novelists) seem to enjoy shifting voices and points of view without explanation or warning, so that rooting each "point of view" in a definite narrator or "character"—i.e. in a fictional subject—becomes virtually impossible. In the New Novel as well as other forms of contemporary fiction, the origin of the narrative voice is as often ambiguous as defined; point of view, as often floating as anchored in one subject.

To experiment openly with shifting perspectives and voices as the most recent New Novels do is something Henry James would probably have frowned upon as "promiscuous,"[1] and Percy Lubbock, his most (too) faithful follower, simply condemned as being characteristic of inferior, deviant works. A "confusion" of narrative perspectives—in other words, any nonsynthesizable plurality interfering with the singularity of point of view—is for James and Lubbock the sign of a badly constructed, even "formless" novel, one whose subject or center is displaced or missing. A plurality of singular and well-defined points of view, on the other hand, is in principle acceptable if the various points of view can be made to focus on a subject; even though James at times seems to admire most the limitation of perspective to a single consciousness and Lubbock attempts to make this a rule. Point of view, thus, for both James and Lubbock is the guarantee of the integrity of form, the essential principle of the "art of the novel."

To read the novels of Samuel Beckett, William Faulkner, Alain Robbe-Grillet, or Claude Simon, to name only these, is to be forced to complicate, rethink, or even put into question the traditional notion of point of view—unless one is content, as some have been, simply to reject a large proportion of contemporary fiction as constituting a bastard or decadent form.[2] But should it really have taken twentieth-century fiction to question the premises and implications of what we could call the Jamesian "theory of the novel," or are there not contradictions within that theory itself which point already to the complexity of the problem? More is certainly at stake in the so-called "formalist" approaches to the novel, which claim to be faithful to James, than a simple process of analyzing and categorizing narrators. It is not simply that the categories associated with point of view no longer apply to a certain form of the novel in the same way that they did to another form; rather the problem lies in the categories themselves, in the assumptions about the novel *in all its forms* which are at the basis of these categories and in the implications of these assumptions. In terms of contemporary theory, it is especially important that these problems be confronted, not just for their historical interest but because the Jamesian tradition is very much alive in Anglo-American theory today as well as in the work of French formalist-structuralist critics such as Gérard Genette and Tzvetan Todorov, who have rediscovered James's theory of point of view and are working in the same general area as the post-Jamesians.[3] Genette and Todorov do refine and complicate the categories used to discuss point of view and voice, but I would argue that their complication and refinement still do not go far enough (and, as we shall see, not even as far as James himself), because they, like the more orthodox Jamesians, never really question the assumptions at work in the categories themselves.

In fact, things are never as simple as they seem or as the "practical criticism" derived from James would want them to be. Within the Jamesian perspective (point of view) on point of view, more is indicated than meets the eye, especially if this eye has already accepted the dictates of point of view and been formed in terms of its theses. What is an eye anyway?—and is there always *an* "I" behind each set of eyes?—at the origin of each point of view? These questions are, in fact, not as easy to answer as they might first seem, even in terms of James himself. Without a clear, precise, certain definition of the eye and how it works—i.e. of consciousness—without the assumption of the identity of an "I" itself at the origin of point of view, the analysis and definition of the novel (its forms) become complicated issues.

For the novel to be a "true," stable form, it had to develop a theory of itself, that is to say, a consciousness of or point of view on itself, and James was very much aware of this necessity. In "The Art of Fiction" he claimed that the English novel suffered when compared to the French in that "only a short time ago it might have been supposed that the English novel was not what the French call *discutable*. It had no air of having a theory, a conviction, a consciousness of itself behind it ... It was ... naïf."[4] If this observation is correct, it is largely due to James himself that the deficiency was made up, that the English novel over-came its naiveté and developed a theory or consciousness of itself to rival the French—so much so that almost a century later the French are returning to James to supplement the deficiencies in their own theory of the novel.

Most critics would agree that the essential element of James's theory of the novel, the very "center" of his theory, is a discussion of point of view.[5] Point of view is for James *the principle* of the novel—its center—that principle around which the novel structures itself as form. In fact, James's theory provides the novel with a consciousness of itself by analyzing the problem of consciousness in the novel; it supplies the novel with a point of view on itself by discussing the problem of point of view. One would not be wrong to say, as many critics have after Lubbock, that for James the "craft" or "art" of fiction begins and ends with the problem of the center. Lubbock is faithful to James when he argues that even a "great novel" such as *War and Peace* "fails" when judged on this formal level. "Here, then, is the reason, or at any rate one of the reasons, why the general shape of *War and Peace* fails to *satisfy the eye*—as I suppose it admittedly has to fail ... It has no centre."[6] To be without a center is to be without a precise, well-defined (to the eye) form; and if one defines form as Lubbock does as "the book itself" (p. 40), then to have failed to establish a center is to have failed to have written *a book* and to have produced instead what James vividly describes as "a formless shape," works which are "fluid puddings."[7]

The faults occurring in a work such as *War and Peace* that has not estab-lished its center are serious, for they threaten the existence of the novel itself as a form. Those occurring in a novel that has a fixed center are superficial and inconsequential, even if it is sometimes by luck rather than skill, knowledge, or calculation that the center is found or put into place:

> One's luck was to have felt one's subject right ... whether instinct or calcula-tion, in those dim days, most served; and the circumstance even amounts per-haps to a little lesson that when this has happily occurred faults may show, faults may disfigure, and yet not upset the work. It remains in equilibrium by having found its centre, the point of command of all the rest. From this centre the subject has been treated, from this centre the interest has spread, and so, whatever else it may do or may not do, the thing has acknowledged a principle of composition and contrives at least to hang together.[8]

The center is the point around which the novel as a form is in equilibrium; it is essential to James's concept of form. And yet the consequences of James's insistence on the center are more than just formal, for the center is always occupied by a consciousness which establishes a point of view, that is, by the presence of a subject.

The center fixes the novel and establishes a point from which the novel emerges and takes form:

> From the moment we proceed by "centres"—and I have never, I confess, embraced the logic of any superior process—they must *be*, each, as a basis, selected and fixed; after which it is that, in the highest interest of economy of treatment, they determine and rule. There is no economy of treatment without an adopted, a related point of view, and though I understand, under certain degrees of pressure, a represented community of vision between several parties to the action when it makes for concentration, I understand no breaking-up of the register, no sacrifice of the recording consistency, that doesn't rather scatter and weaken. (*The Art of the Novel*, p. 300)

The center *rules* and *determines* the form of the novel; form being an "economy of treatment," a closed and unified space. To lose the fixity of the center, in whatever way imaginable, is to "scatter and weaken" the novel's form. James's advice to Mrs. Humphrey Ward in a letter written in 1899 is to stick to a center, the consciousness of her chief character, at all costs: "You don't give [the reader] a positive sense of dealing with your subject from its logical centre... I should have urged you: 'Make that consciousness full, rich, universally prehensile and *stick* to it—don't shift—and don't shift *arbitrarily*—how otherwise, do you get your unity of subject or keep your reader's sense of it?'" (*Theory of Fiction*, p. 155). To shift arbitrarily from one center to another is to lose both the form and the sense of the novel, the form of the novel as its sense.

The center of the novel, as we see in the letter just quoted, is for James more often than not determined as the consciousness of a character in the novel, the consciousness of a fictional subject: "The centre of interest throughout 'Roderick' is in Rowland Mallet's consciousness, and the drama is the very drama of that consciousness... so the beauty of the constructional game was to preserve in everything its especial value for *him*" (*The Art of the Novel*, p. 16). At the center of the novel, then, and fixed in its place, is the presence of a consciousness; the construction or form of the novel is simply the form of the particular consciousness in question. And according to James, any subject, no matter how insignificant, will do as long as it is selected, defined, and fixed. It is not necessarily the nature of the individual subject that makes the novel successful (a unified form) or not, though this is not a totally insignificant question; it is rather the skill with which it has been placed and the construction carried out around it. In fact, as James indicates in his Preface to *The Portrait of a Lady*, there is even a benefit to be derived from the difficulty in working with the "slightest of subjects." He first asks himself if such a subject would not necessarily be quickly exhausted and thus provide what would be a far from substantial center for the novel: "By what process of logical accretion was this slight 'personality,' the mere slim shade of an intelligent but presumptious girl, to find itself endowed with the high attributes of a Subject?—and indeed by what thinness, at the best, would such a subject not be vitiated?" (*The Art of the Novel*, p. 48). The solution, as James told himself—in much the same way that he wrote to Mrs. Humphrey Ward—is to remain focused on the consciousness of the young woman: "'Place the centre of the subject in the young woman's own consciousness,' I said to myself, 'and you get as interesting and as beautiful a difficulty as you could wish. Stick to *that*—for the centre; put the heaviest weight into *that* scale, which will be so largely the scale of her relation to herself'" (p. 51).

This "slight personality," therefore, does in James's terms constitute a *Subject* in the strongest sense. The criteria for determining and placing a subject has less to do with the particular identity or character of the subject, the complexity or lack of complexity of its personality, its high or low intelligence—even though James feels extremes should be avoided in order not to produce "too misshapen a form"—than with its place at the center. Any subject can be a Subject, any consciousness a true and functioning consciousness, as long as from its place in the center, it gives immediate access to "life" and is sincere: "Recognizing so promptly the one measure of the worth of a given subject, the question about it that, rightly answered, disposes of all others—is it valid, in a word, is it genuine, is it sincere, the result of some direct impression or perception of life?" (p. 45). In a letter to the Deerfield School (1889) he further emphasizes this point: "Any point of view is interesting that is a direct impression of life" (*Theory of Fiction*, p. 94, and *The House of Fiction*, p. 46).

The Jamesian subject is posited in a classical philosophical manner as presence. Sincerity is the aspect of a subject totally at one with itself and immediately present to itself, and immediacy characterizes as well its presence to the outside world. The subject-as-consciousness is in fact, in the well-known Jamesian metaphor, a window, and the author's choice of a subject is the choice of one of the infinite number of possible windows which constitute the "house of fiction": "The house of fiction has in short not one window, but a million—a number of possible windows not to be reckoned, rather; every one of which has been pierced, or is still pierceable, in its vast front, by the need of the individual vision and by the pressure of the individual will" (*The Art of the Novel*, p. 46). Too many readers of James have perhaps accepted this metaphor uncritically without analyzing the consequences of the far from innocent equation of consciousness with a window. The metaphor, as it is developed by James, is far more complicated than might first appear.

After James makes his argument on behalf of the immediacy of consciousness and equates the consciousness of the fictional subject at the center of the novel with a window, he makes a further distinction: "These apertures, of dissimilar shape and size, hang so, all together, over the human scene that we might have expected of them a greater sameness of report than we find. They are but windows at the best, mere holes in a dead wall, disconnected, perched aloft; *they are not hinged doors opening straight upon life*" (p. 46, my emphasis). The immediacy in question is a *fictional immediacy*, the immediacy of a fictional subject; it is not a "pure," original, total immediacy. For there is an unbridgeable distance between what the "windows" look out on and the possibility for the author or reader to participate fully, *to be*, in this world (i.e., the window is no door). The shape and place of the fictional consciousness may be the center or origin of a fictional universe that is closed and unified, even if pluralistic, but it always in some sense keeps the "real subject" at a distance. The only entry possible is from behind the window, using the "eyes" of the fictional subject: "But they [the windows] have this mark of their own that at each of them stands a figure with a pair of eyes, or at least with a field-glass, which forms, again and again, for observation, a unique instrument, insuring to the person making use of it an impression distinct from every other" (p. 46). The eyes of the fictional subject work together as *a unique instrument;* they are *one.* They ideally give the exact impression of the world of the fictional consciousness to another consciousness by supplementing and replacing the reader's own eyes, by becoming his eyes. What ultimately guarantees the integrity of the house of fiction, however, and the possibility of the reader being able to assume the place of the fictional subject adequately and completely is that behind the window is another figure, this one supposedly "real" and present in the "real world"—the author himself: "The spreading field, the human scene, is the 'choice of subject'; the pierced aperture, either broad or balconied or slit-like and low-browed, is the 'literary form'; but they are, singly or together, as nothing without the posted presence of the watcher—without, in other words, the consciousness of the artist. Tell me what the artist is, and I will tell you of what he has *been* conscious" (p. 46). Behind the fictional consciousness there is a "real consciousness" which makes use of the fictional to affirm its own presence. Essential to James's theory of the novel, then, and its ultimate origin, is the presence of the author at its source—the fictional universe has its center in the consciousness of a fictional subject behind which stands the "true origin" and subject of the novel: the author and his consciousness.

The ease with which James moves from the philosophical-literary problem of the fictional subject's consciousness-as-window to the presence of the author himself behind the window should not surprise us. Once the principle of the subject-consciousness has been affirmed as the center of form, and since the subject or center of form is *fictional,* that is in James's terms "chosen" and constructed, the question of the origin of that fiction-form must then be raised. The fictional-subject as center and origin is not solid enough ground for the novel, not sufficiently substantial or autonomous. The author-subject will provide the definitive origin and center of the novel outside or behind the novel, behind the particular slit he has pierced, outside the form he has constructed. He will not speak in his own voice or see directly with his own eyes—but *his voice* and *his eyes* will be there behind the consciousness and voice of the fictional subject he has constructed. The author-subject is the "true," transcendent subject of what I would call James's phenomenology of fiction and form. He is present in and behind all voices, in and behind all consciousness.

The goal of the author-subject, then, is to be able to take on another form while remaining identical to himself, to disguise himself all the better to remain himself, to project himself into another in order better to be what he is. The unity of the form of the novel is intimately linked to the skill with which the author is able to possess and be possessed by a fictional other: "A beautiful infatuation this, always, I think, the intensity of the creative effort to get into the skin of the creature; the act of personal possession of one being by another at its completest—and with the high enhancement, ever, that it is, by the same stroke, the effort of the artist to preserve for his subject that unity, and for his use of it ... that effect of a *centre*, which most economise its value. Its value is most discussable when that economy has most operated; the content and the 'importance' of a work of art are in fine wholly dependent on its *being* one" (*The Art of the Novel*, pp. 37–38).

For the author, in what is only an apparent paradox, to find his voice, he must first project it into another through a fiction. For example, James says of Balzac, "It was not 'til well toward his thirtieth year, with the conception of *Comédie Humaine*, as we all again remember, that he found his right ground, found his feet and his voice" ("The Lesson of Balzac," in *The House of Fiction*, p. 68). And James explains a few pages later what finding his own voice actually means: "What he liked was absolutely to get into the constituted consciousness, into all the clothes, gloves and whatever else, into the very skin and bones, of the habited, featured, coloured, articulated form of life that he desired to present" (p. 77).[9] Balzac is most present in the voice and consciousness of the fictional subjects he has created; to speak with the voice of a fictional other is really to speak with his own voice. As long as the fiction is fully possessed by Balzac, as long as it in no way escapes him, then his presence is affirmed and the form of his novels doubly anchored and centered: first in the consciousness and presence of the fictional subjects within the "house of fiction," and second and more importantly in the transcendent, dominant presence and consciousness of the author, who is both "outside" in order to ground the fiction and "within" it in as much as he wears the clothes and uses the voice of his characters. The reader's role is to follow the author and to possess and be possessed by other (fictional) consciousness—to lose himself all the better to find himself.

A novel then can fail in two ways which are intimately related to each other. It can, first of all, fail to provide an effective window onto the "world" through which the novelist and then the reader in his place can look: "The usual imbecility of the novel is that the showing and giving simply don't come off—the reader never touches the subject and the subject never touches the reader; the window is no window at all—but only childish *finta*, like the ornaments of our beloved Italy" (in a letter to W. D. Howells, 1890, in *Theory of Fiction*, p. 66). Any unnecessary ornament—and here the whole problem is how to decide what is simply glitter and what is not—anything that obscures vision and complicates point of view destroys the immediacy of the fictional subject's relation to the world and makes it impossible for the reader to assume his place and his consciousness. This is described by James as an unbridgeable gap between reader and subject, an irretrievable loss of contact, a difference originating witthin fiction that cannot be overcome.

In terms of the author-subject himself and his relation to his own construction, a novel fails when the author does not realize his intention: "What matters, for one's appreciation of a work of art, however modest, is that the prime intention shall have been justified—for any judgment of which we must be clear as to what it was" (*The Art of the Novel*, p. 134). A novel that is successful, one whose form is centered and in equilibrium, one in which there are no unnecessary ornaments and thus no unbridgeable gaps, no loss of immediacy, but only windows behind which the reader and author can look and be at one with the consciousness of the fictional subject, at one with his or her point of view, is a novel that realizes the "prime intention" of its author. The ultimate source of the novel, then, the real center and origin of form, is the founding consciousness of the author.

Given the importance James gives to consciousness and to the intentions of the author, it is not surprising that one of the most convincing analyses of this aspect of his theory has been done by Georges Poulet. Poulet's thesis that the consciousness of the author is the ultimate origin and center of *all literature* is confirmed by James's theory and novelistic practice:

> Moreover, behind the centrality of the principal character, there is still, with James, another centrality, if one can so phrase it, even more withdrawn, that of the author himself. Every central character is for James a means of perceiving things according to the angle of incidency which a creature of his choice gives him. At the back of the consciousness of the character, there is therefore the consciousness of the author. It is like the consciousness of consciousness. Occult, dissimulated into the background, it reigns no less everywhere. It is the center of the center.[10]

For Poulet, all problems concerning form are answered once the consciousness of the author has been discovered, described, and put in its true place—at the "center of the center." What we have seen of James's theory so far seems to support this view completely; his theory of the novel could rightly be considered to be, as Poulet's is, a phenomenology of fiction. The problem of point of view in James has led critics, then, not only in the direction of formalism (the description of point of view and how it works as a form-giving element) but also in the direction of a phenomenological approach to literature (the definition and description of the subject at the origin of form and consciousness). Even though the two positions seem at first to be contradictory, each is derived from one aspect of James's theory, for the contradiction between form and consciousness is at the heart of his concept of point of view.

Form is in James, therefore, as it is elsewhere, a philosophical problem and not a purely "empirical," practical one as some formalists might argue. Poulet is simply more explicit about the philosophical implications of James's theory than the formalist critics indebted to James, whose concept of form is in fact implicitly dependent on the same principle of consciousness developed by Poulet. In the same vein as Poulet, Wayne Booth argues against the narrow, formalist readings of James's theory of the novel which would exclude the "author" from the house of fiction. He is consistent with the James we have seen up to this point when he argues that the "author" is always in some way or another present in his work: "In short, the author's judgment is always present, always evident to anyone *who knows how to look for it* . . . As we begin now to deal with this question, we must never forget that though the author can to some extent choose his disguises, he can never choose to disappear."[11] Booth's term for the presence of the author in the work, this "second self," is, of course, the "implied author," and it serves as the support for his view of form as a unified whole: "Our sense of the implied author includes not only the extractable meanings but also the moral and emotional content of each bit of action and suffering of all the characters. It includes, in short, the intuitive apprehension of *a completed artistic whole*; the chief value to which this implied author is committed, regardless of what party his creator belongs to in real life, is that which is expressed by *the total form* (pp. 73–74, my emphasis). The implied author is the true origin of form, *an ideal* necessary for this concept of form. The implied author "chooses, consciously or unconsciously, what we read; we infer him as an ideal, literary, created version of the real man; he is the sum of his own choices" (pp. 74–75).

Booth's chief argument—that all fiction is "impure," that is, rhetorical—rests on this principle; for in his approach all rhetoric (all form) is linked to the presence of this "subject." But, as in James, the "real author" stands behind the "implied author," who is a product of his choice. The author-subject creates both a second self for himself and the reader, thus making it possible for there to be agreement between them, for the "reader" to be at one, to identify with the "author." For if "the author creates, in short, an image of himself and another of his reader," if "he makes his reader as he makes his second self," then "the most successful reading is one in which the created selves, author and reader, can find agreement" (p. 138). The novel (its form and sense) is threatened when "the narrator's voice rings false in my [Booth's] ears" (p. 363), or when "impersonal narration" leads "to confusion or unintentional ambiguity" (p. 377)—intended ambiguity being permissible because a function of the implied author and thus ultimately consistent with the unity of form rather than disruptive of it. The ultimate threat to the novel is for Booth a moral one which occurs when the author does not "serve larger ends": For "the artist has a moral obligation, contained as an essential part of his aesthetic obligation to 'write well,' to do all that is possible in any given instance *to realize his work as he intends it*" (p. 388, my emphasis). Booth blurs the line between aesthetics and morality; the subject at the origin and center of form is a moral as well as aesthetic principle. The author "must first plumb to universal values about which his readers can really care . . . The writer should worry less about whether his *narrators* are realistic than about whether the *image he creates of himself*, his implied author, is one that his most intelligent and perceptive readers [Booth himself?] can admire" (p. 395).

Strictly "formalist" approaches to the problem of point of view in James may not develop explicitly a concept of the subject as consciousness as do Poulet and Booth, but they *assume* such a subject as the center of form. Depending on a concept of the subject as consciousness, as presence—a fictional

59

subject within the work to serve as the center of the work and a "real" author-subject behind the fiction, responsible for realizing its intentions and presenting a unified, moral-aesthetic form—analyses of point of view have philosophical consequences which cannot be ignored, as they have for the most part by formalist critics. The concept of form as a visible, unified whole is the first and most important consequence of the thesis of the presence of the subject at the origin of point of view—and there is, strictly speaking, really no other concept of point of view but this one. Formal analyses, the "practical business of criticism," may want to ignore the assumptions and implications of their concept of form; but the problems and contradictions associated with the thesis of the subject dominate the problem of form—the tradition and terminology are firmly rooted in them. But this does not mean, however, as we shall see, that James's (or Poulet's or Booth's) concept of the subject must be accepted as-is—for the grounding of form in the consciousness of a subject is *never* accomplished without contradiction.[12] The placement of the center is contradictory in itself; the transcendent subject (outside and inside) does not maintain its position as origin easily, or perhaps at all.

## A Conflict of Eyes

As to perception, I should say that once I recognized it as a necessary conservation. I was extremely conservative. Now I don't know what perception is and I don't believe that anything like perception exists. Perception is precisely a concept, a concept of an intuition or of a given originating from the thing itself, present itself in its meaning, independently from language, from the system of reference . . . I don't believe that there is any perception.

Jacques Derrida, "Structure, Sign, and Play"
(discussion), *The Structuralist Controversy*

That a certain phenomenological, philosophical tradition is implied in the concepts of point of view and voice—form and sense being effects of consciousness, of the presence of a subject—does not mean, however, that the tradition is present as a ruling philosophical-ideological system simply, without contradiction, or that the terms derived from this tradition exist in a simple, transparent form. Within the theoretical writings of James himself, contradictions associated with the thesis of the subject can be found as a complicating, disruptive counterforce to the secure and well-entrenched presence of the fictional subject at the origin and center of fiction and the author-subject as the founding consciousness of all fictional consciousness.

In James's prefaces to his novels, written after-the-fact, when he is himself at a distance from his novels, James finds that the center or origin is not always easy to locate or recover in practice as in theory (even by the author himself); and James's insistence here that the center is an essential element of the construction of the novel as a closed form raises a serious problem for his theory of the novel. Each preface begins with a description of what James remembers as the "germ" of the novel, the seed from which it sprang to become the closed form it was destined to be (at least ideally, in the best of cases). It is in terms of this "germ" that one can determine whether the intentions of the author have been realized and the center firmly in its place.

But, strangely enough, as often as not the "germ" is not recoverable as is. James's memory often fails him, as in the Preface to *The Tragic Muse:*

> I profess a certain vagueness of remembrance in respect to the origin and growth of "The Tragic Muse," which appeared in "The Atlantic Monthly" again, beginning January 1889 and *running on, inordinately, several months beyond its proper twelve.* If it ever be of interest and profit to put one's finger on the productive germ of a work of art, and if in fact a lucid account of any such work involves that *prime identification,* I can but look on the present fiction as *a poor fatherless and motherless, a sort of unrecognized and unacknowledged birth. I fail to recover my precious first moment of consciousness of the idea to which it was to give form;* to recognize in it—as I like to do in general—the effect of some particular sharp impression or concussion. I call such remembered glimmers always precious, because *without them comes no clear vision of what one may have intended,* and without that vision no straight measure of what one may have succeeded in doing. (*The Art of the Novel,* p. 79, my emphasis)

The "prime identification" with his own intentions, with the founding consciousness of his fiction—with himself—necessary to locate the "germ" is lacking, making the novel both "fatherless and motherless," an orphan, without a simple origin or a clearly defined form, one which exceeds the time of engenderment and gestation (twelve months of publication) and the space *proper* to it. The failure to recover the "precious first moment of consciousness of the idea" institutes a lack within the assumed plenitude and presence of the originating consciousness; for without it, "no clear vision of what one may have intended" is possible. A consciousness not completely present to itself and an unclear vision of its intentions displace the center from the center and problematize the integrity of form, leaving the novel without a definite, substantial presence at its origin. The difficulty James has in recalling (making present to his consciousness) his "original intention" clouds his *vision* (his *eyes*) and disrupts every moment of consciousness, fictional or real, by displacing the author-subject not only from his/her position as father/mother (origin) but also from the window behind which he/she (and we, the readers) supposedly stands. An alterity has entered into the process of the engenderment and birth of the "child"—the novel has an uncanny form, familiar and strange at the same time.

In a letter to W. D. Howells (1901), James relates how difficult it is to "identify with" a "first moment of consciousness," which never really occurs *once* or for the first time. This was the case for *The Ambassadors* whose "germ" was the words spoken to Jon Sturges by Howells and then related to James, having been long forgotten by Howells himself: "They presently caused me to see in them the faint vague germ, the mere point of the *start,* of a subject. I noted them, to that end, as I note everything; and years afterwards (that is three or four) the subject sprang at me, one day, out of my notebook ... and my point is that it had long before—it had in the very act of striking me as a germ—got away from *you* or anything like you! had become impersonal and independent" (*Theory of Fiction,* pp. 68-69). The way these words had "got away" from

Howells (or *anything like him*) and become "impersonal and independent," cut off from the intention of Howells, who originally uttered them, reveals the nonoriginal status of any "germ," of any utterance, the aspect of language which makes it understandable and quotable in an infinity of contexts and forms, when the "original" intention of the "original" speaker has been forgotten, lost, or was never known. But does this not also reveal that James's own words (his words or Howells's? or Sturges's? or a fictional subject's?) contain within themselves at the very moment of utterance (whether spoken or written), or at any other moment, the possibility of "getting away" from him and that the intention motivating them is never totally adequate to form them completely and for all times, to master them and give them *a form* or *a sense*. In a certain sense, they have always already gotten away from him, being those of another, of a series of others, always-already there before the author's active intervention, or "springing out" from his notebook at him, from the written page rather than from a unique source in his "lived experience." An other seems to be speaking (writing) in the voice of every "I."

The "before" of the "germ," therefore, is highly problematical even when its specific origin and history are remembered. The conscious origin is never the ultimate origin. The "germ" is "wind-blown" rather than the product of a conscious, intentional, fully controlled act:

> The germ, wherever gathered, has ever been for me the germ of a "story," and most of the stories straining to shape under my hand have sprung from a single small seed, a seed as minute and wind-blown as that casual hint for "The Spoils of Poynton" dropped unwittingly by my neighbour, a mere floating particle in the stream of talk ... Such is the interesting truth about the stray suggestion, the wandering word, the vague echo, at touch of which the novelist's imagination winces as at the prick of some sharp point: its virtue is all in its needle-like quality, the power to penetrate as finely as possible. (*The Art of the Novel*, p. 119)

Stray, wandering, an echo, the "germ" is picked up by the artist in the general dissemination of words, the "stream of talk," "pricking" his imagination, and then planted so that true artistic semination can take place. The "real" birth of the novel takes place here, therefore, whether the moment of insemination is remembered or was ever known in the first place; the true moment of "creation" occurs when dissemination is transformed into semination, when the artist becomes father and mother to his/her work (at the same time receiving and planting the seed). Or does it really happen this way at all? Is the birth really simple, the artist's consciousness definitely present in it, his or her clear vision realized, the offspring taking the exact form of the initial, precise intention of the artist/father/mother at the moment of birth? Is dissemination ever really overcome and controlled with the active intervention of the artist and his/her (its?) consciousness?

So it would seem if we follow James, especially if the consciousness behind the window (the "I" behind the "eyes") is to have its way, if the voice of the author (which one?) behind all fictional voices is to be heard without echo, if the birth of the offspring is to be well-formed, unified, and centered. James's prefaces both affirm the necessity for such a birth and at the same time repeatedly reveal the impossibility of attaining such ideal "perfection." When the parent (father/mother), James, looks back at his offspring in his prefaces, he finds that he has not been able to control and mold the growth, the size, and the shape of his novels:

> I shall encounter, I think, in the course of this copious commentary, no better example, and none on behalf of which I shall venture to invite more interest, of the quite incalculable tendency of a mere grain of subject-matter to expand and develop and cover the ground when conditions happen to favour it . . . "The Awkward Age" was to belong, in the event, to a group of productions, here re-introduced, which have in common, to their author's eyes, the endearing sign that they asserted in each case an unforeseen principle of growth. They were projected as small things, yet had finally to be provided for as comparative monsters. That is my own title for them, though I should perhaps resent it if applied by another critic. (P. 98)

His offspring have become, in spite of his best intentions, textual monsters—formed not according to his will but according to "an unforeseen principle of growth." It seems as if the disseminated "germ," the "mere grain of a subject-matter," disseminates in its turn as much as it produces an offspring modeled after the artist's intention or formed according to his "I" (eyes). Dissemination is in fact general, affecting the before, during and after of "creation" (birth). The control of the artist, the mastery of his consciousness, is relative and limited at each moment of the process.[13]

James admits frankly that he finds this phenomenon incomprehensible in its totality, a matter for the philosopher rather than the artist:

> When I think indeed of those of my many false measurements that have resulted, after much anguish, in decent symmetries, I find the whole case, I profess, a theme for the philosopher. The little ideas one wouldn't have treated save for the design of keeping them small, the developed situations that one would never with malice prepense have undertaken, the long stories that had thoroughly meant to be short, the short subjects that had underhandedly plotted to be long, the hypocrisy of modest beginnings, the audacity of misplaced middles, the triumph of intentions never entertained—with these patches, as I look about, I see my experience paved: an experience to which nothing is wanting save, I confess, some grasp of its final lesson. (P. 100)

The "true philosopher" is, however, no better equipped than James—novelist, theoretician, and, yes, philosopher (as well as brother and offspring to theologians and philosophers)—to understand and give the "final lesson" as to why the "germ" disseminates as much as it germinates, escapes the intention of the author as often as it conforms to it. With the beginning characterized as hypocritical, the middle misplaced, and the final lesson ungraspable, one must wonder how a philosopher or novelist could give a unified sense or form to this "experience" (organize it in terms of *a point of view*) without seriously reducing its complexity and theoretical implications.

The author is, and even must be, the dupe of his plan and intentions, rather than the controlling and originating force behind his work:

> Yet one's plan, alas, is one thing and one's result another; so I am perhaps nearer the point in saying that this last strikes me at present as most characterized by the happy features that *were*, under my first and most blest illusion, to have contributed to it. I meet them all, as I renew acquaintance, I mourn for them all as I remount the stream, the absent values, the palpable voids, the missing links, the mocking shadows, that reflect, taken together, the early bloom of one's good faith. Such cases are of course far from abnormal—so far from it that some acute mind ought surely to have worked out by this time the "law" of the degree in which the artist's energy fairly depends on his fallibility. How much and how often, must he be a dupe, that of his prime object, to be at all measurably a master, that of his actual substitute for it—or in other words at all appreciably to exist? He places, after an earnest survey, the piers of his bridge—he has at least sounded deep enough, heaven knows, for their brave position; yet the bridge spans the stream, after the fact, in apparently complete independence of these properties, the principal grace of the original design. *They* were an illusion, for their necessary hour. (Pp. 296–97)

Mastery is still a goal, therefore, of the author he still wants to impose *his form* on his offspring. To be the unique origin and master of what is actually produced, which invariably differs from his initial intentions, however, the author must admit that the latter were only "illusions." He must not identify with the consciousness of the originating idea but rather with the consciousness behind and at the origin or center of the final product. After the fact, then, consciousness tries to reassert its mastery of a product whose birth and growth it has not controlled. The deviation from the "original vision" is, as James says, "inevitable" (p. 325).

Where then does that leave his argument on behalf of the center and origin of fiction, the very principle of its form, if the consciousness which is supposed to found it only comes in after the fact and is derived? It leaves it in a very shaky, unstable state, to say the least. James admits that in some of his novels the "center" was displaced from where it was ideally supposed to be:

> The usual difficulties... were those bequeathed as a particular vice of the artistic spirit, against which vigilance had been destined from the first to exert itself in vain, and the effect of which was that again and again, perversely, incurably, the centre of my structure would insist on placing itself *not*, so to speak, in the middle... I urge myself to the candid confession that in very few of my productions, to my eye, *has* the organic centre succeeded in getting into proper position... In several of my compositions this displacement has so succeeded, at the crisis, in defying and resisting me, has appeared so fraught with probable dishonour, that I still turn upon them, in spite of the greater or less success of final dissimulation, a rueful and wondering eye. These productions have in fact, if I may be so bold about it, specious and spurious centres altogether, to make up for the failure of the true. As to which in my list they

are, however, that is another business, not on any terms to be made known. (Pp. 85–86)

To James's eye, in very few of his novels is the "organic centre" in position; in these novels the centers are "specious and spurious" attempts "to make up for the failure of the true"—fictions of the center at the center and origin of fiction. These centers cannot be looked at with the same *eye* as the one formed to look at the true, "organic centre"; for out of the corner of his eye, at the very limits of his field of perception, of his consciousness, James is reduced to casting a "rueful and wondering eye" at them for defying him, for resisting his intentions, and his "true eye"—for resisting "his" form. Even if in this day "the reader with the idea or the suspicion of a structural centre is the rarest of friends and of critics—a bird, it would seem, as merely fabled as the phoenix" (p. 85), and even if he practically alone has *the eye* to distinguish between the true, structural center and the spurious, many critics after James have attempted by reading his *Art of the Novel* to form their eyes in conformity with his and attain this "art" for themselves. And yet if they read James carefully, if they see in his theory not only what his "true eye" sees but also what he is forced to see with his other eye, forced to admit in spite of himself, the grounds for distinguishing between the organic center and the spurious, fictional center are none too certain. Ultimately, the works which possess an organic center must remain a secret shared by those who possess the "true eye" for such things; to announce to the world which works are truly centered, as some after James have done, opens a debate which cannot be resolved conclusively, since the distinction between "specious" and "organic" is not a natural one but depends on the formation of one's eye (of one's theoretical orientation or point of view). The question of point of view is in this way forced "outside" the purely literary arena and forced to confront a historical-philosophical tradition it in no way dominates or encloses (forms). The *eye* which sees the true center sees it by suppressing from view everything within it that threatens to displace it or has already displaced it—it sees only the *ideal unity* of form from the position of the *Ideal Subject* by eliminating all contradictions from within the *Ideal*.

As we have already seen, and as James again admits, the displacement of the center is the rule rather than the exception, the "normal" condition and context of the "germ" rather than an "abnormal" one. Even in the most tightly structured of his works, his "greatest successes," the center cannot be simply and unproblematically affirmed. All of his fictions are in some sense "fatherless and motherless," as the origin is never completely original, the center never completely in place, the intentions of the author, his consciousness, never completely master as it comes in after the fact, at each moment, to claim as its own, as its offspring, the "monster" which has been produced in spite of itself. The gaps in memory, the unforeseen and unforeseeable deviations from intention, the blind spots and limits of vision, the echoes in the voice, and the alterity of the fictional center and its predominance over the organic one all lead to a problematization of the concept of point of view which leaves the center and origin of fiction, of any fiction, a much more complex and contradictory problem than is usually thought. Those coming after James have perhaps developed *one* of James's *eyes* to too great an extent at the expense of his other eye; they have defined point of view at the expense of everything that escapes and undermines *the point* of point of view.[14]

The interest in James's "Prefaces," as opposed to more formalist approaches, is that the contradiction at the heart of his concept of point of view is not suppressed, that the conflict between the two eyes at the "origin" of his theory of point of view is not resolved. As one eye is fixed in its place, focusing on and determining the unity of form, the other eye, not quite in focus, barely glimpses at (wonders at) the complex conditions dividing, interfering with, and complicating that unity. It will take the imposition of a unified subject who imposes a reduced set of theoretical "field glasses" on the problem to focus the two eyes together and make them see the same thing in the same way, that is, to make the second conform to the first.

Point of view in its sense as the origin and center of form, the product of a unified consciousness, is thus a reduced and derivative version of the more complicated problem of the status of the subject in any "formalist" theory of fiction. Only when the subject is *assumed* to be a unified presence, to establish the point or origin of point of view and the proper aesthetic distance, does the concept actually work the way it is supposed to—to guarantee the unity and integrity of form as a visible, spatial, or linguistic entity. James does not resolve the question of the subject as the origin of point of view in fiction, or at least not in the way he intended. In fact, the question is raised in his work more often than not in spite of himself, by his other "I" (eye) who (which) is not master, center, or first principle of his (its) own consciousness, point of view or form. Formalist purifications of James have, unfortunately, suppressed this very crucial aspect of his theory of fiction with the result that they simplify the very concept of form in whose name they pretend to speak. The conflict of points of view of the two "I's" (eyes) at the heart of James's theory of point of view, in spite of his best intentions, displaces the subject from the center of form as much as it fixes it in its place and leaves the "house of fiction" without a unique proprietor behind each window. In this sense James's point of view on point of view can hardly be considered *a point* at all.

### The Consciousness of Form
Narrating never goes without saying.

Maurice Blanchot, L'Entretien infini

Claude Simon's novels have attracted the attention of critics interested in the problems of point of view, consciousness, and narrative voice; but two novels in particular—*Le Vent* (1957) and *L'Herbe* (1958)—are usually chosen to serve as examples of how Simon's "early" novelistic techniques constitute a radical complication of these problems and how his "late" novels completely break with tradition. Most critics consider the work of the "late" Simon to be formally more advanced than the "early" Simon, that is, less dominated by the "traditional problems" of representation and expression and more concerned with the problems of textuality and language itself; and they tend to situate that break between these two novels.[15] *The Wind* is seen as complicating the question of point of view but only in terms of problems "exterior" to form and language, problems concerning the signified (that aspect of the text called *histoire*) and arising in this case from the "unreliable" nature of the consciousness and point of view of Montès, the principal character of the novel. *The Grass*, according to this view, breaks with Simon's previous novelistic practice by undercutting the solidity and certainty of point of view from "within," on the level of the signifier itself (the aspect of the text called *récit* or *narration*), thus revealing that for the "late" Simon, the signifier (or "text in itself") has priority over the signified, form over content, *récit* over *histoire*.

Gérard Robichou's *Lecture de L'Herbe de Claude Simon* (Lausanne: L'Age d'Homme, 1976) is the most detailed and developed statement of this argument, which also underlies Jean Ricardou's work on the New Novel as well as that of the majority of formalist critics of contemporary fiction in France. Robichou's delineation of the problem is the following: "*The Wind* is still 'traditional;' it's a novel with characters, plot, setting, evolutionary story-line, even a chronology . . . In addition, the *annecdote which is reported is treated and presented in it as if it existed before its narration* . . . What gives *The Wind* an even more traditional quality is that most of the difficulties of the *récit* are justified in the fiction narrated" (pp. 274–74). *The Grass*, on the other hand, breaks with the traditional aspects still present in *The Wind* by not only being a "reinvention of a 'reality'" but also, and more importantly, a "*visible invention of fiction* (with the accent placed on the phenomena of narrative elaboration)" (p. 276). The assertion that the "*visible invention* of fiction" (and Roubichou himself emphasizes both visible and invention) constitutes as great an advance over "the traditional" must, however, be questioned. To move from the valorization of the signified to the valorization of the signifier, from problems of consciousness founding form to those of form founding consciousness, does not necessarily break with the Jamesian tradition (or any other form of the "traditional") if the ideal of form proposed by the tradition is maintained, and "the visible" still privileged.

One is not born with an eye for form; the eye itself must be formed. If an aspect of James's point of view on point of view has dominated theories of point of view, it is largely in the form and in terms of the categories Percy Lubbock proposed in his reading (reduction) of James. Lubbock's emphasis in *The Craft of Fiction* on the opposition between showing and telling has played an important role in the formation of the "true" Jamesian *eye* and the elimination of "his other eye" from criticism. Making a rule or law out of James's observations on "dramatizing action," Lubbock argues that the reader should preferably "see" things directly without interference from any exterior mediator, and ideally without any mediation at all. Art begins for Lubbock where telling leaves off: "The art of fiction does not begin until the novelist thinks of his story as a matter to be *shown*, to be so exhibited that it will tell itself" (*The Craft of Fiction*, p. 62). It is better, therefore, that the narrator be a character in the book than an authorial voice interrupting and interfering with the story by intervening from the "outside": "It is much more satisfactory to know who the story-teller is, and to see him as a part of the story, than to be deflected away from the book by the author, an arbitrary, unmeasurable, unappraisable factor" (p. 140). But it is better still to eliminate the "deflection" and "interference" from the narrator-character within: "There is a better method, one of finer capacity, then ready to the author's hand, and there is no reason to be content with the hero's mere report ... [For] the story-teller's inner history—it is not clear that we need the intervention of anybody in this matter, and if it might be dramatized, *made immediately visible*, dramatized it evidently should be" (p. 140, my emphasis). The "purest" form of the art of fiction, the *ideal* (of) *form*, occurs when the mind, the consciousness of the hero, is immediately present in itself—present in order to be immediately seized by the reader. "No reflection, no picture, where living drama is possible—it is a good rule; do not let the hero come between us and his active mind, do not let the heroine stand in front of her emotions and portray them—unless for cause, for some needful effect that would otherwise be missed" (p. 145).

Lubbock's position, taken to its logical end, would mean that in the "purest" form of the novel the narrative process itself would be eliminated and the very matter of the novel, its language, negated.[16] In the ideal of the novel Lubbock proposes, the narrator and the author (as scriptor) disappear and language itself becomes transparent so that the reader can occupy the point of view of the novel and be at one with the consciousness present before him in the novel. Dostoevsky accomplished this in *Crime and Punishment*, Lubbock claims, because he "neither spoke for himself (as the communicative author) nor allowed Raskolnikov to speak, but *uncovered the man's mind and made us look*" (p. 144, my emphasis). Here the writer's function is simply to unveil the presence of a consciousness—it seems to have nothing essential to do with language at all. According to Lubbock, James in *The Ambassadors* eliminates himself and his hero, Strether, from being "present" in the book and speaking for (telling) Strether's imagination:

> In the book as it is, Strether personally has nothing to do with the impression that is made by the mazy career of his imagination, he has no hand in the effect it produces. *It speaks for itself*, it spreads over the scene and colours the world just as it did for Strether. *It is immediately in the foreground*, and the "seeing eye" to which it is presented is not his, but the reader's own ... It is rather as though the reader himself were at the window, and as though *the window opened straight into the depths of Strether's conscious existence*. (P. 146, my emphasis)

Lubbock eliminates the presence of the author from fiction because he is an obstacle, because his presence must be overcome by the reader in order to be at one with the consciousness of fiction itself. Lubbock seeks to ensure the place of the reader at *the point* of point of view and thus the immediacy of what he sees: "The spectator, the listener, the reader, is now himself to be placed at the angle of vision; not an account or a report, more or less convincing, is to be offered to him, but a direct sight of the matter itself, while it is passing" (pp. 252-53). Lubbock's position, which has been taken as the basis for a formalist approach to the novel, constitutes then, surprisingly enough, a realism, where all forms of mediation are argued against so that the presence of the thing in itself (consciousness itself) will be present for the eye of the reader, who is placed at "*the angle* of vision"—for there is only one—to grasp. Lubbock thus insures the "purity" of James's theory of fiction by eliminating the "other eye" from it; he reinscribes and anchors *the point* of view in the presence and immediacy of an ideal Subject. This "purification" of James's theory thus reduces its ambiguities and complexities in the name of the ideal James openly pursues, but with serious consequences for that theory. Lubbock's is the "purest" of all the "eyes" of Jamesian tradition—in his approach, form is, or should be, nothing but pure consciousness. Author, reader, and character all occupy the point of origin of this consciousness and merge together in its immediacy. The author's presence may be eliminated but another more immediate, more truly present subject has taken his place.

In taking the position that *The Wind* is formally less advanced than *The Grass* and later Simon novels, Roubichou is making an argument similar to Lubbock's "formalist-realist" argument that the novel in its purest form is the immediate expression of a consciousness—no matter how much Roubichou might explicitly argue against all expressive, mimetic theories of fiction. The two theories agree on the role of consciousness in the novel—they disagree as to how consciousness should be defined. For Lubbock, there would be too much "telling" in this novel, too many "exterior" voices. He would find too many interruptions and contradictions in consciousness to make an argument for the immediacy of any consciousness, including the general narrator's. For Roubichou, there are too many "exterior," superfluous, contradictory anecdotes, too many interruptions in the formation of the form of the novel that cannot be explained totally in formalist terms alone, to consider the novel a pure example of fiction. The novel is never conscious of itself as primarily and essentially made of and from language. In other words, the immediacy of consciousness projected as an ideal in each case is never achieved, and the novel can thus be considered to be deficient in terms of the formalist grounds established by each theory.

Initially, it might seem curious that Roubichou's argument ends up being so close to Lubbock's on this point because they start out from such different positions, one ignoring or even suppressing the role of language in the novel, the other making language the most fundamental and dominant problem for the novel. But Roubichou's argument has in fact the same ends as Lubbock's, even though it is made in different terms. Each seeks the "purification" of fiction, the elimination of all external, mediating, "intrusions" so that the presence of fiction itself—in Lubbock's case, pure consciousness, in Roubichou's, pure text—will be immediately visible to the reader.[17]

In *The Wind*, Roubichou considers the narration of the narrator's difficulties in determining a point of view among the different versions of events told to him to be an intrusion in the formation of the form of the novel, in the consciousness of the novel of itself as form, a way of explaining the complicated formal aspects of the novel in terms of an extraformal, extralinguistic problem. Roubichou is right, up to a point: This kind of intrusion—the narration of the scene(s) of narration—does dramatize and even tend to explain the "origin" of the fiction by fictional "events" and not by the *formal workings of language* alone, but this is not necessarily to deny the role of language. On the contrary, the complicated and even contradictory status of consciousness in *The Wind* affects the "visible," formal structure of the novel and its narrational, linguistic foundations as well. The novel reveals that the concept of the text's consciousness of itself, of its purely linguistic form, is a reductive model for fiction, an ideal of form which cannot be sustained without eliminating from fiction certain of the elements (both formal and not strictly formal) constituting it.

Establishing the center of narration of *The Wind* is a difficult problem, even though the "place" of the narrator is clearly indicated. To use Jamesian terminology, the narrator organizes and "reflects" the others' stories; as a "window" he opens not onto "the world" but onto other "windows." His relation to "what happened," to the events which make up the bulk of the narration, is rarely if even "immediate" (assuming that immediacy is a real possibility). To stand behind the "window" constructed from "his" consciousness (whether it is really *his* or *one* is a question which we will have to consider) is to have only an indirect, ambiguous, incomplete, and contradictory access to "experience" and events, even those seen with "his own eyes," to words, even those spoken with "his own voice." Rather than Montès's unreliability alone, the very nature of narrative and the principle of consciousness (point of view) on which it rests inhibit the smooth and exact (in terms of his or any other consciousness) narration of events. Ultimately Montès himself and the "exceptional quality" of events have only a secondary role in determining the incomplete and conflictual form of this narration.

The narrator of *The Wind* "tells"; he does not "show." For what he tells cannot be shown exactly as it is because the visible is itself divided and contradictory, and thus *telling* here takes the place of and fills in for *showing*. The failure of Montès's consciousness (or the narrator's) to show itself, the failure of the events to be immediately present or visible to his or any other consciousness, necessitates that they be told. *The Wind* is thus constructed in terms of the failure of any consciousness to be totally present to the world and to itself. This means at least two things: first, that for this novel, fiction is not equivalent to or rooted in a traditional concept of consciousness but acts rather as a supplement to consciousness, filling in for the blank spaces of consciousness and adding to what is present in it, recounting its failures more than its successes; second, that at the heart of fiction there is an unavoidable tension between the expectations of consciousness (mainly the desire for order, form, and sense) and the necessarily inadequate alternatives fiction offers to these expectations (by both telling and showing). At the heart of every consciousness, in fact, and not just in "exceptional cases," an inadequacy exists from which fiction arises.

Critics have not been wrong to insist on the particular and peculiar nature of Montès, for unlike a Jamesian personality or "subject" there can be no illusion of penetrating his "consciousness" directly. As a "window" onto the world he is not simply a unique shape, a particular slant, but an opening so distorted, so misshapen, so "fluid," that it threatens the very coming into being of the form and shape of the novel. Within the novel, this misshapen consciousness is seen as a kind of madness; according to the notary, who proclaims himself to be the "most reliable" of all narrators, Montès is "an idiot, that's all. Nothing but a fool, an imbecile" (*The Wind*, p. 9). And as the narrator adds soon after, Montès is "the one who had been the subject of the town's gossip for so long, the man people like the notary had probably still not finished talking about . . . no sooner appearing than arousing rebellion, desire, discord, anger" (pp. 11–12). The "collective consciousness" of the town, as much as it fears and ultimately rejects Montès, in fact needs this madness in order to affirm all the more vigorously its own "rationality" in contrast to it. But this rationality always risks being contaminated by Montès's "madness"; and even the notary must ask himself in the presence of Montès, even if facetiously, which one of them is mad: "that dialogue about which the notary later remarked that by the end of it he had actually wondered which of the two of them, he himself or the other, was the idiot or the lunatic" (p. 24). The rational, ordered consciousness of the community, therefore, can impose itself as the dominant point of view only with the "domestication" of this "wild" consciousness which resists it. The dramatization of narration of *The Wind* is basically of the unresolvable conflict of these consciousnesses.

The narrator of *The Wind* shares neither the perspective of the notary and the other townspeople nor that of Montès, assuming Montès does determine something close to *a point of view* (which is in fact a highly questionable assumption). He seeks to reconstruct as faithfully as possible the events that occurred and to give as complete a narration of them as possible; he must take into account in some way, therefore, both *the* version offered by the notary and the contradictory fragments offered by Montès. In the position of a historian attempting to uncover the "truth" of the past, "things as they really were," the narrator also faces the problem of form; for there cannot be narration of the past without the establishment of some point of view in terms of which the past can be organized. In fact, the search for the "truth" of the past, (for *histoire*), which implies the search for a form adequate to *histoire*, is no more mystified (and no less either) a search than the experimentation with (search for) "form itself" (the *récit*). One problem leads inevitably to the other, and to pretend that the postulate that the *récit* has precedent over the *histoire* is more "advanced" and less mystified than the postulate which states the contrary is in fact to accept that signifier and signified, *récit* and *histoire*, exist as separate entities, and that one aspect of fiction is more essential than another. To analyze the problem of consciousness in *The Wind* is at the same time to analyze the problem of form; to begin the other way, I would argue, is no more "enlightened," no less mystified. It all depends on the assumptions at work and the strategy used.

The notary's perspective in the novel is privileged, since he is a witness to all the events occurring in this small town (the "secretary" of his society);

for sooner or later everyone invariably enters his office for some financial transaction or inheritance. The point of view he assumes and the one around which he organizes his version of Montès's story claims that all actions are motivated by self-interest and economics: "Because as far as samples of humanity go, everything in the world comes in here, believe me, and as far as for people's motives, if I've learned anything in the twenty years I've spent in this office, it is that there's one and only one, and that one is—self-interest" (p. 9). "The single motive of every human action, of all the so-called psychological dramas, and I've seen enough of them acted out in this office to be entitled to talk about them, well, it's self-interest, it's advantage, and nothing but" (p. 14). Establishing such a point of view postulates a principle in terms of which everything can be explained, a fixed perspective and a place (his office) which serves as the center and origin of the "universe" he describes.

The notary's point of view evidently represents a certain social class, or at least a segment of it, "for the notary had that peculiarity, that gift, or, if you prefer, that weakness, of somehow not existing by himself, being instead a medium that seemed to speak not in his own behalf but for the whole town, or at least for what (not a class, properly speaking...not a caste either... rather a certain milieu) considered itself as the town to the exclusion of any other category which was regarded as non-existent" (p. 114). His social function coincides with his "formal" function; the identity of the subject at the origin of point of view is here not that of a Jamesian "individual" but rather that of a "milieu"; the consciousness is that of a certain segment of a ruling class. Nonetheless, in spite of these differences the principle of identity remains the same, whether the subject is individual or collective—the concept of form implied is also the same. The "world"[18] that the point of view of the notary organizes and explains is closed, identical to that which the nineteenth-century novel in general proposes. If we accept *his* definition of the world and the closure this definition imposes on it, the notary is as "omniscient" in this world as any Balzacian narrator, excluding or suppressing from this world anything which challenges his omniscience, anything which resists the sense imposed on it and the place assigned to it (i.e., Montès, and as we shall see later, the wind). Omniscience is simply the ideal form of consciousness; it is the generalization of the individual consciousness rather than being its contrary. The establishment of the notary's point of view as the dominant and central *point* of view would mean that his social class had effectively imposed its order on events and insured that its history would be taken as History itself. The form of any narration from such a point of view would necessarily be closed and integral; the story told as continuous as the unending succession of notaries: "the obscure and victorious army of innumerable notaries like this one" (p. 115).

The notary is not the principal narrator of *The Wind*, however; nor is it certain that he (the "milieu" he represents) has effectively established his (its) point of view, that is, suppressed everything that does not conform to it, that resists its ordering. In the first place, omniscience has supposedly no place in the theory and practice of the New Novel; it is a remnant from another time, one of the elements of the Balzacian novel most severely attacked by Robbe-Grillet in *For a New Novel*.[19] In fact, the novel undermines the notary's role from within; but by describing the context in which "omniscience" is necessarily situated and on which it depends—a closed, centered, stable, hierarchical concept of society and the form of the novel homologous to it—the novel does more than simply *oppose* this concept. For omniscience is not really rejected if the concept of the individual consciousness is retained. As we have seen, certain aspects of omniscience are present in even the most limited points of view, the "slightest of subjects": namely the identity of the subject and its immediate relationship with *its* world. The subject, no matter how slight, retains the essential aspects of the Subject, even if the individual subject's world is more limited than the "omniscient" Subject's. The undermining of omniscience, of Consciousness, from within the novel also affects the more modest and limited concept of individual consciousness and the construction of its "world."

For the "order" and "rationality" of the community represented by the notary, Montès is a *malin génie* who relates to the world "regardless, as the notary put it, of all reason, and even, some went so far as to say, of all shame" (p. 20). For Montès's "point of view" never establishes itself as *a definite point* nor produces a rational discourse, a narration with the logical relationships the novelistic tradition has taught us to expect, "for there was no connection, in his account, between the different episodes or rather scenes he was describing, like those dreams where you suddenly change from one place to another, from one situation to another with no transition ... constantly harried by that furious and impotent sense of urgency, of time running out, inexorable, threatening, disastrous" (p. 87). Montès cannot mount the "effort" necessary to order the world and reduce the world to a manageable, rational, coherent entity to which the notary owes his "omniscience." He is unable to dominate his consciousness, unable to situate himself completely at its origin. Like dreams, his consciousness works according to "exterior," unconscious mechanisms which he does not control;[20] and in addition, at the heart of Montès's consciousness time as a destructive, differentiating force undercuts at each moment the possibility of immediacy, of his being at one with himself and his consciousness.

The "original nature" of Montès's consciousness does not distinguish him from the notary, however, for initially each consciousness, even the notary's, is more and/or less than the reduced, ordered, final state of the notary's. The difference between Montès's consciousness and the notary's is not a difference of nature, but rather due to Montès's inability after the fact to "make sense" out of his consciousness by filling in for what is missing and eliminating what is excessive: "his fundamental inaptitude for being conscious of life, things, events except by the intermediary of his senses, his heart (an inaptitude we ordinarily correct, remedy by an intellectual effort devoted to caulking in the time sequences that have escaped our perception" (p. 153). The irrationality and disorder the notary attributes to Montès's particular and peculiar point of view on things characterizes consciousness in general before it is corrected, rationalized, or rectified—that is, before it is *reduced to a point of view*.

73

An unrectified consciousness is not necessarily *one*, not the attribute of a unique subject or identity. Montès is rarely *at one* with "his" consciousness; it is *his* and *not his* at the same time: "Later he told me he felt something strange happening inside himself. 'As if,' he said, 'I was passing or rather my consciousness was passing back and forth from outside in, then from inside out. I mean as if I were suddenly both of us ... and then right afterwards, with no transition, or rather at the same moment, I could see two of us, tiny insignificant miserable and lost" (p. 103, translation modified). At other moments, before recognition, before distinguishing and making sense out of (giving *a form* to) shapes and lines, there first exists an imprecise blur of colors and forms whose borders are not yet fixed and determined:

> something confused, like a mosaic of faces ... while the pictures in the news-paper, the policeman's sleeve, the outline of the policeman himself blurred ... still staring (now they were nothing but vague spots flecked with silver) at the shapes of the inspector and the priest which drew closer together, melting into one another ... this lasted a moment, then the one black shape formed by the two men changed, distended, narrowed at the center, the isthmus con-necting them growing thinner and thinner finally breaking ... and nothing else (no concept, no idea, and above all no thought) following in his mind: nothing but the mere consciousness of forms, objects. (Pp. 201-2)

Montès's consciousness lacks at these moments, when he is not able to establish himself as an identity at the origin of his consciousness and when the matter of "his" consciousness itself is impossible to *identify* as such, *a concept, an idea, a thought* to anchor and organize this unformed (more than simply formed) plurality. Without such a concept no simple point of view can be established and no simple form produced. Consciousness in this sense is not the origin or center of form, but a conflictual, open plurality which decenters and undermines the closed, visible integrity of form.

The establishment of a point of view and the rectification and reduction of consciousness, therefore, are not original but derived activities—the "eye" neces-sary for such a reduction is formed or trained to see only the visible unity of the "world," to reduce the "world" to this unity. The consciousness which makes possible point of view—i.e. consciousness in its most reduced form—takes place then after a delay, after the fact: "then I saw him give a start, as if his mind suffered a lapse, a delay, as if a series of complicated delays was required for it to receive the images it registered" (p. 110). In the same way, Montès's own voice is not initially "his," not the expression of a subject identical to itself; but it *becomes* "his" after the fact, when he is able to "identify" it after a delay: "Still hearing his own voice articulating the words of refusal as if outside himself, without his having anything to do with it" (p. 203). It *is* possible, therefore, to analyze *The Wind* in terms of the problem of point of view; for even Montès, the "idiot," does constitute (from time to time) *a point of view*. Such an analysis, however, must confront its own limitations, the very reduced space in which it can operate given the limited impact of point of view in the novel, and everything for which such an approach cannot account. To accept point of view as the dominant factor in the determination and discussion of form is to accept the point of view of the notary in *The Wind*—that is, the point of view continually undermined by the novel itself.

The major premise of the novel, stated on the very first page and repeated throughout this and other Simon novels, asserts that consciousness is at the same time incomplete and excessive, its inadequacies supplemented from within by imagination (through "fictions") at the moment of consciousness itself and at each moment thereafter: "And while the notary was talking, telling the story again for maybe the tenth time (or at least what he knew of the story, or what he imagined, having in relation to the events... like everyone else, like the heroes of those events, only that fragmentary, incomplete knowledge... —words, images, sensations—vague, full of gaps, blanks that the imagination and an approximate logic tried to remedy by a series of risky deductions—risky though not necessarily false" (pp. 9–10). Inherent in any point of view, and not just Montès's, and yet suppressed by the concept of point of view itself, is an initial plurality singularized after the fact, a plurality consisting of gaps and blank spaces which are then supplemented and filled in by the imposition of a derived, "logical" order—and this singular order constitutes point of view. The form of fiction cannot, then, be derived totally from the principle of point of view because the latter is itself a derived concept.

The division of fiction into form and content, signifier and signified, or *récit* and *histoire*, then, is not completely pertinent, for no content, signified, or *histoire* is ever simple in itself, a pure event or experience. The "experience" of Montès is already the "experience" of the writer; for consciousness is a complex text in itself, not "outside" and at the origin of fiction as a model or first cause but "within"—never the simple, immediate perception of what is but a complicated, incomplete/excessive text:[21] "That was what he had just lived through: that incoherence, that brutal apparently absurd juxtaposition of sensations, faces, words, actions. Like a story with the syntax—subject, predicate, object—missing from every sentence... and then life recovers its superb and arrogant independence, becomes again that disordered abundance without beginning or end or order, the words fresh again, freed of syntax, that stale arrangement, that all purpose cement" (p. 184). Not being firmly anchored in a point of view, that of a subject at one with itself, the "experience" of this "consciousness" is not and cannot be translated into a developed, well-formed *histoire* but only into one whose origin and end is in formlessness and disorder, which is open-ended rather than closed, a text that is never quite itself.

Imposing a "form" on the novel charts its boundaries, declares where it begins and ends and in terms of what it is organized. The narrator of *The Wind*, however, continually affirms the arbitrary nature of any beginning or end, of any closure, in much the same way that James had to admit that he was unable to master totally the "germination" of his novels. In spite of the narrator's supposed function of imposing order, Montès's "experience" remains fragmented, "open," a narration neither Montès, nor the narrator, nor any other point of view can quite control: "So there I was again, dragged in in spite of myself, as if by a drowning man...I, too, drawn in after him, placed in that perspective of time extending like a gray wall with neither beginning nor end, patched with old peeling posters...fragments of texts with neither beginning nor end, no continuity, juxtaposed, self-contradictory" (p. 156). The search for the original of fiction, the center of its form, remains at one and the same time necessary and ultimately impossible, as endless as the search for "reality" itself on which it depends. It is a process with the characteristics of a *mise en abyme*: "trying to find it (reality), discover it, drive it out of hiding is perhaps just as futile and disappointing as those toys, those Central European dolls that look like old women cupped within the other, each enclosing, revealing a smaller one inside, until you get down to something minute, infinitesimal, insigificant" (p. 10). The origin, then, is never completely original, and the founding consciousness thus always in some way derived, because their foundation is not fixed or determined, the Real itself, but an infinite process from which the "original" is always in some sense missing.

Any account of events made after the fact, therefore, "falsifies" or "fictionalizes" the past because it does not capture the desired immediacy of consciousness: "Only seeing, registering without being quite conscious of it all, so that the account he gave me was probably somewhat false, artificial, as any account of events is bound to be false after the fact, since by the very fact of being described even the most insignificant events assume a formal, consequential aspect" (p. 51). But we have already seen that this process resides within consciousness itself, that the delay responsible for the multiplicity of "false," artificial accounts is inherent in all moments of consciousness and does not begin only after an initial moment of immediacy has been lost. This delay in fact is a fundamental characteristic of consciousness which *all theories* of consciousness attempt to suppress or deny. The lack within the supposed plentide of consciousness is precisely the unstable "space" I have argued that fiction "occupies" as well as the inevitable "fictional" quality of (within) the concepts of consciousness and point of view themselves. Fiction is thus "essentially" neither *showing* nor *telling*, neither pure visibility nor narration, neither pure consciousness nor text, for none of the terms ever exists entirely in itself.[22]

The instability inherent in any point of view, the complex, nonoriginal characteristics of any consciousness (not only Montès's), derives from the instability at the heart of the fictional space itself. For unlike the world projected by the notary, the space in which the narrator says "I" (the space in which Montès and in fact the notary are also located) is an open rather than a closed space, a space which is disrupted by time and change, a space continually being transformed, displaced, and decentered. The uncontrollable force metaphorically connected to this instability, there from the beginning, unchartable and erratic is, in fact, as the title of the novel indicates, the wind: "Through the window I could see the two stunted palm trees in the courtyard tossing in the wind's sporadic gusts. Always the wind" (p. 41). More fundamental than sense, form, and order, the wind blows without purpose, formless and senseless: "and naturally this godforsaken wind, the saraband of papers, leaves, and whirling rubbish hustled about by the March squalls, the indefatigable, permanent gale ceaselessly galloping down the diaphanous sky, growing wild, intoxicated with its own rage, its own useless power, devoid of sense" (p. 43; translation modified and completed). The wind is always there, not as a presence, something to be seen, understood, controlled—i.e. not as *a form*—but as a disruptive and differentiating force wearing away the integrity of the present, carrying with it the debris of the past, continually disordering and reordering.

The particular characteristics of Montès's point of view (the particular shape of the window his consciousness forms) are thus not the explanation and sense, the ultimate origin and cause, of the difficulties the narrator (and the critic after him) has establishing a point of view in the novel; the wind (*The Wind*) has already undermined the solidity, stability, and integrity—the form—of the space in which point of view attempts to establish itself. The eye ("I") of the reader, like that of the narrator, is drawn into the complex and contradictory labyrinth of narration which constitutes *The Wind*, losing in the process the status of an "I" (and thus the "eye" derived from it), as well as *the point* of point of view. What James could only "wonder at" and what he was forced to admit in spite of himself has in *The Wind* become not an impediment to fiction but its reason for being.

## Fictions of Form: Life, Death, and Voice

Form is obstinate, that's its danger.

Maurice Blanchot, *L'Entretien infini*

The argument that *The Wind* is "less advanced" than novels published after it depends on an arbitrary definition of form and formal excellence or "purity," one deeply rooted in the history of aesthetics and philosophy. The argument first separates signifier from signified (*récit* from *histoire*) in order to privilege the former, and ends up idealizing a concept of form over all others. Dominated by an ideal of form as the visible presence of the text itself, that is, the immediate self-presentation or self-consciousness of the text (primarily as signifier), it imposes on fiction a coherent reading, a sense no less restrictive than that given by traditional thematic analyses. An examination of *The Grass* will now reveal the premises at work in the imposition of such a formal ideal and its limitations—and, more specifically, what the ideal excludes from itself in order to maintain its "formal purity."

For Gérard Roubichou, *The Grass* is "visibly" concerned with its own status as narration on a formal rather than thematic level: "a fiction is put in place through a narration which ceaselessly displays its own creative processes. The 'peripeties' of narration have become as important and interesting as those of fiction" (*Lecture de L'Herbe*, p. 103). Not only have the changes in *narration* (the signifier) become as important as those of *fiction*, the story told (the signified), but *The Grass* for Roubichou also reveals that the fiction narrated is a secondary, derived level of the text dependent on *narration:* "the text contains indices which display an elaboration of fiction through the givens of narration" (p. 90). Roubichou's argument is in fact that all fiction is primarily and essentially *narration*, and only secondarily story (*histoire* or *fiction*). The advantage of *The Grass*, therefore, is not that this argument applies to it, for all novels ultimately are open to this kind of analysis, no matter how "realistic," or how "traditional," but rather that it displays and demonstrates the priority of *narration* over *fiction* openly and explicitly, making its formal assumptions visible for the eye to see. The *mise en scène* of the priority of form (narration), the *visible presentation* of its own construction, is ultimately for Roubichou the difference between the "late" and the "early" Simon. Simon's fiction has become conscious of its own formal properties; and not only is this consciousness dominant, the principle of construction around which the novel takes form, but the novel also displays this principle for all to see.

One of the major differences between *The Wind* and *The Grass* for Roubichou is that the narrator of *The Grass* is no longer a "character" in the novel, a "subject" who interacts with other "subjects" as he tries to construct a credible and "accurate" *récit* from the different and contradictory *récits* recounted to him.[23] Because the narrator has no "personality," no "identity," Roubichou calls him an "anonymous narrator" (p. 102): he has no "life," no story of his own to tell, no story to interfere with the story being told, to interfere with our "direct" and "immediate" access to the central consciousness of the novel. The narrative process is no longer an anecdote as in *The Wind*; rather we have a narrator who *shows* the process of narration as a function in a formal system, not as an attribute of any "living" subject. Form points directly to itself as form, as the origin of this or any other *récit*, with no interference from any "outside" source. Lubbock's ideal has been taken one step further and realized as the pure consciousness of fiction of itself.

The "invisibility" of the narrator as a "person" has caused various critics, as Roubichou points out (pp. 48–49, note 40), mistakenly to make Louise the narrator, when she is only the "subject" (in Jamesian terminology) or "point of focalization" (in Genette's)—what Roubichou calls a "means of reference"— and not the origin and source of the narrative voice itself. The question of the origin of this voice and the consciousness associated with it dominates and structures Roubichou's reading of the novel; for the answer he gives to this question—the narrator as the "creative," productive side of language itself, the consciousness of form of itself—is an essential component of the concept or model of form he applies to the novel. In fact, one could say that it is its "center."

The narrator does, in certain instances, put himself in Louise's place and tells us "directly" (i.e. "shows") what she sees and feels: "Louise's position is the spatial reference point of the evocation; and the narrator's *récit* often presents itself as an equivalence of the direct experience of the character" (p. 73). Even though Roubichou calls the narrator's ability to move in and out of Louise's consciousness "surprising" in this instance, there is really nothing "new" or "surprising" about it—the novels employing such a technique are too numerous to mention. Nor is the narrator's anonymity "new" either: for as Roubichou himself admits, most realist texts employ "anonymous narrators." Roubichou is really arguing that what is really "new" in *The Grass* is that the retreat of the narrator-as-person has brought about the advancement of the narrator-as-function, "the visible work of narration."

Thus, for Roubichou, the visibility of the narrative function is the sign of the "highest achievement" of fiction, fiction showing itself for what "it is." "'Louise' and 'the narrator' share the interest of the reader" (p. 135), says Roubichou (p. 135); the Jamesian "subject" shares with the *narrative process* itself center stage. In other words, the *narrative process* has become a possible "subject" for the novel (perhaps even *the subject* of the novel). The novel displays for us its own inception in form; we are present at the very origin or "birth of the *récit*" (p. 122). Something then is *shown* in itself, without any "interference" or mediation from any other "subject" whatsoever, but it is not the consciousness of a "character-subject"—it is rather the consciousness of form itself, of form of itself. We are in the presence of the truth of form, of form as truth.

This brings us back very close to James and Lubbock; the only difference being that while James posited the "truth" and "origin" of fiction in point of view, the particular form of the "subject's" consciousness, Roubichou locates it in the self-consciousness of form itself. The ideal form in both cases, however, remains centered and closed, and its origin can be grasped by (i.e. is visible to) the reader with a "trained eye." Roubichou does not even exclude the presence of the author from the problem of form, for like James he sees the author behind the narrator. The "creative role" he assigns to the narrative function ultimately derives from the writer, Claude Simon himself *in action*: "It can be perhaps better seen now how the narrator is defined. *He is not strictly speaking a 'person,'* but rather the 'novelist in action' in his essential function: the manipulation of language by and through which the novel is written" (p. 134). For Simon, says Roubichou, "to recount is to choose a way to show that one invents" (p. 129). The author-subject, then, is still present at the origin of fiction ("invention"), but only as a "manipulator of language." The narrator is still the "double" of this author-subject, reflecting his "essential" function and characteristics.

Roubichou and other structuralists begin with the assumption that the author's initial "intentions" have a little role to play in the finished product. They make a law out of James's observation on the "monstruous" and uncontrolled growth of his novels. The contemporary novelist who is influenced by structuralist theories of fiction like Simon, *intends* only to be at one with his work, with the finished product and not any initial project which he knows and *intends* to be inadequate. Simon describes the process of "creation" or "production" in the following way in *Orion aveugle* (Geneva: Albert Skira, 1970).

> I know of no other paths of creation than those opened step by step, that is to say word after word, by the march itself of writing. Before I begin tracing signs on paper there is nothing but an unformed magma of more or less confused sensations, of more or less precisely accumulated memories, and a vague —very vague—project. It is only in writing that something is produced [produces itself], in all senses of the term. What is fascinating for me in all this is that this something is always richer than what I intended to do. (Pp. 6–7)

What "fascinates" Simon here seems to fascinate all structuralist critics and all writers influenced by their theory of writing: the productive side of language, what language produces itself, within itself. The role and intention of the author are reduced to observing this "miracle," as Simon calls it, "be produced." This is his reason for writing: "And the most fascinating and perhaps central revelation that the work brings is that these purely formal necessities, far from constituting constraints or obstacles, reveal themselves to be eminently *productive* and, in themselves, *engendering* ... If someone asked me why I wrote, I would answer that it was to see each time this curious miracle be produced."[24] The "wonderment" of James is still present in Simon, but he posits the "productive" side of form as the "origin" of fiction and makes it the principle of his novelistic practice. The author-subject is still present in his work, or behind it, but as a consciousness which like that of the critic comes in after the fact, after form has done its work, to be at one with this "living product" which is practically self-engendered.[25]

Thus, a major problem in the history of aesthetics and philosophy seems to have been dispensed with by the relocation of the author-subject within language considered as a formal system and by the reduction of fiction to its "exterior," "visible" form.[26] The intentions of the author are replaced, however, by an equally questionable concept: the "creativity" or "productivity" of language itself. The great discovery of structuralist thinking, repeated in most of the contemporary criticism of the New Novel, is that language is primary, and that therefore all "creation" must pass by way of it. The narrator of *The Grass*, the double for the "author at work," still "creates" according to Roubichou, but from what language gives to him not *ex nihilo*: "The narrator literally and visibly creates this universe through resources which the language he uses provides him: especially the words and expressions he uses, which constitute so many spring-boards from which fiction is fashioned" (p. 151). Again the work of the narrator (and the author) is *visible*, for how else would we be able to see the narrator "create." The goal of structuralist analyses seems to be identical to that of the author-narrator, to *show* how form is produced or even how form produces itself: in other words, "to valorize ... the creativity of language" (p. 209). It is just as necessary, however, to question the "originality" of form, its "visible creativeness" as well as the premises behind the relocation of the author *in* form, as it was to question the originality of consciousness in James and the location of the author outside the "house of fiction."

Exactly what has changed and what are the consequences of this change when the "creativity" of the author has been replaced by the "creativity" of language itself as an explanation for the origin of fiction and its form? First of all, an emphasis on the "creativity of language" largely ignores the problem of the general context in which the narration takes place, the textual and intertextual network of which it is a part, the historical and philosophical implications of any "product" of form. For "to create" is supposedly to produce something which did not exist before, a form and a sense which are "visibly" different from other forms and senses, even if made out of the materials of language itself. Making language, rather than the author, the active, productive force in "creation" does little to change the concept of "creation" itself, even if it will now be called more often than not "production" rather than "creation" (ex nihilo).[27] As what is produced is emphasized, what interferes with or simply escapes production, being formed into a "product," is ignored. Language is treated as if it were a "living organism," growing and taking on new shapes and forms at all times, an active, productive subject, conscious of itself and its activities. This "subject" has all the attributes of the "living author-subject" in James's theory of fiction, but its consciousness is even more inclusive—nothing seems to escape its "eye" and its consciousness of self. It "wonders" at nothing and seems to control everything.

Or so it seems if we accept this formalist "subject" on its own terms and its consciousness as totally determining. For in order to be conscious of itself as form, it ignores what within form is other than form, not reducible to strictly visible, geometric, logical or functional patterns, not present to the eye at any one moment. In fact, the context of narration in *The Grass*—which is, let us not forget, supposedly the first novel of Simon to practice fully this concept of form—is not the plenitude of life and consciousness, for the narration "takes place" in the proximity of the prolonged death of Louise's husband's Aunt Marie. The proximity of death is more than a theme in the novel, an element of its story (*histoire*); rather death affects all levels of the text, all voices which speak, all linguistic "creations" and productivity. At the formal and thematic center of the novel is the dying Marie; the other incidents narrated—the impending divorce between Louise and her husband, Georges; the ludicrous and perpetual conflict between Georges's parents, Pierre and Sabine; Louise's love affair; the history of the family, etc.—are centered around this barely "living subject." Her "presence" dominates the novel and affects in one way or another all of its elements, but it is a very particular kind of "presence": "So: the old woman—the old fragile heap of bones, skin, exhausted organs yearning for rest, for the original nothingness...at the heart, at the center of the house, reigning, invisible and omnipresent, not only over all the rooms...but even transcending these, extending her presence, her realm, beyond the walls, even beyond the death-rattle [*râle*], as if this need not even be noticed by the ear to be discerned at the foot of the hill, and even farther" (*The Grass*, p. 119).

At the center of this "house of fiction," then, is not the integral presence of a subject but the death-rattle of a dying woman, barely if at all conscious. Unable to speak, to produce meaningful sounds, the death-rattle is the only sound she is able still to utter. It fills her voice and interferes with all other voices; it is an indication of her imminent death, an interference in discourse which seems impossible to flee: "Then Louise stopped listening too, or rather something came between her hearing and the sound of the voice, although she had not actually stopped hearing what that something was...even, she realized, when she thought she was out of reach of the noise, the death-rattle, the powerful bellows...like the regular and terrible pulsations of some organ installed at the very center of the house" (pp. 112-13). The death-rattle is the voice reduced

81

to its most elementary state, at the limits of signification, consciousness, and life itself, meaning and saying (almost) nothing, indicating only the "presence" (nonpresence) of that which escapes meaning and sense, death. Death is at the heart of this voice, not the living presence of a subject.

But in *The Grass* in general, the voice loses its expressive function; as often as not it is cut off from the person who speaks and the sense of the words uttered are ignored or poorly grasped by the person addressed (assuming that this "person" is determinable). The voice has a relative independence from the subject at its source, not totally dependent on the presence and consciousness of the speaker (utterer) or listener (receiver)—that is, on a fixed and identifiable context. Between consciousness and voice there is a gap, a time differentiation, which is supplemented only after the fact: "Then probably noticing, realizing that she was about to speak again, but aloud this time, and doubtless already had been speaking for a while ... because it was in the middle of a sentence her own lips were speaking that she became aware of it hearing herself say ..." (p. 56). As in the case of Montès in *The Wind*, to hear oneself speak is to hear the voice of another. To be at one with one's words is the result of an effort made after the fact, not the initial condition or possibility of the voice—in other words, the origin of the voice is never simple. *The Grass* locates the nonoriginality of the voice, the irreducible relation to an other at the heart of the voice, in the nonpresence (and not the absence) of the subject at the source of the voice, in the subject's proximity to death. The "living voice" is also a carrier of death.

Death is never totally absent from the voice, for the conscious, living presence of the subject (its visible presence to itself and to others) is never the ultimate origin of the voice. The "impersonal"—what Blanchot has called "the neuter"[28] —has always-already displaced this source, complicated it, and rendered it derivative rather than original. The impersonal nature of the origin of the voice, evident in the distance between the consciousness of the subject and his or her voice, and the possibility, even necessity, of the voice escaping the subject's control, are indications of the subject's relation to death, to his/her nonpresence. At the same time the possibility of the voice is its limitation.[29] But this is not to say that the voice is simply a carrier of absence and of non-sense either. Even the death-rattle of Marie, this extreme limit case of the voice, is in no way pure nonsense, for with the intervention of an interpreter-translator, the hunchbacked "mythical figure" (p. 94) who cares for Marie, a "system of communication" of sorts develops between her and the others, her "words" and gestures are given a sense: "And again that sort of cavernous rumble, and the hunchback (for probably ... she also possessed the capacity to understand them, to communicate with them, and this even without the help of words: something like a medium, astride two worlds, so to speak, the living and the inanimate, like a kind of bilingual interpreter able to translate a language no one else would understand" (pp. 95-96). The translator, the medium which conveys (produces) sense from sounds and gestures which are neither sense nor non-sense in themselves, situated between life and death, presence and absence, is a necessary element in the process of the utterance and reception of the voice and its sense. Between the utterer and the receiver (and "behind" each, as their re-source) lies the whole linguistic (and thus historical-philosophical-mythological) system which makes sense possible and at the same time unstable, which allows for the indirect communication of sense but never its immediate enunciation or reception. The "subject" at the origin of the voice is thus never totally determin-ing—nor is the immediate context in which any "speech act" takes place. A non-recuperable, impersonal other is "present" at the origin of the voice as the very possibility of voice—all subjects, all consciousnesses, necessarily come in after the fact.

The voices (the irreducible multiplicity within each voice) of the novel, all of whose sources are in one sense or another problematical, all of which are badly heard, understood after the fact, interrupted or ignored—and this extends to the *narrator's voice* as well as Louise's—do seem to converge and culminate at one "moment" near the end of the novel. The dying Marie, the struggle be-tween Sabine and Georges, and the lovemaking of Louise and her lover have all been intertextually linked, seemingly completing the thematic and formal unity of the novel. All that is left is for Marie to die for the center to be firmly put into place and the plurality and complexity of the various voices and "acts" to be rooted in an *event*, an essential absence around which the novel appears to have been taking form from the start. The absence indicated by this death would seem, then, to constitute the ultimate and definitive sense of the novel, deter-mining it as a form—death would appear to be the center in which consciousness of form originates and around which it structures itself. If this absence were essential and central, *in place*, Roubichou's thesis on the "creativity" and self-consciousness of form could still be pertinent.

Things are not as simple as this, however, because it is impossible to deter-mine within the novel exactly when and even if Marie dies. The event never occurs simply; or rather, it occurs only as repetition. In one sense Marie has never lived, her life being one long, repetitive death agony: "Just an old maid about to die of old age in her bed. If she had ever lived, if all she ever knew about life was anything more than death, if she hadn't already been dead for years and years...A little old woman always wearing those perpetual dark, interchangeable, timeless, and indistinguishable dresses, not even symbols of mourning, of affliction, but perhaps of intemporality, of inexistence" (p. 24). The "event" has already occurred and at the same time not yet occurred, not until the last breath is spent, not until the voice (the *râle*) can no longer enun-ciate at all, not even utter the slightest noise or leave the slightest trace on the mirror: "And Louise: Dead? But she is dead...Wait until she's what? In the ground? Why bother?...What else is she besides a corpse up there in that bed?...But knowing (at the same time she heard her own voice saying it) that it wasn't true...that even when she (Marie) was really dead, when there was no longer any breath to darken, to frost over the mirror...and even when she was buried...she would still not be through being there" (pp. 173–74). As long as there is a voice to utter sounds or breath, and even after, the "event" will not have occurred; and thus Marie's voice (the *râle*) is still a sign of life. At the same time, as we have already seen, the life that it "displays" is one which has already been divided and deferred by death. The voice dominating the novel, through its interference with all other voices, then, is not *one* at all, but divided against itself, a breath (*souffle*), really a "last" breath (*râle*) which is repeated throughout the novel, never indicating either its origin or its end.

The novel performs one final displacement when a voice says to itself (thinks) that which a living voice supposedly cannot say "truthfully": "I am dead." The voice is not that of Marie, however, but that of Louise, lying on the damp grass after making love and repeating over and over, "I am dead." "Louise now lying inert on the grass, motionless, as though dead . . . thinking: 'Now, now I'm dead,' thinking: 'Good. I was so tired so . . .'" (pp. 204–5); "thinking again: 'There. Now I'm dead'" (p. 207); "thinking: 'I'm dead now'" (p. 208). The "real" death of Marie is replaced (repeated "before" and/or "after" the fact) by the proclamation of the death of Louise, the "subject" of the novel, the "means of reference," or the "person" at the origin of "focalization" (depending on the specific theoretical point of view chosen). The absent center (the center as absence) is itself, then, displaced by being repeated.

For, just as the status of Marie is ambiguous, the status of a "subject" whose voice utters, even to itself, "I am dead," is even more so. Is this "subject" dead or alive anyway? Does it remain a "subject" in announcing its own death? Is the statement simply absurd or does it make sense? Perhaps it is the "imagination" of Louise at work (as the author's imagination is at work according to Roubichou), inventing or producing a fictional death for herself as she identifies with the dying Marie and assumes her place at the center of the novel, in the proximity of death. It is this and more, however, for the "fictional death" proclaimed by Louise is at the heart of all voices in the novel, inherent in the very concept of voice itself—the necessary absence of distance between the speaker and his/her voice, the death of the speaker both implied *and* negated within the voice.[30] The problem is to know where such a "fiction" inscribed within a novel (*histoire/récit*) begins and ends, when and how it is born, comes to maturity, and dies, what place it occupies within the production of form and what form the final product (the completed form) actually has. Is a form with such a "spurious center" ever totally visible? Can any consciousness, even its own, be completely conscious of it? Does such a fiction proclaim some truth—for instance the truth of form, of narrative voice, of creativity, of imagination—or does it not rather problematize the whole opposition between truth and fiction, imagination and repetition, creativity and duplication, the visible and the invisible, life and death?

The analysis of the "place" (the "nonplace") of death in *The Grass* reveals, therefore, the lack of "originality" and "creativity" of the narrative process and of the concepts of voice and point of view, and thus renders the "visibility" of form, and the concept of consciousness on which it depends, problematical. Narration is not original in any sense, neither more nor less original than fiction *(histoire)* or consciousness—the whole question of originality or creativity, in whatever form it is raised, is hardly pertinent at all. Narration is not an original invention of the fictional narrator of *The Grass* or of the writer at work, Claude Simon himself, or of language itself. What is original is the displacement of the subject-who-speaks or -who-writes, of the narrator as person or function, from the origin of "life" and his/her own voice—what is original is the necessary conflict between and within voice and consciousness which undermines the certainty and visibility of the context and the form of the narrative process and all points of view.

The chronicle of Marie's life given by her notebooks, the narrative of a woman's life in which "nothing happens," reduces history and narration to their simplest form. As a simple listing of dates and expenses, it reveals the lack of originality of her "life" and of the novel as whole: "the interminable Jacob's ladder rising, extending, notebook after notebook, and it seemed without beginning or end, interchangeable (the notebooks) in time" (p. 184). Where it all begins and ends is an unanswerable question. With Marie? With Louise's "identification" with her? With the narrator's "recapitulation" and "inventions"? With Claude Simon at work? With the fact of language itself? The origin is continually deferred, pushed back further into time and into another form; another origin can always be found in every origin.

The secondhand, nonoriginal quality of Marie's whole existence is equally a metaphor for the novel as a whole, as Louise in some sense continues the process of repetition already at work long before. Like the box which contains the "treasures" of Marie's life, the remnants of her past which she gives to Louise as she is dying, the novel is structured or formed *en abyme:* "a biscuit tin or a cookie jar made out of tin ... and on the lid a young woman wearing a long white dress ... (she was holding the same box in her hand, and the same image was repeated on the cover)" (p. 11). The description of Marie's dresses, pieced together from remnants of other dresses, which in turn had been pieced together so that the "original" dress is no longer visible anywhere, is a metaphor for the complex texture or tissue of the novel, where the whole question of "originality" is not completely pertinent: "sewing their own robes—or rather endlessly twining, readjusting the same dress, making a new one out of two old ones, themselves produced, deriving from preceding dresses, so that a single dress represented ... an ingeneous combination of at least four others ... patched as the cloth frayed, so that finally nothing is left of the original dress but an irregular collection of scraps, themselves replaced as the time came" (pp. 36–37). The concept of *mise en abyme* itself has often served in contemporary theory as the origin of form, as a model or principle which the critic or novelist posits as the truth of fiction when all other truths, all other origins, are assumed to be inadequate—thus in fact using the unending quality of the *mise en abyme* to reinscribe an end or closure within fiction, to impose on it a form which is in appearance open but in fact closed (see chapter 7 below). Fiction, as the *mise en abyme* of itself, becomes a totally self-enclosed, self-sufficient, and self-conscious "object." *The Grass*, however, indicates that such a use of the *mise en abyme* is as problematical as any other imposition of an origin or truth onto fiction, even one which supposedly is the "truth of fiction itself."

The effect of the *mise en abyme* in the novel is not one of self-mastery at all, not a new truth to replace old truths, not a new visibility of form to supplement older versions. The *mise en abyme* rather indicates that which within form is not strictly visible, that which escapes simple perception in the present:

> The old can on whose lid the picture of the young woman lying on the grass and the same curly little dog with the blue ribbon repeated themselves, indefinitely reproduced a size smaller on the lid of the same box the young woman was holding in her hand (actually, that is visibly, only twice, the third cookie tin being already so small that the young woman was nothing more than a mere spot on the green of the grass, and the little dog a speck, but the idea of this endless repetition whose perception escaped the senses, escaped sight, precipitating the mind into a dizzying anguish). (P. 153)

The *mise en abyme* is itself a theoretical, speculative fiction, for the repetition on the box of the two figures is not infinite, not really abyssal at all. It is only the "*idea* of endless repetition," with the third repetition of the figures become a blotch of color or a vague point, hardly visible at all. Its visibility falls off into formlessness, with the infinite series only suggested, not actually visible. The *mise en abyme* as an origin or center for form is just as theoretical, speculative, "fictional," or "spurious" as any other. It is "spuriousness" itself. Furthermore, its effect produces anguish in the subject at the origin of consciousness rather than certainty, the anguish produced by that which is not masterable, not formed, not visible in any simple sense.

*The Grass* consists of a disruptive series of transformations of narrative voice and perspective, a patchwork of memories, voices, and texts; and thus it cannot really be used to argue either the "originality" of the narrative process over the story narrated, or the presence of the author-at-work behind the narrator and other figures of the novel, or the visible, original, creativity of language itself. I have emphasized in my reading of *The Grass* the elements of fiction which cannot be formalized or finalized, made visible to be seen and given a sense, in order to show the limitations of structuralist-formalist approaches to fiction. Formalist theories which argue for the integrity and presence of form as the essence of fiction ultimately suppress all traces, fragments, and undefinable differences which escape simple, formal, visible delineation—they attempt to negate all traces of time and death which are at work in form from the start. A truly living voice full of the presence of a subject (any subject, real, fictional, or formal), is a strict impossibility. Form as a centered, integral concept is a theoretical fiction derived from fiction in an attempt to master fiction from within, to impose an ideal sense on fiction which is in agreement with its assumed "nature."

It is not that formalist studies of voice and point of view have no place in literary studies, but in the form they have traditionally taken and in the form they are now taking, they are limited by the concepts and oppositions which determine their concept of form. To define fiction in terms of its dependence on the concepts of point of view, voice, or the originality of the narrative process is to limit the possibilities of fiction and to eliminate everything from within fiction which is not visible to the eye, even the "best-trained" one. In this way the definition, form, and sense of fiction is limited by other fictions—the fictions of voice, consciousness, point of view, and the narrative process, for instance—which in their turn must be investigated and questioned. Positing form as a self-engendered, productive, "living," linguistic entity does not resolve the problems or overcome the limitations of voice and point of view—on the contrary it simply repeats them by rooting consciousness in a "formal" rather than a "human" subject. Whether *form* takes priority over *consciousness* or *consciousness* over *form* ultimately makes little difference—the same ideal of form is retained in each case, and an "I" behind the "eye" is kept in its place at the origin.

# F O U R
## Representation or the End(s) of History: Dialectics and Fiction

The Spirit *(Geist)* is an artist.

Hegel

### The Origin(s) of Representation: Lukács's *Theory of the Novel*

By searching out origins, one becomes a crab. The historian looks backward; eventually he also *believes* backward.

Nietzsche, *Twilight of the Idols*

Literature is considered to be representational when it produces a *figure* of either a particular and recognizable historical, social or psychological reality or, in a more abstract manner, a *figure* of an ideal, mythical, metaphysical reality—when it presents or makes visible the essential or characteristic traits of some space or context other than the strictly literary. This "extraliterary" space is assumed to exist before its representation and thus to be the origin of representational literature, to be present in itself before it is re-presented in literature—which means that the space is defined by other means than strictly literary ones and assumed to exist in itself before it is "figured" and recognized for what it is in literature.

Whether the essence of this space is defined as the realm of the Idea, of Truth, of the Real (or the real), of society, of history, of the collective subject (as *Geist* or *Weltanschauung*), or the individual subject, it inevitably will fall within the spectrum of possibilities limited at each end by positions which have in the history of philosophy (and especially since Marx) been considered to be polar opposites: idealism and materialism (especially in its historical form). Ever since Plato, philosophy in its various forms has claimed for itself mastery over this extraliterary space, a privileged access to whatever truth is presumed to exist there. At the same time philosophy has relegated literature to a derivative role, at its best imitating or expressing this (philosophy's) truth, at its worst distorting, confusing, or subverting it. All idealisms and materialisms seem to share this definition of the relationship of literature (of all art) with its exterior; they differ simply over the nature of the truth contained there and the way this truth is made present or distorted in literature.

The novel has a special place in the history of theories of representation, for no literary genre seems more intimately intertwined in its history and theory with this question in perhaps its most specific and limited form: what is and is not a faithful and complete portrayal of the real? The novel has been considered by most theories, with a few notable exceptions,[1] to be the realist genre par excellence[2]—it is usually considered to have instituted a break with classical modes of literary expression in order to represent *directly* "everyday reality."[3] The question that largely goes unexplored in theories of realism of this type, which are largely impressionistic and rooted in a fairly naive empiricism, is the nature of the process of representation itself; and thus a certain unquestioned concept of representation tends to dominate, determine and limit all theories of realism.

Dialectical theories of the novel also accept its fundamentally representational nature and tend for the most part to consider it to be *the* bourgeois genre in both a historical and ideological sense. Historically, its "true birth" (or at least its "rebirth" and dominant period) coincides with the decline of feudal, aristocratic society and the rise of the bourgeoisie; and, ideologically, it is the genre which best represents the ideological interests of the bourgeoisie, the genre in which the bourgeoisie most completely and adequately searches for and finds its identity, the images of itself it needs to serve its own interests. In other words, the novel is the privileged mode of representation of the bourgeoisie in a fairly limited period of history. These theories by and large thus also accept a linear view of history in which the birth and development of the novel are given a rational, dialectical sense and made to follow and coincide with the "dialectical progression" of society. More than any other genre, the novel is thus limited to the historical space defined by representation and rationality, the space occupied and determined by philosophy (in its idealist *and* historical-materialist forms); and more than any other genre it seems to accept its assigned place here, to resist least the sense philosophy and history give to it. The only differences between philosophy and the novel seem to be those of rivalry over whether it better than philosophy or history represents the real, whether its form of "fictional" representation and rationality is not more adequate to the task than philosophy's or history's "nonfictional" representations. It would seem difficult, if one takes seriously the history of the novel, to argue with the statement that the novel has been presented as the most historical and the most philosophical of genres.

Historically, the theorists of the novel (and the novelists themselves) who have equated the novel with realism and thus linked it to the rationality of philosophy and history have done so in order to give it worth and stature, in order to raise it up from its premodern status of an "inferior," nonserious, "bastard" mixture of forms to that of a true, "noble," serious genre. As Auerbach has argued, realism is the "emancipation" from "the doctrine of the ancients regarding the several levels of literary representation" (*Mimesis*, p. 489). For the more empiricist theories of realism, it is precisely because the novel is a mixture of forms, of discourses, of dialogues and monologues, of narration and description—that is, because it is not predetermined as a form by tradition or abstract theory—that it is representational, in *immediate* contact with the random material of social, historical or even psychological reality. Its initial plurality, however, is nonetheless limited by the necessity to represent and make sense of "what is," and "what is" is ultimately rational.[4] The initial heterogeneous mixture of forms, which institutes a break with "traditional literature," is structured nevertheless in terms of an ideal, but an ideal that is seemingly more historical than that of traditional, hierarchical, theological genres, though just as determining. What fiction is or should be is predetermined by the concept (image) of the real, which is assumed by the theory and projected onto it. Whether the theory of the real is implicit or explicit, empiricist or dialectical, fiction will ultimately be governed by it, made to take its form and assume its sense—that is to say, fiction will be considered worthy of philosophy and history (realist) only in so much as it is as rational as philosophy and history are assumed to be.

One way to confront the limitations of representational theories of fiction and to criticize the rationality that philosophy imposes on fiction (and on the history of literary theory) is to reject both philosophy and history, as well as the philosophical, rationalistic, prosaic side of fiction, in the name of a "pure aesthetics," of a "poetry" more fundamental than rationality, which philosophy coming in after the fact can master only by being contaminated by it—that is, not really master at all. This is basically Nietzsche's position in *The Birth of Tragedy*,[5] where he sees Plato not only as the first metaphysician but also as the first novelist, and thus places the birth of the novel long before the emergence of the bourgeoisie as a specific class. Like the German Romantics before him, he sees the origin or at least the precursor of the novel in the Socratic dialogues,[6] which for him are philosophical attempts to recuperate, to rationalize art (poetry) for the purposes of philosophy:

> But where unconquerable propensities struggled against the Socratic maxims, their power, together with the impact of his tremendous character, was still great enough to force poetry itself into new and hitherto unknown channels. An instance of this is Plato, who in condemning tragedy and art in general certainly did not lag behind the naive cynicism of his master; he was nevertheless constrained by sheer artistic necessity to create an art form that was related to those forms of art which he repudiated ... If tragedy has absorbed into itself all the earlier types of art, the same might also be said in an eccentric sense of the Platonic dialogue which, a mixture of all extant styles and forms, hovers midway between narrative, lyric, and drama, between prose and poetry, and so has broken the strict old law of the unity of linguistic form ... Indeed, Plato has given to all posterity the model of a new art form, the model of the *novel*—which may be described as an infinitely enhanced Aesopian fable, in which poetry holds the same rank in relation to dialectical philosophy as the same philosophy held for many centuries in relation to theology; namely, the rank of *ancilla.* This was the new position into which Plato, under the pressure of the demonic Socrates, forced poetry. (*The Birth of Tragedy*, pp. 90-91)

The birth of the novel and Western philosophy are identical for Nietzsche, each serving to reduce and control the impact of a poetry which is more fundamental than either the novel or philosophy. But the Platonic dialogues ("novels") do not do this simply for Nietzsche, for in rationalizing (condemning) poetry and art in general Plato was "constrained by sheer artistic necessity" to assume its form—philosophy, in making poetry its handmaiden, in turn becomes poetry's. The mixture constituting the Platonic dialogues (novels) is not only that of styles and forms, but also of poetry (literature) and philosophy: philosophy becomes poetical as it makes poetry philosophical; rationality is forced to take on the disguises of fiction in order to make fiction rational. Representational theories of fiction, like the aesthetic theories to which they seem to be opposed, assume that it is possible to resolve or transcend this "contamination," to return to a state before representation (either to the real itself or to pure poetry) in which representation itself could then be grounded. I will argue against both realist and aesthetic positions that it is in fact the "contamination" constituting representation that is truly historical and not its resolution in either poetry or reality.

The conflicting theories of the birth and definition of the novel are opposed over whether the novel is a rational, homogeneous totality which effectively reflects the rationality and unity of the real itself or an irresolvable, heterogeneous mixture of philosophy and poetry which reveals the limitations of both, the failure of each to mold fiction in its own image. What is at stake in the conflict besides the definition of representation and the status of both poetry and philosophy as separate entities is the concept of history itself. In terms of this problem, the work of Georg Lukács occupies an especially critical position, if for no other reason than it repeats in a very particular form the conflict over how the novel is representational—over how it relates to its historical context and represents the concept of history itself. The work of the early Lukács treats the novel as a heterogeneous mixture of conflictual elements which is unable, strictly speaking, because it is cut off from the essence or presence of the world itself, to represent the world as it is. The late Lukács, theorist of realism, restores to the novel its unity and treats it as one of the privileged modes of representation, as the dialectical resolution of contradictions and the true reflection of reality. But the opposition itself between early and late is perhaps misleading because, as we shall see, the work of both the early and late Lukács is dominated by the same ideal of representation that defines, limits, and ultimately gives or even puts an end to history—even more quickly and massively, in fact, in his later "historical" work than in his earlier work.

For Lukács, the differences between his early and late theories of representation are rooted in one essential difference: his early work is idealist, his later work dialectical and materialist. There is for him, as for the great majority of both his critics and followers, a radical epistemological and political break between his "pre-Marxist" and "Marxist" work.[7] Thus he refers to the early Lukács in the 1962 Preface to *The Theory of the Novel* in the third person: "To put it briefly, the author of *The Theory of the Novel* had a conception of the world which aimed at a fusion of 'left' ethics and 'right' epistemology (ontology, etc)" (p. 21); elsewhere he considers this work "a reactionary work in every respect, full of idealistic mysticism, wrong in all its estimates of historical development."[8]

At the same time Lukács is aware that the break with "idealism" did not occur all at once (assuming that it does occur at all), for in his 1967 "Preface to the New Edition" of *History and Class Consciousness* (translated by Rodney Livingstone; Cambridge: MIT Press, 1971), he criticizes this collection of texts all originally written after his conversion to Marxism but condemned immediately by the Communist party. In 1967 Lukács considers these texts to be a "deviation from Marxism" (p. xvii) rather than its reactionary opposite, as is the case for *The Theory*, closer to "true materialism" but not yet totally "materialist." Of the overlapping of Marxist and idealist influences, Lukács says:

> If Faust could have two souls within his breast, why should not a normal person unite conflicting intellectual trends within himself when he finds himself changing from one class to another in the middle of a world crisis? ... When I recall my none too numerous and none too important literary essays from that period I find that their aggressive and paradoxical idealism often outdoes that of my earlier works. At the same time the process of assimilating Marxism went on apace. If I now regard this disharmonious dualism as characteristic of my ideas at that period it is not my intention to paint it in black and white, as if the dynamics of the situation could be confined within the limits of a struggle between revolutionary good and the evil of bourgeois thought. The transition from one class to the class directly opposed to it is a much more complex business than that. (P. x)

Here Lukács is much more flexible than he is elsewhere—refusing to paint or represent the period in "black and white," as good or evil—accepting at least as a momentary step along his "way to Marx" the simultaneous influence of conflicting tendencies within his thought, the unresolvable (at least at this moment) duality of his position.[9]

Even in making the realization of the subject-object identification in his own work a "sociohistorical" rather than a "logical and philosophical" process (p. xxii) as he claims it is in Hegel, there is still doubt in Lukács's mind as to whether he has really succeeded in "standing Hegel on his feet" and overcome idealism—that is, truly historicized his theory:

> But is the identical subject-object here anything more in truth than a purely metaphysical construct? Can a genuinely identical subject-object be created by self-knowledge, however adequate, and however truly based on an adequate knowledge of society, i.e. however perfect that self-knowledge is? We need only formulate the question precisely to see that it must be answered in the negative ... Thus the proletariat seen as the identical subject-object of the real history of mankind is no materialist consummation that overcomes the constructions of idealism. It is rather an attempt to out-Hegel Hegel, it is an edifice boldly erected above every possible reality and thus attempts objectively to surpass the Master himself. (P. xxiii)

If the essays of *History and Class Consciousness* fail in their attempt to rectify Hegelian idealism, but simply extend it, the problem remains as to how one is to determine the point where (and even if) the real break with idealism occurs, where and how the system is turned right side up and its head and feet, the sky and the ground, the ideal and the material, no longer confused. Lukács says in the same preface, "My own uncritical attitude towards Hegel had still not been overcome" (p. xxxv), implying that later it will be; but if the concepts, oppositions, strategies, and practices governing his later work can be shown to participate fully in the Hegelian idealism denounced, then the oppositions between early and late, idealist and materialist, ahistorical and historical, can hardly be accepted at face value. That Lukács continually struggles with and against Hegel turns out to be the most interesting aspect of his theory; when he speaks with the authority of the subject who knows the way beyond Hegel, who has truly overcome the "idealist theory of representation," then he falls even more completely within the idealism of the Hegelian system he has supposedly negated and overcome.

In his Preface to *The Theory of the Novel*, Lukács claims to have in the period after *The Theory* "arrived at a genuine historico-systematic method... in opposition to the vulgar sociology of a variety of schools during the Stalin period" (p. 17). The problem remains, however, that the only way to posit such a pure or purified Marx ("Marx's real aesthetic") is by privileging (idealizing) *a* reading of Marx which synthesizes his "two souls" (assuming he had only two and that each was integral) into one and assumes not only that the conflicts and contradictions on Marx's own way to "Marx" were overcome but also that Marxist thought is, as Lukács wants his own form of Marxism to be, "a new, homogenous outlook" (Preface to *History and Class Consciousness*, p. x). Marxism, for Lukács, is fundamentally the true, homogenous, totalized system; it is the rectification and transcendence of the Hegelian idealist system. Marxism is the *Aufhebung* of the idealist *Aufhebung;* it is "to subject the Hegelian heritage to a thoroughgoing materialist reinterpretation and hence to transcend and preserve it" (p. xx).[10] In other words, in a sense that will soon become clear, Marxism is for Lukács *the representation* of Hegelianism.

In *The Theory of the Novel*, Lukács employs the Hegelian (really pre-Hegelian) distinction between the epic and the novel: the novel originates in the dissolution of harmony and totality that supposedly defined Greece. The loss of this idealized, mythical Greece produces the historical situation in which the novel emerges out of the epic as the form of this loss, the "expression of transcendental homelessness" (p. 41).[11] The harmonious totality figured by Greece also serves as the utopian end toward which the novel strives and yet which it can never regain. The picture drawn of the origin is not simply an idealization of a mythical Greece, but also of a state which Lukács claims is definitely lost, nonrecoverable, though still yearned after nostalgically. At the origin of history is an ahistorical ideal which governs history by its absence. Though governed in its history by this ideal, the novel itself does not really participate in the ideal or take on its form; its failure to regain, to be adequate to this origin is posited from the start. History is thus a division within, or a break with, a harmonious origin. The novel is historical in that it never completely finds its way home and thus never completely finds its way at all—and this is precisely its advantage over all other forms after the fall from Greece.

The "unhealthy despair" which the later, Marxist Lukács finds characteristic of *The Theory* can probably be rooted in the statements positing the irretrievable loss of the Greek totality, for this loss of the origin could imply that any attempt to discover, project, or reestablish any totality whatsoever is as futile as the attempt to return to Greece itself. Thus the antiutopian statements of *The Theory* are not simply signs of the pessimism of the war period and thus idealist or, even worse, reactionary products of this time as Lukács claims. Their specific function is to criticize all utopian idealisms, all romantic, ahistorical, nostalgic attempts to return to (or project into the future), to recreate or equate, Greece. Lukács sees such attempts as predominately aesthetic or formalist attempts to reduce the world to the sphere of art: "Henceforth, any resurrection of the Greek world is a more or less conscious hypostasy of aesthetics into metaphysics—a violence done to the essence of everything that lies outside the sphere of art, and a desire to destroy it; an attempt to forget that art is only one sphere among many, and that the very disintegration and inadequacy of the world is the pre-condition for the existence of art and its becoming conscious" (*The Theory of the Novel*, p. 38). This criticism of aesthetic idealism, of romantic nostalgia, is hardly one with which the later Lukács would disagree as such; what he finds "unhealthly" must be then the contamination of all utopian projects (of all ends assigned to history) which the loss of the Greek ideal produces in *The Theory*. In *The Theory* there is no distinction made between good and bad, idealist and realist, impossible and possible totalities, as there will be in his later work; all totalities in *The Theory* are modeled after Greece and are therefore lost.[12] Representation of the totality—true representation—is therefore an impossibility after the epic age of Greece.

The novel, however, does not give up the search for totality, nor can it without becoming "inconsequential"; it is for Lukács the privileged mode of the theo-retical, speculative search for totality and true representation. The hero of the novel is a "seeker" (p. 60), but one whose search is endless, the new totality nowhere visible, an impossible and yet necessary dream from the past. The novel is an unrealized (unrealizable) totality, conceived by and forced to remain within the boundaries established by the figure or theory of the absent totality. The novel is historical insomuch as it searches for but never ultimately finds the sense and form of the totality. History here is the difference between the lost, ideal origin and the representations which supplement its absence.

The way to the novel, then, is not clearly marked; the process of the formation of the novel contradictory; the status of the novel as a totality far from assured. The totality constituted by a novel can in fact only be abstract: "In a novel, totality can be systematised only in abstract terms, which is why any system that could be established in the novel... had to be one of abstract concepts and therefore not directly suitable for aesthetic form-giving... In the created reality of the novel all that becomes visible is the distance separating the systematisation from concrete life... Thus the elements of the novel are, in the Hegelian sense, entirely abstract" (p. 70). Thus, the abstract totality which the novel attempts to impose on concrete life can only result in the repeated assertion of the distance separating it from life, its representations from reality itself—that is to say, the opposite effect from the desired epic *representation of presence*.

In a certain sense, then, representation as such never occurs; historical reality is never re-presented as it is. Curiously enough, the conditions under which rep-resentation is possible—an initial state of epic harmony or presence—are the same conditions which make it unnecessary. The total, ahistorical presence of the origin has no need to be, and in fact cannot be, re-presented, because it *is present* in itself. Within this presence, there is no need for representation for the original *is;* without it, when the harmony and presence of Greece to itself have been divided, removed at a distance, or lost, no totally effective representation of presence itself seems possible, because the way back to the origin has been irreparably cut. This irresolvable contradiction at the heart of Lukács's theory of representation is not specific to him but is in fact basic to all theories of representation.[13]

The conflictual, paradoxical status Lukács gives to the novel leads him, following the German Romantics, to assign irony a central place in the formation of the novel. He first seems to give irony a totally dialectical, Hegelian definition: "the self-recognition and, with it, self-abolition of subjectivity" (p. 74). But it is immediately clear that irony does not really form a simple dialectic, for the basic dualities which constitute it remain unresolved: "The antagonistic nature of the inner and outer worlds is not abolished but only recognized as necessary" (p. 75). Irony is not, then, the novel's last resource for constituting itself, for guaranteeing its own autonomy—at least not initially. Irony, as Lukács uses it here, turns the novel against itself and thus seems in fact closer to that of the German Romantics criticized by Hegel than to that of Hegel himself—an irony which Hegel considered perverse, dangerous, and (self-)destructive because it knows no bounds and undercuts the possibility of any synthesis or totality whatsoever.[14] For Lukács, "this irony is directed both at his heroes ... and against his own wisdom, which has been forced to see the uselessness of the struggle and the final victory of reality. Indeed, the irony is a double one in both directions" (p. 85). The struggle to represent reality from this ironic perspective is seen as never totally successful or finalized; the knowledge gained of reality is a knowledge of limitations and insufficiencies, not a positive knowledge, not the re-presentation of *what is.*

Irony points to the instability of the novel as a synthesized, totalized form: "But the parts ... can never lose their inexorable, abstract self-dependence: and their relationship to the totality, although it approximates as closely as possible to an organic one, is nevertheless not a true-born organic relationship but a conceptual one which is abolished again and again" (pp. 75–76). Unlike the epic, which is "homogeneously organic and stable," the novel is "heterogeneously contingent and discrete" (p. 76); the relationship its form establishes between its parts is continually being constructed and abolished. Lukács argues that the synthesis the novel must achieve in order to become an organic form is never realized simply, and perhaps not at all. The novel is given the paradoxical status of a form consisting of a mixture of heterogeneous elements, a form that is never quite able to do more than reveal its own inadequacy as form. The process must begin over and over again: "The composition of the novel is the paradoxical fusion of heterogeneous and discrete components into an organic whole which is then abolished over and over again" (p. 84). Irony is the novel's way of covering over the instability of its form, a way of acknowledging and denying in the same gesture the presence/absence of the organic totality it strives to achieve: "This aspect is only a symptom of contingency; it merely sheds light upon a state of affairs which is necessarily present at all times and everywhere, but which is covered over, by skillfully ironic compositional tact, by a semblance of organic quality which is revealed again and again as illusory" (p. 77). Irony is the trope which points to its own illusory nature, to the nonorganic, fictional, or artificial aspects of form. Irony does not resolve the conflicts and heterogeneity of the novel—at least not initially—but rather maintains and even reasserts them.

Just when it seems as if Lukács's position might become subversively anti-Hegelian and in order to limit and thwart the seemingly destructive aspects of irony, Lukács recuperates irony by making it the principle of "form-giving" (of structure), a negative certitude in itself: "The writer's irony is a negative mysticism to be found in times without a god. It is an attitude of *docta ignorantia* towards meaning, a portrayal of the kindly and malicious workings of the demons, a refusal to comprehend more than the mere fact of these workings; and in it there is the deep certainty, expressible only by form-giving, that through not-desiring-to-know and not-being-able-to-know he has truly encountered, glimpsed and grasped the ultimate, true substance, the present, non-existent God. That is why irony is the objectivity of the novel" (p. 90). Irony, then, is not a concept which in itself could be considered an alternative to the Hegelian concept of art as a totalized form; for this negative principle of certitude is *a principle* nonetheless, and in terms of it the novel ultimately can become a totality, using the complex heterogeneity of its parts as the basis for its own totalization: "Irony, the self-surmounting of a subjectivity that has gone as far as it was possible to go, is the highest freedom that can be achieved in a world without God. That is why it is not only the sole possible *a priori* condition for a true, totality-creating objectivity but also why it makes that totality—the novel—the representative art-form of our age: because the structural categories of the novel constitutively coincide with the world as it is today" (p. 93). We seem to have finally found our way to our destination in the novel as representation and to "ourselves" and our own self-recognition, to "the world as it is today." But the detours, rifts, contradictions, and uncertainties which constitute the way to the novel from the epic are not easily contained even within a negative *Phenomenology*[15] or theology, the form given by irony not easily closed off, its limits definable, its totality visible. The objectivity of irony is tenuous, unstable—the totality it forms in spite of Lukács's desire to have it otherwise (or both ways) problematical. Irony finally does lead to the novel becoming representative, for even a position of "not-being-able-to-know" can serve as a principle of representation, can itself be represented (ironically) as the world and be representative of the world; but it does not lead there directly or without contradictions.

It must be evident by this time that *The Theory* cannot be classified as the simple application of Hegelian categories to the definition and history of the novel. Lukács's approach is massively indebted to Hegel as it traces the (almost) dialectical development of the novel (as an historical subject) through stages of exteriorization, interiorization, and self-recognition (of its limitations) and applies by and large exactly as-is Hegelian terminology to the novel.[16] But it is also more than the mechanical application of Hegelian categories to the novel, if only for the reason that Lukács has taken the profoundly "un-Hegelian" genre of the novel to study—un-Hegelian quite simply because unsynthesizable, untotalizable, not sufficiently dialectical.[17] The novel never adequately and totally becomes *a subject* in the Hegelian sense; it is never completely brought to self-awareness and thus never becomes a totally philosophical, speculative subject—one which represents itself. Thus, no theory can completely account for it or master it, for the non-synthesized mixture of heterogeneous parts resists being raised up to the level of pure philosophical speculation. *The Theory of the Novel* itself falls short of its goal to be *the theory* of the novel, just as the novel falls short of itself and historical representation. For this very reason Hegel criticized and "put in its place"[18] (though not simply) what we usually refer to as Romanticism as the final dissolution of art, and for this same reason the novel in *The Theory* ultimately escapes being enclosed by theorizing, speculation, or rationalization, refuses to be simply representative, to represent either or both the individual subject and the world—and this becomes its theory.

I have emphasized up to this point in Lukács's *Theory of the Novel* the internal contradictions which undermine his (or any other) attempts to theorize, to represent for speculative thought, what are presented in his own terms as the "unrepresentable" aspects of fiction and historical reality—the original distance separating the novel from the real, differences between the two which cannot be overcome in simple representation. Lukács's concept of irony is a critical concept inasmuch as it takes into account these differences and yet resists either falling back onto a naive relativism or a subjective or transcendental idealism to account for them or to resolve them. Nevertheless, the mythical, ideal origin, the homogeneous totality, finally has its way, and Lukács is unable to sustain the ironic position described up to this point—precisely it is a position which cannot ever be totally assumed or sustained. The temptation of the orgin is too great. In his chapter "The Romanticism of Disillusionment," Lukács introduces a new element into his discussion of the novel which, he claims, like the "certitude of a negative irony," brings about a successful resolution to the problems of totalization and representation: the problem of "real time" in the sense of the Bergsonian *durée*. Historicity will make representation possible again, or to put it another way, representation is again possible as the end of each moment of history and of history in general, when history is unified and has an end.

Time at first seems to be at the heart of the heterogeneity of the novel, a "corrupting principle" at the heart of all experience, a product of the loss of the organic, ahistorical homogeneity of the epic: "In the epic the life-immanence of meaning is so strong that it abolishes time... In the novel, meaning is separated from life, and hence the essential from the temporal; we might almost say that the entire inner action of the novel is nothing but a struggle against the power of time" (p. 122). Time is thus the best indication of the irresolvable rift or fissure at the heart of the novel, the sign of the non-epic quality of the novel and its historical-philosophical period. But time is also—and this is in Lukács's own words, his "discovery"[19]—the solution to the heterogeneity and the seemingly irresolvable contradictions which constitute the novel. Time in this sense is posited as the fundamental continuity of lived experience, the essentiality which overcomes the accidental nature of any isolated experience: "Beyond events, beyond psychology, time gives them [the characters] the essential quality of their existence: however accidental the appearance of a character may be in pragmatic and psychological terms, it emerges from an existent, experienced continuity, and the atmosphere of thus being borne upon the unique and unrepeatable stream of life cancels out the accidental nature of the events recounted. The life totality which carries all men here becomes a living and dynamic thing . . . a thing existing in itself and for itself, a concrete and organic continuum" (p. 125). Now the contradictions and oppositions discussed earlier are seen as only apparent, for Lukács has "discovered" a way to make life itself a continuous temporality and thus "a concrete and organic continuum." The novel seems to have finally found a way to figure itself as a totality, to figure adequately its essence and that of life; through time, it seems to overcome the "destructive irony" which previously characterized it and thus to attain epic dimensions. Time, which is the sign of the break with the epic, is also the way back to the epic and the recapturing of the origin; *representation* is now (again or for the first time) possible.

The novel *figures* this totality through hope and particularly through memory, for experience itself in the present grasps the divisive, destructive nature of time rather than its continuity: "the experiences of hope and memory; experiences of time which are victories over time: a synoptic vision of time as solidified unity *ante rem* and its synoptic comprehension *post rem. In re,* there can be no simple, happy experience of this form or of the times which have produced it. Experiences of this kind can only be subjective and reflexive; nevertheless there is always in them the form-giving sense of comprehending a meaning; they are experiences in which we come as near as we can, in a world forsaken by God, to the essence of things" (p. 124). Hope and memory are form-giving, totalized experiences, true representations. Before and/or after the fact, the victory over the destructive aspects of time can occur; like philosophy, the novel, when it is the representation of experience through memory, becomes true representation, the interiorization and totalization of experience, the synthesis of all fragmentation.[20] By a ruse of reason, of memory, a novel, Flaubert's *L'Education sentimentale,* achieves in *The Theory* what the absolute Spirit achieves in the *Phenomenology;* it achieves what the epic *is* by definition and what the novel seemed irremediably to be cut off from: the harmonious totality of the subject at one with itself and the world.

> The objective structure of the world of the novel shows a heterogeneous totality, regulated only by regulative ideas, whose meaning is prescribed but not given. That is why the unity of the personality and the world—a unity which is dimly sensed through memory, yet which once was part of our lived experience—that is why this unity in its subjectively constitutive, objectively reflexive essence is the most profound and authentic means of accomplishing the totality required by the novel form. The subject's return home to itself is to be found in this experience, just as the anticipation of this return and the desire for it lie at the root of the experience of hope. It is this return home that, in retrospect, completes everything that was begun,

interrupted and allowed to fall by the way—completes it and turns it into rounded action. The lyrical character of moods is transcended in the mood of experiencing this homecoming because it is related to the outside world, to the totality of life. (Pp. 128–29)

If this novel, and thus the novel in general, can overcome, that is synthesize, its own fragmentation as it does here for Lukács, then *The Theory of the Novel* ends up being much less pessimistic than has been claimed. Its negativity is simply a slight detour, a moment on the way to the positivity indicated in *L'Education sentimentale;* the homelessness of its origins overcome in this "homecoming."

The novel, then, appears on the philosophic-historical stage simply as a step on the way from the epic to a renewed novel-epic,[21] a negative moment, a moment of alterity to be sure, but one which culminates here in the assumption and transcendence of its own negativity. In fact, with *L'Education sentimentale* we have finally arrived at the true novel, all previous "great novels" having a "tendency to overlap into the epic," this one being the "only real exception to this and ... therefore best suited to serve as a model of the novel form" (p. 129). And yet the novel, when it has succeeded in becoming most fully itself—that is, by definition other than the epic—paradoxically achieves at the same time epic proportions, realizing through the assumption of negativity what the epic *is* simply and immediately. Even in his most negative, "pessimistic" work, Lukács recuperates the novel (dialectically) for speculative thought. The stage is already set for his later work. Theory has triumphed over fiction, Hegel over irony, the totality over the contradictions constituting it. Representation has been maintained as the truth of the novel—but only after a long, complicated, historical-philosophical "journey." The dispersive, conflictual heterogeneity constituting representation continues to haunt it from within even as it is being resolved, that is, represented.

## The Idealism of Dialectical History: "The Ends of Man"

For greatness and force are truly measured only by the greatness and force of the opposition out of which the spirit brings itself back to unity with itself again ... for might consists only in maintaining oneself within the negative of oneself.

Hegel, *The Phenomenology of the Spirit*

Even though the theme of history is very present in the discourse of the period [the period of *Being and Nothingness*], the history of concepts is very little practiced; and, for example, the history of the concept of man is never examined. It is as if the sign "man" had no origin, no historical, cultural, or linguistic limit whatsoever.

Jacques Derrida, "The Ends of Man"

In *The Theory of the Novel,* Lukács situates the problem of the representation of reality within the context of a fall from an ideal state of total presence, and conceives of history both as the movement away from this origin and the attempt to regain or duplicate it. The contradictory responses given to the problem of representation are derived from the assumptions inherent in the positing of this origin and its eventual projection onto the beginning as well as the end of history. The novel is on the one hand the endless, conflictual, and necessarily inadequate search for the representation of the lost totality and thus the repetitive assertion of the differences or distance between the ideal origin of history and its contradictory representations. On the other hand, as the correction or supplement to this inadequacy, the novel is seen as the most adequate representation of reality—either an ironic, negative certitude or the representation of the continuous temporality constituting life. As long as the ideal origin of history is not itself put into question, even as a lost origin, the concept of the novel as a heterogeneous mixture of irresolvable historical differences will only be a momentary departure from the ideal determining history as its origin and to which it inevitably must return as its end.

The ideal, homogeneous presence Lukács ascribes to Greece as the lost origin of the novel and history functions in his work as a historical ideal; but, as an ideal, presence can take other forms in other contexts, depending on the nature of the theory of representation implied in the particular approach to the novel. Even in approaches claiming not to be representational at all, one can find such an ideal at work. Paul de Man in his short essay on Lukács emphasizes, as I do here, the central role irony plays in *The Theory of the Novel* and even claims that "Lukács's originality resides in his use of irony as a structural category." De Man is well aware of the dual nature of irony in Lukács as both a disruptive and unifying principle, one which is both discontinuous as well as structural: "This discontinuity is defined by Lukács as irony. The ironic structure acts disruptively, yet *it reveals the truth of the paradoxical predicament that the novel represents* . . . For if irony is indeed the determining and organizing principle of the novel's form, then Lukács is indeed freeing himself from preconceived notions about the novel as an imitation of reality. Irony steadily undermines this claim at imitation and substitutes for it a conscious, interpreted awareness of the distance that separates an actual experience from the understanding of this experience" (p. 56, my emphasis). De Man's argument differs from mine, however, in that he sees Lukács's use of irony as *an alternative* to what he calls "Lukács's later dogmatic commitment to realism" (p. 55), which, he claims, is in fact already evident in his concept of temporality.[22] For de Man irony "reveals the truth" of the novel's situation and brings Lukács very close "to reaching a point from which a *genuine hermeneutic* of the novel could start" (p. 57, my emphasis). But this starting point de Man feels is lost in the "dogmatism" of Lukács's theory of realism: "The later development of Lukács's theories on the novel, the retreat . . . from a theory of art as interpretation to a theory of art as reflected imitation (Wiederspiegelung) should be traced back to the reified idea of temporality that is so clearly in evidence at the end of *Theory of the Novel*" (p. 50). It seems clear that for de Man a "genuine hermeneutic" rooted in irony is the true alternative to a theory of literature as representation; it constitutes the truth of literature, which theories of representation are unable to represent.

This alternative, however, is not a real alternative; for de Man's "genuine hermeneutic" is also a representational theory of literature under a different guise. Interpretation for him is also rooted in an original presence which has been "lost" and which the critic must strive to regain, to re-present—the original presence of the novel to itself, the truth or "insight" it contains within it.[23] The ideal, homogeneous presence figured by Lukács historically as Greece reappears in de Man as the definition of, or model for, literature itself. In this sense both the strictly representational theory of literature de Man opposes and the hermeneutical approach he proposes ("art as interpretation") assume a total presence at the origin of history, or at the origin of and within the novel itself, and in this way put an end to historical differentiation and thus to both *representation* and *interpretation*—though never simply and definitively.

The work of the later Lukács which argues that the dialectical representation of the real is the essence of the novel is not in fact as radically different from *The Theory* as he claimed or as is often claimed by critics attempting to praise one phase of his work at the expense of the other. His later work seems more historical than his early work in the sense that (1) the abstract typology used to classify the novel in *The Theory* is replaced by a dialectical (really evolutionary) historical model, (2) more concrete historical details are given in the analysis of specific novels, and (3) the motive force of history is apparently located within history in the class struggle rather than in some idealist realm dominating history from the outside. The same Hegelian categories that defined his earlier typology, however, are used to define his historical periodization, and his materialist, historical approach is in fact even more firmly rooted in the assumptions concerning the origin of history as an ideal presence than *The Theory of the Novel.* When applied both to specific novels and to history in general, Lukács's concept of the dialectic provides the means for representing and thus resolving the differences and contradictions which constitute history and separate the novel as an essentially representative art form from its ideal origin in the harmonious and undifferentiated presence of the Greek totality. History in this sense is simply, then, the interval between the loss and reinstitution of the ideal origin; for the Lukácsian dialectic negates, all the better to retain, the essence of the origin which it projects onto the end of history. Dialectical history in this sense is totally subservient to the philosophical (metaphysical) ideals of homogeneity and total presence—it is the resolution and thus denial of historical contradictions and differences.

In his later, Marxist work, the historical period of the original epic is seen in the same utopian terms as in *The Theory*, as a kind of "primitive unity" of a society in which there is "an absence of contradictions between the individual and society."[24] There is less overt, lyrical nostalgia for the lost times of the epic, however, than in *The Theory*, because the primitive totality of Greece, this "historical childhood of humanity," as Marx called it in the *Grundrisse*, will not really be lost, as it is at least initially in *The Theory*, but negated, retained, and raised to another level in the new socialist state at the end (beginning) of history. The epic will then be possible again, but this time in the form of a mature, adult, self-conscious, developed totality manifesting the same harmonious conditions as its "childhood" but on a higher level. The lost Greek totality still governs history and its representations—it is now not only their origin but also explicitly their end.

In defining representation in dialectical terms, Lukács not only reduces the novel to the "adequate representation" of the workings of *a form* of history, but he also reduces history to a fixed representation—but one inevitably implies the other. In his Marxist work, the novel is treated in Hegelian terms as an adequate form, typical of its sociohistorical situation. Lukács now considers the novel to be successfully able to represent, to synthesize the concrete oppositions of its historical period: "The novelistic form is a contradictory, paradoxical, and, for the classical mind, unfinished form, but whose artistic greatness is due precisely to the fact that it reflects and figures artistically the contradictory character of the ultimate class society and this in a form adequate to its contradictory character" (*Ecrits de Moscou*, p. 68). The realist novel has thus become one of the privileged modes of the now successful representation of history, equal to science and dialectical history itself as the "reflection of the real."[25] The search for adequacy now, at least in "truly realist" novels, Lukács asserts, has a successful dialectical solution, the contradictions of the real are not avoided, suppressed or denied, but negated, conserved, and transcended in form. Representation becomes equivalent to the *Aufhebung*, but this is less of a radical break with his earlier position than its extension or even resolution (representation). The question that must be asked, however, is what within Lukács's historical system makes such a resolution possible? What guarantees that the dialectic will work the way it is supposed to when it does work? What separates true, realistic representation from its nondialectical opposite?

The opposition which governs Lukács's view of representation and his view of history is not really between idealism and materialism or even between nondialectical and dialectical thought. More fundamental than these is the static and, I would claim, ahistorical opposition between prose and poetry, which is never questioned by Lukács and which determines his view of history *from above*. Poetry is posited following Hegel, and in an even less problematical fashion, as an unquestioned positivity, the manifestation of an essential harmony or presence, and prose as total negativity and divisiveness. Ideally, poetry is the expression of a free subject totally at one with itself and the world (i.e. a Greek subject); and insomuch as poetry is still possible in the period after Greece, it is a manifestation of the same epic, harmonious totality as Greece, the same homogeneity described in *The Theory*. It does not, however, manifest these epic properties simply and immediately but rather through a mediated, dialectical process: "The inner poetry of life is the poetry of men in struggle, the poetry of the turbulent, active, interaction of men."[26] Prose, on the other hand, does not have the double sense for Lukács that it has for Hegel: as both the "prose of everyday life" and thus a decline from the immediacy of poetry and the prose of philosophy and science which constitute an *Aufhebung* of poetry.[27] For Lukács, prose is only the term of division and alienation of the exterior, capitalist, social reality, totally destructive of the integrity proposed by the poetic. The poetic is even more ideal for him than it is for Hegel (or even Nietzsche), it is the eternal presence that underlies all history as an ideal, the point from which history emerges and the end toward which it heads. The ideal governing Lukács's view of history and realism is then not only a utopian, social ideal but more fundamentally an aesthetic ideal—poetry is the before and after of the class struggle.[28]

The third historical period delineated by Lukács in the development of the novel, that of "the poetry of the *Tierreich*,"[29] is privileged because in it realism (poetry) is able to transcend (negate and overcome) the most extreme obstacles produced by the division of labor and the capitalist class society resulting from it. Capitalism has practically eliminated the possibility of epic poetry and the positive representation of a typical hero—the prosification of life being almost totally dominant. It is here, at the extreme limits of its history, at the point of complete alienation from itself, that the novel reaches its greatest heights, that within the novel as in philosophy, "bourgeois ideology achieves... its great, final syntheses" (*Ecrits*, p. 115). The figure of the real that is presented by the novels of this period is the most complete because it is a synthesis of the most serious and radical contradictions possible, because it has overcome practically absolute prosification and conserved the poetry that constitutes all realism as synthesis. The realism of this period is the antidote to Romanticism, which, according to Lukács, is incapable of overcoming the opposition prose/poetry but which fixes and objectifies it by making poetry not the synthesis but only the term of opposition, "a subjective and impotent protestation against prose" (*Ecrits*, p. 117).

In his essay "Balzac and Stendhal," included in *Studies in European Realism* (New York: Grosset and Dunlap, 1964) and written about the same period as the essays of the *Ecrits*, Lukács equates the realism of this period, and thus realism in general, with the dialectical overcoming of Romanticism: "They [the great writers of the age] therefore had to attempt to overcome romanticism (in the Hegelian sense), i.e., to fight against it, preserve it and raise it to a higher level all at the same time. (This was a general tendency of the time and by no means required acquaintance with Hegel's philosophy, which Balzac himself lacked). We must add that this synthesis was not achieved completely and without contradictions by any of the great writers of the age. Their greatest virtues as writers rested on contradictions in their social and intellectual positions which they boldly followed through to their logical conclusion, but which they could not objectively solve" (pp. 67-68). Realism and dialectical philosophy are thus the same thing; realism in fiction is the *Aufhebung* of the oppositions constituting Romanticism: subjective/objective, poetry/prose, individual/social, etc. Realism raises fiction to the level of speculative thought, it proves its greatness, just as the Spirit does in Hegel's *Phenomenology* by manifesting itself in its other, by figuring and synthesizing the radical contradictions which constitute it.[30]

For Lukács the truly great realist is not the one who has a correct, progressive ideology—that is what he calls "vulgar sociology"—but rather the one who is able to overcome the contradictions of his ideological formation and in whose work ideology does not function as a simple and determining a priori. Great realists are all writers who are able to transcend their ideology positively, that is in the direction that history itself (i.e. Lukács's version of Marxist-Hegelian history) would, or should, or must take; and this struggle against themselves, against their class prejudices, is a sign of their heroism and greatness, as well as the definition of their realism. Realism, true representation, then, is always seen by Lukács as the end result of a dialectical process, of the struggle against ideology, its negation, and its transcendence. In his essays on Balzac's *Les Paysans* he states that Balzac's greatness is a result of his having done the opposite of what he had intended:

"Yet, for all his painstaking preparation and careful planning, what Balzac really did in this novel was the exact opposite of what he had set out to do; what he depicted was not the tragedy of the aristocratic estate but of the peasant small-holding. It is precisely this discrepancy between intention and performance, between Balzac the political thinker and Balzac the author of *La Comédie humaine* that constitutes Balzac's historical greatness" (p. 21). To have simply had a correct view of the peasantry would not have been enough to warrant Balzac being classified as great; his greatness is entirely a function of his overcoming his ideological, distorted view to arrive, in spite of himself, at the correct one. The process of overcoming ideology is the essence of realism for Lukács.

Simple observation of the real is in fact never sufficient, because observation is governed by ideology. The realist novelist is, therefore, not a simple observer but a participant as Lukács stresses repeatedly in his critique of Zola and naturalism. But realism remains a form of observing, nevertheless; it is simply a higher form, *the true form:* "But however greatly he may distort reality in these novels by a propagandist, exhortatory, nontypical bias, the great realist and incorruptibly faithful observer breaks through everywhere, rendering even sharper the already existing contradictions" (*Studies*, p. 24). The naturalist novelist-as-observer only sees what is; the realist sees the contradictions in what is visible which will be assumed and given sense in his narration and in history: "Balzac *did not see* this dialectic of objective economic evolution and, as the legitimist extoller of the aristocratic large estate that he was, he *could not possibly have seen* it. But as the inexorable *observer* of the social history of France he *did see* a great deal of the social movements and evolutionary trends produced by this economic dialectic of the smallholding. Balzac's greatness lies precisely in the fact that in spite of all his political and ideological prejudices he yet *observed with incorruptible eyes* all contradictions as they arose, and *faithfully described them*" (pp. 38–39, my emphasis). Balzac could not see the entire economic dialectic working itself out, for it would take Marx to see this; but Balzac does see the essential contradictions which will make up the dialectic. It will take someone with the eyes of a Lukács, borrowing the eyes of Marx and assuming the absolute position of Hegel to see everything. The eyes of the observer still dominate Lukács's theory of realism; the real is still speculative, to be seen.

There are thus two kinds of observing in question here: one realist, that is, dialectical, synthesizing, totalizing and which produces true narration; the other "mere reflection"—undialectical, contradictory, fragmented, producing only description. The greater the realist, the "higher the level," the more totalized view of reality he is able to attain. In commenting on a dialogue from *Les Paysans* between the peasant Fourchon and a priest, Lukács argues that the totally unrealistic (i.e. unnatural) dialogue is a necessary aspect of the novel's realism: "It is obvious that an old French peasant in 1844 would not have used such words as these. And yet, the whole character and everything Balzac puts into his mouth are absolutely true to life, precisely because they go beyond the limits of a pedestrian copying of reality. All that Balzac does is to express on its potentially highest level what a peasant of the Fourchon type would dimly feel but would not be able to express clearly. Balzac speaks for those who are mute and who fight their battles in silence" (pp. 42–43). The idealism inherent in Lukács's realism and his use of the dialectic is evident here; perhaps all realisms, insomuch as they assume a Real, even a contradictory, dialectical real, share in this idealism. For it is not a question of what a peasant said or would have said (another form of idealism perhaps) but what a peasant *should have said*, or *really meant* by whatever he said, or could say, or simply felt. The author, Balzac, as realist, like the philosopher-critic Lukács, *knows* and *sees* what the peasant meant or should have meant and thus speaks for the silent peasant—silenced by the whole speculative, dialectical process as much as by his society. He supplies the peasant with an ideal, speculative discourse, a discourse raised up to the highest level of meaning, the highest level of the real. Through Balzac speaking for the peasant, the real is made visible; its true, realist (ideal) sense is conserved by the dialectic.

In his attempt to distinguish naturalism from realism Lukács stresses the process of "abstraction" within all great realisms and the necessity for this process: "The concrete presentation of social interconnections is rendered possible only by raising them up to so high a level of abstraction that from it the concrete can be sought and found as a 'unity of diversity,' as Marx says. The modern realists who as a result of the decline in *bourgeois* ideology have lost their deep understanding of social interconnections and with it their capacity for abstraction, vainly attempt by concretizing details to render concrete the social totality and its real, objectively decisive determinants" (p. 44). Not to grasp the unity to which the contradictory nature of the particular must be raised in order to be understood (truly seen) is to fall short of realism, but to impose an abstract formalist unity on the fragments of the real is utopian and idealistic in Lukács's own terms.[31] And yet overall Lukács is far more indulgent of the latter, perhaps because the grounds for distinguishing between his own position and utopian idealism are not as clear as those which distinguish the fragmented, nontranscendable, nontotalizable from the totalizable (the Hegelian from the non-Hegelian).

In fact, as Lukács himself admits, his theory of realism is an essentialist doctrine; it consists in finding within what usually passes for realism the essential core of the real. In comparing Stendhal with Balzac he says that Stendhal "like Balzac himself, by conscientiously uncovering the true driving forces of the social process, strives to present to the reader the most typical and essential traits in every social phenomenon. In this analysis the two greatest realists of the past century meet and join hands; they are at one in their rejection of all attempts to drag realism down from this height of the essential" (*Studies*, pp. 70–71). "A further point of contact is that they both regard realism as transcending the trivial and average, because for them realism is a search for that deeper essence of reality that is hidden under the surface. Where they diverge widely is in their conception of what this essense is" (pp. 83–84). Like all metaphysics, Lukács's theory of the real makes distinctions between the essential and inessential (accidental) aspects of reality, those which constitute the totality and those which do not. The essential and the real are the same thing for Lukács, and the way one distinguishes them from their inessential, unrealistic opposites is determined by whether they participate in and encourage, or on the other hand escape from and resist, dialectical transcendence.

True realism is poetic, a synthesis of divergent, contradictory elements, and one of the essential elements of this poetry is the type. Present in any realist novel but missing from all naturalist novels, the type is the synthesis of the general and the concrete: "The general is thus always concrete and real because it is based on a profound understanding of what is typical in each of the characters figuring in it—an understanding so deep that the particular is not eclipsed but on the contrary emphasized and concretized by the typical" (*Studies*, pp. 54-55). The type, then, serves an important formal function in Lukács's theory of the real, figuring in itself the unity which the work as a whole must establish in order to be considered realist. The type is a dialectical principle of synthesis which is a microcosm of the work as a whole in that it is the highest synthesis possible of the individual and the particular: "The central category and criterion of realist literature is the type, a peculiar synthesis which organically binds together the general and the particular both in characters and situations. What makes a type a type ... is that in it all the humanly and socially essential determinants are present on the highest level of development, in the ultimate unfolding of the possibilities latent in them" (Preface to *Studies in European Realism*, p. 6; written in 1948). The type points back to the Greek epic hero, who was immediately and spontaneously at one with his society, and forward to the "new socialist man," who will be again restored to himself and at one with society. Like realism itself, the type is an intermediary unity—arising out of the contradictions resulting from the loss of the origin—between an innocent, lost unity and a mature unity to be regained. By definition the type is eschatological and thus poetic in Lukács's sense;[32] the type guarantees that history will reach its end. It is already a representation in miniature of that end.

The notion of the type, and thus realism itself, conserves the ideal of the "complete human personality" within it at a time when the ideal cannot be realized as such: "The central aesthetic problem of realism is the adequate presentation of the complete human personality" (Preface to *Studies*, p. 7). Lukács's concept of Marxism is—and in this he is consistent from *The Theory*, through *History and Class Consciousness*, to his last works—primarily oriented toward the restoration of this ideal:

> The Marxist philosophy of history analyses man as a whole, and contemplates the history of human evolution as a whole ... It strives to unearth the hidden laws governing all human relationships. Thus the object of proletarian humanism is to reconstruct the complete human personality and free it from the distortion and dismemberment to which it has been subjected in class society ... The ancient Greeks, Dante, Shakespeare, Goethe, Balzac, Tolstoy all give adequate pictures of great periods of human development and at the same time serve as signposts in the ideological battle fought for the restoration of the unbroken human personality. ("Preface" to *Studies*, p. 5)

The ideal of the "complete and human personality," of "harmonious man,"[33] precedes and determines the dialectical process charted by Lukács from epic to novel and ahead/back to epic. Poetry is the expression of, the representation of, such an ideal of man, and at all stages of the process the adequacy of any figures (of any individual or collective subject) is measured against it. The adequacy of the type is a function of the path leading from the Greek ideal[34] to the restored totality of the new Greece at the end of history and of the knowledge or vision one has of both the ideal and the process. In this sense, Lukács's view of history is ultimately as circular as Hegel's, originating and ending in the poetry and harmony of an ideal state of presence.[35]

In Lukács's history of realism, 1848 marks, after Greece, the other crucial turning point in history—in many ways it is a repetition of a break or disruption in history as great as that which separates the epic from the non-epic periods in *The Theory*. Lukács claims that in 1848 the bourgeoisie turned against its own ideals (the ideal of man) and replaced them with the struggle for economic and political power: "During these days the bourgeoisie for the first time fights for the naked continuance of its economic and political rule ... It is the June battle of the Paris proletariat which produces a decisive change in the bourgeois camp, accelerating to an extraordinary degree the inner process of differentiation which is to transform revolutionary democracy into compromising liberalism. This change affects all spheres of bourgeois ideology. It would be altogether super-ficial and wrong to suppose that, when a class turns its back so radically upon its earlier political aims and ideals, the spheres of ideology, the fates of science and art can remain untouched" (*The Historical Novel*, p. 171). For a Marxist there is a strange separation in Lukács's analysis between ideals and ideology. His argu-ment is not that the "bourgeois ideals" are in themselves from the start in some sense compromised by political and economic interests and thus historically determined—that the ideals themselves are ideological—but rather that a turning away from the ideals results in a transformation of ideology, a fall back into "class ideology in a much narrower sense" (*The Historical Novel*, p. 171). The utopian ideal, the ideal of "harmonious man" that is conserved in all truly poetic, realist literature and regulates Lukács's view of history, here as elsewhere, escapes criti-cal investigation—it reigns constant throughout, dominating either by its absence or presence. It is a metahistorical (idealist) rather than historical principle.

The reason that Lukács claims that this is the first time the bourgeoisie turns completely against its ideals and fights for its own interests is that he needs to posit a "before-1848" which, although not untouched by contradiction and compromise, maintains the ideals in spite of contradictions (in the positive hero, the type, and the realist novel in general). The "after-1848" is like the after-Greece in its relation to the "before," and Lukács feels it necessary to condemn it in its entirety as "sick" or decadent (see "Healthy or 'Sick' Art?" in *Writer and Critic*), to resist it as other "heroic individuals" have done, in order to conserve intact the ideals turned away from by the bourgeoisie and now maintained and repre-sented only by the proletariat, the new, true, universal, historical subject, the totally adequate synthesis of general and particular. The ideal governing history has not changed; only the subject embodying or representing it has. Thus the historical subject which the proletariat is supposed to represent is actually derived from or modeled after an ahistorical Subject dominating and transcending all history.

If Balzac is the best example of the "great realist," Zola is, of course, the example of the fall from realism into naturalism. The opposition, narration/description, which Lukács uses to indicate the difference between realism and naturalism is also derived in fact from the more fundamental opposition between poetry and prose, description being a reaction to the ever-increasing prosaic nature of life: "The dilemma *narrate* or *describe* is as old as bourgeois literature, because the creative method of description was born in the immediate reaction of writers to reality becoming fixed in prose and prohibiting the spontaneous activity of men" (*Ecrits*, p. 128). Description is the technique born of prose, and dominates when capitalism has destroyed the "ideal of harmonious man": "The predominance of description is not only a result but also and simultaneously a cause, the cause of a further divorce of literature from epic significance. The domination of capitalist prose over the inner poetry of human experience, the continuous dehumanization of social life, the general debasement of humanity—all these are objective facts of the development of capitalism. The descriptive method is the inevitable product of this development ... The poetic level of life decays—and literature intensifies the decay" ("Narrate or Describe," *Writer and Critic*, p. 127). Poetry is paradoxically the essence of true narration (the dialectical process); description on the other hand is a product of the prosaic fragmentation of reality and of true ideals. The capitalist prosification of life destroys the last remnant of the ideal carried on from the Greeks; for Lukács, capitalism is really the end (again) of Greece. In this sense, his later Marxist work can be seen to repeat the basic schema of *The Theory of the Novel* with the fall now occurring twice rather than once. 1848 is really the repetition of the loss of Greece, its final repetition, the ultimate decadence and distance from the poetic ideal before its eventual recovery in the historically new, but essentially the same, proletariat subject.

If "form is the highest abstraction" (*Writer and Critic*, p. 50), then post-1848 literature remains on the lowest level of undialectical marginalism. This is not just a formal insufficiency and an ideological insufficiency for Lukács but also a moral insufficiency. He sees the case of Zola to be a great "literary tragedy," for Zola was "one of those outstanding personalities whose talents and human qualities destined them for the greatest things but who have been prevented by capitalism from accomplishing their destiny and finding themselves in a truly realistic art" (*Studies in European Realism*, p. 95). The "tragedy" of Zola is simply the reverse side of the "heroic realism" of his predecessors; for Lukács's history of realism is really a history of the great men of literature struggling against their times, their ideology, and even themselves, and in the best of cases overcoming all these obstacles to achieve true realistic "greatness."[36] Not only does Lukács's concept of realism maintain and depend on the ideal of "harmonious man," but in "turning things right side up" it leaves the "bourgeois concept" of the author as a struggling, heroic individual in place also.

If Lukács's theory of representation is "dogmatic" and reductive of the complexity of history and the novel, this "dogmatism" does not really originate in his concept of historicity in *The Theory of the Novel* as de Man claims, nor with his conversion to Marxism as others claim—in the same vein, the more concretely historical orientation of his later work in no way rectifies ("puts on its feet") the idealism of his earlier work as Jameson and readers more sympathetic to Lukács have argued. Rather the ideal, harmonious presence he attributes to the origin of history in Greece dominates both his early pre-Marxist, idealist work and his later Marxist, materialist work, though not simply and without contradiction. The origin of history is never really lost for Lukács; for representation is the dialectic at work in fiction to ensure that the presence of harmonious man, that "his" poetry, will be conserved and projected forward onto the end of history. To transform a phrase of Lukács from *The Theory of the Novel*, in this view of history, the historical journey is over as soon as the voyage begins. The presence of harmonious man as the essence of all representation (and interpretation) has put an end to the conflicts, contradictions, and differences of history. Representation in this abstract, dialectical sense is the end of history.

## History or the Irresolvable Contradictions of Representation

Genealogy does not oppose itself to history as the lofty and profound gaze of the philosopher might compare to the molelike perspective of the scholar; on the contrary, it rejects the metahistorical deployment of ideal significations and indefinite teleologies. It opposes itself to the search for "origins."

History becomes "effective" to the degree that it introduces discontinuity into our very being... "Effective" history deprives the self of the reassuring stability of life and nature, and it will not permit itself to be transported by a voiceless obstinacy toward a millennial ending. It will uproot its traditional foundations and relentlessly disrupt its pretended continuity... The forces operating in history are not controlled by destiny or regulative mechanisms, but respond to haphazard conflicts.

Michel Foucault, "Nietzsche, Genealogy, History"

In the previous sections of this chapter I have shown that Lukács's dialectical definition of realism posits an ideal origin and end to history and assumes the existence of an ideal Subject ("harmonious man") outside and above the conflicts of history, a Subject whose presence (progressive) history has the role of reinstating. If this historical ideal is accepted, all representation which is not strictly dialectical, which does not resolve and raise to a higher, more visible, speculative (essential) level the contradictions of history, and all critiques of teleological, eschatalogical forms of history and philosophy (and fiction) are by definition "sick," ahistorical, and even reactionary. But if on the contrary, the ideal origin of history (in Greece or anywhere else) and the Subject it implies are put into question by revealing their ahistorical nature, representation can no longer function as *the end* of history but becomes, rather, one of the conflictual elements constituting history and undermining any end which might be assigned to the historical process.

There are, of course, positions which are either overtly or implicitly anti- or ahistorical and ideologically reactionary; and perhaps any critical position which challenges the utopic, teleological (metaphysical) characteristics of traditional and even dialectical history runs the risk of essentializing or dehistoricizing (idealizing) the "nonrepresentational," not strictly dialectical elements of history and fiction as alternatives to the abstract imposition of the dialectic (of philosophical sense and rationality) onto fiction. But it is not enough, as we have seen, to criticize opposing positions for being ahistorical to ensure that one's own is truly historical and avoids the pitfalls of idealism. By positing a state of harmonious presence at the origin and end of history, Lukács dehistoricizes and essentializes (idealizes) his own dialectical approach—the dialectic and the theory of representation derived from it are not in fact alternatives to idealism but its support.

Could a novel still in any way be considered to be "representational" if its representations of the past were not determined by either a historical or an aesthetic ideal, if its representations were indications of the contradictions of history, of history as the conflict of opposing forces, rather than their resolution (suppression)? Is it possible to "free" the concept of representation from the long historical-philosophical tradition governing it—or at least make it exceed the limitations imposed by this tradition—without falling back onto a sterile, textual, or aesthetic idealism, or a naive, formalist empiricism which cuts fiction off from the historical and philosophical problems with which it necessarily interacts and which in fact have always-already invaded its language and representations?

The answers to such questions can never be simple because representation neither serves philosophy nor breaks totally with it. All representation, in spite of the speculative ends it might be assigned, exceeds the boundaries imposed on it by philosophy; for no representation, whether in fiction, history or philosophy, no matter how idealistic, no matter how purely philosophical, no matter how complete its resolution of contradictions seems to be, ever really accomplishes its ends simply, without leaving behind unresolved, unrepresented, "fictive" (not strictly rational) traces or remainders of these contradictions. In addition, no representation is ever really free of the historical-philosophical heritage it carries on within it, even as it claims to break with it. No representation, no matter how "poetically pure," ever breaks totally with the idealism and rationality of philosophy (in whatever form) but carries on in some way remnants of its historical-philosophical heritage which continue to mold it, to make sense out of it (and to make this sense visible in it) and to interfere with its purity. Representation is in this sense a problem with no definite resolution; thus conceived, it does not put an end to history but is precisely an indication of the conflictual, contradictory nature of history itself in its nonteleological forms.

Claude Simon's *Le Palace* (1962; translated by Richard Howard as *The Palace;* New York: George Braziller, 1963) treats representation as a formal (narrational), thematic, and historical problem it is unable to resolve. *The Palace* is not written from the position of an ideal Subject who knows the truth of the past or who is representative or typical of a past moment and who thus dominates history, but rather from that of a crisis within history undermining all representation, all attempts to capture the past. Irresolvable contradiction, loss, repetition, and conflict within history—rather than some harmonious state of presence—are presented in the novel as the origin and end of representation; and thus the negative aspects of history (of the dialectic) dominate *The Palace*. But to label the novel a pessimistic, anti- or ahistorical work, as Michel Deguy does,[37] is too simplistic. *The Palace* is not the simple alternative to "optimistic visions" of history, but rather a radical investigation and critique of history and fiction as modes of representation of the past that in no way attempts to do away with history, to transcend it, or to ignore it. Representation is a contradictory process in the novel which constitutes, limits, and eventually undercuts the integrity of both history and fiction; and the "crisis of representation" thematized and practiced in *The Palace* necessitates that history and fiction be conceived as open rather than closed processes or forms.

The chief contradiction within representation as it is conceptualized and dramatized in *The Palace* is that it is unstable, ungrounded, impossible to bring back to any definite *presentation* that is not in itself already a representation. Both the assumption on the one hand of a "before-representation" in which all representation would originate—of an "outside," of a real untouched by representation but existing only in itself and as itself—and on the other hand of an "after-representation" in Lukács's sense as the resolution of contradiction and the highest synthesis or sense of the real itself, are seen precisely as ideals which the representation of the past undermines in the very process of striving to attain them. Representation in *The Palace* is original and potentially infinite, unbounded by any unique origin or *telos*, any unique before or after. Discovering or positing the origin and end of its representations is precisely what the novel refuses or is unable to do, for this would be to transcend the crisis constituting it and to step outside of the contradictions of history. It is only from a transcendent, metahistorical position that such contradictions could ultimately be resolved, and this resolution itself could never be achieved simply and without contradiction, as the novel shows by situating such attempts within rather than outside the crisis itself.

The local, historical crisis represented in *The Palace* is that of the Spain of the Civil War; more precisely, it consists of the conflicts and divisions within the Republican forces themselves, of a revolution destroyed as much from within as from without.[38] The local crisis, however, points to a crisis within all history— it is a repetitive aspect of history itself. The Republic is described for the most part in the terms of the most cynical of the characters of the novel, "the American," as a corpse; but the putrifying smell which permeates the book is not only that of the city but also that of history itself and only specifically in this instance of the already badly decomposed, and yet newly born, Republic: "until someone opening the window remembered that it was not the hotel . . . which stank this way, but the entire city, as if it were in the process of putrefying yellowish, dusty and fossilized above the suffocating labyrinth of its sewers" (*The Palace*, p. 19); "'like a sewer grating,' the American said, 'and if you lifted it up you'd find underneath the corpse of a still born child wrapped in old newspapers—old, that is, a month old—full of enticing headlines. That's what stank so much: not the cauliflower or the turnips on the slum stairs, not the blocked latrines: nothing but carrion, a fetus with its oversized head swathed in printed paper, nothing but a little macrocephalic corpse, dead before its time because the doctors hadn't agreed on their diagnosis, and thrown into the sewers in a shroud of words" (pp. 20–21). Putrification and the smell of sewers and decay are the dominant images associated with the failure of the Spanish Republic to sustain itself, but this failure is not confined to one moment or place but seems to spread to the general movement of history itself, to contaminate all of history with its negativity. Spain appears to constitute a moment of absolute negativity in history, a moment which in its turn resists being negated and overcome, one of the moments of history which displace history from its projected course and from its assigned end.

In *The Palace* the assumptions which would allow for a positive transcendence of negativity through its representation in history—the assignment to it of *a place* and *sense* in history—are treated ironically and undercut. The gimmick *(truc)* necessary to negate the past and master the future and thus to understand history as a whole is missing or has been lost, the contradictions constituting any transcendence or simple representation of the past impossible to deny: "But how was it? How was it? No doubt there was something he hadn't been able to see, something that escaped him, so perhaps he too could gain a footing, get inside, gate-crash this tangential, comestible and optimistic derivative of metaphysics baptized carp or History, by means of which, if you knew how, you could apparently derive yourself in a manner that was if not agreeable and coherent at least satisfying, as was proved by the excremental derivative of reason baptized rhetoric, and after all it couldn't be so difficult since so many people managed it ... There had to be a gimmick to it" (pp. 147–48). The uncertainty of the representation of the past (of history and memory) when the origin and end of history are no longer assumed to be present, when the sense or direction of history is in question (precisely because of moments like Spain), cannot simply be dismissed as constituting a subjectivist view of history (as Lukács argues); for it is the subject itself, as an individual or collectivity (type), that depends on teleological views of history for its support. The derivation of the individual subject itself, the realization-projection of the subject as a unified presence ("harmonious man"), is problematical when history is not accepted in its "domesticated," rational, metaphysical form as the optimistic resolution of contradictions: as either History or Rhetoric.[39]

The Spain of the Civil War and history in general are not presented in completely negative and cynical terms, however; for the "American's" voice is only one of the many voices or fragments of the past and the present which constitute the "narrator's" voice and the complex point of view of the novel: "able to hear that part of himself which had the form of a lanky American ... having a dialogue with that other part of himself which had the form of a bald man ... or rather those three fragments of himself which were an American, a Rifle *[l'homme-fusil]* and a young fledgling" (pp. 171–72).[40] The American's voice cannot be totally ignored, but it is not totally determining either; the same is true of negativity. It is not the essence of history any more than its resolution would be. The negative, destructive representations of past and present that "the

American" insists on as the truth of history would simply be the opposite of the optimistic representations he caricatures in others. The narrator's memory (and thus the representation of the past produced by the novel) consists of a conflict of voices and representations of the past, rather than their resolution or synthesis. The narrator is adrift in the representations of the past; his voice and his subjectivity are products of the conflict and do not dominate it.

The past is retained and represented (produced) in *The Palace* largely as a collage of images (memory traces, descriptions in history texts, illustrations, photographs, etc.)—its representation is predominately visual or photographic.[41] The class struggle in Spain and the momentary success of the revolutionary forces, for example, are represented in the photographs of Marx and Stalin, which literally take the place of the engravings of scenes and portraits appropriate to the ruling classes that had hung on the walls of the hotel before. "Tacked on the walls (but not exactly in the places where the lacivious prints had been taken down, so that the paler rectangles were clearly visible) and opposite each other...two glossy photographs of the same size...one showing the head of a man with a beard and hair of a biblical prophet...the other of a smiling man with a square face and a black mustache, dressed in a dark jacket with a military collar" (p. 20). The images of the revolution replace those of a class society, covering but not completely eliminating this prerevolutionary past whose traces are still evident in the border surrounding the portraits of the heroes of the revolution. If one considers history to be reduced when, as in *The Palace*, it exists predominately as the visual representation of events, this reduction itself is complex because within and around all images, in the very presence of the image itself, the traces of the past are not effectively negated. The present of representation is never pure because the image exists only as a replacement and/or repetition of other images, in conflict with what it replaces.

*The Palace* suggests that the desire to explain, to understand, to domesticate and give sense to death motivates attempts to retain the truth of the past through representation. But like the people of the city trying to understand the sense of the death of General Santiago, the search is endless because death has no sense; it is not strictly representable: "'As if they were looking for something,' he thought. 'Something they're afraid of, something hidden in the city and whose nature and even whose name they don't know'" (p. 142). "Perhaps they were going in circles in the city in search of the unfindable enemy, of that thing which had no name, no face, no appearance, condemned to wander forever like that Jew in the legend who couldn't rest, like those flocks of anxious, plaintive and wild birds he saw fluttering endlessly as they wailed over something invisible, some carrion, some dying beast, some monster, some sick Leviathan already beginning to decompose though still alive" (pp. 245–46). The question of who killed Santiago and for what political ends it was done could in principle be determined, proved, and represented as a historical truth, but the question of death in a more general sense, haunting history as its unconscious, is indeterminable. The repetition of the question of who killed Santiago in the headlines of newspapers and on the banners in the procession takes on the form of the more general and unanswerable question of what is the origin and reason for death in general:

¿QUIEN A MUERTO? ¿QUIEN A MUERTO? ¿QUIEN A MUERTO?

the personal pronoun used as though out of a kind of modesty, or prudence, or precaution . . . so that the real translation (that is, what everyone really read wasn't "Who has killed?" but "What has killed?" as if they were wondering in astonishment about the name, the nature of an infection, a disease. (P. 125)

The representation of the past can never quite negate and transcend the indications and traces of death inscribed within it; memory and history as antidotes to death are thus never successful in overcoming its effects.

Memory is uncertain because it is rooted in the distance separating present and past rather than in the presence of either or in some assumed continuity linking them together: "And they (the four men—who, with him made five) standing there, appearing out of that nothingness to which they were to return almost immediately after a brief, violent and meteoric existence during which he would see them behave like beings of flesh and blood" (p. 38). The representation of the past in memory has its origin and end not in the presence of a present now past and a synthesis to be achieved, but in the nothingness of absence and death. The mode of existence of all subjects in representation is that of "being-like the living" and is never equivalent to that of the "living" themselves. Even the relation of the subject to itself is not immediate but theatrical or cinematographic—that is, staged, constructed, repetitive, without a stable foundation in any past or present moment: "Then he saw himself, that is years later, and he, that residue of himself, or rather that trace, that stain (that excrement, so to speak) left behind himself: the ridiculous figure one sees stirring, absurd and presumptuous, over there, far away . . . bursting in without even having been asked to do so, like those actors, those movie hams dead and long since forgotten and still ready to revive on the silver screen the same stupid scene . . . then once again oblivion, the nothingness in which they no doubt remain somewhere, costumed, made up, tireless, starving for applause" (pp. 24–25). The represented subject—and there is no subject in *The Palace* which exists before or outside of representation—is always a caricature of itself (of an ideal self). Representation has invaded all relationships, even the most intimate relationship of the subject with itself, in the past and in the present as well.

If photography (and particularly the cinema) is a privileged metaphor or mode of representation for Simon, as Michel Deguy has claimed, it is not because his novels are "of their time," representative themselves of a particular modern, negative, alienated *Weltanschauung*.[42] Rather, photographic or cinematographic representations point explicitly in Simon to an aspect of representation—to a contradiction within representation—which traditional concepts ignore or suppress by regulating representation in terms of an ideal presence of the original itself and claiming that adequate (essential, ideal) representation is possible, that the perfect double or replica of the original is equivalent to the original itself. In photography there are no original copies, as there are in painting for instance, for the "copy" is infinitely repeatable and reproducible. As Walter Benjamin has argued, photography undermines the concept of an authentic, unique, original representation and frees art from its "parasitical dependence on ritual." Art, for Benjamin, now modeled after photography, should no longer be judged in terms of its relation to a fixed tradition but rather in terms of the multiple effects it produces in various historical contexts: "Instead of being based on ritual, it begins to be based on another practice—politics."[43] Representation in *The Palace*, if it is fundamentally "cinematographic" as Deguy claims, is so in Benjamin's sense, indicating the original, conflictual repeatability (and thus historicization) of past and present and not the existence of their ritualistic presence.

The figures and representations of the past in *The Palace* are a heterogeneous mixture of reality and fiction, linked to the original moment and space of experience ("inhabiting it") but never adequate to it: "standing there, then, unexpected and even slightly unbelievable, slightly unreal, slightly out of date, among the ghosts...as if they themselves were something like specters ready to return (which they did) to the place from which they had come" (p. 39). They are real insomuch as they have been preserved in a kind of immobility (as if) on a photograph, but fictional insomuch as the very act of conserving, of fixing and retaining these images necessarily transforms them: "And later he seemed to see them, immobilized or preserved as in a photograph, in that kind of petrified and grayish matter which is the past, that gelatin which keeps things and people indefinitely, as though in alcohol, slightly distorted no doubt, but intact—or rather, as far as they were concerned, not entirely, because no doubt they had never been intact" (p. 40). Representation cannot restore an intactness that never was. In fact the "visual" image in Simon, even and especially the photographic image,[44] is never exact, never the presence of what is, photographed retained exactly as is, but rather a conflictual, divided space which gives rise to a multitude of possible interpretations. The image can thus never be perceived simply as is; it must be read and interpreted. In this sense, history is not simplified when it is reduced to photographic images, at least not any more than it is in any form of representation; for images do not function in *The Palace* as simple, empirical, "subjective" presentations of surface reality and thus are not "naturalistic" in Lukács's sense.[45] The collage they constitute manifests the unresolved contradictions of history rather than their ideal, represented, synthesis.

The narrator, himself, asks the question that should be asked of all realisms, all attempts to represent the past: what ends does representation serve? The answer given by the novel, if it can be called an answer, is as double and contradictory as representation itself. The narrator's efforts to recapture his past are motivated by a desire either to give sense to his experiences and leave some trace of his presence, of his own subjectivity, after him, or, on the contrary, to distance and free himself from the events narrated:

> Wondering what it was that impelled a man to tell his story ("or to tell his story to himself," he thought: "the only difference being that he's doing it aloud now"), that is to reconstruct, to reconstitute by means of verbal

equivalents something he had seen or done, as if he dare not admit that what he had seen or done hadn't left any more trace than a dream, thinking: "Unless it's the opposite, unless he hopes that once it's told, once it's put in the form of words, it begins existing all by itself, without his needing to endure it any longer ... as if he were trying to tear, to fling from himself that violence, that thing which had seized on, made use of him." (Pp. 85–86)

Representation derives its force on the one hand from a desire to solidify and unify the traces constituting experience, as if to constitute a unified image of oneself (or of an ideal self), a totalized image of what one was and did, and at the same time, on the other hand, from a desire to expunge from oneself the unformed, unpresentable violence of experience, the work of time and death, and to produce not a metaphorical equivalent of oneself or the sense of one's existence but the irreducible and repetitive loss of this unity.

In this sense all representation is constituted by both production and loss. Like the description of the city (as well as of history as a whole), representation is at the same time the "giving birth" to and "abortion" of reality: "The city, as they approached the center of it, now revealing in places the vestiges of what had been not a battle... not, then, a conquest, a rape (since it had not been the victim of an invasion, assailed from the exterior), but apparently torn apart by something that had come out of, or rather that it had wrested, expelled from itself, more (blood and ordure) like a kind of childbirth, or perhaps an abortion" (p. 101). The reality of any event is in the multiple, nonsynthesizable, dispersive representations produced from it. The impossibility of any adequate and sufficient representation produces a series of partial and contradictory representations which in turn multiply and complicate the effects of the original event. Representation in this sense could be defined as the potentially infinite repetition or rewriting of the real, the continual reinscription in different contexts of any event—it largely exceeds the boundaries determined by traditional realisms and by any other theory of the subject. To equate representation with the successful resolution of all differences, contradictions, or loss is to assign *a sense* or end to the process and to cling to the fiction of a whole, integral, totally present, present —it is to reduce seriously the contradictory status of the process of representation itself.

To accept the reduced version of representation imposed by the limitations of realism is always in some sense to reject, to reduce or even to oppose history. According to "the American," the revolution in Spain is "aborted" not only because of the fascist revolt against it or the differences dividing the left, but also because the revolution acquiesced and began to identify with a certain image or representation of itself projected by the press: "a stinking mummy swathed and strangled by the umbilical cord of miles of enthusiastic phrases punched on the typewriter ribbon by the enthusiastic army of foreign correspondents of the liberal press. Victim of the pre-infantile disease of the revolution: the sponsorship and the esteem of the honorable Manchester Guar ..." (p. 21). The acceptance of the adequacy of any representation is in some sense the artificial end of historical conflicts, the idealistic resolution of historical contradictions through the positing of a unified image or representation. The revolution terminates in a bureaucratic mound of paper and regulations as if to assure itself a proper status and to protect itself against the kind of revolt that originally constituted it; "stifled under the bureaucratic accumulation of paper in which all violence and all rebellion is reabsorbed" (p. 216); by "the deafening clatter of typewriters that came through the doors, insurmountable, annihilating every impulse, every velleity of rebellion" (p. 219). The acceptance of representation in its simple sense is a kind of bureaucratic solution to the conflicts of history, an acquiesence to the demands and false security of realism without the will or the force to maintain the potentially irresolvable contradictions of the struggle.

The return to the past, to the traces, fragments, and debris of memory and history is both necessary and inconclusive: all reconstructions or rewritings of the past are necessarily repetitive and open-ended. Representation is a mixture which is never quite dissolved and given a unity or sense: "this vast and confused mixture of forms, smells and noises" (p. 237). Another return to the past (another representation) can and must always be made because no one representation is ever conclusive; the past always awaits its final representation: "Then he would go in, he would climb the three flights because the elevator wouldn't be working, or rather would be jammed for good—and he would go into the office ...they would all be there, the schoolmaster, the Italian, the bald man, the American...perhaps a little desiccated, a little mummified, a little dusty... and they would receive him, without smiles, without effusions, without even a visible sign of sympathy...as if they had been expecting all along, even after so many years, that he would finally come to find them again" (pp. 247-48). The conditional tense used here—*entrerait, monterait, serait,* etc.—indicates not only that another rewriting or reconstruction of the past can always be made but also that any reconstruction of the past is provisional. In this sense the past is always written in the conditional—the conditional of unresolved contradictions—as is the present.

The "return to the past" in *The Palace* fails to produce an "adequate," totalized, complete representation, fails to overcome the deaths, absences and contradictions constituting it, to unify the fragments and traces of events and experience. If anything, the "return" only repeats and accentuates the difference between and within past and present, between the figure of the student that the narrator was and the plurality of voices and figures he now is: "Then he stopped listening to him altogether, stopped hearing him (that is, that part of himself that diminished, shrank, reduced itself as fast as it could until it had the size and the absurd voice of a tiny doll dressed as a monkey...hearing himself say aloud (that is, that other part of himself which was now sitting on a bench in the middle of that other part of himself which was the huge esplanade" (p. 242). The figure of the general narrator, the subject of memory and of representation, remains at the end divided and plural, hardly *a subject* at all—the unity desired and searched for in the return to the past remains an unattainable, illusory, and yet in some sense necessary, ideal.

The city in Spain to which the narrator returns in an attempt to discover the truth of the past is represented in *The Palace* but not in the sense that the violence, contradictions, and political and ideological conflicts of its past and present are overcome in a present or a projected future which effectively figures—that is, resolves or synthesizes—these conflictual elements. The city is represented in terms of excess and loss, never adequate to itself or its representations: "The city too abandoned, desolate... Like one of those queens in confinement left alone in her palace because no one must see them at that moment, giving birth, expelling from her sweat-drenched loins what must be given birth to, expelled, some tiny microcephalic monster (the American said), unviable and degenerate— and finally everything growing motionless, collapsing, and she lying there, ex- hausted, expiring, without hope that it can ever end, draining away in a tiny, incessant and futile hemorrhage ... a tiny and invisible fissure in the very center of the body" (pp. 251–52). At the center of the (representations of the) city, then, there is an invisible fissure which it can never close, an internal difference separating it from itself, inhabiting it as its other. When representation is not assumed to resolve negativity and difference, there is, strictly speaking, no end to representation and no simple origin for it.

From the perspective of Lukács the indeterminacy of representation of *The Palace* would constitute an ahistorical, subjectivist position; from the perspective of *The Palace*, Lukács's position itself constitutes an idealist position which can- not be sustained. What certainly is in question in the conflict between the two positions is the sense of history itself: for one, it is dialectical and totalized; for the other plural, conflictual, and open-ended. The question that remains unan- swered at the end of this analysis is on the basis of what is one to decide between the positions. Can one really make such a choice? Does the conflict itself have a simple resolution? Can it be represented and, if so, in whose terms and for what ends? The ends of representation are thus still in question when representation is taken as the end of history and when it is not—these conflictual ends in any case constitute no end at all.

# F I V E

# The Times of History and the Orders of Discourse

I affirm, against Ranke or Karl Brandi, that history-as-*récit* is not an objective method, still less the supreme objective method, but a philosophy of history ...

Fernand Braudel, "Time in History"
(really "The Times of History"), in
*On History (Ecrits sur l'histoire)*

We must elaborate—outside of philosophies of time and the subject—a theory of discontinuous systemization.

Michel Foucault, *The Discourse on Language*
*(L'Ordre du Discours)*

## The Questions of History: Temporality, Subjectivity, Order

I am afraid we are not rid of God because we still believe in grammar.

Nietzsche, *Twilight of the Idols*

That excremental derivative of reason baptized rhetoric ...

Claude Simon, *The Palace*

The question of the relationship between history and fiction is hardly new, for it has often been argued by historians and literary critics alike that an intimate relationship exists between these two forms of discourse. For no period of history does this relationship seem more evident than for the nineteenth century, when the novel and history are considered by most historians to be at the most dominant, prestigious stage of their development, to have fully realized the potential of their respective forms. The nineteenth-century or "classical" novel has traditionally been accepted as the norm, the model for what the form and the essence of the novel are or should be—assuming for a moment that the novel possesses *a* form and has an essence—just as the prevalent ideal of what history is or should be is largely a nineteenth-century concept. It has often been argued with some justice that in the nineteenth century the novel explicitly models itself after history (Balzac, Stendhal, Dickens, Tolstoy, etc.), and it would even be accurate to say that the novel has for much of its history claimed to be a form of history. This means at the very least that a certain form of the novel and history share the same basic assumptions about the historical nature of the world and about the narrative form best suited to capture or represent it. The "world" that both this form of history and fiction attempt to represent is assumed for the most part in the nineteenth century to be a closed universe; and the narrative form according to which they both order themselves is posited as being equally closed and continuous. The individual or collective subject is clearly indicated as the vital force of history and the novel in this period, as the origin of its own life and actions, a unity (small and large) whose "life" is the matter of history and the novel. The "life" of this subject is assumed to be a continuous, temporal process with a definite beginning and end, and the *récit* which narrates this "life" is necessarily one which attempts to be as continuous and uninterrupted as history or "life" itself is assumed to be.

The so-called classical novel has been challenged, undermined, or simply rejected as the proper form of fiction numerous times since its "dominant period," and Alain Robbe-Grillet's *For a New Novel* is thus only one of many critiques of this form and its traditional assumptions. It is the terms of his critique, however, which interest me here. As I have argued in chapter 1, Robbe-Grillet explicitly rejects the nineteenth-century model and its premises: the belief in a metaphysical, preconceived Sense which governs the novel from the outside (*For a New Novel*, pp. 11–12); the acceptance of "Man" or human nature as the subject of the novel (pp. 52, 56–57); as well as all other anthropocentric aspects of the novel, including the necessity to present unified characters or heroes (pp. 27–29) and to use a continuous narrative technique which conveys the impression that there are no blanks, no interruptions, no discontinuity or repetition in the movement of time (p. 30). In the name of a *New* Novel and a *new* realism he argues for a *new* narrative model, one in which discontinuity will dominate, where Sense will be replaced by a plurality of senses, and where the novel will be open-ended rather than closed.

If Robbe-Grillet can be considered in some sense representative of a certain form of contemporary fiction, can it be said, then, that the contemporary or New Novel has radically and definitely broken with history, that it no longer shares its assumptions, models or forms, that it has, as many have argued, become a- or antihistorical? This can be argued only if history is conceived in its "classical," nineteenth-century sense; for just as Robbe-Grillet demands that the New Novel break away from the "classical novel," it could be said that there are "New Historians" who reject the nineteenth-century concept of history in order to propose a radically "new" concept. The defense and illustration of the New History that parallels Robbe-Grillet's *For a New Novel* would be found in such works as Fernand Braudel's *On History* (translated by Sarah Matthews; Chicago: University of Chicago Press, 1980) and numerous texts by Michel Foucault— especially *The Discourse on Language* and *The Archaeology of Knowledge* (Translated in the same volume by A. M. Sheridan Smith; New York: Pantheon, 1972). In *The Archaeology* Foucault in fact uses the term, "new history," to describe his work and that of the Annales school and to distinguish it from traditional history.[1] In much the same manner as Robbe-Grillet, Foucault attacks the "classical" form of history for its teleological assumptions: for positing history as a unified process of Sense rather than a plurality of discursive acts, for its dependence on a generative, progressive temporal model, and for its assumption of temporal continuity. Like Robbe-Grillet, he directs his critique against the transcendent unity of traditional history and the metahistorical Sense it imposes on all (historical and fictional) discursive practices. In this way, he attempts to undermine the supposed neutrality of the classical *récit* as a model for both history and fiction writing.

But there is a crucial difference between Robbe-Grillet's critique of the classical, Balzacian novel and Foucault's of classical, Hegelian history. Robbe-Grillet attacks continuity, the Real, Human Nature, and Sense in the name of the individual subject—in particular, in the name of the random, unstructured workings of a subject's consciousness, its presence to itself in the world. As we have seen, his critique is made in the name of a phenomenology of perception: "Man is present on every page, in every line, in every word... The objects in our novels never have a presence outside human perception, real or imaginary" (p. 137). Foucault's critique is directed specifically against the priority of the subject and is overtly antiphenomenological. Consciousness—whether it be that of a collective subject or Spirit *(Weltanschauung)* or of an individual subject—is for Foucault the principle of traditional history, the basis for, rather than the alternative to, Sense: "If there is one approach that I do reject, however, it is that (one might call it, broadly speaking, the phenomenological approach) which gives absolute priority to the observing subject, which attributes a constituent role to an act, which places its own point of view at the origin of all historicity—which, in short, leads to a transcendental consciousness" ("Forword to the English Edition," in *The Order of Things* [New York: Vintage Books, 1974], p. xiv). Foucault's archeological approach to history is overtly antisubject,[2] and in this area as in others he owes much to the work of the Annales historians and especially to Fernand Braudel, who, as early as 1950, had already laid the grounds for such a direct critique of the individual subject in history—a critique which in fact should be traced at least back to Nietzsche and Marx:

> But it must be said that, in history, the individual is all too often a mere abstraction... The question is not to deny the individual on the grounds that he is the prey of contingency, but somehow to transcend him, to distinguish him from the forces separate from him, to react against a history arbitrarily reduced to the role of quintessential heroes. We do not believe in this cult of demigods, or to put it even more simply, we are against Treitschke's proud and unilateral declaration: "Men make history." No, history also makes men and fashions their destiny—anonymous history, working in the depths and most often in silence, whose domain, immense and uncertain as it is, we must now approach. (*On History*, p. 10)

As we have seen in chapter 1, since the time of the publication of *For a New Novel*, the theory and criticism associated with the New Novel have moved away from Robbe-Grillet's early statements and, like Foucault and Braudel, find the subject to be derivative, an abstraction, the principal obstacle to the development of a "science of discourse." The phenomenological subject is now treated as a mystified concept which obscures the "true workings" of the text, a false or imaginary unity imposed on fragmentation and multiplicity from "outside," an origin for a metaphysical order in which to root form and sense. Theorists and critics (and most of the novelists themselves) accept that the subject must be "rejected" as Foucault says, "transcended" as Braudel urges, or "dissolved" in Lévi-Strauss's words (*The Savage Mind*, p. 247). For the most recent theory of the New Novel, as for the New History, the subject is a derived concept rather than an original one; situated in discourse, in the Symbolic (Lacan), or at the intersection of various series and structures, the subject is dominated by the contexts and orders which enclose it.

For Foucault—and for the present generation of New Novelists and critics— the notion of temporal continuity is intimately linked to the notion of the subject in its various forms. Foucault claims in fact that as long as history and fiction are dependent on notions of continuity and synthesis, the concept of the subject will continue to dominate in spite of any efforts to undermine it:

> If the history of thought could remain the locus of uninterrupted continuities ... if it could weave, around everything that men say and do, obscure syntheses that anticipate for him, prepare him, and lead him endlessly towards his future, it would provide a privileged shelter for the sovereignty of consciousness. Continuous history is the indispensable correlate of the founding function of the subject: the guarantee that everything that has eluded him may be restored to him ... Making historical analyses the discourse of the continuous and making human consciousness the original subject of all historical development and all action are two sides of the same system of thought. (*The Archaeology of Knowledge*, p. 12)

The concepts of the subject and of historical and narrative continuity have been so intertwined in history that they seem inseparable. This is why Foucault claims that those who attack him for being antihistorical (Sartre, among others) are not defending history in general but a very narrow view of history based on the dominance and originality of the subject:

> But you shouldn't be deceived: what is being mourned with such vehemence is not the disappearance of history, but the eclipse of that form of history that was secretly, but entirely related to the synthetic activity of the subject; what is being mourned is the development *(devenir)* that was to provide the sovereignty of consciousness with a safer, less exposed shelter than myths, kinship systems, language, sexuality, or desire ... what is being mourned is that ideological use of history by which one tries to restore to man everything that has unceasingly eluded him for over a hundred years. (P. 14)

The question remains, however: what is history when it is not dominated by a concept of the subject and not dependent on the related assumption of temporal continuity and the possibility of establishing a closed order? What form does such a history take? What order underlies it and makes it possible?

In *The Archaeology of Knowledge*, in order to answer these questions, Foucault refers explicitly to the work of the historians of the Annales school, to whom, he admits, his own theory of history as discontinuity is indebted. The "new questions" that Foucault feels must now be asked of history, those questions which are to replace the "old questions" of unity and synthesis, are largely those asked by the Annales school: "The old questions of traditional analysis ... are now being replaced by questions of another type: which strata should be isolated from others? What types of series should be established? What criteria of periodization should be adopted for each of them? What systems of relationship... may be established between them? What series of series may be established? And in what large-scale chronological table may distinct series of events be determined?" (pp. 3–4). Traditional historical questions have, for Foucault, then, been replaced in the "New History" by questions of strata, series, periodization, and long duration—the Order and the Time which History was thought to provide are thus replaced by the orders and times of various and conflicting histories and discursive practices.

From the very beginning of his research, in the preface to his monumental *La Méditerranée et le monde méditerranéen à l'époque de Philippe II* (Paris: Armand Colin, 1966; originally written in 1946), Fernand Braudel states that the goal of the historian should be to complicate the form of temporality usually projected onto history in order to ensure its unity. He posits three general forms of temporality, three general temporal series, in opposition to the assumed temporal unity of traditional history: (1) "a history that is almost changeless, the history of man in relation to his surroundings"; (2) "a history of gentle rhythms... a social history of groups and groupings"; (3) "a traditional history, history, so to speak, on the scale not so much of man in general as of men in particular... 'l'histoire événementielle,' the history of events" (*On History*, p. 3). Braudel thus demands that the concept of the Time of history be replaced by a more complicated and particularized notion of the "times of history": "Thus we have been brought to the decomposition of history into successive levels. Or rather to the distinction, within historical time, of a geographical time, a social time, and an individual time. Or, again, to the decomposition of man into a succession of characters" (p. 4). It is clear that for Braudel the "decomposition of history," the complication of its form as a simple, continuous *récit*, implies also the "decomposition of man," *the subject* of history, into various and contradictory "characters." Here Braudel's critique of traditional history can be compared with Robbe-Grillet's critique of the traditional novel, for if the fundamental unity of time is no longer assumed, if the continuity and unity of "life" are no longer accepted as given and the related concept of man no longer taken as a natural, universal concept, then the traditional form of *récit*, whether in history or fiction, can no longer be accepted as natural either. Braudel is here demanding exactly what Robbe-Grillet will later demand: a "new" form of the *récit*—a *new history* and a *new novel*.

The other major element of Braudel's critique and reformulation of historical discourse—long duration—also works to complicate the form as well as the sense of history. Braudel describes long duration as the "curious phenomenon" of how certain regularities are carried over from one time period into the next, from one social structure or institutional formation into the next—even across revolutions, "epistemological breaks," and radical discontinuities. The notion of long duration does not, however, reinstate a principle of continuity or unity within history—rather it is evidence that history is never simply progressive. It also reveals that no historical present is ever entirely present, for each present is at the same time itself and not itself, having broken with the past in order to be considered present and yet carrying on at the same time past elements, structures, and series practically unchanged. "All the cycles and intercycles and structural crises tend to mask the regularities, the permanence of particular systems that some have gone so far as to call civilizations—that is to say, all the old habits of thinking and acting, the set patterns which do not break down easily and which, however illogical, are a long time dying" (p. 32). Long duration makes the work of even the "new historian" more difficult because it continually cuts across the various temporal series into which he has decomposed history: "Among the different times of history, the *longue durée* often seems a troublesome character, full of complications, and all too frequently lacking in any sort of organization. To give it a place in the heart of our profession is not a simple game and would entail more than a routine expansion of our studies and curiosities... For the historian, accepting the *longue durée* entails a readiness to change his style, his attitudes, a whole reversal in his thinking, a whole new way of conceiving of social affairs. It means becoming used to a slower tempo, sometimes at the limits of motion" (p. 33). Decomposing or pluralizing history is not enough, then, and the historian must do more than simply enlarge the scope of his research to take into account this new factor. Braudel demands that he/she also rethink the way history is conceived and narrated—long duration demands a *new style* or form of history.

The chief error of traditional historians for Braudel is that they choose one of the times of history for *the time* of history and thus reduce the differences between temporal series, excluding those which cannot be formulated in terms of, or brought back to, the one chosen. This is what he calls the "historicist error" (p. 34); it is to conceptualize all problems in terms of the same theoretical model or frame, to narrate all history in terms of the same *récit*. For, as Braudel argues, "there is never any problem, ever, which can be confined within a single framework" (p. 15). The conceptual and formal frame with which the historian encloses data is never neutral—just as the form of narration he/she uses to order or arrange material is never inconsequential. The form and the frame of history have theoretical and ideological effects on the production and sense of history—not to question them is to accept a traditional form of history and the restricted field in which it works, no matter how many "new" or "nontraditional" subjects are added to the list of "legitimate" historical subjects.

According to Braudel, history is and should be continually at the "crossroads" (p. 200), in all senses of this term: that is, in a process of perpetual self-questioning as to its own status and place, and situated at the various points where different series, orders, and times intersect with each other and break with each other. The perspective or point of view of history can then never be transcendent or metahistorical, or even anchored in one completely defined and fixed position within history—the point of view of history is on the contrary a function of the conflictual aspect of the various orders and series which constitute history and which no perspective completely dominates. To determine *a* point of view within history is to restrict the form and sense of history—it is to do the one thing that Braudel claims the historian should never do: reduce the conflictual plurality of history. He argues that the historian must maintain "a clear awareness of this plurality of social time" (p. 26). History here has lost the certainty of its base in a simple notion of unilinear, evolutionary, or dialectical temporality and its anchor in a fixed and determined perspective. For Braudel, the historian's task is not to synthesize the plurality constituting history (which is not, it should be clear by now, a simple pluralism) but to maintain it, to analyze the differences between series and how they intersect and conflict with each other. History is for Braudel fundamentally conflictual, and where it is going is precisely part of the conflict constituting it, rather than a question resolved before the fact through a choice of a certain narrational or conceptual mode: "the future is not a single path. So we must renounce the linear" (p. 200).

Foucault argues in the same vein that history should no longer be considered to be homogeneous, for the unity at the basis of traditional forms of history can no longer be assumed: "History has long since abandoned its attempts to understand events in terms of a play of cause and effect in the formless unity of some great evolutionary process, whether vaguely homogeneous or rigidly hierarchized" (*The Discourse on Language*, p. 237). The basic assumptions at the heart of traditional history which serve to unify it—basically those of consciousness, subjectivity, and continuity—are for Foucault ideological concepts which, for the purpose of ordering and giving sense to history, reduce its complexity, "police" it to make it conform to the interests of the dominant institutions and ruling classes, and control its possible forms and senses. The questions of the subject, of continuity, and of order in history, because they are no longer accepted as givens by the "New History," no longer given transcendent or metahistorical status above, outside, or at the origin of history, are precisely the questions with which history must deal if it is not to simply repeat the limitations and restrictions of traditional history. If the arguments of Braudel and Foucault are to be taken seriously, it seems clear that there can be no truly critical history which does not in some form or another confront such questions—for both the form and the sense of history are at stake in the responses given to them.

The discipline itself of history[3] is thus no longer seen by the "New Historians" as constituting a closed space unto itself. The questions which history must now confront—those of the subject, of temporal discontinuity, of the conflictual plurality of the various orders constituting it—are in fact not simply historical questions in a narrow sense. They are questions which are also being pursued in philosophy, psychoanalysis, sociology, anthropology, linguistics, and, I would argue, fiction too. Of all contemporary novels, the novels of Claude Simon are probably the most involved with such historical questions, and no novel more that the one I shall analyze in this chapter, *La Route des Flandres* (1960) (*The Flanders Road*, translated by Richard Howard; New York: George Braziller, 1961). All of Simon's novels explicitly and persistently return to the fundamental historical questions raised by Braudel and Foucault: the multiple and contradictory status of the past, its complicated relation to the present, the ideological and formal implications of the way "life" is ordered by history, and the way that the individual subject is defined and its place determined in and by history. My reading of the novel in terms of these theoretical/practical, historical/ literary questions will have a dual purpose: (1) to analyze the role of these questions in the novel and the effect they have on the narrative form of the novel, and (2) to emphasize the fundamental relationship that I argue exists between fiction and history (historical theory and discourse) in general. The argument for the existence of such a relationship does not depend on the reduction of the complexity or relative specificity of either term, nor does it accept either term as an unproblematical given—that is to say, it neither makes history into a form or subset of fiction nor fiction into a form or subset of history. To be more specific—the following section investigates how the question(s) of history is (are) raised and formulated in *The Flanders Road* and the effects of this particular formulation on the writing of fiction and on the writing and theorization of history. I should also add that even though the so-called "New History" and "New Novel" have made it possible to ask these "new questions," neither has provided satisfactory answers to them. Each in turn provides or imposes order on history and fiction—no matter how plural or discontinuous these "new orders" may be—and these discontinuous orders need to be questioned and put into question just as much as the traditional orders that have already been rejected. The chief problem with the theories of the New Novel and the New History is that, as powerful as their critique of the order and time of traditional history and fiction is, they leave uninvestigated the ideological and formal implications of their own orders and times.

## The Debacle of Order

Social time does not flow at one even rate, but goes at a thousand different paces, swift or slow, which bear almost no relation to the day-to-day rhythm of a chronicle or of traditional history.

Each "current event" brings together movements of different origins, of a different rhythm: today's time dates from yesterday, the day before yesterday, and from a long time ago.

Fernand Braudel, "Time in History,"
in *On History*

Order is a kind of compulsion to repeat which, when a regulation has been laid down once and for all, decides when, where and how a thing shall be done, so that in every similar circumstance one is spared hesitation and indecision. The benefits of order are incontestable ... We should have the right to expect that order would have taken its place in human activities from the start and without difficulty; and we may well wonder that this has not happened.

Sigmund Freud,
*Civilization and Its Discontents*

All of the novels of Claude Simon are marked by a fundamental uncertainty concerning the workings and sense of history, an uncertainty which permeates all levels of reality, all forms of knowledge, and all action. This uncertainty is first of all due to the fact that the traditional foundations for history, the epistemologies, ideologies, and narrative techniques used to order, form, and make sense out of the past and relate it to the present, prove themselves to be contradictory and reductive in dealing with the complexity of the past. In Simon's novels there seems to be no solid foundation on which to construct an historical order—both the subject and the referent of history are pictured as being deficient in various ways and are repeatedly undercut in the novels as the origin or foundation of history. The concepts of progress, development, continuity, enlightenment, rationality, etc. which constitute and give direction to traditional history are presented in Simon's novels not as innocent, metahistorical assumptions underlying the course of history and determining its sense and narrative form, but rather as naive ideals which restrict the form of history to that of a continuous *récit* and in the process suppress the deviations, contradictions, and gaps from within the narration of history. Simon's novels attempt to resist this form of historical-narrational reductionism by continually multiplying the ways any (hi)story is told, by contradicting with an opposing version any (hi)story which takes itself to be definitive.

The problem of historical certainty is not just an epistemological problem but is a formal problem as well. It is important to investigate, then, the effects the questioning of the grounds of traditional history has on the *writing* of both history and fiction. What are the narrative-historical effects when a traditional concept of history as continuity is not taken as a given, as the model for all *récits?* What forms of fiction and what forms of history emerge from the radical questioning of the foundations of history? Is history still possible after such a questioning? Is fiction? The traditional sense of history as an evolutionary or dialectical movement toward some assumed or well-defined end orders history in terms of its "victories"—all "defeats," all losses, disruptions, or deviations from the path to the posited end are recuperated or transcended in the process itself. But what results when negativity is taken seriously and resists being negated or transcended (recuperated), when it continues to interfere with the positivity history is supposed to constitute? History constructed or narrated in terms of loss, disintegration, and discontinuity is history thought of in terms of its limitations, as the dispersion and contradictory multiplicity of various orders and times (temporal series). History, of course, does "go on" as the cliché states, but where it is going becomes problematical, a conflict within history rather than its origin or end. In fact, historical uncertainty in Simon does not inevitably result in a sterile and conservative pessimism as some might assume (even though this is a risk for any radical critique or questioning of this type); rather it constitutes a critical perspective aimed against all idealisms and utopias and their reductionary effects on historical thinking.

If history has traditionally been thought of either as the presentation of an accurate picture of the past, "things as they really were" in Ranke's phrase, or as the determination of well-defined historical periods within the continuous movement of a positivist evolution toward an end, then there is nothing further removed from this concept of history than the novels of Claude Simon. Discontinuous, contradictory, intermixing fact and fiction, fantasy and reality, as well as past and present, Simon's novels state clearly and repeatedly that they are unable to resolve the historical questions which haunt them. If history is supposed to determine a *knowledge* (even an "archeology of knowledge"), then

Simon's novels are "failures" as history, unable to determine and represent the truth of the past they question. The questions asked of history in the novels in fact produce no valid, uncontradicted responses—history in its dispersive multiplicity, is continually falling back into fiction, unable to establish itself against fiction as *the form* of true discourse.

Insomuch as they raise fundamental historical questions, rather than being opposed to historical investigation as both a narrow historicism and formalism might claim, I would argue that the novels of Claude Simon have an important place within the ongoing critique and rethinking of both history and the novel. The historical uncertainty at the basis of his novels takes the form of a narrative uncertainty affecting history and fiction at the same time and in the same ways. This means that in Simon's work the initial disorder or "debacle" of history is never completely overcome, never effectively made to conform to any other, supposedly more fundamental order—neither to a metaphysical order nor to an empirical one, and certainly not to any order of discourse or language which might be claimed to underlie them both. The "order of discourse" is no more certain, no more systematic, nor more totalized, and no more fundamental and determining than the traditional "orders of history" explicitly put into question. The problem then is more complicated than replacing one order with another, than arguing that one order is more essential than another.

It is not sufficient, I would argue, simply to reverse the hierarchy between history and fiction, referent and language, content and form, as most contemporary critics of the novel tend to do in order to make history into a more naive, totally unselfconscious form of fiction.[4] These critics are not wrong to question the so-called exterior order of history as the model for fiction (or for history writing either for that matter); nor are they wrong to criticize the restrictive qualities of the concept of mimesis governing the relationship between history and fiction when history is taken as a given, unquestioned empirical order. The problem with this formalist position is that a critique of the absolute priority of history leads immediately to a rejection of history and to the replacement of the order history was supposed to establish with one that is just as restrictive and just as problematical: the order of discourse or of language itself. As Serge Doubrovsky has argued in his analysis of *The Flanders Road*, to give total priority to the order of language—which he calls "the postulate of a scriptualism"—is just as naive as to give total priority to the referent, to history or experience in itself: "Impossible here to give priority in the genesis of writing either to 'fiction' (the experiences that the writer would like to communicate and for which he must invent a language—the postulate of a naive realism) or to 'narration' (a language developed *ex nihilo* and which then goes off in search of 'experiences' to figure—postulate of the scriptualism defended by Jean Ricardou)."[5] The simple reversal of the relationship between history and fiction, the absolute privilege given now to language as a closed system or order (or to a metahistorical system of tropes as in the case of Hayden White)[6] simply replaces one questionable order with another, equally questionable order—it leaves the notion of order in general unchallenged.

Jean Ricardou is only one of many critics to have emphasized the conflict between order and disorder in his discussion of *The Flanders Road*. The various critics who have treated this aspect of the novel appear to agree that the real for Simon is initially chaos, contradiction, discontinuity—a complex plurality of forces—and that the novel tries to give form to the "debacle," to reconcile this "disorder," with the "artificial order of language."[7] In this perspective, the disorder of "experience" and linguistic, narrative order remain separate entities until they are brought together through the mediation of an individual subject or consciousness, that of either the author, a character in the novel, or a formal subject (scriptor) located in language; and language is the means by which this mediation is accomplished.[8] But does the novel really support this view? This is an especially important question because history is also taken as the attempt to institute order where there is disorder, to make sense out of chaos. The question must be asked as to how the order of language can be claimed to have succeeded where the order of history failed. It will be necessary in order to answer this question to examine the grounds for the different orders that appear in the novel and the particular situations out of which they arise; for language and history are not in fact the only orders in question. Order and disorder are never abstract terms in the novel but always specifically defined and related to particular historical, social, and textual forces.

The fundamental, though not totally determinant, order in *The Flanders Road* is the social order, a hierarchy dominated by and providing privileges and economic benefits for the ruling classes. The divisions in the remains of an army retreating from the debacle of Flanders repeat with specific differences its divisive structure and conflicts. Captain de Reixach, leading his men through a leisurely and aristocratic retreat at the risk of their lives, simply employs a knowledge and exercises a traditional prerogative granted him by society: "Keeping his horse at a walk because he had ancestrally learned that you have to let an animal breathe if you've demanded a violent effort of it, that was why we were advancing aristocratically cavalierly at a majestic turtle's gait" (p. 318). De Reixach's actions seem to indicate that the aristocratic and military codes are completely stable; for they seem to be identical to those of his ancestors, as if no time had elapsed between generations, as if nothing had changed: "Repeating, doing over what a hundred and fifty years before... what another de Reixach, then, had already done" (p. 85), and this, even and especially in the face of death: "for instance his reaction of drawing his saber when that burst of gunfire came from behind the hedge: there was a moment when I could see him that way his arm raised brandishing that useless ridiculous weapon in the hereditary gesture of an equestrian statute which had probably been handed down to him by generations of swordsmen" (pp. 10-11). But is this herarchical order really an Order in an absolute sense: static, universal, and complete? To answer in the affirmative is to express the view of the ruling classes themselves. Does this order really only begin to crumble with the massacre of de Reixach's troops and the general debacle of the French Army in Flanders, because some "outside" event, occurring through chance or necessity, disrupts it? Or does it begin to lose its stability and universality for the first time when de Reixach gives up his military career for a marriage outside the aristocracy? Or, then, if this is not the first instance and origin of disorder, perhaps it can be found a century and a half before, when his ancestor joins the Convention? Or back further, in some mythical past at the inception of the family and the aristocratic order itself? The impossibility of finding a first instance or origin for disorder indicates that it was there from the start, that order was only apparent, not actual, that this class was never totally coherent, unified, or dominant.

In situating the social order in which the de Reixachs have a privileged place, the novel clearly indicates that it is historical, developing out of particular economic and social conditions, and limited in time and scope. By the time of the war, the aristocracy is an anachronism, persisting in the bourgeois order which is supposed to have replaced it. The army, as an aristocratic institution, also functions according to the old order and old traditions. In fact if the French Revolution marks the end of the rule of aristocracy in history, the rout of de Reixach's calvary—itself a remnant from another time and from a different kind of war— reveals that the status and privileges of the aristocracy were never totally destroyed and that the present still contains within it many elements of the past, and of a distant past at that. De Reixach is "behind the times," living in an order which history has left behind, but at the same time very much a part of his times —he lives in the past, but in a past which plays an important (reactionary) political role in the present.

The past is visibly present in the portrait of de Reixach's ancestor. This portrait obsesses Georges, a distant cousin of de Reixach and the principal narrator of the novel. It supposedly captures the identity of the ancestor (of the "model aristocrat"), and it serves as a model for both de Reixach's behavior and the interpretations given it. It orders and frames the past and the present; it gives sense to the ancestor's life and that of de Reixach. But all apparent orders or frames are spaces of conflicting interpretations, theories, and (hi)stories rather than their resolution.[9] Blum, a prisoner with Georges after the "debacle," reconstructs the *double history* of de Reixach and his ancestor from evidence given by Iglesia, the Captain's jockey and aide. He reverses the order of history by using de Reixach as the model for the ancestor's life: "and Georges: 'No, you're mixing it all up. You're confusing him with ... and Blum': ... his great-grandson. That's right. But I think you can still imagine it" (p. 198). Due to the number of conflicting versions, no simple before and after can be established; the past is read in terms of the present, the present in terms of the past. Each frames and is framed by the other. Georges's mother, defending the family honor, dismisses Blum's theory, that the ancestor was killed by his wife's lover, a story already prevalent at the time of his death: "His grandmother had always told her it was a legend, a piece of slander, scandal spread by the servants in the pay of political enemies—the *sans-culottes*, her grandmother said, forgetting that he happened to have been on their side" (p. 86). She clings to the version agreed upon by the family: "According to the tradition the version the flattering family legend it was to avoid the guillotine that the other one had done it had been forced to do it" (p. 91). For the family, the painting depicts a man true to aristocratic ideals, capable of heroic action and even suicide in order to remain faithful to them. It proves their worth and right to dominate.

When Georges looks for the trace of the bullet in the room where the ancestor was supposed to have died, he sees in the hole in the painting and its badly smudged surface the confirmation of the ancestor's suicide. The painting has received after-the-fact the bullet intended for the ancestor himself. Georges's efforts to judge and even to reconcile the different versions of the (hi)story are never completely successful, however; for no one version resolves all contradictions. The ultimate evidence which would determine the truth remains missing. The painting remains a space of conflict as it inserts the ancestor's history into that of de Reixach and reinscribes one time-span in another, so that they are difficult, if not impossible, to separate. The painting itself becomes a persona (a "subject") of the novel, as real, as alive, as active (generating historical-fictional narratives) and as contradictory as any other. When each present is thought of as complex and when the evolutionary model for history is complicated or undermined, de Reixach and his ancestor become "contemporaries."[10] In this way the hegemony and persistence characteristic of ideology and social institutions problematize the linear flow (order) of history and divide the present into conflicting series and orders. A moment in history long past (that of de Reixach's ancestor) has a greater influence on (forms) the present than do moments of a more recent past.

The social order, which is posited as universal and unilinear in order to benefit its privileged classes, actually consists of a multiplicity of time scales and time spans, each having its own relatively autonomous historicity. In spite of its static and timeless appearance (de Reixach's world and that of his ancestor seem in many ways to be identical), it is subject to the destructive workings of time. It has a specific kind of historicity, that of long duration, which gives it the appearance of structural stability; but it is not eternal, for time simply works at a much slower rate on this level. Changes which occur are sometimes not evident til long after the fact: "as if war, violence, murder had somehow resuscitated him in order to kill him a second time as if the pistol bullet fired a century and a half before had taken all these years to reach its second target to put the final period to a new disaster" (p. 80). The destruction of an order and the suicide/accidental death of an aristocrat have taken over a century to be accomplished; but of course it is neither exactly the same order nor exactly the same aristocrat who are ultimately destroyed.

The aristocratic social order has from the start, in fact, been threatened from within—through revolts, suicides (especially of women who have less to gain from its maintenance than men), revolutions, and the conflicts resulting from its hierarchical structure. It is not a simple system where all relationships are determined by one principle or in terms of one force, but a complex network of opposing and attracting forces, a system of conflictual interaction rather than one of unilateral cause and effect. The model for all social orders in the novel is the fluid system of the relations existing among the four principal figures of the novel:

131

"the four men bound together by an invisible and complex network of forces impulses attractions and repulsions interconnecting and combining to form by their resultants so to speak the polygon of sustentation of the group which itself constantly shifts because of the continual modifications produced by internal or external accidents" (p. 308). The social order as it is presented by the novel is a disordering element itself, not a totalized Order which only begins to disintegrate when it is interfered with by outside forces or events. It is without a solid foundation and originates in conflict.

The different social groups present in the novel form relatively autonomous orders coinciding with relatively autonomous temporal series, interconnected but not unified. The peasants whom the regiment passes along the route of its retreat, for example, are hostile to the segments of society which have produced the war and have no interest in protecting the soldiers. Like the aristocracy they live according to another time; they are "of the past." The war is more alien to them than to the aristocracy, because it is for them neither a means of attaining economic superiority or national security, as it is for the bourgeoisie, nor a theater in which to reenact ancestral gestures and customs, as it is for the aristocracy. For the peasants the war is completely negative, a destruction of their lands and their way of life, a violent disruption of the historicity they are closest to, a geographic, cyclical, practically stable temporality. The bitter hostility between them and the soldiers arises out of their distance (temporal, spatial, national, and linguistic) from the forces and interests of the war.

As the principal narrator, Georges occupies a special place in the various social orders; he is located at their points of intersection, but not at their center. His mother is a relative of the de Reixachs ("I think that we are more or less cousins," both de Reixach and his wife, Corinne, say to Georges at different times), and his father, a professor, is the son of an illiterate peasant who has left the land and gained access to the privileged classes through his mastery of the written word.[11] Georges is neither completely aristocratic, nor bourgeois, nor peasant; he is not situated in a clearly defined, stable space but is a product of, and occupies various places of, conflict among the classes. Though he is the principal narrator (even though it is impossible ultimately to distinguish his voice from Blum's and that of the other soldiers) and the principal point from which the novel speaks (though there is never one source for the novel), Georges does not dominate the novel as subject, identity, or original consciousness. The novel emerges from the place(s) he occupies rather than *from him*.

The moment of narration, the "present" in which the narrative voice (or narrative function) is located, is not simple or unique. Each present is a fusion of other moments, which are never really completely past. Simon's much discussed use of the present participle blurs the absolute distinction between past, present, and future, not in order to collapse all time into an eternal present as some have argued, but to differentiate (complicate and defer) the present, to give it duration. The present carries within it traces of the past; it is a reconstruction from these traces rather than a given. No exact *point of reference*, no anchor for the narrator, can be postulated ("the passage of time itself, that is, invisible, immaterial with neither beginning nor end nor point of reference"; p. 29); and thus no inscription in any one context is ever absolute or final. As the history of his family, "that cohort of ancestors crowding behind him, the ghosts surrounded by legends" (p. 59), molds de Reixach's behavior and values, so the voices of the past, of those dead—his ancestor's and here also Blum's voice—interrupt and invade Georges's thought and voice: "maybe I was still talking to him, exchanging with a little Jew dead now for many years boasts gossip obscenities words sounds" (p. 283). It is often difficult to identify the origin of a voice because it is never simple, never the living presence of an identifiable speaker totally at one with him/herself: "and Georges (unless it was still Blum, interrupting himself, clowning, unless he (Georges) wasn't having this dialogue under the cold Saxon rain with a little sickly Jew—or the shadow of a little Jew, and who was not much more than a corpse—one more corpse—of a little Jew—but with himself, that is, his double, all alone under the gray rain, among the rails, the coal cars, or perhaps years later, still alone... still having a dialogue with that double, or with Blum, or with no one)" (p. 189). The subject-speaker and subject-receiver have both been displaced; each is divided by a fundamental relation to absence and death. Communication, therefore, does not take place in the present, and neither does narration; and thus no formalism modeled after a simple form of communication which assumes such a present can account for the complicated narrative (dis)orders in play here. The order of narrative is no more certain than any of the other orders undermined in the novel.[12]

Given the complexity of the social and narrative orders and the different temporal series associated with each, it is not surprising that the time span of the events associated with the retreat in Flanders is not simple either. The war moves along at various speeds which do not coincide exactly with the temporality of any of the social groups but cut through them all. The times of the war are usually extreme. At one moment the war accelerates the destructive aspects of time, death, and decay: "Have you noticed how fast it goes, that acceleration of time, the extraordinary speed with which the war produces phenomena—rust, stains, putrefaction, corruption of bodies—which in ordinary times usually take months or years to happen?" (p. 208). At another moment, or even at the same moment, it seems immobile, unchanging, infinite: "time somehow motionless too, like a kind of mud, of mire, stagnant" (p. 119)—or irrelevant: "trying to remember how long we had been in that train a day and a night or a night and a day and a night but it didn't have any meaning time doesn't exist" (p. 19). To attempt to define the time span of the novel, then, is to be confronted with a multiplicity of times and narrative perspectives: any unity, any synthesis of this multiplicity, any unilinear narrative sequence must be imposed on the novel at the expense of this multiplicity. The sense of any event (and thus its place in a temporal order) is thus never exact; it can only be determined as it is reinscribed and displaced after the fact by other events—in other words, as it is continually rewritten.

As Ricardou points out in "Un Ordre dans la débâcle," *The Flanders Road* often moves from moment to moment, from series to series, from order to order, by means of devices inherent in language, thus emphasizing its so-called "material nature" as text. Through a play on words *(calembour)* the narration abruptly changes direction in mid-sentence, the multiple significations of the same word or sound serving as the intersection of various series: i.e. "saumur" indicating at the same time "salt" and a prestigious military school (Ricardou, p. 48). An assumed resemblance (not an identity) between events occurring at different times (i.e., the death of de Reixach's ancestor and his own death) accomplishes the same purpose. The novel continually moves back and forth between similar events (the retreat of the calvary and the defeat of de Reixach in a horse race), between narrative voices, between different senses of the same word in different contexts, and between the different series produced by a sound within a word. The novel is narrated by means of a sequence of these intertextual bifurcations which themselves occur at different speeds—some after pages of development, others within a single phrase. The *histoires* (historical-fictional narratives) are told, interrupted, contradicted, and modified throughout the novel because no one version of any story, any event, or any temporal series is definitive in either a historical or formal sense. It is the conflict between versions that emerges as the dynamic principle of the novel. All temporal orderings are artificial and limited; no meta-order is ever established.

The problem of the order(s) and time(s) of history should not be discussed, however, without also raising the question of the nature of the historical or fictional text in general, as well as the question of language itself. In *The Flanders Road* there are at least two concepts of writing (and of knowledge) advanced, one optimistic and "universal" (idealistic), the other cynical (and equally idealistic), attacking all writing (historical, philosophical, or fictional) as useless and vain. The first, the belief in books as the means of capturing the Truth, expressed in its most naive and absolutist sense, is that of one figure in particular, Georges's father, the son of an illiterate peasant become professor. For him books are sacred and reading, a religion: "That's why he talks so much Because all he can manage is that ponderous stubborn and superstitious credulity—or rather faith—in the absolute pre-eminence of knowledge acquired by proxy, of what is written, of those words which his own father who was only a peasant had never managed to decipher, lending them, charging them with a kind of mysterious magical power" (p. 36). Books constitute an absolute Order which resists conflict and contradiction, a tradition within which the solution to all the problems facing humanity can be found: "He's so proud of having been able to learn how to read that he's deeply convinced that there's no problem, and particularly no problem standing in the way of humanity's happiness, that can't be solved by reading good authors" (p. 226). The most distressing aspect of the war for Georges's father is the temporary setback it inflicts on the "progress of humanity's happiness" through the destruction of the library at Leipzig, where "the best" of what past generations had left behind had been housed:

> To add to the concert his own laments by sharing with me his despair at the news of the bombing of Leipzig and its apparently irreplaceable library ...
> "this world where man strives to destroy himself not only in the flesh of his

children but even in what he can best achieve and bequeathe: History will say later what humanity lost the other day in a few minutes, the heritage of several centuries, in the bombing of what was the most precious library in the world, all of which is infinitely sad, your old father." (P. 227)

The novel presents the father's view of writing—writing as a closed system rooted in the Truth, writing as a self-sufficient and totalized Order (whether it be ontological or formal)—as pure idealism, equivalent to the belief that the social order dominated by the aristocracy is stable and universal. This view is idealistic because it is absolutist, because it pretends to resolve all contradictions and to synthesize all diversity. To speak like a book in this sense, as Blum accuses Georges of doing—Georges, who has inherited more from his father than he acknowledges (p. 226)—is to use "useless and empty words" (p. 37), words which are meant to cover over and repress everything which does not have a simple and precise sense (or form), everything which resists the Order books attempt to establish. The Order of knowledge conceived by the father establishes itself through exclusion and retreat; like the social order, it is based on the idea of privilege: "My father absolutely insisted that I get myself ploughed at the Ecole Normale. He absolutely insisted that I profit at least a little from that marvelous culture which centuries of thought have bequeathed to us. He absolutely insisted that his son enjoy the incomparable privileges of Western Civilization" (p. 226). The father's conception (ideology) of books is rooted in the particular situation and status of the professor in society. It is in his interest to affirm the *written* as a transcendent order of Truth—it supports his social position and emphasizes the distance which separates him from his own illiterate father: "His father's voice heavy with that sadness, that intractable and vacillating obstinacy in order to convince himself, if not of the usefulness or the veracity of what it was saying at least of *the usefulness of believing in the usefulness of saying it*, persisting for itself alone" (p. 36, my emphasis). Like all apparent universals, the relativity and partisan nature of this position become evident when one asks what is the particular situation from which universality is proclaimed and in whose interest it works.

The literary-political source for this idealization of the Book is Rousseau,[13] who haunts Simon's novels and who is evoked here as the inspiration for the ancestor's class betrayal and for his naive confidence in the total success of the revolution, "the pathetic and grotesque costume lying there crumpled mausoleum of what (not power, honors, glory, but the idyllic shady dells, the idyllic and sentimental reign of Reason and Virtue) his readings had given him a glimpse of" (p. 205). The ideological configuration is basically the same although almost two centuries separate Georges's father and de Reixach's ancestor: a belief in the idealist order created by knowledge and books, which in one case results in political action, taking the side of the sans-culottes, and in the other, total inaction. The ideology persists, though well-worn, just as the painting of the ancestor is passed from generation to generation. In the ancestor's case, when history cannot be made to conform to the utopian ideal, suicide (Georges's solution to the enigma of his death) is the result: "Imagining him then, seeing him conscientiously reading one after the other each of the twenty-three volumes of sentimental, idyllic and confused prose, ingurgitating pell-mell the prolix and Genevese lessions in harmony and *solfège*, in education, silliness, effusions and genius, that incendiary chatter of a jack-of-all trades vagabond, musician, exhibitionist and crybaby which would ultimately make him press against his temple the sinister icy mouth of that ..." (pp. 84–85). The caricature of Rousseau presented here serves as a model for all idealist, utopian orders which are assumed to transcend the contradictions of history. Georges's father's position is simpler—a radical denial of everything which is not found in his precious books or which cannot be accounted for by them. For this ideological position, history will conform to the principle of its origin and will lead inevitably to its utopian end, or it will not exist at all.

What is denied or rejected does return however to contradict the view of history which ignores defeats and betrayals, which sees only the positive side of all events. In *The Flanders Road* the complete annihilation of the army in Flanders is more than just a temporary setback which will soon be overcome by the next phase of history. What de Reixach with the proper aristocratic aloofness calls a "bad business" (p. 166) is rather a serious and substantial loss, a radical disruption in history and the "progress of mankind": "his brigade no longer existed, had been not annihilated, destroyed according to the rules ... of war, normally, correctly ... but so to speak absorbed, diluted, dissolved, erased from the general-staff charts without his knowing where nor when ... his brigade somehow evaporated, conjured away, erased, sponged out without leaving a trace" (pp. 206, 208). The threat is of total dispersion and annihilation; "but what would you call that: not war not the classical destruction or extermination of one of two armies but rather the disappearance the absorption by the primal nothingness or the primal All of what a week before were still regiments batteries squadrons of men, or better still: the disappearance of the very notion of a regiment a battery a squadron of men or better still: the disappearance of any notion of any concept at all" (p. 305). Destruction, disintegration, defeat, loss, death—i.e. time in a radically negative sense—oppose at each step of the way the naive belief in continuous progress and development and undermine the assumed unity of history: "the world stopped frozen crumbling collapsing gradually disintegrating in fragments like an abandoned building, unusable, left to the incoherent, casual, impersonal and destructive work of time" (p. 320).

The cynicism of Georges concerning the value of books and knowledge, articulated from the position of total defeat and death, conflicts with his father's idealism, "to which I answered in return that if the contents of the thousands of books in the irreplaceable library had been impotent to prevent things like the bombing which destroyed them from happening, I don't really see what loss to humanity was represented by the disappearance of those thousands of books and papers obviously devoid of the slightest utility" (p. 228).[14] But it is not a question of choosing between the two positions, between absolute, naive optimism and gloomy, regressive nihilism, between Georges's argument against books and knowledge and that of his father, who gives them an absolute value. Rather the novel is constructed in terms of the conflict between the two positions, in terms of the inadequacy of either as a universal statement. The novel continually under-cuts and situates all positions which pretend to be universal—and most definitely the order of language (of books) itself, in whatever way language is defined: idealistically or "materialistically".

Simon's novels explicitly put into question the tendency of written history to reduce and diminish the complexity of its relation to the "real" ("the ephe-meral, incantatory magic of language, words invented in the hope of making palatable—like those vaguely sugared pellets disguising a bitter medicine for children—the unnamable reality" (p. 186), its proclivity to universalize or natur-alize its ordering or inscription of the "real" and to ignore all but the most inof-fensive forces and events: "History leaves behind it only a residue excessively confiscated, disinfected and finally edible, for the use of official school manuals and pedigreed families... But actually what do you know?" (p. 190). *The Flan-ders Road* repeatedly evokes the margins of history, what has been repressed, excluded, and rejected in order for one version of a historical event to become accepted as the official version (part of the textbook heritage), for one historical order to be accepted rather than another. It acknowledges the relativity of the border or enclosure of any pictoral or written inscription. Writing for Simon is a repeated process of reordering and reinscription from the traces of history and at the same time an assertion of the limitations of any one order or inscription. Writing disperses what seems to be unified and sets up various and contradictory systems of relationship between orders in the very process of ordering.

This is not to say that the novel accepts these limitations or cynically rejoices in the impossibility of exact knowledge. It refuses to valorize either the destruc-tive, chaotic, fragmented working of time and death or the reassuring certainty of any supposed order. Georges and Blum never give up their desire to know, but they are continually confronted with the impossibility of transcending time and their own situation in order to achieve knowledge. As he attempts to under-stand the sense of de Reixach's death and its causes (and thus the sense of his own life and his family's history), Georges reveals that he would have to be at least double to possess this knowledge, self and other at the same time, behind de Reixach and ahead of him, a principle of Hegelian synthesis of the past, pres-ent, and future: "But how to know, how to know? I would have had also to be the man hidden behind the hedge, watching him advance calmly toward his death down the road" (pp. 301-2). Only then could the totality of the enigma of de Reixach's death (and life)—and his own—be resolved: "Between us—I following him and the other man watching him advance—we possessed the totality of the enigma (the murderer knowing what was going to happen to him and I knowing what had happened to him, that is after and before, that is, like the two parts of an orange cut in half and that fit together perfectly)" (p. 319).

But even if this doubling of perspective and the synthesis of past and future were possible in the present—and assuming that Georges and de Reixach's assassin have the knowledge they are claimed to have here—something would be missing from the totality "at the center of which he rode ignoring or wanting to ignore what had happened as well as what would happen, in that kind of nothingness (as it is said that in the center, the eye of a hurricane there exists a perfectly calm zone) of knowledge, that zero point" (pp. 319-20). Without this principle of unity at the center, without the living presence of a subject certain of itself, and without a founding consciousness, the circle of interpretation or recall (of history) cannot be effectively closed but must continually be formed and re-formed. At the center of this and other orders there is a lack, a fundamental disorder—the destructive space of death and time. Rather than the presence of a consciousness and supplementing its absence are the systems of reinscription, of representation, which produce, like a mirror with many sides, looking "out-side" as well as in—"he would have needed a mirror with several panels" (p. 320)—conflicting images, reproductions, fictions, histories. The original, the real in itself, is always in some sense lost in the complex process of cross-reference, reflection, and reproduction. The complexity of the temporal and spatial orders prevents the construction of a true meta-order which would dominate and ac-count for all other orders; and the novel continually returns to the points where the different orders, all disrupted by absence and death, intersect, break apart, and reform: "watching, impotent, the slow transmutation of his own substance, starting with his arm that he could feel dying gradually ... devoured not by worms but by a slowly mounting tingle that was perhaps the secret stirring of atoms in the process of permutating in order to organize themselves according to a differ-ent structure" (pp. 247-48).

Without the possibility of a transcendent leap outside of the contradictions and disintegration perpetrated by time and death, an Order that is sufficient and inclusive cannot be constituted. If history and the novel have traditionally been thought to be thus ordered and to be moving forward toward some specific end, it is only at the expense of certain forces, like a map that accounts only for those routes that can be reduced to straight lines and charted as continuous and well-marked, with a clearly indicated beginning and end: "The whole of the battle which had just taken place therefore could be represented on the general staff map ... this schematic representation of the movements of the different units not of course taking into account the accidents of the terrain nor the unforseen obstacles occuring during the course of the fighting, the actual trajections having the form of broken lines zigzagging and sometimes intersecting and getting em-broiled in each other" (p. 304). *The Flanders Road* follows this/these zigzag, repetitive, discontinuous, multilinear route(s), for the novel refuses to posit a unilinear narrative-historical direction or to privilege one level of the text, one time, one order, at the expense of all others. The narration of multiple versions of each event, told from different perspectives and according to different systems of organization and disorganization, is not meant to indicate, however, that the accumulation of enough versions of an experience or a historical event would capture its totality, this time as a synthesized multiplicity, the sum of all its versions. On the contrary, it indicates that the event, the document, the date, the moment of narration—any element of history, no matter how small—is itself the space of conflict among different forces and interests, and that the resolution of any particular conflict by the imposition of an order only produces another conflict. As there is no end to time and history (how would it be determined?), there is no end to conflict.

Simon's novels, then, assume a radically critical position on history, inserting negativity where it is repressed; complexity, conflict, and contradiction where they are supposedly surpassed. Loss, destruction, and defeat at the same time constitute and interfere with Simon's narratives; and this produces a continual process of reconstruction, reordering, and reinscription. A superficial reading might lead one to believe that Simon views history as cyclical, in the sense of an eternal return of the Same (of an historical identity or essential subject). But the form and sense of history in Simon's novels is, as I have argued, repetitive and not cyclical, the return of difference rather than identity. Each repetition and return produces new conflicts and contradictions and never results in their simple resolution. Without the assumptions which would determine the institution of Order (social, temporal, linguistic, or ontological), repetition and plurality are the basic characteristics of Simon's narratives, of the *histoires* which constitute his texts. An order, then, cannot be found or posited *in, under, around* or *above* the debacle.

If the Simonian novel is haunted by historical questions, it ultimately returns these questions to history without a solution but with a difference—for it reinscribes them in a space which is not that of traditional history. By their radical critical perspective on these questions, by their continual undercutting of all historical finalities, and by their contradictory formal complexity, Simon's novels demand that history do more than simply provide answers to them. They demand that history also investigate continually how and in terms of what system (what order) it provides these answers and in whose interests it imposes an order on the debacle. Finally, they demand that history begin to question itself as a particular narrative form, not only in terms of what is accepted (written down) as history, but also in terms of what does not fit into any "continuous" narrative form, what is "lost" or rejected but nevertheless "written" in the blank spaces of history, in its margins. The questions of history, as they are returned to history by Simon's novels, demand, then, not *an answer*, a resolution of the debacle and an imposition of order, but rather that history assume a critical perspective on itself: that it not be content to be the simple narration of "what happened," that it not accept as such any sense, order, or form as definitive or fundamental.

The historical uncertainty and negativity at the heart of Simon's novels, therefore, serve a critical rather than a nihilistic function; for to undercut idealisms, utopias, formalisms, and other forms of historical and narrative finality is to work not against history but rather against those forces and forms which reduce, simplify, and attempt to transcend the contradictions, differences, and negativity at the heart of history, seen here as a complex narrative system of conflicting series and orders rather than a monolithic, unilinear narrative continuity.

# S I X

## Diachrony and Synchrony in Fiction/History: Reading *Histoire*

### The Limitations of Spatial Models: The Novel as Painting

There is a language which is tacit and painting speaks in its own way ... Like a painting a novel expresses tacitly.

Maurice Merleau-Ponty, *Signs*

Painting—that's what I like best in the world. I am a failed painter.

Claude Simon, "Interview"

Much has already been written and continues to be written about the ahistorical and even antihistorical nature of structuralism. In fact, the history of structuralism in France is also the history of this critique, dating from the earliest responses to Lévi-Strauss's work and continuing even today. That the critique is more or less the same form has been repeated over the last twenty years indicates at the very least that the conflict is a serious one and the issues at stake are unresolved—and perhaps unresolvable in any simple sense. Unresolvable in any case when the critique of structure is made in the name of History as an external force, an idol;[1] when diachrony as a positive, unquestioned given is brought in to negate and do away with synchrony; when time is used to conquer and open up the "prison-house" which language taken in spatial terms has constructed.[2] Unresolvable because one term of the opposition immediately calls up the other—the attack against structuralist thought in the name of dialectical thought is part of the very definition of structure. One term derives its meaning in opposition to the other: structure is opposed to history, space is to time, analytical thought to dialectical thought, etc. It would be difficult to find a philosophical movement which did not in some way deal with the problem and take sides on the issue. The opposition itself is the given, a seemingly unresolvable duality basic not only

140

to our time but to Western thought in general. The opposition is not really between history and its Other as Sartre and others have argued in an attempt to defend history, but one inscribed within history, a conflict basic to history, at the origin of historicity itself. It cannot be resolved by simply taking one side over the other or by problematizing one side at the expense of the other; for this is to remain within the dualist opposition and to accept the premises lying behind it and the more devious "prisonhouse" of metaphysics.

This is not to say that the critique of structuralism made in the name of history does not have validity and does not touch on some of the ideological suppositions underlying the methodology and reveal some of its limitations. But behind the critique more often than not lies an equally questionable theory of history ready to take the place left vacant by the exorcising of structure. Lévi-Strauss's response to Sartre in *The Savage Mind* attempts both to defend the positive contributions structuralism has made toward developing a critical historical methodology and to point out the serious ideological limitations of Sartre's own concept of history. For structuralism did originate, at least in part, in opposition to a simple, evolutionary (i.e. historicist) sense of history—one that was inadequate in its attempts to account for cultural (especially linguistic and communicational) phenomena and belittled or totally ignored other cultures and their history by implying that they were ahistorical or primitive. Lévi-Strauss's critique is most effective when it points out the ideological implications of the concept of the self in Sartre's system and the latent ethnocentrism in modeling all history after our own.[3] But this is not to say that Lévi-Strauss's work itself necessarily overcomes all such limitations; it is in fact more complicit with that of Sartre than Lévi-Strauss realizes.[4] The opposition which forces one to choose between two equally limited ("emprisoned") positions must itself be undermined if the ideological limitations Sartre and Lévi-Strauss each finds in the other are to be exceeded. The question is not, therefore, synchrony *or* diachrony; for they have always been thought together as an opposition in terms of the same origin. Rather it is how to complicate this simple opposition in order to avoid being determined by it completely—how to think space in terms of time and time in terms of space.[5]

The opposition between diachrony and synchrony is not only historical in the general sense alluded to above but basic to structuralism itself. If structuralists exclude dialectical thinking, as has been argued, the exclusion is not a simple one. It is at least double. The Saussurian model itself is more complex than usually thought. Saussure defines the proper object of linguistics to be *la langue*, the socially rooted, systematic side of language, as opposed to *la parole*, the individual, evolutionary side (*Course in General Linguistics*, translated by Wade Baskin; London: Peter Owen, 1974, p. 8). Language is at the same time an institution and a product of the past, an established system, and continually evolving. *Langue* and *parole* are interdependent, each supposing the other, instrument and product of the other at the same time. Saussure determines that the institution or system (*la langue* as a structure) is "the sole object" of linguistics (p. 20), however, even if "historically" *la parole* always precedes *la langue* (p. 18). This is Saussure's first "exclusion" of diachrony, but it does not mean, however, that

141

for him there can be only one approach to the study of *la langue*. He argues rather that synchronic and diachronic approaches are both possible and necessary and he gives the following diagram (p. 98) to illustrate the place of diachrony in relationship to synchrony in a synchronic approach to language.

$$\text{Language} \left\{ \begin{array}{l} \textit{Langue} \\ \textit{Parole} \end{array} \right. \left\{ \begin{array}{l} \text{Synchrony} \\ \text{Diachrony} \end{array} \right.$$

The opposition between synchrony and diachrony repeats itself within the area of study devoted to *la langue*, within structural linguistics itself—it does not simply separate linguistics from its other. If diachrony has been excluded in order to define *la langue*, it reappears with *la langue* to differentiate it further; and another "choice" must be made: synchrony or diachrony? Diachrony, then, is not so much being excluded or denied as situated within synchrony, which in turn is situated by being opposed to diachrony. Diachrony is both the limit or end of synchrony and a moment of it—outside and inside at the same time.

Following Saussure, structuralists tend to be obsessed with the spatial foundation for diachrony and to read temporality in terms of the system of which it is a part. Roland Barthes uses the Saussurian model as his base but argues against Saussure's concept of the univocity of discourse and the successive ("vulgar") concept of temporality he feels is complicit with it: "Contemporary analysis tends to "dechronologize" the narrative continuum and to "relogicize" it ... To be more precise, the goal is to give a structural description to the chronological illusion; it is up to narrative logic to account for narrative time. To put it another way, temporality is no more than a structural class of narrative *(récit)* (understood as discourse); just as in language, time exists only in the form of a system. From the point of view of narrative, what we call time does not exist, or at least it only exists functionally, as an element of a semiotic system.... "True" time is only a referential illusion."[6] Barthes here does not deny all diachronic aspects of discourse but rather refines and develops the notion of temporality by refusing to accept it as an unquestioned given. The spatialization of time, if it is in the last resort a limitation and reduction of time, serves also to undercut the illusion of simple, linear historicity. There is more in question here than the exclusion of diachrony, for history is not so much denied as reinscribed in a space different from that usually constructed by historians.

What I am saying here is perhaps very simple—so simple it is most often overlooked. It is that certain aspects of the historical process are perhaps better accounted for by thinkers who do not accept history as an unproblematical given, precisely those thinkers who have been considered by some to be a- or antihistorical. Their work has played a role in questioning the simple, evolutionary model for history, in showing that the monolithically singular and unified view of history as well as the continuity often assumed to be fundamental to history (the dialectic establishes more often than not a continuity rather than emphasizing the conflictual aspects of history and its plurality), are not natural givens but ideological presuppositions rooted deeply in Western civilization. Dialectical thought is never innocent or natural but implies a system at its base which encloses and structures it. As Lévi-Strauss argues, history is never an absence of system or code but a particular kind of code: "History does not therefore escape the common obligation of all knowledge, to employ a code to analyze its object, even (and especially) if a continuous reality is attributed to that object. The distinctive features of historical knowledge are due not to the absence of a code, which is illusory, but to its particular nature: the code consists in a chronology" (*The Savage Mind*, p. 258). The analysis of the assumptions behind the structuring of the codes, the series of dates and events at the basis of history, constitutes in this sense a critical approach to history rather than an antihistorical position. Neither the tools of the historian nor his construction of historical series is value-neutral, and if structuralist analyses of historical discourse have served to undermine the supposedly objective status of history, its direct and immediate links with the real, historical investigation can certainly benefit from it.

Something is lost, however, when diachrony is read in terms of synchrony, when after a critical investigation of the codes, series, oppositions, and even the subjects of history, history becomes simply a function in a larger system. But what is lost or excluded is not so much the complexity and conflict at the heart of history but the complexity of space. What structuralists reduce ultimately by accounting for all diachronic elements in spatial terms is the concept of space itself, for at the heart of structuralism is the implicit assumption that there is one space and that all space is one. The structuralist space is closed, unified, and centered, but the assumptions behind the centering and closing off of space and the consequences of these assumptions are rarely questioned.

Saussure reveals that he is aware that in describing language in spatial or structural terms the problem is not just the delimitation of all temporal factors but the construction and delimitation of space itself (*Course*, p. 102)—but after admitting the problem exists, he chooses not to pursue it. Rather he eliminates the problem by basing the delimitation and unity of the state of language on the assumed and admittedly approximate unity of the word and then proceeds as if unity were a natural given. His justification?—the speaking subject makes a similar assumption: "Anyone who speaks a language delimits its units by a very simple method—in theory, at any rate. His method consists of placing himself within speech *(la parole)*, seen as the source material of language *(la langue)* and of representing it as two parallel chains, one of concepts and the other of sound images" (p. 104, translation modified). For Saussure, one must assume the basic unity of words as well as the space in which they circulate, because even though this unity cannot be proven, it is necessary for structuralist methodology, "concrete" (p. 114), and therefore part of the "natural reality" of language. "Language then has the strange, striking characteristic of not having entities that are perceptible at the outset and yet of not permitting us to doubt that they exist and that their play *(jeu)* constitutes it" (p. 107); "for in spite of the difficulty of defining it, the word is a unit that imposes itself on the mind, something central in the mechanism of language" (p. 111).[7]

The reductionary aspects of structuralist thought, then, are not due to the simple exclusion of diachrony per se but rather to the exclusion of all space which is not unified, autonomous, and closed. Lévi-Strauss claims that *la pensée sauvage* (more faithfully translated perhaps as "untamed thought"), modeled after language, is "timeless" and "totalizing"—it accounts for everything, synchronic and diachronic elements alike (*The Savage Mind*, pp. 245, 263). But it is totalization itself that is questionable here, as questionable as Sartre's concept of totalization based on the individual subject as first principle, which Lévi-Strauss rightly criticizes. Linearity and closed space are interdependent concepts rather than absolute and uncommunicating opposites. To argue against one for the sake of the other, as Barthes and Lévi-Strauss do, is not an effective strategy; for a closed system is simply another form of linearity, dependent on the same principles of construction. The simultaneity attributed to space and the linearity attributed to time are both effects of presence, means of reappropriating the present in its integrity and imposing a final sense on temporal and spatial configurations.

These are some of the problems the synchronic/diachronic opposition raises and masks at the same time by seeming to demand a resolution which can come about only at the expense of either temporal or spatial complexity—a reduction to the dictates of a final, monolithic sense: either a fully enclosed unified space or a continuous, evolutionary temporal order. The opposition not only plays a role in determing the categories and methodologies of anthropology and history but also those of literary theory and criticism, for it is central to any theory of literature insomuch as it determines how texts are read by predetermining whether a text is considered a diachronic or synchronic entity. In Claude Simon's novel *Histoire* (1967; translated by Richard Howard; New York: George Braziller, 1968)—and in fact in all his work—this opposition plays a central role not only as a thematic, philosophical problem, but also as part of the formal configuration and construction of the novel. A critical reading of Simon's theoretical statements and of *Histoire* itself from a perspective privileging neither term of the opposition reveals the grounds for the formulation of the opposition, the configuration it takes in Simon's theory and novelistic practice, and the consequences of this particular formulation in terms of the two senses of *histoire* suggested by the title of his novel: (1) story or fictional narrative, and (2) history, a particular reading and construction of the past. Fiction and history—still another formulation of the opposition itself with form supposedly being in the last instance the principal characteristic of fiction (what defines it) and with temporal progression or succession being the "essence" of history. The way outside the opposition is not simple, for at each level it seems to be reinforced rather than broken down.

Simon has formulated the synchronic/diachronic opposition, which he sees to be the central problem of his theory and practice of writing, in the following manner: the obligation to "write successively" what is "perceived simultaneously."[8] "The question is no longer to describe successively things which occur successively in a duration, but to describe a score of simultaneous sensations or images with the only instrument we have at our disposal: language, that is to say a duration" (Knapp, p. 185). Simon's model for experience is spatial, a simultaneity limited to the present, bordered on one side by the just past and on the other by the soon to be. Experience in the novels, enclosed in the space constituted by the present, most often is modeled after perception; but as we have already seen, and as Michel Deguy has argued, perception in Simon is never exact.[9] The space of experience, which is the origin of life and the novel—"the point of departure for every writer (in any case for me) is the perception, the knowledge I have of the world" (Knapp, p. 184)—is not ordered but chaotic, fragmented, plural. One never experiences (sees) exactly what is and the world is never exactly what one sees. The origin is not simple and original, therefore, but what is original is a chaotic plurality, the disorder inscribed in the space of experience.

For Simon the problem of time comes in after the fact, at the same moment as the problems of language and order, and it is equivalent to them. Language is for Simon primarily duration, a putting into a temporal sequence or order what is initially unordered in the present moment of experience. The writer is defined as a producer of order: "Writing consists of introducing order into, or rather producing order from the confused and chaotic perception we have of the world" (Du Verlie, p. 7). Simon's sense of language here is a linear one, modeled after *la parole* in Saussure's opposition. Language comes in as a remedy, a means of correcting and making sense out of the prediscursive plurality of space, of inserting an origin there where there are many conflicting ones. The linearity of a text, however, is not its end; for the ultimate goal of the writer is not linear but spatial order. The writer must "overcome that obstacle which the linearity of language constitutes in order to try to satisfy the need for simultaneity which seems at first irreconcilable with it"(*Nouveau Roman: Hier, aujourd'hui*, 2:90). The novel must transcend its own language, its own linearity, and constitute a space in which linearity is simply an element. "Time in the novel cannot be linear, pasted on—a thread onto which events are to be placed one after the other as in clock time; but on the contrary a sort of inclusion, a sort of gelatin or transparent plastic material in which all the elements of the novel are enclosed and in which they coexist simultaneously" (Knapp, p. 185). The space of the novel "where all its elements coexist simultaneously" is a formal space, a closing off and end of all diachrony, the system *(la langue)* behind all discourse *(la parole).* It is not the initial, chaotic simultaneity of experience but a new, constructed simultaneity, a new spatial order. The novel must be "framed," the parentheses closed; for to leave the novel open is to neglect formal problems, a weakness Simon finds in the Surrealists. "What the automatic writing of the Surrealists produced was too often (if not always) parentheses which were opened but never closed (precisely because of this scorn for formal values). The parentheses must be closed: *the work must be closed in on itself in order to constitute a totality*" (Knapp, p. 189, my emphasis). If the parentheses are not closed, the work will have no form, no center, no unity, and cacophony (a meaningless and formless linear discordance) is the result (*Entretiens*, p. 18). The writer produces a linear order (language in its temporal dimension) that must be read in terms of the space in which it is inscribed. The work is fundamentally a closed entity, a "structured system" (*Nouveau Roman* 2:81)—to be "framed" in a formal sense, then, the novel must become a painting.

A novel is like a painting for Simon (the writer is a "failed painter" trying to be a successful one in another medium) in the modern sense of painting as a "nonrepresentational art." The writer is seen as working with (or on) language to produce shades of meaning, colors, and forms, and not simply to construct coherent stories. A novel as a nonrepresentational artifact has a formal rather than a hermeneutical sense; it is a spatial rather than a temporal entity. "Literature, which has traditionally projected a coherent view of the world, is now grappling with its fragmented form; and like the modern painter, the modern writer is reassembling the pieces in a new order" (Du Verlie, p. 8). The work, however fragmented, must be unified; in fact that is its definition: "book, that is to say unity" (*Nouveau Roman*, 2:88). The unity of a work is a formal, visible unity. Like the "logic of painting in itself," there exists an "internal logic of the text" (p. 78), which necessitates that the text too constitute "a coherent pictorial totality" and be judged in terms of its "pictorial credibility," of formal rather than representative criteria (p. 81). Neither Simon nor the great majority of critics reading him ever questions the assumptions underlying the "spatialization" of the novel which he and they propose, the transcendence of linearity in space and the closing off or unification of space. He (they) proceed(s) as if formal unity were not problematical but a natural given, as if "pictoral credibility" were a universal, objective criterion, unlike the constraints of "representational credibility" which he wishes to do away with.

The consequences of using a formal, pictorial model for the text are, however, serious. The text is given a flat, spatial configuration so that once it has been read from beginning to end and "closed," it can be grasped (understood) in its entirety by the reader. "And the book having been closed, the reader can all the same, if not in terms of all the details he might want to return to in reopening the book ... at the very least in its totality, 'grasp the whole visual field in one stroke'" (p. 86). This unity of the whole, present to the reader who knows how to close the book properly, is precisely its formal credibility, its presence: "its pictorial perfection, a credibility, a presence" (*Entretiens*, p. 21). The "true continuity of writing" replaces the "scriptural cacophony" of conventional novels whose model for continuity is the sequence of events rather than the formal dictates of space (*Entretiens*, p. 18). The continuity of the text is thus a "more profound continuity because its articulations, its connections, its progression depend now only on the qualitative relations among the elements constituting it" (*Entretiens*, p. 22). According to Simon a text should always be read, therefore, in terms of its logical consistency, its formal configurations, its origin and end in space. Simon thus does not move outside the Saussurian model at all. The limitations of his statements are those of the model he and others at least implicitly use. Form now becomes equated with sense; "a new order" is assembled. What is not seen is that form can be as monolithic a model for sense as representation, that form, to the extent that it occupies a closed space, is simply the other side of representation, retaining the dualist opposition on which representation depends.[10]

A reading of Simon's novels reveals that the solution which his theoretical statements bring to the synchronic/diachronic problem is not adequate and not in complete conformity with his writing. Space in fact is never closed or "framed" within the novel, nor is it an adequate frame for the novel. Painting does not enclose and account for the novel, for it is situated within the novel and thus implicated in its conflicts. The relationship between language and painting (time and space) is not simple, causal, or *pre*formative but one in which one term continually undermines, takes the place of, and adds to the other. The example of Stendhal, which Simon has used in many places to describe the "act of writing," in fact undermines rather than supports the simple spatial/temporal opposition and, among other things, questions the idea of writing as a simple act which takes place in the present.

> Contrary to the traditional formula: something to say—act of writing, I believe that what really happens is: act of writing—something being said. Or to put it another way: one always writes only about what is happening *at the moment of writing*. Stendhal himself had the same experience. While writing *Henri Brulard* he realized that instead of describing (with the greatest possible fidelity, according to him) how he crossed the Great Saint Bernard Pass with the Italian army, he was actually describing an engraving of that event which he saw much later and which "took the place of reality." What he might also have added, if he had been more observant, was that he was not even describing that engraving (for which he would have needed at least one hundred pages), but that he was *writing* "something" that, in its turn, was taking the place of that engraving. (Du Verlie, p. 5)

The moment of writing *(le présent de l'écriture)* is thus never simple—the present never full but a complex moment of replacement and supplementarity. The "present of writing" is not a present at all but a process of reinscription of the traces of the past within a space which in turn will provide the material for another open and divided present. Diachrony has penetrated synchrony from the start and vice versa. Neither is absolute origin or end (frame) of the other—all origins and ends are partial and relative. The present moment of experience is "chaotic" because it is not simply spatial, not simply present, but already within itself historical, carrying along with it traces of the past—the present moment of writing also. Neither the novel nor painting, nor the novel as painting, nor experience itself, ever ultimately constitutes a real simultaneity. The closing off or spatialization of fiction can only be accomplished at the expense of its complexity, its pluridimensionality, in the name of the integrity of the present.[11] Simon's "structuralist" solution to the synchronic/diachronic opposition is not adequate, therefore, because it too accepts the dictates of the opposition and privileges one of its terms over the other.

To ask which model, diachronic or synchronic, should determine a reading of *Histoire* (of any fiction or history) is to ask which elements of the novel should be emphasized and which should be underplayed, situated or even neglected—that is whether diachrony should be read in terms of synchrony or synchrony in terms of diachrony. In spite of Simon's theoretical statements, the question does not have a simple answer and is poorly phrased in this form. The novel should be looked at as a nonfinalized, conflictual texture of meanings, open to the readings history will bring to it, and nonreducible to any present, spatial or temporal. A dual strategy twice over is necessary for reading such a text, one in which the reader must be prepared to look in order to see the novel as a painting and to listen in order to hear the novel as discourse, but prepared also, to paraphrase Merleau-Ponty, *to look at discourse* the way the deaf look at those who speak and *to listen to painting* in order to hear it speak its "tacit language" (*Signs*, pp. 46–47). All this at the same time—in the complex, synchronic-diachronic present of reading or writing.

### Noise and the Visual: Openings in the Structure or Frame of Fiction

D: Daddy, when they teach us French at school, why don't they teach us to wave our hands [as the French do]?

F: I don't know. I'm sure I don't know. That is probably one of the reasons people find learning languages so difficult . . . Anyhow, it is all nonsense. I mean, the notion that language is made of words is all nonsense . . . there is no such thing as "mere words." And all the syntax and grammar and all that stuff is nonsense. It's all based on the idea that "mere words" exist—and there are none.

Gregory Bateson, "Metalogue: Why do<br>Frenchmen?" In Steps to an Ecology<br>of Mind

*Histoire* is a novel, like many others, that models itself after memory; but memory here is not a given, not assumed to be the exact retention of the past. The past evoked through memory in *Histoire* is uncertain, fragmented, contradictory: "But exactly, exactly?" (*Histoire*, p. 70). For what is left of the past in the present are its traces: discourse (the documents, letters, and voices of the past) and visual "representations" (paintings, photographs, postcards). Fragments, debris, and residue left over from what was, but without unity or continuity, "like the permanent and solidified residue of some limitless, permanent and so to speak domesticated affliction, expressed outwardly in passive and respectable formulas" (p. 17); "trying to imagine under the rubbish, the fallen blocks, the debris, what had been" (p. 84); "fragments, flakes torn from the surface of the enormous earth" (p. 10). Because the past never comes back in itself, exactly as it was, but only as pictorial and linguistic traces of itself, the principal problem becomes one of reconstruction. What to do with this mass of material? To treat it as a painter (or an archeologist) would and to reconstruct it according to spatial demands, isolating and privileging synchrony, or as a historian would, constructing a temporal series in which one moment follows the next? The choice is not simple because there is such an abundance of fragments of different sorts of material that no single order—synchronic or diachronic—could effectively account for it all. Any choice of one order over another would define and limit the material to be used in the reconstruction; and in order to exceed these limitations it is through a complex process of construction, deconstruction, and reconstruction that the novel takes form—an open, nonfinalized, self-reflexive form, constantly calling attention to its own limitations and instability.

Memory in the traditional sense is rooted in the desire for the origin, a desire to retain the past exactly as it was and to make the present the accomplishment of the past. The source of this desire for the origin is the subject in whose interests memory works. The context of this subject is the family, which defines a structure, an enclosure where the subject takes on an identity and becomes what it is, equal to itself. Memory within this enclosure protects the identity of the subject and is a means of recalling the sense of the subject to itself. Here, memory is exact, the "truth" retained exactly as it was, the subject secure. The identity of the subject is assured by the identity (integrity) of the family, and the family is one as the subject is one. The family seems to have overcome the problem of the reconstruction of the past by offering a substantial, "natural" context in which the reconstruction can take place.

The space that seems to contain the history of the family, the space in which the family possessions are stored, the space synonymous with the family name, is the very same space from which the principal narrator speaks and remembers—the family home.[12] Here his memory is triggered and the past reconstructed. The family and the space equivalent to it, the home, have persisted regardless of diachronic change, in spite of the deaths of individual members, divorces, wars, or other catastrophes—regardless of all events taking place either inside or outside. The family is the underlying structure that makes the history of the individual possible, the term of long duration as opposed to the short duration of each individual. The family constitutes a space more basic than evolutionary time, and the events which occur there, closed off to change in the short term. The family home thus becomes the space of memory, the frame that encloses the novel, the guarantee of the originality and the autonomy of the subject inscribed there. Or so it seems if one accepts the thesis of the family and the autonomy and originality of each individual member.

The novel begins, however, not at a moment when the integrity of the family and the space the home constitutes are affirmed, but rather at a moment of crisis, the selling of the family home and the possessions within. The principal narrator, divorced, perhaps even widowed, alone in a half-empty crumbling house and about to sell off what remains, recalls his life (or has his life recalled to him). He may desire the enclosure the family home is supposed to provide, and his memories may be a result of this desire, but what comes back to him is anything but integral, his memories anything but exact, the history of the family anything but linear and continuous. This crisis is simply a repetition in a long series of crises within the family which question its status as a closed unity and the principle of identity at its center. The history of the family and his own history turn out to be more about conflict, absence, and discontinuity than about harmony, presence, and continuity. The family has only been able to maintain its "ideal" status by means of a repression of everything which might disturb it, everything foreign to the principle of identity—and so it is the crisis which is original to the family and not the closed space of the home.

The home retains the voices of the family past, the discourse of the family history. Inside the house the narrator hears again in memory—or for the first time, since memory is constructive and productive and not simply mimetic—the words that were spoken there, the words he himself heard and those passed on to him as part of the family heritage. The discourse of the family history combines all the voices the home contains. As it is recalled it is not a unilinear history because once the voices have been cut off from the living presence of the speakers at their origin, with the absence and/or death of the speakers, their arrangement in a simple chronological order either in terms of the events they narrate or in terms of their moment of utterance becomes problematical. The voices tend to become blurred, one voice mingling with another, one generation indistinguishable from another, and one discourse recalling another not necessarily linked with it temporally, thematically, or logically. The moment of utterance, the identity of the speaker, and the referent are very easily lost in the confusion of voices constituting memory. But as long as the home is thought to be a closed space with a substantial center, the disorder of memory can in theory be overcome, a simple, evolutionary chronology established. The thesis of the family is that all crises are superficial, all disruptions, absences, deaths inconsequential, for its history is continuous. It demands that all voices of the past, all discourse, and thus all history have their roots in the subject as origin and first principle.

The thesis of the family also demands that discourse be unilinear, the simple expression of sense. But before voices are heard and identified and before the discourse of the past can be arranged and made sense out of, something is heard which resembles discourse, the linear chain of sense and communication, but which is not discourse (sense). The novel begins and the past is rooted in noise (cacophony), not sense—in "murmur" *(rumeur)*.[13] The noise of a branch moving in the wind just outside, practically touching the house, is both a noise from the past and a noise which evokes the past, a noise not unlike the unformed, unrecalled rustling of the past: "and behind you could discern being communicated closer and closer a mysterious and delicate murmur *(rumeur)* spreading invisibly through the dim tangle of branches" (p. 11). Within this noise other, more precise noises can be isolated: birds chirping in the tree; the old women and men who used to come to visit the narrator's grandmother "chirping" to each other, his grandmother, mother, uncle and others talking. A series of exchanges is set up in the novel between the different sets of noises as they overlap each other, with one set giving way to and evoking the other. "As if those invisible shudders those invisible sighs that invisible palpitation which populated the darkness were not simply the noises of wings, of birds' throats, but the plaintive and vehement protests persistently emitted by the feeble ghosts gagged by time death but invincible unconquered still whispering still here eyes wide open in the dark chattering around Grand-mère at that one pitch which was now permitted them" (p. 2). The division between discursive and prediscursive (sense and non-sense) is secondary, therefore, because both are fundamentally and originally noise.

Discourse has been traditionally conceived in terms of simple communication: the exchange of messages and the production and reception of sense. A subject who is the origin of discourse and emits messages, one who receives them, and the linear chain between the two constitute this model.[14] With this model, the discourse of the past can be reconstructed without serious problems as long as the origin and end of the chain are intact or can be restored. But if discourse is fundamentally noise and not sense, problems arise. Discourse will continually give way to and be threatened by its foundation in noise (non-sense, plurality of senses), noise which can in turn produce a sense (many senses) not intended by the "original" emitter or understood by the "original" receiver. Noise subverts the linear flow of discourse. Discourse misinterpreted, not heard exactly as it was uttered, forgotten, or heard outside of a closed system of sense, will be received at least in part as noise. At its origin is this possibility. When the noise *(rumeur)* of the past, traces left behind from previous discourses, is reordered as discourse, this is what we usually call memory or history. The "disorder of memory" and thus its inexactness are due to noise within the discourse of the past, to the impossibility of eliminating all noise from discourse, of simply and conclusively rooting discourse in any subject or in any intersubjective relationship— of giving the past a simple sense. Noise threatens the family history from within.

No system, no matter how apparently closed, no matter how "sacred," is safe from the noise within it. In fact the assumption that communication in its ideal form contains no noise is logically prior to the definition and delimitation of the system which constitutes it; the assumption of a closed system determines that there will be no noise, that sense will be unequivocal and univocal. The "sacred," symbolic system of the Church is the ideal model for discourse. Rooted in a system of truth, the sense of the words of the mass, repeated throughout the ages in the same form, seems free of noise; and yet the sense of the words is easily undermined when the closed system of truth is not posited as a given. Lambert, a childhood friend of the narrator, continually perverts the "sacred sense" of the Church Latin and Greek. "Intoibo ad altare Dei" becomes "En trou si beau adultère est béni;" and "Kyrie Eleïsson," "Bite y est dans le caleçon" (p. 43)— translated by Howard as "Keep the pay and lay the Son" and "Come Spermatozoon" (p. 31). The "sacred language" of the Church provides him with an arsenal of puns because the possibility of reinscribing the sounds and multiplying the sense of the Latin and Greek of the mass in other "nonsacred" contexts is fundamental to these and all languages. The "sacred sense" can only be sustained through a repression of all other senses, through a mystification of the status of discourse and its inscription in a closed system. Discourse, without this mystification, is plural not unilinear, a complex texture of meanings and forms and not a system of communication in the traditional sense. Non-sense and a plurality of senses underlie all sense. The "nonoriginal" situation of all discourse in *Histoire* is not the transcendent, ideal model provided by "the sacred," but the following: "the voice seeming to resurge with the light, rising getting louder by degrees as the latter spread, mere sound without any more presence than the tinkle of bracelets again becoming words then sentences perhaps simply set end to end with the sole purpose of making noise" (pp. 151–52). Signification and communication in the simple sense are not the norms for discourse but exceptions, a moment within discourse, discourse taken in its most reduced sense. Noise is the (non)origin and end of discourse.

There is another model for discourse offered in the novel, which is nonlinear and not dependent on a closed system for its foundation. Here discourse is seen as a complex and open system of cross-references without a definable and simple end, a practice evident in Lambert's puns. The two models conflict directly throughout the novel but most evidently in the lessons in Latin translation given to the narrator by his Uncle Charles in his enormous library—in the midst of so many words in so many different languages, of inscriptions on page after page of text, of so much history written down, recorded, and filed neatly away. For the Uncle, the library is closed and self-sufficient. All words have a simple and precise meaning, all books also. When a Latin phrase gives the young student trouble, the solution is simple. "Have you ever bothered to look it up in the dictionary?" (p. 106). The Uncle knows how *to close* (make sense out of) his books. But for the student, as much fascinated by the form of words as by their sense—"conscious of the fascination exerted upon me by the inscriptions in Cyrillic characters" (p. 180)—the dictionary is much more than a storehouse of sense where the answer to any problem concerning meaning can be researched and resolved. The dictionary does not eliminate noise but multiplies it. Words are not given a simple and definitive sense but rather are broken down and sent off in many different directions at once, "ready to fall apart (the words), one would have said, into a dust of fragile brownish particles of rust that seemed to escape from the pages of the dictionary" (p. 89).[15]

The dictionary is incorrectly seen as an enclosure for words just as the library is not an effective enclosure for books (and thus written history), for they do not effectively limit the sense of words or books. They are part, rather, of an open system of reinscription and cross-reference which has no simple origin and end. Sense here is multiple rather than univocal: "the crude violent Latin words which their unfamiliar, somehow exotic look, their uncertain meaning, charged with an ambiguous, multiple power" (p. 86). We are thus now able to situate more precisely the "space" of memory the novel (in spite of the family thesis) actually constructs. The complex process of remembering does not take place completely within the house (within the family) but rather in one particular room of the house, the uncle's library, which is for the reasons indicated above the opening in the enclosure constructed by the thesis of the family. Memory can never be, therefore, the passive return to what was, because the house retains the voices and the documents of the past in the same form that the library its books, the dictionary its words—that is to say it does not contain them. No simple ordering of the past is possible without the active suppression of other orderings. The voices, the discourses, the events, and the documents of the past are combined in memory to produce versions of the past, but no one version is definitive. The orders of discourse and memory are problematical when it is the library rather than the house as a substantial entity in which they are inscribed, when memory is conceived as part of an open, inter-textual network rather than a closed communications system.

Taken in itself, the discourse of the family history is uncertain, contradictory, impossible to keep within the family house and to order effectively. There are in fact too many openings in the enclosure the home is supposed to constitute— too many absences which affect the linearity of discourse. Noise interrupts the family history when discourse is not rooted in the subject, when the moment of its utterance and thus its sense are problematical. All is not lost for the family, however, for it has another remedy for absence, a way of overcoming such threats to its integrity. The principle (the center) of the family is the identity of each subject within the family. The family in question here in Simon's novels is, as we have seen, the bourgeois family, often with some connection to an aristocratic past whose ideology continues to play a role in constructing its self-image. The disruptions caused by the death of individual members or by other absences (divorces or even the perpetual travels of the narrator's father) are the principal threats to the family's history. The family's remedy for absence is the portrait of each individual member hung within the home as the visible proof and guarantee of the continuation of presence. One dies in the family not to disappear but to become immortal; and the sign of this immortality is what remains after death, the portrait.

The integrity of the past of each family is assured by its gallery of paintings, its album of photographs. The subject *is* because it can be painted or photographed, and by being painted or photographed it enters into the family history and assures that its voice will continue to be heard and be attributed to itself. There is no conflict between self and other here because all others are identical to self; the other who is admitted into the gallery or album is never an alterity but a double. It is as if there were only one actor on the stage of the family history (of all history as it comes down in history books with portraits of the "great men and women"), so similar are the portraits, "as if the same model with the same pensive, pitiless and disabused countenance posing for the same painter had put on at some theatrical costumer's their successive garments, reincarnations, sporadic reappearances of a single character repeated down through the centuries in the same calm perfidious and weary attitude" (p. 67). Anyone or anything that might threaten the identity of the family has been excluded or "domesticated," made to look like everyone else. The family history with its "origin" in the portrait is nothing but the continuous series of its portraits and the voices that can be anchored in them. Its veracity, its continuity, and the closed nature of the space it occupies are all rooted in the visibility, in the images, of the individual agents it guards within it. As the frame of the painting or the border of a photograph enclose the identity of the person captured there, so the family is safely enclosed in the home. But the visible realm is in fact no more substantial than the discursive or the historical; to root the identity of the family and each individual subject in the visible is to indicate the limitations of what I have called the thesis of the family. The breaking down of spatial unity here accompanies the complication of temporal linearity.

Identity is defined in terms of space because it is a question of an image, of what can be captured by the eye in the present constituted as a fully enclosed space. To capture the essence of the individual in a portrait is to immobilize the individual, to spatialize all diachrony. It is to give the illusion of presence. The family clings to this illusion as a means of negating absence. The narrator's mother overcomes the father's continual absence by means of his photograph: "I could see it now see him I mean that enormous enlargement she had had made and hung on the right wall parallel to her bed... like one of those apparitions surrounded with a halo of light... like some divinity... the way she had doubtless never stopped seeing him ever-present the unforgettable image floating immaterial and aureoled" (pp. 8-9); "the way he would be for eternity in that portrait" (p. 213). Absence is presence here, the father still present there in the family no matter where he is. All change is secondary to the permanence of the portrait.

In reconstructing his father's life, the narrator has as material for the reconstruction only the portrait and the postcards sent to his mother from Africa, Asia, and South America. The postcards depict the places his father visited; on the back a few banal, clichéd expressions and a signature. They are glamorized, romanticized, theatrical representations of these faraway places; in actuality, reductions of the colonialized Third World to its exotic characteristics, to what a tourist would expect to see there, to what someone in the home would expect a tourist to see. It is as if the colonized world existed only to be on display for its European masters' pleasure, "the laconic signature lettered with an accountant's care on the reverse of tropical landscapes, of photographs of prostitutes disguised as ethnographic documents" (p. 11). What one sees is not what *is* but a theatrical representation, a travesty, what a Westerner expects to see, a difference which is exotic but not dangerous, a sign of his domination, an inverted picture of himself. Just as the father never leaves the house no matter how much he travels because his identity is secure there in his portrait, he also never leaves Europe (according to the family thesis) but finds Europe and himself everywhere; for the European has imposed his own image and customs on the colonized world. "And a restaurant too: as if... it had been shipped just as it stood from Lannion or from Agen: first of all loaded or rather incorporated, embedded in the sides of the streamer... dragged across swamps, virgin forest and jungles by lyre-horned ox teams; and finally set down between the casino of the thermal resort, the Basilica of Lourdes and the Lycée, Jules-Ferry... completing the civilizing and ceremonial grouping sprung up among the huts of Negroes and the giant date-palms... costly, distinguished, rachitic but indestructible, like the very symbols of the indestructible superiority of the white race" (pp. 112-13). Identity results from the suppression or domination of difference. The portrait, taken as the sign of the father's presence, his identity, suppresses all diachronic differences and all cultural and racial differences. *Man* is modeled after the image the European constructs of himself, the image of self he projects as universal to all men and women.

Diachronic difference does not trouble the immobile, unchanging spatialization of the father in the portrait because diachrony is ordered and linear. The postcards do not disturb the closed tranquility of the house or the portrait because they arrive at regular intervals, confirming rather than challenging the integrity of space: "the last card or cards received the last of those insistent messages that were somehow brutal by their very tranquility their regularity their patient laconism milestones in what was for her only immutable immobility a time always the same always recommenced hours days weeks not succeeding but simply replacing each other in the serenity of her immutable universe" (p. 22). Linearity is complicit with the closed space of the family, with immobility.

As long as we accept the thesis of the family and remain within it, diachrony poses no problem. The mother clings to the illusion of the father's presence at the center of the family because she has been assigned that task by him (by the family structure which favors him); she is responsible for the preservation of his and the family's identity. She too is a victim of identity—the father's—at the cost of her own life. She takes over from the grandmother to guard the family (masculine) treasures, to preserve the integrity of space, to watch over the realm of the dead. She is dead as the family is dead, as she replaces the dead grandmother and is almost indistinguishable from her. Immobility is not only the sign of identity but also of death. The family—and particularly the women left behind to preserve it—is a "universe of motionless shadows, the circle of old queens stiff and whining the assemblage of black and bejeweled shapes"; its voices not signs of the living presence of speakers but carriers of death, "continuing (the voices) that kind of *lamento* I could hear as a child" (pp. 14–15). Even though the portrait is the basic unit of the family, the sign of the identity of each member, it is also a sign of death: "disclosing one or another of the pictures which, in their heavy gilding, seemed to participate by their immobility, their permanence, in this funereal and melancholy rite" (p. 15). The women growing old in the family are already portraits of themselves, made up to hide old age and only revealing it more, unchanging and unreal, "able to see her, cadaverous and made up ... not a human face but a thing: that same mask, grotesquely made up with violent colors ... and the man walking so to speak behind the protection of this face which no longer belonged to him ... quite frozen drained or rather deserted by all life ... and even the portraits hanging on the walls participated in an unreal world in the process of decomposing, crumbling falling to pieces around this living corpse with its made up, decorated head, immobilized once and for all in a bright affable rictus" (pp. 46–48). The women have no history of their own, for their place is in the house—while living they are already dead, already fixed portraits, already "ghosts." They can only passively receive history from the outside as they receive the postcards. While the role of the men is to come and go inside of the family home, the women remain inside to keep it unified. The women who do not accept this role—and there are many instances hinted at within the family history—threaten through divorce and perhaps even suicide (the wife of the narrator) the integrity of the family and its history. The family tries to suppress such revolts as best it can. They are not ever mentioned directly; it is as if they never occurred.[16] Maintenance of the integrity of the family is a mortal occupation for the woman, often even if she attempts to refuse it. Enclosed space is deadly—is death.

If, however, the portrait is not accepted as the basic unity of identity, if the arbitrary nature of the space enclosed by the borders of the portrait is made evident and the portrait is not equated with the truth or essence of the individual portrayed, then certainly diachrony and other spatial configurations cannot be completely contained by it. The father as he is reconstructed in the novel is not reducible to his portrait if the portrait is not first valorized. The novel rejects the thesis of the family by showing the principles around which this thesis is organized and at what costs its integrity is maintained. The portraits then have no more profundity than the postcards found in the mother's desk drawer. The father's portrait is no more the sign of his presence or identity than the scenes on the postcards are real. With the portrait and the postcards on equal footing, the father loses center stage and loses his status as an identity. Space loses its dominance and priority over time, and at the same time its unity. It is not closed to the outside but rather penetrated continually by exteriority. The portrait and the postcards function as a *collage* of the father—not pretending to capture his identity the collage replaces the idea of the essential self and opens up the closed space of the family to time, disintegration, and other spaces, all of which in fact were at work within it from the start. The ideology of identity reduced the complexity and intertextuality of the collage to that of the portrait—a reduction of space and time, but more importantly a repression of women and cultural others —while the novel as a whole situates memory, as a form of collage, outside the family (even or especially when it is triggered inside). Identity thus gives way to difference when the outside and the Other cannot be kept outside. The space of identity then is never effectively closed.

The model for looking at (for reading) all portraits is not supplied by the thesis of the family but rather by a group portrait found among the mother's postcards, a group portrait which is "ruined" in terms of content and technique. Part of the photograph effectively captures a "family scene," Uncle Charles ceremoniously being offered tea by his artist friends; but the presence of a naked model disturbs its familiarity—"a scene which exuded something unfamiliar and even unreal, not only by reason of the contrast between the simultaneously domestic, respectable and even formal atmosphere: the tea being served, the classic plate of little cakes, the studious young man...and on the other side, on the divan, the presence of the naked model" (p. 237). In addition, the right side of the photograph is blurred, and the figure of the Dutch painter in whose studio it was taken appears in triplicate—"the right side of the photograph occupied in the foreground by the blurred image (not vague if you look more carefully, but having moved, shifted position) of the Dutchman, or rather by three images of the same face" (p. 225). The tension between the two aspects of the photograph is evident to the eye: the tension between the fixed, immobile quality of the figures who are as they should be—the familiar and acceptable family scene—and the scandalous, naked model; between those who did not move and seem effectively present there, identical to themselves for all times, and the triple figure of the painter. What is indicated in the photo is the arbitrariness of any social identity and of any immobilization, of any spatialization of duration, "so that while the other persons present, retaining for those several seconds the position they had taken when the shutter opened, seemed to deny time, giving the illusion that the photograph is one of those snapshots, one of those knifelike slices made in duration and in which the figures flattened, enclosed within precise contours are so to speak artificially isolated from the series of attitudes preceding and following, the lightning like trace left by the face during its various changes of position restoring to the event its density, postulating...the double series of past and future instants" (p. 226). The indication of identity and otherness and of a "before" and an "after" within the photograph itself does not posit a total-ization of society or a continuity of time in which the photograph, capturing a moment which could be attached to others in a continuous flow, would find its place. The "before" and "after" inscribed within the space of the photo reveal that time is inscribed in any spatialization, that otherness disrupts identity, that no present is full and complete in itself but contains traces of the past and the future within it (as it becomes a part of another present in which it is trace rather than presence). This is true of any photograph, any portrait, not just a "ruined" one. To *read* a photograph is to produce a double series (at least) of discourses around it (before and after) and generating from it; it is to inscribe it in an intertextual synchronic-diachronic network and to open up its arbitrary frame or border to the differences of society and the times of history (a con-flictual plurality). Visual representations abound in Simon's texts not really as outside stimuli for the composition of his texts, not as reference points outside, but as textual elements themselves, which are given multiple and contradictory readings. The essential difference between visual "representation" and discourse, synchrony and diachrony, is not pertinent within the text. It is an illusion of the outside (the *hors texte*), what in the novel considers itself to be the inside—that is to say an illusion and projection of the family.

There is another *reading* of a visual representation given in *Histoire*, one which could be said to undermine the rigid synchronic/diachronic opposition by chal-lenging the way in which space is enclosed and time ordered. This reading is given to the engraving of the city of Barcelona hanging in Uncle Charles's study. The engraving and the Spanish themes it evokes—particularly of the Spanish Civil War (*Le Sacre du printemps* and *The Palace*, as we have seen, develop this theme more fully)—are introduced by a condemnation. Corinne, the narrator's cousin, expresses the family view of the narrator's actions in Spain: "Guess what Papa wrote and he de Reixach looking up politely raising his eyebrows and she That fool has run off to Spain and you can imagine on which side" (p. 132). It is bad enough to have left the family in order to attempt to play an active role in history (the family acting to negate all history that is not written within the enclosure of its borders), but unforgivable to have fought on the side of the Republic against the Church, the aristocracy, and the values to which the family clings. The family condemnation is repeated later in the novel, but this time from the perspective of the narrator's childhood friend, Lambert, who has become an important figure in the Communist party and sees himself as the "guardian" of the sense and direction of "progressive history," able to judge exactly the path history should take (should have taken). The narrator and Lambert have the following exchange: "I heard you were in Spain—yes—very romantic he said... me, I'm not a romantic young bourgeois he said I fight against fascism wherever it is...I heard you were running guns for the Anarchists—no I was running guns

157

period without bothering about—those guys are bastards didn't you know that? All they do is create division in the ranks of the..." (pp. 251–52). Anarchy, the threat to spatial and temporal order, is the enemy of both the family and Lambert, not just in its political form but in its *form* (formlessness) itself. The conflict at the heart of the Spanish Civil War can be read within the context of the engraving of Barcelona (but not only in the terms that either the family or Lambert want it to be read), for the engraving delimits a space of conflict, revealing what both the family thesis and Lambert's linear view of history repress. There can be no neutral reading of the engraving because the nineteenth-century Barcelona depicted in it can only be looked at from the conflicting perspectives of history. There is no way to return to a time completely before the Civil War or to an Eternal Spain which would transcend (repress) these events. The war is written there in nineteenth-century Barcelona, not present in itself but inscribed between the lines in the perspectives and history contemporary viewers (readers) must bring to it.

The readings of the engraving given in the novel are constructed around a basic opposition between what is seen and what is heard, between the eye and the ear. This opposition in turn produces a whole chain of oppositions of the same nature: between order and disorder, space and time, unity and dispersion, continuity and conflict, etc. The opposition, however, is not rigid. The eye is the synchronic principle (space is to be perceived); the ear the diachronic (history like discourse is to be heard). The eye is rooted in the present; the ear in the past (memory is equivalent to the voices and murmurs of the past). The engraving can be *read* (perception is only one element of the complex process of reading) in terms of one of its elements but only after a negation of all others. The eye can look, therefore, blind to anything but itself (i.e. deaf); and it will see order: "something exemplary, calm and educational in which everything was in its place, respectable and orderly" (p. 136). The order of the city is a product of repression—a repression performed by the eye of all social differences and of the "before" and "after," which posits the visible as a universal model. This repression is homologous to that of a political and economic system that produces slums and prisons in which to control its deviants and yet sees them too as model—"and even model prisons, model slums" (p. 137); a system whose monuments indicate the interests it caters to—"the elephantine monuments raised to the glory of Industrial Production or the God Commerce" (p. 133). For this eye the city is one, tranquil, and static—"the city itself, the virtual entity formed by this concretion the color of dried earth, apparently immobile and static" (p. 135)—a city conforming to its own interests and design.

The eye, however, does not initially see this tranquility and order—they must be imposed on what it sees after the fact. What the eye initially sees (hears) and represses is the conflict and confusion of the city, evident in its noise: "What the eye saw rising toward it first was that vague complex and heavy murmur which by a graphic transposition... seemed to emanate from that swarm of minutely drawn details in the foreground... gradually becoming series of vertical lines, then merely dots, in rows of thousands, hundreds of thousands, infinitesimal, obsessive" (p. 134). The first moment of perception is also one of noise. Rather than separate the eye and the ear in a sterile opposition (synchrony and diachrony), the eye must be allowed to hear as well as see—what I have called here *reading;* "So that quite a long interval of time elapsed before your eyes—not your ears: the eyes—perceived faint noises, isolated, identified later by the mind recognizing them and diversifying them only long after they had been emitted, as if they had needed a considerable delay in order to traverse this shapeless magma" (p. 135). Time is always-already at work within the space which the eye *looks at and listens to;* and therefore perception in the simple sense can only take place after a delay, after all noise has been eliminated, all disorder and conflict repressed—and thus the "simple sense" of perception is never really simple at all.

The city is "dedicated, consecrated in advance ... to violence" (p. 133), as is Spain, because the economic and political order desired by the ruling classes can only come about with the violent repression of the conflict and contradictions inscribed within it, with a repression of all differences in order to establish a system, a structure, a space, which is closed and consecrated to Industry and Commerce. The impossibility of maintaining such an order is evident in the act of repression itself. The history of Spain can be read within the engraving of Barcelona precisely because its frame is not absolute; and thus the space it constitutes is open to history, to the history (the traces of the past and future) already inscribed and to be inscribed within it. The double condemnation of the narrator's actions in Spain by the family and Lambert cannot effectively determine either the structure of the city (the frame of the engraving) or its history but are a part of the conflict within them.

Visible representations are no more immediately linked to the "Real," therefore, than discourse. Enclosed space present for the eye to see is just as much a reduction of space as linearity, the continuous movement from one moment of the present to the next, is of time. History must be read synchronically in order to undermine its assumed linearity, and space must be read diachronically in order to undermine its apparently closed nature. A dual, intertextual strategy is needed in order *to read* any painting or discourse in a nonreductionary and thus truly historical sense.[17] In spite of what Simon argues in his theoretical statements, a critical reading of *Histoire* reveals that neither in history nor in the novel are the parentheses ever really closed, and that the illusion of a closing off, of an arrival at or movement toward an end, may be a necessary moment of both history and fiction (as well as painting), but it is nothing more than that, a momentary illusion. Something always escapes repression; something always remains to interfere with the pure presence of form and with the historical identity desired.

The origin of life, of experience, of history, of memory, and of fiction, therefore, should be thought of in terms of the *interplay* between synchronic and diachronic models and not posited in either one alone. Structure is only an arbitrary enclosure of time and space and must give way to history and the plurality and complexity of space; at the same time history, whose origin and end can only be determined (posited) ideologically, is rooted in structure and a plurality of conflicting temporal series. Perhaps Merleau-Ponty was not as frivolous as he might first have seemed to proclaim that history should be modeled after language and the arts, diachrony after synchrony (*Signs*, p. 73), as long as his statement is completed in accordance with the logic of his argument to say that language and the arts should at the same time be modeled after history, synchrony after diachrony—all "at the same time," in the complex space/time of the text, of *Histoire* (fiction/history).

# The Dogmatism of Form: Theory and Fiction as *Bricolage*

The characteristic feature of mythical thought is that it expresses itself by means of a heterogeneous repertoire, which, even if extensive, is nevertheless limited. It has to use this repertoire, however, whatever the task at hand, because it has nothing else at its disposal. Mythical thought is therefore a kind of intellectual bricolage.

Claude Lévi-Strauss,
*The Savage Mind*

The work of the writer, work which in so far as it concerns me is artisinal (consisting of strokes of the pen, cross-outs, and additions) to such an extent that to describe it I can find no better word than *bricolage*.

Claude Simon,
"Interview'

Completely engaged in what Simon, quoting Lévi-Strauss, calls a *bricolage*, the practice of fragmentation and articulation achieves such a level of perfection that it permits a theoretical leap forward.

Jean Ricardou,
"'Claude Simon,' textuellement"

## From Structuralism to Pluralism: The Heritage of *Bricolage*

The only weakness of *bricolage*—but, as a weakness, is it not irremediable?—is a total inability to justify itself through and through in its own discourse. The already-there status of instruments and concepts cannot be undone or re-invented.

Jacques Derrida, *Of Grammatology*

A text that reveals its operations and "machinery" explicitly for all to see, that proclaims clearly and with a single and insistent voice its plurivocity, that thematizes its discontinuity and multiplicity, that insists on and continually returns to the "nonrepresentational" character of its "figures," the originality or perfection of its self-generated fictions, would seem at first glance to be far removed from the so-called "dogmatism" of representational theories of fiction. The "nonrepresentational text" refuses to be an example of anything but itself; it refuses, breaks with, or complicates all relations to any "outside" that might be used to explain it, give it a sense, or predetermine its form. These operations it performs on itself before any operation originating outside the boundaries it determines for itself can be performed on it.[1] The "nonrepresentational text" is a text in its purest form, a text that has eliminated from within itself or transformed into itself all "pre-texts" or *hors-textes*. This text *is*, and what it is is only itself.

Taken on its own terms, the argument on behalf of "non-" or "antirepresentation" is quite convincing; however, a critical analysis of these very terms reveals that the theory and practice of what I would call "ultratextuality" is hardly what it claims to be. In fact it is as "dogmatic," as restrictive, and as predetermining as the representational theories it opposes. In order for a "pure text," one which is only itself, to be produced, all elements which cannot be made to originate totally within it or made to take on its form must in principle be excluded from it—and this includes all theories of textuality which the text itself does not explicitly propose or figure. The theory and practice of ultratextuality attempts to resolve the conflicts and contradictions of theory and fiction, not by making the text a simple example of the "real," as in representational theories of fiction, but by encompassing or "framing" all theory and all "reality" within the closed space fiction (the text) supposedly determines.[2]

If the "ideal (of the) text" for such ultratextual theories is a text which is only itself, such an ideal is neither posited nor realized easily. Strategies and concepts are needed both on the theoretical level in order to institute a break with the long mimetic tradition dominating theories of fiction and on the level of practice or literary production to ensure that all potential openings to the "outside" are immediately closed off, that all representational effects produced by the language of a text are confined to the representation of the text of and to itself. Traditional theories of fiction and traditional novelistic practices then are not ignored as much as they are opposed; and thus the "ideal text" is not original at all, but a derived product, dependent on very particular premises and operations of exclusion and opposition for its nonrepresentational ideality. It is by functioning in a certain way and avoiding "representation" that a text realizes its potential and becomes truly and fully *a text*. It is not truly itself if these operations are not performed.

The key concepts and strategies for the most recent theory and practice of fiction in France are in fact, not surprisingly, borrowed from the theory that made such an ultratextual position possible through its emphasis on the fundamental role of language in all of the "sciences humaines" as a model for all social, mythological, symbolic, political, and semiotic systems. I am referring here to the structuralism of Lévi-Strauss and his use and reformulation of Saussurian linguistics. As in all such cases, this borrowing is hardly insignificant or neutral. In particular, the most important concept borrowed from Lévi-Strauss by the most radically formalist of contemporary theories of fiction is the concept of *bricolage*. *Bricolage* plays a central and dominant role in the theory and practice of "ultratextuality" precisely because it seems to offer a sure strategy for breaking with what Jean Ricardou calls the "ruling ideologies of representation and expression" by emphasizing only the purely functional aspects of any textual system, its internal, "essential" workings. Lévi-Strauss introduces the concept of *bricolage* in *The Savage Mind* in order to explain the complexity of what he calls "magical" or "mythic thought," which, he argues, is as complex and sophisticated as "scientific thought." When he opposes the work of the *bricoleur* to that of the engineer (the ultimate metaphysician or technician whose language is totally dependent on his project and "invented" in terms of it—p. 17), it is certainly in order to differentiate between radically different kinds of logical orders, but it is also—and here *bricolage* is privileged—in order to posit a means of "communicating" between the orders, of overcoming the distance and misunderstanding separating the "rationality" of the culture of the engineer (and of the anthropologist) from the "magical thought" of the culture he desires to penetrate. *Bricolage* then is at the same time one of the terms of the opposition and the means of breaking it down.

For the anthropologist to apply dogmatically the terminology, concepts, and strategies of his own historical-philosophical tradition to another culture would be to accept the classification traditionally given to cultures outside the Western tradition as primitive, as less advanced stages on the way to our own supposed maturity—to make the Other into a greatly reduced version of oneself. To attempt to leave one's own culture totally behind and become the Other ("going native") is equally limited, and in fact impossible. Lévi-Strauss has always condemned these two forms of ethnocentrism—the denial *and* the mystification of the "cultural Other"—and in order to avoid them he proposes using a strategy of *bricolage* common to *both cultures* to analyze myths, which are determined by him to be essentially forms of *bricolage.* He thus hopes to preserve the specifity of the myths by treating them on their own terms with a logic appropriate both to them and to his own tradition—*bricolage* persisting in his own culture in art, poetry, and games.[3] In this way the premises and prejudices of his own rationalist culture and tradition are supposedly broken with and neutralized. *Bricolage* is then the fundamental characteristic of myths—the essense of "untamed thought" *(la pensée sauvage)*—insomuch as it is the technique used to organize the material with which they work, the way they function or operate; and it is equally the theory and strategy used to analyze the nature of myths and determine their form (structure) and sense.

Almost as soon as the concept of *bricolage* appeared in *The Savage Mind,* it it was appropriated by literary critics; and the history of this appropriation is a part of its current use in the theory and practice of contemporary fiction. Gérard Genette in an essay entitled "Structuralisme et Critique Littéraire," which was first published in a special issue of *L'Arc* (no. 26, 1965) devoted to Lévi-Strauss, defines the critical act in general (and especially literary criticism) as a form of *bricolage* and thus places the critic in relation to the text in the same position as the anthropologist to the myths he studies—but with one crucial difference. For Genette, the critic is a *bricoleur* but the material he analyzes is not itself a form of *bricolage* but rather the product of a novelist-engineer: "The engineer 'investigates the universe, while the *bricoleur* focuses on a collection of residue from human works, that is to say on a subset of culture.' All that must be done is to replace in this last sentence the words 'engineer' and 'bricoleur' respectively by *novelist* (for example) and *critic* to define the literary status of criticism" (*Figures I;* Paris: Seuil, 1966, p. 147).[4] The first step in the appropriation of the concept of *bricolage,* then, affects only the critical act itself—Genette still sees the practice of the novelist in mimetic terms as "representing a (the) world."

163

The next step is to make *bricolage* not only characteristic of all critical activity but also of the work of the novelist himself. This is the step that was taken first by Roland Barthes and then later by Jean Ricardou and Claude Simon himself. For them the differences between novelist and critic have been essentially eliminated because both are considered to be *bricoleurs*. The essence of their work is to "tinker with" the various elements of language and produce figures, meanings, and forms which are claimed to be "pure products" of language and to reflect only the way language itself operates and which have no relation to any "outside." In this way both the novel and criticism are declared to have escaped from the long rationalist, mimetic tradition previously determining them and to have avoided the limitations of the "ruling ideologies" associated with it, just as Lévi-Strauss hoped to avoid or overcome the "rationalism" of his own tradition. The critic today is required by the theory of fiction as *bricolage* to develop a strategy which is supposedly of the same nature as that of the texts he studies. The novelist, on the other hand, is also required to be worthy of such theory and critical practice by being only a *bricoleur* and avoiding all "investigation of the world" (the supposed activity of the metaphysician-engineer), any meanings or representations which are not self-generated or self-reflexive. *Bricolage*, by taking over the entire theoretical-practical field, has seemingly silenced the "engineer" and the metaphysician, as well as the entire historical-philosophical tradition supporting them, once and for all.

Before assuming such a concept and strategy, however, Barthes, Ricardou, and Simon and the other novelists and critics practicing textual *bricolage* should have perhaps paid more attention to its formulation in Lévi-Strauss and to its repetition and transformation in critical theory since then. This is what I propose to do in this chapter in order to show that a theory of *bricolage* does not work entirely the way it is supposed to, that it continues in spite of itself, though not simply, the mimetic tradition with which it claims to break. Jacques Derrida's critical analysis of *bricolage* in his essay on Lévi-Strauss entitled "Structure, Sign, and Play in the Discourse of the Human Sciences" (in *Writing and Difference*) is an invaluable starting point for such an investigation because it situates within the history of philosophy the concept of structure dominating recent critical theory and reveals the contradictory status of *bricolage* within this history. By ignoring or suppressing the internal contradictions of a concept which is central to the theory and practice of contemporary fiction, the vast majority of critics and novelists using it on the contrary limit the scope of their own activity and produce a "dogmatism" as restrictive as the one they are reacting against.

*Bricolage* is conceived by Lévi-Strauss as a concept and critical strategy directed against his own historical-philosophical tradition, one which attempts to use pragmatically the concepts and tools of analysis of the tradition but in a way which avoids its ideological limitations and assumptions. As Derrida argues, "This is how the language of the human sciences criticizes *itself*. Lévi-Strauss thinks that in this way he can separate *method* from *truth*, the instruments of the method and the objective significations envisaged by it ... Lévi-Strauss will always remain faithful to this double intention: to preserve as an instrument something whose truth value he criticizes" (p. 284). The *bricoleur's* work is considered by Lévi-Strauss to be pure instrumentality because, unlike the engineer, he supposedly has no fixed project (to create, represent, or express the truth or the real, for example) and simply works with the material and instruments he finds "at hand," the remnants of past projects which are "at hand" not out of any necessity or because they were chosen specially for any defined project. In *The Savage Mind* Lévi-Strauss defines the *bricoleur* in terms that contemporary formalist theory will later adopt.

> The "bricoleur" is adept at performing a large number of diverse tasks; but unlike the engineer, he does not subordinate each of them to the availability of raw materials and tools conceived and produced for the purpose of the project. His universe of instruments is closed and the rules of his game are always to make do with "whatever is at hand". . . that is to say, a set of tools and materials which bears no relation to the current project, or indeed to any project whatsoever, but is the contingent result of all the occasions . . . to maintain it with the remains of previous constructions or destructions. The set of the "bricoleur's" means . . . is to be defined only by its instrumentality . . . because the elements are collected or retained on the principle that "they may always come in handy". . . Each element represents a set of actual and potential relations. (Pp. 17–18; translation modified)

The *bricoleur's* work is defined by its instrumentality, by relationships and arrangements (new projects and structures) fabricated out of elements which have already served other purposes in the past, remnants of other relationships, arrangements, and structures, products of other histories. To stress the instrumentality of *bricolage* as an end in itself is to emphasize the functional side of products, the potentially generative nature of all elements "at hand." For not only does any element of any structure occupy a place in relation to other elements of that structure, but it also contains within itself the potential to be in another place as part of a different arrangement with other elements, and even to generate from itself a new arrangement, a "set to be realized" (p. 18). The product of the *bricoleur* is incidental, a "byproduct" rather than a finished projected product; the essence of *bricolage* is the process of production itself, not its end. The engineer may strive to reach an "outside" of language (an *au delà*), to project, determine or impose a definite sense on the "outside," but the *bricoleur* is content to remain "within" the universe determined by his instruments and his material and to signify only by *how* he manipulates the instruments and the material with which he works (p. 19).

It should be sufficiently evident by now why the concept and strategy of *bricolage* are so appealing to contemporary formalist literary theory and practice. *Bricolage* situates the writer completely within language conceived as a closed system of signs; and, more importantly, it puts the problem of sense and the related problem of representation (problems of the "outside" of language) "in brackets" (p. 18), considering them to be not at all pertinent to the "essence" of the literary (or critical) act. This act, or "activity," as Roland Barthes called it in his essay entitled "The Structuralist Activity" (in *Critical Essays*), which

165

in many ways announced a program which is still that of the contemporary practice and theory of fiction, is defined as being essentially *technique:* "technique
is the very being of all creation" (p. 216).[5] Ultimately, the concept of *bricolage*
allows both the writer and critic (the distinction becomes less and less pertinent)
to use the concepts, strategies, and oppositions (i.e. the language) of the Western
philosophical tradition as if they were neutral instruments emptied of their heritage. The *bricoleur* at one and the same time acknowledges in principle the constraints imposed by this tradition on all "production," on all "activity" of any
sort, and yet proceeds as if these constraints no longer come into play to influence in any way the new arrangement. *Bricolage* is a critical concept insomuch as
it admits the primacy and necessity of language (of codes) and thus the historical
sedimentation any element of language carries with it in no matter which context it is placed. But in spite of this admission of principle, theories of *bricolage*
more often than not leave unanalyzed the effects of this "carrying over" on each
new arrangement of elements and assume that the heritage is neutralized when
the arrangement can be argued to grow out of the elements themselves. By emphasizing technique and instrumentality, as we shall see, problems of sense and
representation do not immediately disappear.

The concept of *bricolage* takes on its sense in Lévi-Strauss by being opposed
to the work of the engineer; and, as Derrida argues, the opposition is not a neutral one. For Derrida, the engineer is a myth created by the *bricoleur* (by the
theoretician of *bricolage*) against which to distinguish himself. But if the concept of *bricolage* is taken in its most radical sense, it must also apply to the work
of the engineer, and then the opposition itself and the specificity the *bricoleur*
claims for himself are also threatened.

> If one calls *bricolage* the necessity of borrowing one's concepts from the text
> of a heritage which is more or less coherent or ruined, it must be said that
> every discourse is *bricoleur.* The engineer, whom Lévi-Strauss opposes to the
> *bricoleur* should be the one to construct the totality of his language, syntax,
> and lexicon. In this sense the engineer is a myth: a subject who supposedly
> would be the absolute origin of his own discourse and would construct it
> "out of nothing" would be the creator of the Word, the Word itself... As
> soon as we cease to believe in such an engineer and in a discourse which breaks
> with the received historical discourse, and as soon as we admit that every fi-
> nite discourse is bound by a certain *bricolage* and that the engineer and the
> scientist are also species of *bricoleurs,* then the very idea of *bricolage* is men-
> aced and the definition in which it took on its meaning breaks down. (P. 285)

The *bricoleur* needs the myth of the engineer, and yet at the same time, by his
insistence on technique as the essence of his activity and on the "already-there"
status of his (of all) instruments and material, he also undercuts the transcendent
and totalized status of the "activities" of the engineer. Structuralist theory in
general and the theory of fiction derived from it are caught in the same contradiction—they need the myth of a classical literature and the concept of representation associated with it (products of the "ruling ideology," Ricardou would say)
in order to differentiate themselves from the mimetic tradition; and at the same

time they continually undermine such "theological," metaphysical concepts by arguing that the "essence" of all literature, even the classical, is some form of *bricolage*. The "newness" of the New Novel, of structuralism or poststructuralism, is undermined as it is proclaimed.

If mythical thought, *la pensée sauvage*, is fundamentally *bricolage*, it is so unconsciously or "naively," without an explicit awareness or self-consciousness of its own instrumentality.[6] The structuralist interpreter of myths, a *bricoleur* of *bricolage*, by decomposing and recomposing myths in order to make their structure and instrumentality more comprehensible, that is more visible, provides this intelligibility or visibility after the fact.[7] But to proclaim a theory and practice of literature as *bricolage* is to follow "consciously" a particular model, to program all interpretations and productions to fit the dictates of *bricolage*. Thus one would not be wrong to say that the *bricoleur* is not at all without a project. His project is simply to be without a project; but this project is as absolute, as "theological," as metaphysical a project as the engineer's—it is simply the reverse of it. The project to be without a project is the project to reveal or unveil how things *function* in themselves. The engineer, as Derrida argues, is a disguised *bricoleur*, but the *bricoleur* is at the same time, I would add, a disguised engineer. The theory and practice of the most recent fiction in France, of the "New New Novel," can be considered in this way to produce a repeated confrontation with the contradictions inherent in the concept of *bricolage* and yet inevitably to fail to realize fully the project to be nothing but *bricolage*, that is, pure instrumentality, pure form.

Roland Barthes, for instance, in "The Structuralist Activity," argues that structuralism results in the breaking down of traditional oppositions between creative and critical works because both have the same goal: in each case, "the object is recomposed in order to make certain functions appear" (p. 216). Structuralist critics perform the same function as "structuralist artists"; "They all do nothing different from what Mondrian, Boulez, or Butor do when they piece together a certain object" (p. 215). Creation, or more in line with structuralist terminology, artistic production, has become as critical (or theoretical) as criticism has become "productive." Ignoring totally the heritage of such a position, Barthes claims that what is new in all "structuralist activity" is a lack of concern for the problem of meaning (the problem facing the engineer) and an emphasis on how meaning is fabricated: "What is new is a mode of thought (or a 'poetics') which seeks less to assign full meaning to the objects it discovers than to know how meaning is possible, at what cost and by what means. Ultimately one might say that the object of structuralism is not man endowed with certain meanings but man fabricator of meanings... 'Homo significans': such would be the new man of structural inquiry" (p. 218). Such statements as these seem to put this essay completely within the problematic of *bricolage* as it will later be used by Ricardou and Simon to define the New Novel. Barthes seems to be implying what Simon and Ricardou will declare openly: that true literary and critical activity must be opposed to that of hermeneutical, representational approaches. Meaning for Barthes seems to have become a false concern or, at the very least, an uninteresting one, one that is not entirely pertinent to either literary production or criticism.

In the same essay, however, Barthes admits what most critics after him (and he, himself, at a later stage) will deny, even though he fails to draw any conclusions from his admission: that the emphasis on the literary "object" as a functioning system, on the "internal machinery" of literature or on its "modes of production," does not avoid the problem of representation. The "structuralist activity" is for Barthes, at least in this essay, still mimetic.

> We see, then, why we must speak of a structuralist *activity:* creation or reflection is not, here, an original "impression" of the world, but a veritable fabrication of a world which ressembles the original, not in order to copy it but to render it intelligible. Hence one might say that structuralism is essentially an *activity of imagination*, which is also why there is, strictly speaking, no *technical* difference between structuralism as an intellectual activity, on the one hand, and literature in particular, and art in general, on the other; both derive from a *mimesis* based not on the analogy of substances (as in so-called realist art) but on the analogy of functions (what Lévi-Strauss calls *homology*). (P. 215)[8]

The problem of representation is just located on a different level in structuralist approaches than it is in realist theories; in no way can it be considered to have disappeared.[9] As fiction strives to become more and more structuralist, that is, a purer and purer form of *bricolage*, it is continually confronted by the problem of representation, a problem thought to have been left far behind. The ever increasing formal complexity of the recent novels of Simon, for instance, as well as the equally complex, if not even more exaggerated, technical nature of Jean Ricardou's readings of his novels, I would argue, follow from the fact that the problem of representation has not been done away with and that "new" techniques must continually be found to undermine what already "used" techniques continue to reinforce. No matter how complex the strategy, however, no matter how complete or pure the technique of *bricolage*, to break totally with the "ruling ideology of representation" (if that is what it is) is impossible, and this repeated "failure" provokes the continual search for "new," more successful, and thus more complicated formal techniques. At best, the theory associated with Simon's most recent novels and the complicated machinery uncovered within them or proclaimed overtly by them (which is more and more the case) serve a critical function in the questioning of and experimentation with the form and concept of fiction. At the worst, they serve to support a "dogmatic," ultratextual position which leaves uninvestigated central questions of theory and fiction —uninvestigated because they are wrongly assumed to have already been resolved.

The undeclared assumption of recent formalist theories of the novel seems to be that the more formally or technically complicated the novel, the further it leaves behind all questions concerning sense and representation, the more its instrumentation shows and the more complex its machinery, the less mimetic its nature. Barthes, who was always sensitive to changes in emphasis in avant-garde theory and one of the first to proclaim such changes (even if he rarely analyzed their impact), in *S/Z* (translated by Richard Miller; New York: Hill and Wang, 1974), moves away from the position taken previously that all "structuralist activity" remains mimetic. What he now calls the "plural text" in its *ideal form* never establishes any singular sense and thus can never be constrained by any theory of representation. It naturally demands an equally "pluralistic" theory of interpretation to account for it.

> To interpret a text is not to give it a ... meaning, but on the contrary to appreciate what *plural* constitutes it. Let us first posit the image of a triumphant plural unimpoverished by any constraint of representation (of imitation). In this ideal text, the networks are many and interact, without any one of them being able to surpass the rest; this text is a galaxy of signifiers, not a structure of signifieds; it has no beginning; it is reversible; we gain access to it by several entrances, none of which can be authoritatively declared to be the main one; the codes it mobilizes extend *as far as the eye can reach*, they are indeterminable ... The interpretation demanded by a specific text, in its plurality, is in no way liberal: it is not a question of conceding some meanings, of magnanimously acknowledging that each one has its share of truth; it is a question, against all in-difference, of asserting the very being of plurality, which is not that of the true, the probable, or even the possible. (Pp. 5–6)

By refining Lévi-Strauss's concept of *bricolage* and explicitly having it apply now only to "signifiers" (a tendency already implicit in Lévi-Strauss), Barthes's new position is simply a refinement and extension of his earlier stance rather than a rejection of it. It seems that at a certain point an emphasis on the signifier (on instrumentality) inevitably becomes an assertion of the signifier as an end in itself, and it is at that point that a break is declared with all theories of representation. "Plurality" in the form of technical or formal complexity will prove, however, to be an ineffective means of overcoming the constraints and limitations of representation, of totally undoing all representational effects in a text (assuming such a project is undertaken). Barthes's earlier statement about the mimetic nature of formalist theories which emphasizes how a text functions rather than what it means was perhaps too quickly forgotten by Barthes himself and others following after him. Technical or formal complexity and pluralism are in themselves theoretically naive concepts (and practices); in themselves they undermine nothing.

### Speculations of Fiction: The Theory of the *Mise en Abyme*

*Mise en abyme* is every internal mirror reflecting the totality of the narrative *[récit]* through simple, repeated, or specious reduplication.

Lucien Dallenbach,<br>
Le Récit spéculaire

The so-called nonprinciple of *mise en abyme* functions in deconstructionist commentary as a universal shield which protects texts from difference rather than opening them up to it.

Frank Lentricchia,<br>
"History or the Abyss: Poststructuralism,"<br>
in After the New Criticism

Jean Ricardou has held an important, and one could even say dominant, position in terms of the formulation of the theory of the New Novel since the publication of his first collection of essays, *Problèmes du Nouveau Roman* (Paris: Seuil, 1967).[10] It is for this reason that I have referred to his work frequently in previous chapters and why I feel it necessary to return again to it, especially in an analysis of the "dogmatic" tendencies of recent formalist approaches to fiction. But it is not just that Ricardou is often cited by critics working on the New Novel and treated as an authority that makes returning frequently to his work necessary. As important is that many novelists take him as an authority too, and no novelist more than Simon himself. For better or for worse, Ricardou's ultramechanistic theory of fiction has begun (at least in part) to determine the form, the techniques, and the "strategies of production" of a significant number of contemporary novels. Ricardou's role is no longer just that of the critic who comes in after the fact and unveils the "machinery" of the works he studies; for in the case of at least Simon, certain novels can be seen as responses to Ricardou's theory of the novel, attempts to generate fictions according to the principles established (or uncovered in previous works) by Ricardou.

As we have seen, Simon's novels from the beginning have included within them, as elements of fiction, theoretical questions, speculations about the nature of fiction and demonstrations of how fiction is formulated in terms of these questions. What is different in Simon's recent novels (and in other contemporary novels) is that the theoretical questions have become more and more "dogmatically" formalist and faithful to Ricardou's theory of the novel and the structuralist heritage it continues. It is not the interpenetration of theory and fiction that is the problem here; this has always been one of the most interesting aspects of Simon's work, and my argument from the start has been that the irresolvable conflicts generated by such a confrontation or interpenetration are an inevitable and necessary part of the dynamics of any novel. The problem is rather the monolithic nature of the theory now confronted in the novels or, more accurately, the lack of confrontation between theory and practice and the agreement and harmony reached between them. The problem is one of the *programming* of fiction after an ultraformalist theory of fiction, for such a structuralist (or poststructuralist) form of fiction is too predictable. In following closely the development of Ricardou's theoretical position and analyzing the form it takes in the recent fictions of Simon, my purpose is to make clear the limitations of the position and to situate and undermine its "dogmatism." Fiction, when it pretends to generate its own theory of itself and to master itself totally is just as "dogmatic" as any theory supposedly originating "outside" which has as its goal the total explanation and mastery of fiction. "Dogmatism" is not then an attribute of any theory or group of theories alone, but it can also be characteristic of the speculative, theoretical side of fiction as well—and most certainly of fiction which claims to engender and figure both itself and its own theory of itself.

In *Problèmes du Nouveau Roman* the principal elements of Ricardou's extreme (post)structuralist position are already in place. The strategies and techniques of analysis, as well as the statement of principles, become more refined and complicated in his later work, but the underlying assumptions governing his definition of literature as fundamentally and essentially *technique* (here called *narration*) do not change. The necessary complication of technique, as I have already suggested, is built into the structuralist position itself. For if criticism and theory serve to make fiction more aware of itself, and especially of its instrumentality or "internal operations," and if in fact the definition given to "true" fiction demands the "theoretical" awareness *(prise de conscience)* of itself as it does here, then fiction either is destined to repeat endlessly the same thing—what it is—and soon to exhaust itself in the sterility of this repetition, or must infinitely complicate the way this awareness is achieved as well as the techniques used to figure this awareness. What the novel is for structuralist approaches —a formal, closed, narrative-linguistic system—does not change, once what it is, its "essence," has been determined. All that is left to change are the techniques of analysis and production which capture this "essence" and which assure that all elements from the nonessential, nonlinguistic outside are eliminated.

Ricardou's main point in these early essays is to undermine the "realist illusion" by insisting that the narrative level *(narration)* of any *récit* has priority over the story told (fiction), that the signifier has priority over the signified: "*Fiction* does not at all reflect the world through the intermediary of a *narration;* it is, through a certain usage of the world, like the designation in reverse of its own *narration*" (p. 25). The primacy of the narrative level is, however, for Ricardou more than simply a thesis he is trying to prove or a discovery he claims to have made. His claim is rather that he is simply restating what fiction already states or figures in itself. In other words, for Ricardou it is not enough to claim that fiction is primarily *narration,* but more importantly he argues that fiction itself *must be aware* of its "essence" and *must reveal or figure* this awareness to the "discriminating reader." Because of the primacy of narration, two theoretical positions are supposedly refuted—"evacuated," he says (p. 44), but it might be more correct to say obfuscated—the "realist" and "abstract formalist" positions.[11] Each predetermines the form and nature of fiction before the fact: realism by determining that fiction conform to or reflect a preexisting reality, and formalism by determining a fixed grammar of the *récit* that all fiction in some way is destined to follow—i.e. the former on the level of the signified, the latter on the level of the signifier. Ricardou's position is that fiction is never predetermined and thus it can never represent or be an example of any preexisting form or content—it is a radical form of *bricolage.* If it represents, it represents only itself and its own particular form: "All *fiction,* at the very least by intuition, tends to produce an image of the narrative principles which found it ... In addition, *fiction* should include, in its allegory, its allegorical relation to *narration,* and, in the text, the awareness *(prise de conscience)* of the text" (p. 55). The only "true" theory (representation) of fiction is the one given by fiction of itself as primarily *narration,* that is, language. If fiction is never *pre*determined for Ricardou in its form or content, it nevertheless is (pre-)determined by him to function in a very particular way.

For Ricardou, fiction is essentially this self-awareness itself. In fact, he establishes a hierarchy among various forms of the *récit;* and through an analysis of the Oedipal myth he concludes that the highest form of fiction, the form which most completely manifests the "essence of fiction," is the one which most explicitly "dramatizes" the way it works: "Such is the ultimate lesson of the Oedipus fable for us. We summarize it by the theorem: the greatest narratives *(récits)* are recognized by this sign that the *fiction* they propose is nothing other than the dramatization of their own functioning" (p. 178). At its best, the story told is the story of how the story is told; fiction in its "purest form" is the fiction of how fiction is constructed and functions.

As there is a hierarchy established by Ricardou among the various forms of the *récit,* there is also a hierarchy of techniques of dramatization. The pun *(calembour)* is privileged because it uses the play of sounds (of signifiers) to complicate sense and in this way calls attention to the supposed priority of the material, linguistic nature of fiction over its referential nature. Fiction "displays" this primacy of the signifier especially when it uses the pun as a "structural element," producing a "bifurcation" on the narrative level which causes a break in the continuity of the story told and sends it off in at least two directions at once (p. 48). This "structural use" of the pun, argues Ricardou, reveals that language is not a neutral, passive instrument serving some "outside" end or sense; but totally defined by its own instrumentality, it is its own end.

The pun may not even be *in fact* a dominant element in the novels studied by Ricardou in the various essays of this collection, especially not as a governing, structural element; but it is nonetheless central to the theory being elaborated because it reveals that a logic other than the explicit, surface logic, the logic of what Ricardou calls "established meaning," determines the form of the *récit.* The pun displays the underside of language, the "unhibited play" of words before they are made to serve meaning: "Words become centers of semantic irradiation and under the crust of their immediate sense, tend to recompose among themselves, step by step, the connections of an underlying language, which is free and mobile ... Freed from the tyranny of established meaning, which would make language serve it, language ... obtains meanings in the making" (pp. 52–54). The pun indicates that within language itself *bricolage* is at work, that *bricolage* is not an operation performed on language from the "outside," but is language free of all the constraints of sense and operating on its own terms, its elements combining and connecting with each other only in terms of their "material" existence as signifiers. Fiction is completely itself in these moments when it gives in to and structures itself according to the "free play" of its signifiers, a process which complicates and undermines "established meaning." The pun is the sign that fiction is aware of its true essence and is able to structure itself accordingly.

The central concept governing these essays—the definition of fiction as essentially self-reflexive, a mirror turned inward on itself—is of course the concept of the *mise en abyme,*[12] which dominates in one form or another so much of contemporary theory. In his second collection of essays, *Pour une théorie du Nouveau Roman* (Paris: Seuil, 1971), Ricardou goes a step further and complicates the concept of the *mise en abyme* by insisting not only on the self-reflexive nature of fiction but also on the self-generative aspects of selected texts which are even higher on the hierarchy of texts manifesting the "true" and "essential" properties of fiction. If self-reflection is a mirroring process of the first degree of complexity, a more advanced stage of fiction, a stage closer still to the "essence" of fiction, is arrived at when a second-degree mirroring is attained, a reflection of the doubling process itself: "Far from being a stable image of everyday life, fiction is a perpetually doubling entity. It is from itself that the text proliferates: it writes in imitating what it reads ... Every *mise en abyme* is already the sketch of these internal mirrorings ... Even better, we know that it often reflects the functioning of the text. If it happens to reflect the doubling itself, it forms in a sense a mirroring of the second degree" (p. 262). When fiction attains this second-degree mirroring, it gives the appearance of having effectively closed itself off to anything that is not itself, and Ricardou takes this appearance or fiction for reality. By mirroring the process of mirroring, fiction has supposedly determined that all of its elements originate entirely within itself, somewhere within or between the mirrors constituting it: "Thus the *récit* shows itself to be at the same time mirror of a mirror and mirror of itself" (p. 100). An awareness of self inevitably seems to lead fiction to this second stage of awareness, an awareness of being aware, and of being aware that what it is aware of is entirely itself.

There is an important critical side to Ricardou's argument that should not be ignored in spite of the ultraformalist implications of his theory. For by insisting on the fact that fiction is a product of a certain form of "work," and analyzing "the exact work that produces the text" (p. 22), Ricardou is claiming that fiction has a critical function—in fact the first essay in this collection is entitled "La Littérature comme critique." By analyzing the techniques and strategies within fiction that are "productive" of fiction, the initial effect is not to suppress all questions having to do with the signified as such but to show that no sense is possible apart from an underlying textuality that has produced it and continues to be carried on in it. Sense and problems of representation are not so much suppressed or "refused" as contested, put into question: "The signified is in no way then refused ... but submitted word by word to a permanent critique by the play of writing, which prevents it from coagulating and from hiding the work which forms it. Thus at the center of literature, writing is contestation itself. It is this critical power, you can be sure, that is more than anything else hidden by the diverse approaches that travesty literature" (p. 32). When Ricardou's analyses serve to delineate the critical function of fiction as a form of contestation of preestablished meaning, they are in fact the most successful, and I do not want to deny that at times they have this effect. But given the premises that underly even this critical stance—fiction defined as a self-generated, self-enclosed system —Ricardou very quickly leaves behind the critical position momentarily taken here and reduces the tension or conflict between signified and signifier to the "pure formal play" of the signifier. Fiction does not remain a form of "contestation" for him; because it is fundamentally only itself, it has nothing really to contest.[13]

If the second degree of mirroring leaves the outside of the text even further behind than the first degree, it is because it is a strategy and theory programmed explicitly to do exactly this. The model for this textual strategy for Ricardou is to be found in the work of Raymond Roussel, especially in Roussel's exploitation of the pun: "For the Rousselian manufacture [ of fiction] ... it is a question, given a sign, of finding another sign having if possible with the first an equivalency of *signifiers:* it is the signified of the second sign that is the tangible result of the operation. As Roussel remarked, 'this procedure is in short related to rhyme'" (pp. 92–93). It all amounts to a fairly simple proposition, which is a reversal of traditional theories of textual production based on the model of translation or the search for signs adequate to the meaning derived from the "original" —instead of the signified determining the choice of the signifier, the signifier now determines the production of the signified. Ricardou's theory of fiction becomes more and more the theory of the pun or what he calls "the Rousselian activity" (taking Barthes's "structuralist activity" one step further). As we shall see, Simon's later novels (as well as Ricardou's own novels) are for Ricardou the full manifestation of this "activity"—Simon (Ricardou) is Roussel radicalized and perfected.

The "Rousselian activity" or the "activity of the pun" is, Ricardou claims, a "pure productive activity" (p. 94)—"pure" because it depends on only itself and on no outside force whatsoever. The only virtuosity given to the author in such an operation, therefore, is the virtuosity of abstracting himself from the process and letting the virtuosity of language take over: "With each rigorous agreement of a group of signifiers, every author experiences as a matter of fact a paradoxical metamorphosis: at the moment when his perfect ability shines forth he is himself the object of an evacuation ... *So visibly active, it seems that it is to language alone that the credit for the formula belongs each time*" (p. 95, my emphasis). The *je* ("I") of the author-subject must be "evacuated" by the author so that the *jeu* of signifiers can take over—the only active, productive subject at work in such an operation, in fact, is the text (language) itself as absolute origin and end of itself. The text is a *jeu* (play, game) which (who) announces itself as *je* (I): "I am a rebus" (p. 102), "I am a written text" (p. 105), "Here is the person who can read me" (p. 106) are the titles Ricardou, speaking for the text-subject, gives to various sections of his essay on Roussel. The purpose of Ricardou's theory of fiction is, therefore, double: (1) to make fiction an absolute, ideal *Subject,* subject and object of itself, having eliminated all other subjects and objects from itself; and (2) to put his theory of the text and himself in the position of speaking for (and as) Fiction itself. The highest form of fiction is fiction that becomes what it essentially always-already is—itself and nothing but itself.[14]

But what is fiction in itself in this configuration?—what is the *in itself?* In fact, for Ricardou, *fiction is nothing* (the in itself is nothing)—it is only the process or operation of showing itself, of showing the process of showing: "Fiction, in the weaving of its themes, is completely occupied with indicating itself as a text. That is to write, very precisely, that it *is nothing.* It is vertiginously that which, vertiginously, applies itself to showing what it is. Always separated from itself by the perceptible renascent displacement of a new designation of self, its stability is always differed" (p. 105).[15] The *nothing* constituting the text, then, even if it is not a predetermined context of any sort is *something* nevertheless: the process or strategy of a certain form of production which necessitates the *mise en scène* of the process itself. This is the essence of "Rousselian activity:" "Turning successively inside out the roles of rhyme and text, the Rousselian chiasma opportunely reminds us of the evidence, which is much too often ignored, that no element is ever predestined. Whatever the case, it is always a strategy that assigns each element its function" (p. 116). What precedes and predetermines fiction in Ricardou's theory is the decision that fiction, in order to be itself, must be confined to representing the strategies and operations constituting it, the processes of the representation and engenderment of self. What dominates Ricardou's theory of fiction is not the signifier itself (assuming such a concept makes sense) but, rather, a certain formulation of the signifier. The "royal way to the unconscious" of language, to language as essentially *bricolage*, as the formal "play" of the signifier, many pass by way of the pun, but it is nevertheless a very definite and limited concept of language (and thus of the signifier) that is in question in such a theory.

## Textual (Re)Productions: the Operations of Self-Engenderment

Romanticism is neither literature (the Romantics invent the concept) nor even simply a theory of literature (ancient or modern), but *theory itself as literature*, or, another way of saying it, literature producing its own theory of itself. The literary absolute is also and perhaps above all this absolute *literary operation*.

Philippe Lacoue-Labarthe and<br>Jean-Luc Nancy, L'Absolu littéraire

Every sign, linguistic or nonlinguistic, spoken or written (in the current sense of the opposition), in a small or large unit, can... break with every given context, engendering an infinity of new contexts in a manner which is absolutely illimitable. This does not imply that the mark is valid outside of a context, but on the contrary that there are only contexts without any center or absolute anchoring *(ancrage)*... It would have been better and more precise to have said "engendering *and* inscribing itself," or being inscribed *in*, new contexts. For a context never creates itself *ex nihilo;* no mark can create or engender a context on its own, much less dominate it. This limit, this finitude is the condition under which contextual transformation remains an always open possibility.

Jacques Derrida, "Limited Inc abc..."

When Ricardou comes to the study of Claude Simon's most recent novels,[16]—the works he considers to have most fruitfully continued the practice of the "Rousselian activity" of the pun—he emphasizes in his readings the operations and programs of self-reflection and self-engenderment almost to the exclusion of all others. For instance, in his reading of Simon's *La Bataille de Pharsale (The Battle of Pharsalus)* entitled anagrammatically "La Bataille de la Phrase" [Sentence] *(Pour une théorie du Nouveau Roman)*, Ricardou claims that his purpose is "only to emphasize the frequent dispositives by which the text engenders itself" (p. 118). But in "only" emphasizing this aspect of the novel, Ricardou is doing much more than his modest statement might indicate: he is establishing a definite theoretical position which has become more and more rigid and "dogmatic" with each essay and as Simon's novels are more explicitly and completely programmed to be

read according to his theory of fiction. All the conflicts and contradictions between and within theory and fiction seem to have been resolved because both
theory and fiction have been programmed either to avoid or to transcend all
such differences between them.

To undermine the apparent "harmony" of theory and fiction and show the
limitations of this "mutual programming" in no way implies that Ricardou is
wrong to insist on the role of puns and anagrams in Simon's recent fictions or in
fiction in general (the pun being the effect of the play of the signifier as sound,
an anagram being an effect of this play on the level of the spatial order or arrangement of the signifier as letter). In the first place, to ignore the "matter" of fiction—as theories which concentrate on the signified and accept a simplistic concept of representation do—is to reduce its complexity. Ricardou's attacks on
such theories, even if overstated, are necessary and justified. Second, Ricardou's
approach to Simon's fictions cannot be considered wrong if it can be shown that
Simon himself shares Ricardou's approach to fiction and has attempted to model
his novelistic practice after Ricardou's theory. Simon has in fact frequently
acknowledged the beneficial role contemporary theory in general and Ricardou's
work in particular have played in his own understanding and practice of fiction
writing: "As for criticism (I mean a certain criticism), you know as well as I do,
and perhaps even better, the completely new importance that it has taken on and
all that certain recent work has taught writers of *fictions* about their art. Concerning this importance and the relationship 'criticism-fiction' of which you
spoke, I think it is good to remember the percussive formula of Jean Ricardou:
'the reading that writes!'"[17] In an article devoted to the response of various
New Novelists to the work of Ricardou, Simon is even more specific: "If everything that the formula 'reading that writes' uncovers and highlights can in fact
be found in my books, it has illuminated for me certain obscure mechanisms by
means of which that strange thing born of the work of the writer is gradually
organized and produced . . . His analyses, his 'unveilings' (as much of others'
work as of mine) have played a role in the slow evolution of the conception
that I have of my art."[18]

The apparent "harmony" between theory and fiction proclaimed by Simon
here is misleading, however, for I would argue that even here the relationship between the two is more complex and even more conflictual than it seems. Theory
comes in after the fact to reveal how fiction works; but fiction is then written
after the fact to be what theory has shown it to have always-already been, and
now to be even more.[19] The process is endless; something is always added, something lost. Neither theory nor fiction totally encompasses the other; neither has
the last word. The question, then, is not how Ricardou is wrong but, rather, how
—even when he is right (and because he is right) and in total agreement with
Simon's practices and Simon's novels with his theory—even then, and even because of this harmony, there is discord and conflict between and within theory
and fiction, even if it is suppressed by the harmonious project governing both.

As we have seen, Simon, himself, sees two important breaks in the evolution
of his novelistic practice: the first occurring with *The Grass* (the implications of

which have already been discussed in chapter 3) and the second, which is a radicalization of the first break, with the final chapter of *The Battle of Pharsalus:*

> With *The Grass*, on the contrary, it seems to me that something fairly different occurred. A turning point was taken. But it was only in writing *Histoire* that I began to have a clearer consciousness of the powers and internal dynamics of writing and to let myself be guided more by what writing *said*—or "discovered"—than by what I wanted *to make it say*—or "recover." As for the last part of *Pharsalus* (another turning point), it results from the fact that I finally understood that one never writes—or says—anything except what occurs *at the present moment* of writing. (*Entretiens*, p. 17)

The new break instituted by *Pharsalus* is due not to this novel being of a fundamentally different nature than those that came before it but, rather, to the growing consciousness Simon began to have of the "internal dynamics of writing." From this point on in his writing, he tried to interfere less with what writing said on its own and to follow it more rigorously. The contradiction in such statements is quite evident: if "one never writes—one never says—anything except what occurs at the *present moment* of writing," how can Simon talk about substantial breaks in the evolution of his own writing? What does it mean to have "let oneself be guided more by what writing *was saying*—or discovering—than by what one wants to *make it say*," if all fiction is in fact basically what "writing says?" What Simon really means is that in *Pharsalus* and in the novels following it he will make repeated attempts to eliminate from his fictions anything that cannot be made to originate from within fiction itself; not just to make fiction work the way it will work no matter what he wants or does, but to have the subject fiction as *the only subject* of fiction.

Fiction as an operation of pure productivity, as the uninhibited play of language, supposedly remains within itself and is (even more?) only itself. The purity of the productive system or instrumentality, as well as the uninhibited nature of the play of the signifier, come into question because they are products of an inhibition or exclusion, of a "sacrifice" as Simon puts it: "It is always necessary to sacrifice the signified to plastic necessities or, if you prefer, to formal ones" (p. 26). The "free play" is not free but limited in theory to one level of the text to the exclusion of all others. In order to have his texts conform exactly to the theory used to interpret them, in order that this theory and his texts say the same thing, and in order that his fictions represent only themselves and the theory of themselves they contain within them, the "sacrifice" of the signified to the dictates of the signifier is necessary. The gradual elimination of all problems of the signified (of representation, history, sense, etc.) alone can guarantee that fiction is really what this theory and practice project it as being, but the consequences of such a "sacrifice" are evident within both the theory and practice of such fictions.

*The Battle of Pharsalus*, however, is not yet the ideal, totally self-enclosed, self-reflexive, self-generated text that *Fiction* is supposed to be, even if Ricardou's analysis "La Bataille de la Phrase" at times reads as if it were. For no fiction can ever attain this formalist ideal, no matter how much it sacrifices the signified. Perhaps there is a simple explanation as to why this particular fiction fails to attain the ideal which has nothing to do with the ideal itself. Perhaps it is due to a confusion of motives on the part of the author, resulting in a plurality or mixture of contradictory programs engendering the novel. Perhaps Simon still interfered too much with the workings of fiction itself. As Simon says in an interview, the novel had a complex and multiple (even contradictory, one could say) origin. It was engendered not simply from within itself but from various "outsides," from a complex intertextual network (Simon's other fictions, his readings, history, his experiences, his "life," etc.).[20] And in another interview, when asked how a more recent novel, *Triptych,* was "engendered," Simon replied: "That's a very difficult question to answer: so many factors play a part in the engendering of a text" ("The Crossing of the Image," in *Diacritics,* p. 4). But it is only when these "other factors" are eliminated or when the intertextual, historical "outside" is overcome or neutralized by the text itself that there is true self-engenderment. Simon's anecdotal references to personal experience as the source, or at least as one of the sources of *The Battle of Pharsalus,* may seem to many to be theoretically naive; but they are in fact no more naive than Ricardou's reduction of the process of engenderment to that of the text totally engendering itself from itself—a position which Simon will soon make his own. When the only experience engendering a text is the experience of the text of itself, both experience and the text have been seriously reduced.

In "La Bataille de la Phrase," Ricardou proceeds as if the question of engenderment were already resolved—assuming that the text does "engender itself," his goal is *only* to reveal the internal, textual "generators" and analyse how they work. His reading of *Pharsalus* is perceptive and at times ingenious in its analysis of specific details of the text, but, like all forms of "close reading" or what I would call textual empiricism—in fact like all approaches—it has criteria according to which it selects and analyzes the details it privileges. Like the *bricoleur,* whose project is never really random and ungoverned by any laws whatsoever, but more like the totalizing project of the engineer that the theory of *bricolage* can admit, the textual critic as *bricoleur* also has a project and models his reading after it. To show how a text engenders itself is to organize one's reading around the principle of self-engenderment and foreclose the possibility that other principles or programs inform the text and are part of its "system(s) of production." It is to confine fiction to the self-enclosed space of *a text* (in its most reduced sense); and no matter how one might claim the complicated "play of the signifier" to be within this space, the confinement of fiction to such a space is not a neutral activity.

The justification in *Pour une théorie du Nouveau Roman* for such a position, developed in Ricardou's essays on Simon as well as in his analyses of Valéry, Roussel, Sollers, and, of course, of his own fiction, depends on particular assumptions concerning the "essence" of fiction. The mechanisms of self-engenderment that Ricardou finds in modern texts are for him not specific to these texts but are at work in all texts, even if not explicitly or overtly proclaimed by the texts themselves. Like the pun, the mechanisms of fiction in its purest sense "have been at work from the very beginning of time" (p. 121). What modernity has accomplished—roughly since Mallarmé and even more overtly with the New Novel—is the full realization of the essence of literature at work from the very beginning of history, but most often repressed or condemned. When Ricardou analyzes a text in terms of its "generators," he is in fact claiming to analyze the literariness, specificity, or essence of that text, as well as the essence of literature in general. All the rest is not literature.

As the title of his essay on *The Battle of Pharsalus*—"The Battle of the Sentence"—indicates, for Ricardou, the essential conflict of the novel is internal to the text. Its "secrets" are to be found within it. As a kind of metaphor for all metaphors, even its title signifies the "essence" it contains, which will be revealed and made even more visible by Ricardou's article: "In this sense, on the cover, *The Battle of Pharsalus* is a metaphor discovering the secret title whose anagram it is. There is no doubt that this dispositive allows us to read better" (p. 156). The battle then is not a real battle at all but one between fiction and itself fought entirely within the confines of a space delineated by a concept of textuality in its most reduced form and won before it is fought. Fiction defined as a self-engendered, self-reflexive, closed system has to win all battles—it has no serious combatants with which to do battle other than itself. All other combatants have been eliminated from or neutralized within the field of battle (the text) before the war begins. The war is not only over; it never really begins.

Paradoxically, the principal generator of *The Battle of Pharsalus* is a fragment from another text—"Achilles Running Motionless" ("Achille immobile à grands pas") from Paul Valéry's "Cimetière marin"—which serves as an epigraph to the novel.[21] Ricardou goes to great lengths to show how this fragment doesn't have an "expressive function" and determine *the sense* of the novel, its signifieds, but rather how it engenders the signifiers and structure of the novel: "But suppose that instead of coming in after the fact in an illustrative role, the fragment serves as an explicit thematic program. Then the role of the epigraph is transformed into that of generating fiction" (p. 122). For Ricardou the essential elements (that is, the formal and thematic elements) of *The Battle of Pharsalus* are engendered from this origin and this origin alone. The sense of the novel is not what it means but how it is engendered and takes form. The transitions of the text are supposedly made according to the rules established in the fragment, already at work in "Achilles" before they are at work in *Pharsalus*—even the particular textual strategy necessary to read "the entire text" (p. 126) correctly is already indicated in Valéry's poems. For Ricardou, the fragment "Achilles" from "Le Cimetière marin" evokes the entire textual system of the poem in which it originally stands, and at the same time it engenders a new text, *The Battle of Pharsalus*, and thus becomes part of a new textual system which works according to the same mode of operations as its original context. Once the new system has been engendered, the original textual system is no longer seen as an outside but rather as part of the new system itself: in fact, it becomes its origin and center. The novel can be said to be "self-engendered" insomuch as it makes its origin its own—that is, brings it entirely within itself. Textual *bricolage* is at work here as a fragment of a text "at hand," which is itself a fragment of the entire linguistic system, engenders another text which will be dismantled in its turn to engender other texts, and so on.

But there are some serious problems in Ricardou's argument. The first and most obvious is that if "Achilles" really determines the form and structure of *The Battle of Pharsalus*, this form of textual engenderment is as monolithic and "dogmatic" as the most reductionary, representational theories of engenderment, which posit the "real" as the absolute origin of and model for a text. Second, as in all theories of *bricolage*, the original context of the textual fragment must be totally neutralized if the new context is to be considered as a closed, self-engendered textual system. This means that the new context must totally enclose within its borders the original context, and it does this by making its epigraph the center of its textual system and not an outside "authority" dictating its sense. In this way the epigraph can be said to be entirely within the new context just as it is physically within the covers of the book. In order to argue that a text is a closed system, Ricardou must reduce the contradictory, double status of its origin(s)—the origin being both inside and outside at the same time—and make it occupy primarily the center of the text.[22] In fact, "Achilles" is only a pretext for his reading of the novel, a means of justifying his reduction of the novel to a pure, linguistic system. It is, however, only one of the many pre-texts informing the novel, pre-texts which in fact prevent this or any text from being totally closed in on itself and being only itself.

This epigraph, then, which serves as the principal "generator of fiction" within fiction, is not really a simple origin, nor is it totally brought inside the text. It is a complicated textual fragment itself, one whose form and sense are not self-evident, whose "machinery" is not explicit. In originating his reading of *Pharsalus* in this fragment and in claiming, moreover, that the novel itself originates or engenders itself here, Ricardou is treating "Achilles" as if it were a given, its themes, sense, and instrumentality self-evident. Ricardou's analysis of "Achilles," which consists in isolating and valorizing certain of its themes, figures, and textual operations, governs his reading of *Pharsalus*, not the textual fragment "in itself." What is supposed to close the text off to itself in fact opens it up to various thematics and textual operations that no fiction or theory, contrary to Ricardou's argument, can be shown to master or contain.

For example, because the novel begins and ends with the evocation of the color yellow—"Yellow and then black in the wink of an eye then yellow again" (pp. 3, 187) are the first as well as the last words of the novel[23] —Ricardou looks for and of course finds its source in the "sun" of the last lines of the fragment from Valéry's poem:

And the sun . . . a tortoise shadow for
The soul, Archilles running motionless

"The sun" is not a neutral or accidental element of Ricardou's analysis. It reflects in itself the whole definition of fiction he is attempting to elaborate and apply to *Pharsalus.* The novel is as circular as the sun. As the "real sun" engenders light from itself which reflects back on itself, as the sun is its own source of light and color, so the sun "snatched" from Valéry's poem and present in the epigraph radiates and generates the life of the novel from within the novel. On the thematic level, Ricardou finds numerous effects of this sun: "the sun," aureoled with saffron," "triangle surrounded by divergent gold rays" (p. 3); "urine" (p. 4); "puddle of spilt beer," yellowed photograph" (p. 5), etc., etc. (*Pour une théorie du Nouveau Roman*, p. 129). But *jaune* in French is not only the color yellow; metaphorically it is a sign of "being cuckold" (p. 130). *Jaunes* is also the name given to strike breakers. The color yellow, whose source is the sun of "Achilles," is not just a color (a signified); it is also a word (a signifier) and thus anagrammatically engenders a whole series of words from itself (*nuage, jeuna, auge, ange*, etc., p. 132)—the list goes on for half a page and is not meant to be exhaustive. The repetition and transformation of the yellow of the sun (as signifier and signified) throughout the novel are for Ricardou *visible signs* of the process of self-engenderment as well as the means by which different levels of the novel are linked together, not on the level of the plot (of the signified) but on the level of the text itself (the sun itself): "That is to say that this color plays a role of mediation in many different processes of rapprochement" (p. 130). The sun and all its attributes (as signifier and signified) dominate Ricardou's reading of *Pharsalus.* The novel is seen not only as engendering itself from Valéry's sun, which has become its own, but as modeling itself after the sun, opening and closing within its own (the sun's own) light and reflecting itself in it.[24]

And yet all words, figures, metaphors, themes, etc., have a history of previous uses which no textual operation, no matter how "generative," completely transcends. Textual *bricolage* is never purely productive, therefore, for its figures, metaphors, and operations are by definition "used."[25] Even if one emphasizes the productive chain, as Ricardou does, rather than the thematic network, one is still assuming a common point at its origin and therefore some principle or characteristic which is common to all elements of the chain. The operations of generation that link together the different forms and senses of the sign *jaune* can only work if there is some similarity between the different forms and senses (a common source) and if the same sort of operation is performed each time. Ricardou assumes that the sun is yellow, that it gives off light, and that it is round, etc., and these commonsense and very naive assumptions linking the sun to its products are necessary in order for him to perform the kind of textual analysis he does. The origin of the text in itself should be questioned because the closure the text is assumed to constitute can only be argued after its original opening to other thematics, other histories, and other forms of generation have been repressed or "sacrificed."

In Ricardou's analysis it is as if the themes, metaphors, figures, and operations of a text had no history themselves, as if the productive mechanisms of each text totally and originally determined anew, with no recourse to any preproductive history, the place and sense of each metaphor as well as its link to all other elements of the text. This is perhaps the most troublesome problem with any theory of the self-engenderment of fiction—it assumes a radical break with any pre-texts, with the intertextual network preceding its engenderment—that is, a break with history, theory, etc. It considers all aspects of the intertextual network constituting the so-called outside to be either totally foreign to it and radically outside or, on the contrary, not outside at all but part of *its system of production* and dependent on it. Everything must be made subservient to the new (con)text in which it is inscribed and made totally dependent on the text's operations and programs or be considered totally irrelevant. Originality (self-engenderment) consists then of the *exclusion* of all outsides as such from the text.[26] When, for instance, passages from Marcel Proust's *A la Recherche du temps perdu* are quoted within *Pharsalus,* they are for Ricardou signs of the radical originality of their new context, "a space henceforth violently productive, *an entirely new fiction.* There is no doubt then that this irrefutable radicalization is demonstrated in *The Battle of Pharsalus* precisely by the *active insertion* of certain passages from *Swann's Way*" (p. 153, my emphasis).[27] The difference between "active" and "passive insertion" of fragments of other texts into a new (con)text is that in the first case the textual fragment is totally assumed by the new (con)text and becomes part of the new (con)text's generative system and operates according to its program; in the second, the fragment would seemingly interfere with this closed system of operation by inscribing within it (and not passively) remnants from other contexts the new (con)text cannot totally neutralize or make its own and which it must passively accept and be transformed by.

Obviously, it should not be a question of choosing between the two possibilities: between (1) the "originality" of a purely productive text which makes its own all intertextual references and thus can be claimed to be self-engendered, and (2) the text as a passive product of operations originating outside and over which it has no control and which are not its own. Ricardou's theory of fiction, insomuch as it claims that true fiction is self-engendered, like all theories of *bricolage* forces one to choose each time the new (con)text and treat all other previous contexts and uses which conflict with the new as if they were ultimately not pertinent at all. It thus reduces the history and origins of a text to the origin contained within the borders of the text itself, seen as a closed, self-engendered system.

Part of Ricardou's argument on behalf of the self-engendered, self-reflexive text depends on taking at face value the figures or descriptions that the text gives of itself. Because these figures are found in the text, Ricardou treats them as if they had a special status—as if they were true, appropriate models for fiction simply because they were generated inside the text and not imposed on it from some theoretical-philosophical outside. I have already referred to one of these figures, that of the sun, and especially in terms of its circularity. *Pharsalus* not only engenders itself from its own epigraph—from "Valéry's sun" in this case— but it forms itself in terms of the circular form of the sun. This is accomplished when the novel ends with a description of a table on which stand various objects as well as a blank sheet of paper, as if the "writer-scriptor," referred to in the novel only as "O" (another circle), were as in Proust, about to begin the novel the reader has just read, using the objects in front of him as stimuli from which to engender the novel. The apparent paradox of a novel which figures itself as beginning at its end is easily resolved by Ricardou—the figure the novel is giving of itself through this paradox is one of its own essential circularity.

> The paradox declaring virginal and initial the last and 187th page leads to the consequence, through an inevitable reversal, that it is the virginal and initial page which is last and 187th. In short, it is a question here, as it was for Proust and Joyce, of opposing each tentative of naturalist reduction with the fact of circularity. By the terms of the text, or of the turn of its circularity, the person who takes up a pen could not be a writer getting ready to represent what he sees or to express what he feels. *O* stripped of his identity by the work of the text is caught in its web and product of his product, he is a scriptor. (P. 155)

Even though Ricardou ignores the metaphysical overtones of the project of total, textual circularity, evident as well in the projects of Proust and Joyce, it is clear that *The Battle of Pharsalus* does explicitly figure itself in terms of such a circle and repeat within its pages the figure of the circle in various forms. The question that should be asked is whether we should accept without question the figures of self (the metaphors, images, or representations) fiction gives. Is the paradox of circularity as easy to resolve as Ricardou claims? Are all outsides really brought entirely inside the circularity of the text? Are these figures or fictions of fiction any more valid, any more certain, any more true than those proposed by any other theory or fiction? That fiction in its purest, formalist state, in striving to be only itself, programs itself in terms of circularity in an attempt to attain an ideal state of textuality does not mean, however, that it succeeds in eliminating all contradictions from within its figures of itself and from within its programming. Ricardou has perhaps followed too "dogmatically" or slavishly the figures or fictions of fiction and taken one of its many fictions of itself for its truth or essence.

And yet there is sufficient debate and commentary even within this one novel over the meaning and nature of art and literature to make us question whether the novel is monolithic in the way it figures or represents itself, or even whether it can decide how to represent itself. In any case, this question is certainly not resolved in the novel as it is in Ricardou's reading of the novel—no one figure or fiction of fiction can be said to dominate or determine all others. No one fiction can be said to be the "true fiction" of fiction, its theory of itself at work within it. To analyze just one of the other figures of fiction presented in the novel, the one closest to Ricardou's theory of fiction—the text as machine[28]—should be sufficient to show the necessary contradictions within this or any other textual representation of textuality, in whatever form it is presented, and why the question of the form of fiction cannot be resolved within fiction—assuming it can be resolved at all.

The novel is composed of various intersecting narrative series, and as part of the series narrating the search for the historical battleground at Pharsalus—and the context of the discovery should not be ignored—a machine is discovered abandoned in a field. "Everything looked abandoned. On the one side of the bare ground at the edge of the cottonfield there was an old McCormick reaper-binder out of commission and rusty lying on its side a tangle of plates wheels and gears bristling with broken rods—like some wreck cast up by the sea stranded after a flood. There for a very long time" (*Pharsalus*, p. 22). The search for historical truth has a specific role in the novel, even if this truth is never attained, for the battlefield cannot be conclusively identified, delineated, and separated from its surrounding environment. The search for the battlefield discovers this machine instead of the true, identifiable, historical space of conflict. To supplement the absence of the exact location of Pharsalus, which has been obscured by history, the novel gives an exact, detailed description of a machine. The text-as-machine has taken over from the text-as-reflection of historical truth; the machine has the function of supplementing the absence of a successful end to the search for historical truth. Ricardou passes much too quickly over the formal and theoretical role of the search for historical truth in all of Simon's novels, but in his reading of *Pharsalus* this is an especially serious omission, which leads to his exaggerated insistence on the text as an end and origin of itself. Even if the search for historical truth each time proves to be contradictory, endless, or even illusory in each of Simon's novels, the search itself should not be ignored. It is one of the contexts of the discovery of the contradictory properties of textuality. It is thus one of the many origins of the text, one of the ways in which the text figures itself, as Ricardou points out; but it is equally and at the same time one of the ways in which the text figures its own inability to represent itself effectively or to be at one with itself.

The text is a machine in the sense that it works according to its own internal laws of which it is, at least ideally, aware: "Everything in it is the effect of a textual elaboration that is subjected to rigorous laws," says Ricardou in another essay devoted to this novel ("L'Essence et les sens," in *Pour une théorie du Nouveau Roman*, p. 209). The ultimate proof of his case, as Ricardou goes on to say, is that the text itself explicitly points to these laws; "but a decisive proof is furnished when the text itself designates the scriptoral movement which produces it" (pp. 209–10). *Pharsalus*, in particular, works according to the "law of intersection," as if the different series constituting it were chains of a machine. "This book is fashioned through intersection. Two sets intersect if they have a subset in common; this is the case for metaphor... as for rhyme" (p. 202).

The reaper-binder seems to be such a perfect analogy for Ricardou's purposes that it is curious he devotes so little time to analyzing it. He mentions in passing what kind of machine is described and indicates that the text itself is also a kind of reaper-binder; but he does not make the observation that the machine works internally according to the same techniques or laws which govern its external productions, that internally it is propelled by means of a series of intersecting chains and gears, and externally it produces bundles of hay (in the form of tightly wrapped strands) by binding what it reaps from the field and leaving behind on the field the marks or inscriptions of its passage in the form of intersecting lines. The machine is in this sense a kind of writing machine, one would think a perfect metaphor for the concept of fiction Ricardou is proposing in that its external productions parallel and are formed in terms of its internal construction and operations—that is, all its products are generated out of itself in the sense that they take on *its form*. It operates on all elements which might seem initially to exist outside to make them function according to *its rules*, to give them a new form and sense, to produce them anew as analogies or images of itself. Nothing in the path of the reaper-binder seems to escape reaping and binding.

Perhaps, however, Ricardou has a reason for avoiding a detailed analysis of the machine, for it is not described in the novel in an operative state. It is a reaper-binder (writing) machine that is no longer productive or functioning but abandoned, missing parts, a far cry from the ideal (textual) machine it might be made to represent under other conditions.

> As it stands, the machine is evidently incomplete; several of its parts are missing, either because it has been damaged in an accident or because, as is more likely, since the machine is useless anyway, these parts have been removed in order to replace corresponding ones in another machine, or quite simply in order to be utilized as they are, that is, as plates, planks or rods for fences or some other purpose ... As if the metallic and unusable whole were gradually being invaded by a parasitic though also metallic vegetation creeping into the interstices of the machine and finally paralyzing it. (P. 102)

The machine, then, is a metaphor not just for the productivity or even the internal functioning of the text but also for the gradual loss or wear implied in any process of production. The machine does not and cannot stay exactly the same and still produce—production implies at the same time destruction. Every machine—even and especially a textual machine—is "destined to end some day, abandoned to the sun, the rain, the wind, rusting, gradually falling to pieces ... apocalyptic and anachronistic" (pp. 103-4). The ideal text-machine, because it is self-contained, admits no loss that it does not recuperate immediately within itself and compensate for—through a potentially infinite process of mirroring of itself, the text-machine supposedly remains always identical to itself. The machine described in the novel, however, is subject to the destruction of time and history and testifies to this destructiveness—it is never simply productive. The ideal text-machine must somehow negate, suppress, or in some other way overcome this destructiveness in order to be itself; it must exist outside of time. Ricardou's concept of fiction as a circular, functioning machine, therefore, is limited to one moment of the text's operation, to an ideal present before loss and destruction have occurred, before any of its parts have been used or put to other uses by other *bricoleurs*, whether they be literary, historical, or philosophical, before any parts are missing or worn. Ricardou, then, was right to avoid a detailed discussion of the machine described in the novel—it would be impossible to deal with this machine and the problem of temporality and loss it implies and still maintain the ideal of fiction he supports. The text-machine is never quite equal to itself except before it has begun to operate, that is only as long as it remains an ideal whose destiny is outside of time in an eternal, aesthetic or "scientific" present unaffected by loss and destruction, a present in which there is no wearing away of its productivity or operations. The "science of the text," the study of its so-called material existence, is then as idealistic as the idealisms attacked by Ricardou in the name of science.

The machinery or laws of a text, then, can account only for a part of its total and contradictory operations, for no one operation or series of operations can ever fully explain the form or the sense of a text except ideally. Pure production, the engenderment and maintenance of all the parts and products of the text-machine, as well as of the machine itself, is an ideal that no machine can ever achieve, an ideal that contradicts the very operations that are supposed to constitute it—even those of the *bricoleur*. We shouldn't forget: pure, total production is also the ideal (myth) of the engineer. No machine is ever able to neutralize its preproductive history, the historical heritage of which it is a product; no machine is able to escape from or even contain the gradual destruction *(usure)* of its parts as it operates. Its preproductive history (the heritage of its parts) as well as its postproductive fate (the consequences of its products and of itself) are part of its operations from the start and interfere with its ideal functioning. The text-machine never undoes or reinvents for itself the instruments, concepts, and forms constituting it. Even in figuring itself and its own machinery (laws), it is never itself, never the pure textual machine formalism would make it to be. It never totally neutralizes the various outsides informing it, just as it never passively accepts them or is formed completely in terms of them. The ideal circularity of the text has gaping holes in it; the text never quite comes back on itself; it never constitutes a perfect closure.

## The Borders of Form: Textual Voyeurism or the Contradictions of the Visible

Every vision of no matter what color, is this screen-thought (which makes possible the profusion of other thoughts)—*(Vorhabe)* (and sedimentation).

Maurice Merleau-Ponty,
"Cinq notes sur Claude Simon,"
*Entretiens*, no. 31.

And the effect of formality is always linked to the possibility of a system of framing at the same time imposed and erased.

Jacques Derrida, "Parergon,"
*La Vérité en peinture*

In Simon's most recent novels the strategy of *bricolage* remains in effect: what changes from novel to novel is the way in which this strategy is formulated, the specific tactics used. Because no one program or strategy proves to be entirely successful in realizing the ideal of the production of a pure, self-contained, self-engendered fiction, no matter to what degree the process of self-engenderment and reflection is taken, Ricardou in his most recent essays has begun to emphasize, to an even greater extent than before, the fragmentation and plurality of all "truly" modern texts, as if fragmentation or technical complexity alone were sufficient to do away with all representational effects. *Conducting Bodies* is, on the narrative level, probably the most fragmented of Simon's texts, the one where the different points of intersection between series (consisting of the repetition and transformation of a theme or signifier) are multiplied to the greatest extent. If form is defined in spatial or geometric terms (as formalists have always assumed), it would be fair to say that this is the most formally complicated of Simon's fictions.

Simon himself seems to suggest this when, in order to emphasize the formal, technical complexity of his novel, he describes the "production" of *Conducting Bodies* as an exercise in *set theory:* "Could one not try in fiction to reunite sets whose elements are connected in function of their qualities rather than simply aligning a succession of elements one after the other" ("La Fiction mot à mot," in *Nouveau Roman: Hier, Aujourd'hui,* 2:79-80; Simon also includes a sketch of the intersection of two sets to illustrate his point). Simon (like Ricardou, whose critical work he is following here—but who really is following whom?) seems to consider this mathematical-logical procedure to be a purely neutral technique which in itself has made all problems of traditional logic, psychology, plot, epistemology, etc.—i.e. all problems of representation—irrelevant. He sees this formalist, narrative technique as a radical alternative to the traditional sense of narration defined as the account of the actions and experiences of an individual or collective subject. Here narration is only the combination of elements of language (the "word to word" of his title) in terms of their intrinsic qualities. Exploiting what he calls the *mot carrefour* (the word or signifier found at the intersection of various sets), Simon's novel moves from series to series abruptly and without any other transition except that provided by the *mot carrefour* itself, as signifier and signified. The series seem to generate their own logic of composition—no coherence is imposed on the various series from the outside. In this way, then, fiction is seen as composing and writing itself.

This shift in emphasis in Simon's novelistic techniques toward even more purely formal techniques and away from problems of self-reflection per se parallels a shift in emphasis in Ricardou's latest collection of essays, *Nouveaux problèmes du roman* (Paris: Seuil, 1978). Here Ricardou seems less interested in the problem of textuality in general and more concerned with describing the specific characteristics of what he calls the "modern domain," fiction defined chiefly in terms of fragmentation and dispersion. Simon's *Conducting Bodies* serves as a privileged example of this modernity.

> Neither accomplished unity, nor perfect dispersion, the text is produced from active contradictions, notably between what breaks apart and what connects. From which two large categories can be drawn: what could be called the old domain (where contradiction is dominated by the effects of reunion) and what could be called the modern domain (where contradiction is dominated by the effects of breaking apart) ... What confuses the reader of *Conducting Bodies* is that from the first lines on, there are incessant bifurcations due to an aggressive and complex fragmentation of fiction. (*Nouveaux Problèmes,* p. 198)

Ricardou stresses, even more than Simon, the contradictory plurality of the "unity" of the modern text, of what he calls after Barthes (see *S/Z*) the "discoherent," "plural order": "Far from incoherency, discoherency is a contradictory coherency" (p. 231). Ricardou is thus still working under the assumption that the more complicated the form of the novel, the more the novel takes on its sense only in terms of that form, and the further behind it leaves all problems of representation and expression.

Ricardou is content in this essay, entitled "Le Dispositif osiriaque," to chart the various forms of fragmentation in the novel as well as to point to the logical, linguistic rules governing the breaks or interruptions in the various series established, as if ideally that should be enough to establish the antirepresentational "modern" status of the novel. And yet the contradictory, dispersive fragmentation of the narrative level of any novel, even one as fragmented as *Conducting Bodies*—and Ricardou does seem to treat it as a limit case—does not even realize the desired ideal of antirepresentation or pure textuality, as both Ricardou and Simon are forced to admit. The novel is a "failure" in terms of the ideal both assume for fiction, for critics were still able to read it and explain the fragmentation of its form in terms of a dominant thematic (wandering) that they attribute to a central subject, namely a narrator who is ill and unable fully to participate in or be at one with various experiences which he "lives" and "recalls" in a particular "discoherent" way (to use Ricardou's term). As Ricardou says, the fragmentation of the form of the novel cannot prevent it from being interpreted in terms of a dominant subject who experiences such fragmentation in his life. The theme of fragmentation thus ultimately gives the novel a sense and a unity: "*Conducting Bodies* presents a sick man in a North American city and a sick man in a South American city and nothing prevents the identification of the one with the other" (p. 232). The work is a "failure," therefore, because it leaves open this possibility of interpretation, because its form is not pure or plural or discoherent enough to eliminate the possibility of its being assigned an origin outside, of its being explained in terms of a "nonlinguistic," "extratextual" subject. The question remains whether such a project is realizable in general, for only if even the possibility of representation can be eliminated from fiction can the ideal of ultratextuality, pure fiction, fiction that is only itself, be achieved.

Simon himself feels that he has written such a novel—not a perfect novel but one that does realize fully its goals or program, a novel in fact that the failure of *Conducting Bodies* made possible.[29] The project or program that *Triptych*, in Simon's mind, successfully realizes is not just any program, but rather the one underlying the various strategies analyzed up to this point, which is at least implicitly assumed to be the program that best manifests the very essence of fiction itself: fiction irreducible to any realist or representational schema whatsoever. As Simon says, "I had the project of writing a novel which would be irreducible to any realist schema, that is to say, a novel where the relationships among the different 'scenes' or 'sets' would in no way be constructed from any sequence or determinism of a psychological order, or from any similarity of situations or themes (like that of wandering without end which dominated *Conducting Bodies*), and where moreover there would be no privileged character, time or space" (*Claude Simon*, p. 424). *Triptych* may not be the perfect novel, but if it in fact has successfully realized Simon's stated project, then it certainly is a pure fiction.[30]

The general strategy to bring about such a success is fairly simple (the strategy, not necessarily the writing itself). It is to inscribe or frame each series—in this novel as the title indicates, there are three major series—within one of the other series as a painting, engraving, or film, thus emphasizing the purely fictional status of each series, its origin within fiction rather than outside of it. The strategy is a combination of past strategies—it combines the fragmentation of Simon's recent serial novels with the principle of the *mise en abyme*, where now each series represents not only itself but one or more of the other series as well. In this way the text as a whole is not simply the repeated reflection of images or fictions of itself but a more complex process of the reflection, intersection, and cross-reference of the plurality of series constituting it. The novel is still programmed to be self-contained; and Simon claims that it comes even closer to realizing this ideal than previous novels because all transitions are made on purely linguistic or textual grounds, in terms of "considerations," as Simon calls them, supposedly indigenous to the material essence of the text.[31] In other words, this strategy is supposed to guarantee that fiction will contain within itself not only its own origin (one series engenders another and is in turn engendered by another) but also its own plurality and fragmentation. Ideally, nothing will escape it because the only possible explanation for fragmentation is linguistic in nature; the novel is the experience of language (of) itself and not of a subject outside language (as still could be argued for *Conducting Bodies*). Nothing seems to escape its frame or borders because to escape from one series is to be immediately thrown into another. In this limit case what has to be questioned is the process of framing itself—that is to say, in terms of what premises is the frame of the novel put in place?

In *Triptych* the three principal series are identified by the place where they occur: the seashore, the countryside, and the city. The unity of each series (which will of course be broken down) is initially one of place. Each series (each place) contains the other two series (places) and is at the same time contained by them; each is presented as a representation or fiction (painting, photograph, film, postcard, etc.) in the other two series. The novel opens, for example, with a description of a postcard depicting a scene by the seashore. The postcard is on the table in the kitchen of a farmhouse which is then described. The events constituting the city series are evoked later in the novel by being represented by a poster on the wall of a barn in the country series announcing a coming film and then later described as part of the film itself. And finally, on the wall of a hotel in the series at the seashore there is an engraving depicting the barn on which the poster is attached. The events of the city series are also elements of a film seen in the country series—the events of the country series are part of a film shown in a movie theater in the city. The process of cross-referentiality and the intersection of the three series is thus potentially infinite, but it is contained within a reduced frame and confined to the three series that are defined in terms of a unity of place. It is in fact the reduced frame that makes possible the infinite process of exchange between the series.

Ricardou is correct in arguing—in " 'Claude Simon,' Textuellement" *(Claude Simon: Colloque de Cerisy)*—that a reversal (actually there is a series of reversals) takes place in the novel as each series frames, encloses, and thus dominates the other two series only to be framed, enclosed, and dominated by them in its turn. But even in arguing that the novel is a radical example of "discoherency," of "contradictory multipolarity" (p. 25), and thus acknowledging that no one frame or series *within* the novel totally dominates the other two, Ricardou never puts into question the novel itself as the frame of all frames, the series of all series—the only one which is never reversed or dominated by any other. The more "discoherent" the interior of the novel, the more absolute the frame of the novel itself becomes for Ricardou. He never asks, nor can he without seriously undermining his own ultraformalist position, What is the frame or context of the framing of fiction in on itself? What makes possible the frame of all frames? In general, what links all formalisms is their reluctance to question the frame they impose on a text to make visible its "visible" form.

The novel taken in formalist terms as the complicated interplay of these three series is equivalent to one of the models it gives of itself: a puzzle. "The puzzle is almost completely together. Some twenty small pieces with sinuous contours are spread out in a disorderly array to the right of it" (*Triptych*, p. 168). The formalist description and interpretation of the novel given by Ricardou takes the form of putting the pieces of the textual puzzle together and even of giving the rules or laws—it claims to be scientific—which allow one to find the way to put it together, to finish the puzzle and make sure it fits completely together as it should within its frame. Ricardou, when he accomplishes such a task, is being, as we say, "faithful" to the text. He is in fact doing nothing to the novel that the novel itself has not demanded be done to it, and in fact nothing that has not already been represented in the novel as already having been done; for near the end of the novel there is a description of a puzzle being completed: "Leaning forward...the man with the powerful but heavy build sets the last little piece in place with his right hand and the last little island of black lacquer disappears" (p. 170). The closed frame of the puzzle encloses, gives form to, and establishes relations between the complicated pieces constituting it, determining, however, that there is only one way to complete the puzzle, that the puzzle has one and only one form. In a puzzle, the ideal order of form simply awaits the pieces to be put together in "the right way."

Sylvère Lotringer, in "Cryptique" *(Claude Simon: Colloque de Cerisy)*, is one of very few contemporary critics to criticize such formalist, "scientific" approaches to fiction, which, like Ricardou's, treat all texts as if they were puzzles to be put together within the supposedly closed frame provided by language.[32] The model of the puzzle and the logic implied in the model which is applied to the text are elements of what Lotringer, borrowing from Derrida, calls an "operation of mastery," products of a "restrained economy."

> The reader is invited, in this perspective, to confront the diverse sections of the text, to uncover the correspondances, to note the similarities and differences, to describe relations, in brief, to summon the elements to constitute a Summa, a Monument of Sense. A procedure which is eminently classical and in no way contributes to bringing the reading to its critical point...One

always ends up completing a puzzle. All it takes is enough time. Disorder is never irremediable: it constitutes only a simple moment of hesitation in the service of an operation of mastery. The dispersion of pieces never ceases to proliferate under the reassuring image of an original totality which is initially hidden only in order to be reestablished in all its rights ... Each piece of the puzzle holds "its place" from all eternity. It is enough to identify it and to assign to it, according to its own configuration, the site that belongs to it. The puzzle, in its closed, restrained economy, is a secure game. Meticulously closed in on itself, completely framed. The game of science and the game of meaning. The game of the science of meaning. (Pp. 313–15)

The writer-*bricoleur* and the critic-*bricoleur* who construct, deconstruct, and reconstruct such puzzles are masters of their craft (i.e. engineers); but, as Lotringer rightly points out, their craft is more limited than they would claim. The fragmentation, disintegration, or dispersion of the sets or series constituting a novel is a momentary detour on the way to their eventual reunification within the book as a whole, the frame of all frames. The logic on which Ricardou's analysis depends is supposedly totally linguistic in nature, neutral, and thus "scientific", and if this were so, it would constitute a closed frame since it would give the rules in terms of which all framing would be carried out.

But there is no universal agreement as to what language is or how it works, no irrefutable logic that could be claimed to be at work in all linguistic theories and practices. The logic in question in Ricardou's radical structuralist approach, as in other linguistically based formalisms (such as that of the Russian Formalists), is derived from the assumption that language itself constitutes a universal and closed system; and it stresses the *visibility* of linguistic operations in the determination of the form of the novel.[33] Form is constituted by the visible operations of language at work in the novel—the frame of all frames. The form of the entire novel encloses a space of pure linguistic visibility and guarantees that the visible enclosed in this space is pure. The novel's main function is to call attention to this linguistic visibility, to stage it, to make visible the visible. Neither in this essay nor in any other does Ricardou question the limitations of his concept of linguistic visibility; nowhere is the logic which guarantees the integrity of the visible ever investigated in itself. It is postulated and applied. The frame of the visible is accepted uncritically simply because it is visible itself. It guarantees the integrity of the visible, and its integrity is guaranteed because it is visible.

And yet there is still another problem with the concept of visibility assumed by Ricardou (and other formalisms) when it is used to interpret *Triptych* (or any other novel), for no novel can successfully model itself after only one form of visibility, nor can it ever become a *purely visible form*. *Triptych*, like Simon's other novels, questions the status of the visible, both in general terms and in terms of its own form. The problematic status of the visible in *Triptych* is in fact more than "visible proof" of the limitations of the visible, of the mechanistic, logical-linguistic structuralism Ricardou carries on from the Russiam Formalists, Lévi-Strauss, Barthes, and others, a structuralism that he in turn propagates and radicalizes. It could be said that Ricardou's is the most extreme form of structuralist-formalism seen so far. The visible, logical workings of the text are for him totally determining, even when the text itself questions the grounds for such determination.

If each of the three major series (assuming that there are only three) constituting the triptych of *Triptych* is visibly enclosed by the other two series and in turn visibly encloses and thus engenders the other two, the text also and just as visibly displays or narrates the contradictions of visibility itself, and especially the contradictions of the visibility of form. Ricardou's analysis concentrates too heavily on the operations of the text as a supposedly completed form in itself; and not enough attention is paid to the process of the formation of form, to the conditions which make form possible. The delineation or even production of form is itself a product of an operation or analysis, not an initial condition. The product, if it is to be considered a "successful" form, must realize the philosophical-aesthetic ideal which is part of its program from the start—that is, it must overcome all the contradictions in the process of the formation of form. Form, then, is never simply and initially visible; its operations are visible only after the unquestioned operations of the formalist critic have been made to work on the text and (re)form it according to a formalist model.

In *Triptych*, however, the formation, construction, or production of form is a problem, not a given; the *writing* of (in) the novel is much more complex than the program Simon claims he followed and the one that is most visible to the text. One aspect of the problem is that of perspective: there is no one position from which to see the integrity of form clearly and without interference. No perspective guarantees this integrity, not even the perspective of the text on itself, assuming this could be established or were given by the text in a self-evident, visible, "scientific" way. Perspective distorts as much as it makes visible; it hides as much as it uncovers. This is perhaps most evident in the text in terms of the problem of focus. To concentrate on one element of form or one program linking together the various elements constituting form—colors, shapes, patterns, etc.—is always to leave other elements out of focus or to suppress them from the frame constituted by the particular perspective. These out-of-focus elements, traces of forms or colors, are never totally eliminated, however, but act as a ground against which the distinct and purely "visible" features of the form that *is* in focus take form.

Near the beginning of the novel the related problems of perspective and focus are raised in the following passage: "Viewed from this angle, the umbels are taller than the church steeple. In fact, it is not possible to look at both the umbels and the steeple at the same time. If one fixes one's gaze on the umbels, the church steeple in the distance appears as a vague gray rectangle, stood vertically on edge, topped by an equally vague violet-colored triangle... On the slender pedicels supporting the heads of the flowerlets... the downy hairs stretch out, join, and intermingle, forming a sort of snowy haze" (pp. 2-3). To isolate and focus on certain of the elements constituting the visible is to give form to them; but this can be done only by leaving outside the field or frame of focus other elements whose frame or arrangement is fluid rather than fixed, elements which constitute a mixture of shapes, colors, and forms rather than an established form. The exchanges between elements not completely fixed, not completely in focus, is fluid, not reducible to one pattern or operation. No one frame can contain them. They are not formless but not completely formed either—they take the form of a "snowy haze," whose borders are not distinct, whose inside and outside are never completely separated. The limits or borders of the field in focus are not sufficiently fixed or clearly enough defined to guarantee the integrity of form; for the border or frame necessary to separate form from formlessness links inside to outside as much as it separates the one from the other, permits the exchange and mixture of elements inside and out as much as it limits and closes the inside in on itself. Even if a single perspective could be posited from which to frame or put in focus the entire visible field, and even if this perspective were posited as that of fiction on itself, the frame defining the "in itself" could hardly be taken as an absolute guarantee of form. To use a cinematographic term appropriate to the problem and to the novel, no focus is ever deep enough that it can include everything within itself in focus. The determination of any field or frame must necessarily leave out of focus or at the borderline of focus elements outside its frame against which focus is established. The frame of a field is precisely the problem—no matter how visible the operations that seem to define such a field, they are never visible enough, never exact enough, never themselves in focus enough to determine a closed frame. What is always a little out of focus is the frame itself and the operations defining it and those against which it defines itself.[34]

Without a clearly defined frame within the novel to separate inside from outside, the superimposition of scenes, of the three principal series one onto the other, is the most "visible," "productive" mechanism at work in the novel. Superimposition, as we have seen, is the normal situation in this novel, not an exceptional or deviant one. But is superimposition, then, only or principally a *formal exercise*, as Ricardou and Simon argue, one whose sole or at least chief purpose is to make visible the linguistic operations at the origin of the production of the novel? Without denying the "fact of language" and returning to a naive realist position, it is possible, however, to question the dominant, all-engendering position given to language from this perspective, to question language as *the Origin* or *Subject* of fiction.

Very near the beginning of the novel, two scenes are superimposed. Both picture the two boys associated with the country series in situations in which they are described as staring intently: the first "innocent," as they are staring at a trout they are hoping to catch, and the second erotically charged, as they stare through the hole in the barn wall at a couple making love. One of the operations that allow the two scenes to be superimposed and produce a complicated mixture without a definite frame is a "linguistic operation," which depends on the multiple senses of various key words to evoke the two scenes at the same time. Words like *ventre, bassin, lit, mousse,* etc., refer at the same time to the trout in the stream and the lovers in the barn: *ventre* (the woman's belly and the trout's underside); *bassin* (the river basin and the man's pelvis); *lit* (the river bed and the lovers' bed) (pp. 7-8), etc., etc. The characteristic of words to be "knots of sig-nification,"[35] to evoke simultaneously a multiplicity of senses, seems to account for the superimposition of the two scenes—a visible, linguistic operation seems to be the unique origin of and a sufficient explanation for the complex visibility of the scene. Pure linguistic visibility seems to underlie and explain the complexity (impurity) of the visibility of the scene itself.

But the linguistic operations described above are not the only ones at work in the scene(s). Besides the multiple and thus superimposed senses of various signifiers, those mentioned above and others which inextricably link together the two scenes, color plays a homologous role. For example, the blue of the water is superimposed on the seemingly blue color of parts of the woman's body, the clear color of the trout on other parts of the woman's body. Other pictorial effects have the same purpose—for example, the trout meandering in and out of sight resembles and is visually interchanged with the man's penis entering and withdrawing from the woman. All this is completely visible in the text, and the text seems to be entirely constructed in terms of both this linguistic and pictorial visibility. Nothing seems left to be accounted for. And yet there is still another operation, another part of the "machinery" of the novel which links the two scenes and which a purely formalist approach intent on describing only the visible operations of a text, but avoiding the question of visibility in a general sense, necessarily ignores. This other operation is especially important because it situates and points to the limitations of the visible; and by not dealing with it in any way Ricardou's formalist reading ensures that the visible itself will not be questioned as the foundation for his approach.

The operation in question, an operation underlying both scenes, their super-imposition, and the question of visibility in general, is one of desire and voyeur-ism. The desire to see characterizes the two boys mentioned above from the start; they are voyeurs, continually hiding in order to look without being seen themselves. They look surreptitiously at the few frames of film of a naked wom-an on a bed which they have found or have stolen from the makeshift movie house (the woman in the seashore sequence); they hide in the bushes to spy on a girl changing into her bathing suit; they look from outside the movie house through a crack in the wall at the erotic movies being shown there; and they stare at the lovers in the barn. Their obsessive stalking of the trout is inextricably linked to and superimposed on other scenes of voyeurism on a general level, then, because they all have the same form—they are all motivated by the same desire. The novel, in fact, tells us much about this desire to see and to make visibility the dominant realm, about the desire to make desire a purely visual activity.

Voyeurism is a hidden pleasure, a pleasure that results from being hidden. A voyeur can never enter into the scene being spied on, never participate in it except at a distance—to be seen seeing is to lose the supposed neutrality of one's per-spective on the scene and the imaginary integrity of the scene itself. Voyeurism is thus the ideal situation in which to see, for the invisibility of the voyeur pro-duces a frame that encloses a scene of total visibility and creates the illusion that everything is seen as it "really is." As long as the voyeur remains hidden, the contradictions in the scene spied on and of his own perspective can be ignored. Total invisibility produces then a scene of total visibility, a scene in which everything "essential" is visible. But the frame which guarantees the integrity of the visible for the voyeur and his ability to identify totally with what he sees—and thus his pleasure—remains intact only as long as he remains hidden. The only way the voyeur can react to being caught seeing, the only way he can protect himself and maintain the ideal status he projects onto visibility, is to flee—as the boys do when they are seen spying on the young girl. The frame projected around any scene of voyeurism is as fragile as the voyeur's own, hidden, "invisible" perspective on it. There are in fact no other examples of a "successful" framing of the visible in the novel, of a successful transcendence of the contradictions and incompleteness of the visible, than these fleeting moments of voyeurism. They serve as the model for the frame the novel itself is supposed to constitute. Voyeurism is the operation that makes the visible totally visible and that makes language conform to the dictates of such visibility.[36]

In the novel, voyeurism is largely associated with the two young boys, but given that all the love scenes spied on by them and described in the novel are also films, the spectators for these representations—"invisible spectators" (p. 66) —are also voyeurs. The novel makes voyeurs out of its readers also through its detailed description of the love scenes, at least until the point that voyeurism itself is situated and undermined by being exposed for what it really is—a *mystification of the visible*. Only the voyeur, whose interest is in maintaining an invisible ("scientific") perspective on the novel could refuse to see the way in which voyeurism is undermined by the novel and how the frame projected onto the visible from this perspective, as from any other perspective "visibly" undermined in the novel, does not really enclose the scene it frames—precisely because it gives value (visibility) only to those elements which are simply visible, which present themselves to be seen. Only a voyeur would flee the consequences of the loss of his privileged perspective and the inscription of his own desire and perspective within rather than outside and dominating the scene. Only a voyeur would want to maintain that the visible is an objective, value-neutral space, that his interest in the visible is a totally disinterested interest.[37] Only a voyeur would take one of the many fictions of fiction and make it an all-inclusive reality.

The novel, by situating the perspective of the voyeur and making visible his naive, masculine[38] interests, further complicates the problem of how the visible can be framed. All frames in the novel are relative and interested—no one frame, even that of the novel itself revealing or making visible its own visibility so that it will be perceived and privileged by the reader, is ever adequate, closed, or fixed. It is always possible—and it is absolutely necessary—to frame any operation of framing within another frame, to situate it, and to undermine its privileged status in order to show how interested and relative all framing operations are, no matter how "scientific" or "purely aesthetic" they might claim to be.

The visible mechanistic operations of the text so cleverly delineated by Ricardou are in no way irrelevant to the analysis of *Triptych;* but they are certainly not totally determining either, unless we refuse to step back from the perspective of the ultraformalist critic or textual voyeur and question his perspective and the frame with which he encloses the novel. Like the movie projector described in the novel, the "mechanical operations" of the text cannot be denied. They are visibly and audibly present (as the projector is audibly present in what it projects) in the text between the lines and in its blank spaces, and without them there is no text: "In the brief intervals of silence between the thundering voice of the off-screen commentator and the bursts of music serving as an accompaniment, one again perceives, like a permanent background noise, the regular crackling noise of the projector" (*Triptych*, pp. 21–22). The "background noise" generated by such machinery can perhaps be ignored when the text runs smoothly (even if it shouldn't be ignored), when the eyes of the critic are turned only toward what is produced and not toward how production works. But in a text which continually "breaks down" and whose narrative continuity is repeatedly fragmented, the operations of the machinery of the text are too evident to be overlooked—its noise is even louder precisely because of the breakdowns in the operation of the machine, and not because the machine works perfectly and with no noise at all: "At this moment the image jumps about several times on the screen, which immediately thereafter is crisscrossed with a rapid, chaotic succession of black and white streaks and finally remains completely blank a dull gray color now, as a broadside of whistles and animal cries rises from the rows of spectators" (p. 36). The repeated breakdowns and noise of the machine are nonoperational elements of its operations, and they indicate that the operational level of the text is itself divided by conflicts, contradictions, and wear. The machinery of the text runs no more smoothly than the projector: "At this moment the voice grows hoarse, gradually fading away into articulated sounds as black and white patches alternate and collide with each other on the screen, like fragments of broken glass" (p. 76). The visible, like the discursive, is rooted in noise, that which is neither strictly visible nor audible, neither form nor sense.

The operational level of the text cannot be privileged over all others as Ricardou's formalism would have it, therefore, because it cannot overcome the divisions, conflicts, and noise within its machinery that cause it repeatedly to break down, to project more and/or less than its program. All operations have only relative efficacity—they too, like the visibility they produce, are subject to disintegration, blockage, and ultimately to destruction: "the film jamming in the projector at this precise moment and the two protagonists remaining frozen in this position as though the life had suddenly drained out of them and time had stopped, the image that was only a passing phase, a simple transition, suddenly taking on a solemn, definitive dimension... until, as though to confirm the impression that a catastrophe has occurred, a blinding white spot appears, the flame-red edge of which rapidly grows larger and larger, indiscriminately devouring the two bodies locked in embrace, the farm implements, and the walls of the barn, the lights then coming on, and the screen blank now, a dull uniform grayish color" (p. 148).

The repeated breakdowns of the text-machine and its operations do not constitute, however, a supplementary operation which the text then can program and control. The fragmentation Ricardou thinks he has made operative or productive is never completely brought within the frame of the text—it is never totally visible. Ricardou's ultraformalist approach attempts to negate or neutralize the destructive, inoperative, nonproductive, not strictly visible or representable elements of the text-machine; but no matter how detailed and complicated his description of the textual operations is, it will always be limited by the interest any formalism has in keeping its own interests hidden, in keeping the frame it projects around the visible elements of the text intact, and the destructive aspects of the text and its operations in control and working smoothly.

As Lotringer argues, but not necessarily for the reasons he gives,[39] fragmentation in the novel is maintained up until the end, up to and exceeding the frame of the novel: "Fragmentation is maintained as such, a dissemination without reserve and not the obsession of completeness" (*Claude Simon: Colloque de Cerisy*, p. 331). The novel ends not with the completion of the puzzle, as Lotringer also points out, but with the scattering of its pieces outside of its frame. "With the same slow movement, the man's head returns to its initial position. He sits there motionless for a few seconds, then suddenly his right hand violently sweeps back and forth across the surface of the table, breaking up the puzzle and scattering the little pieces all about" (*Triptych*, p. 171). The solving of the puzzle—the description of the operations of the text and how its different parts visibly fit together—is only one step in the process of analysis. The completed, finalized, "formed" form, therefore, must be considered to be only an arbitrary frame for operations which consist as much of disintegration, dispersion, and destruction as production, formation, and construction. No frame, even the one the novel visibly gives to itself, ever adequately accounts for the conflictual operations at work within the text or keeps the products of these operations totally within itself. No formal operation or theory ever quite succeeds in making totally visible the operations of a text, even when the text on which it operates has already been programmed successfully to be only itself and to have eliminated all outside subjects from within its frame. The contradictions within the framing of even a successful fiction continually interfere with the frame and force the products of the operations constituting the frame outside of its control and mastery. The closure offered by formalism, even in its most radical form, then, is a partial, reduced closure that accounts for only a very small portion of the text's operations and products.

## The Subject Still in Question: The Blinding Insights of Blindness or the "True Voice" of the Text

Rousseau's text has no blind spots: it accounts at all moments for its own rhetorical mode.

Paul de Man,
*Blindness and Insight*[40]

Just as various and conflicting metaphors or models of fiction abound in the most recent novels of Simon, a multitude of figures of the writer (scriptor) are also produced. But Poussin's "Blind Orion Searching for the Rising Sun," which gives its name to the volume published by Simon in the series "Les Sentiers de la Création" (*Orion Aveugle;* Genève: Skira, 1970), provides the figure of the writer closest to Simon's (and Ricardou's) theory and practice of fiction. Simon asserts as much in the interview entitled "The Crossing of the Image":

> The complete title of this painting is, "Blind Orion Searching for the Rising Sun." That seemed to symbolize my own work: the writer advancing blindly in his language, groping in the midst of a forest of signs toward something he will never attain (Picasso once said: "I never did the painting I wanted to do") - ... And this allegory is all the more complete given that Orion is, as you know, a constellation and that as the sun, toward which it advances, rises, the constellation disappears. The writer (the scriptor) is, in a similar manner, erased by the text which he has written and which was not the one he had projected. Isn't that extraordinary? (P. 52)

Orion is the dominating figure of the writer-scriptor for Simon because he is the perfect figure of the *bricoleur*. He is blind, unable to follow on his own the path to his destination or project. Left to himself, he is never totally sure of his way, but groping and stumbling, he is more product of his means (a *bricoleur* in and of language) than master (engineer) of his language. His existence is only nocturnal; he has no recourse to the light provided by the sun to see things as they are or to represent them as they are or should be, no means of his own to plot his way to these ends. Pure technician, he is totally enclosed in his language—his blindness functions to make visible the visibility of language enclosing or framing his landscape, horizon, and text. The *bricoleur* never realizes any preconceived project; when the light of day shines on his products, what is visible is not his presence or that of his project, but that of the workings of language (his landscape) itself.

This interpretation of Orion as *bricoleur* which Simon presents in various theoretical statements is incomplete, however, if it stops with the description of Orion's blindness; for this adequately accounts neither for Poussin's painting nor for the place of Orion-*bricoleur* in Simon's fictions. It is blind to a very important aspect of Orion's blindness. For Orion is not alone, and he does not really wander in a totally random way within the landscape or frame of language, nor proceed without regard for any project whatsoever. Orion is guided by a project: to find the sun and have his sight restored. And he is guided in this project by a small figure perched on his shoulders whose role is hardly without significance: "One of his arms held out ahead of him groping in the empty space, Orion, the blind giant, advanced on his route in the direction of the rising sun, his step guided by the voice and indications of a small figure perched on his muscular shoulders" (*Orion Aveugle,* p. 19). The blind, stumbling giant is not so blind and stumbling as all that, for his blindness is supplemented by the voice and indications of the small figure on his shoulders who sees the way and keeps Orion on the path toward the sun. Blindness is in this description supplemented by the visible insights of the all-knowing, all-seeing figure who, because he is perched on the shoulders of a giant (the writer), has a privileged perspective from which to see—he sees the entire landscape—and therefore sees more than he ever could were he confined to his own reduced perspective. If the writer must blind himself to his own project in order to let language have its way and show him the way, he will always have need of a small, supplementary figure (the theorist) who knows and sees everything, who knows particularly what language is and how it works, and who keeps *in sight* what a true text is at all times. Without this voice directing him, Orion would, in total blindness, deviate from his path and destroy the countryside around him and the people on his path (p. 143). Without having first the in-sight of what language is, its workings would never be visible in themselves when the sun finally does rise and Orion disappears into a text that is pure language, the pure visibility of the text to itself. Language, in spite of fragmentation and "discoherence," speaks with one voice—that of the small figure (theorist) who knows and sees all there is to see.

The goal of this little figure directing Orion—the attainment of the pure visibility of the sun and the restoration of total (in)sight—is an ideal one: "servant perched on his shoulders, indicating with his finger to the blind face an ideal goal" (p. 129). Orion may not be able to see his indications but he does hear his voice—the visual gesture is for us, invisible spectators of the painting and the text, following the blind giant on his way and sharing in the insights of the all-seeing figure. In other words, the voice of the formalist theorist (here Ricardou) and the theory of ultratextuality he proposes are there to assure the writer-*bricoleur* that his steps do lead where they are supposed to lead; and his descriptions or indications of the path taken by the blind giant "on his way to language" are made to convince us that this path is indeed the right one. Orion the writer, in Simon's (Ricardou's) theory, walks in fact with a sure step following the operations of language the figure on his shoulders has made visible to him—he is not really blind at all but always guided by the insights of this figure. If he does not ever attain his ideal goal completely, it is not because of his blindness but actually because the ideality of the goal itself indicated by the small figure is contradictory and not visibly present in the sense they both assume. The figure in fact sees too well to question its ideality; the way is too visible to let the giant grope, stumble, or wander too long. The dogmatism of form is precisely the ideal visibility of language sought after by the writer/theorist/*bricoleur*, a visibility which is a product of a feigned blindness which nevertheless knows its way to the ideal. The program of blindness, the program to have no program, is that of the *bricoleur* which we have been following throughout this chapter. Contrary to the thesis of blindness, the ideal it pursues is in fact too visible, too "dogmatically" present in the recent theory and practice of fiction (and not just contemporary French fiction) for us to take it for other than what it is: a feigned blindness serving the "insights" of a rigidly formalist, linguistic-rhetorical position.

The theory of fiction as *bricolage* which demands that the project of the writer be sacrificed so that the ideal visibility of language, the truth of the text, will be all that is visible in the text reencloses fiction within a frame that is as restrictive as that imposed on fiction by the so-called "ideologies of representation and expression." The conflicts and contradictions between theory and fiction are not resolved when fiction takes on the project to be its own theory of itself, to be only "pure," visible textuality. No blindness is blind enough, no in-sight perceptive enough, to ensure the realization of such a project. The project of *bricolage* is really the ultimate project, the project which pretends to do away with all other projects by blinding itself and us to its interests as it moves insightfully toward the realization of its ideal goals. The conflictual interplay between theory and fiction, however, continues despite all attempts to resolve the conflicts between them on behalf of either of the terms. The subject of fiction is never totally itself, no matter how visible it makes itself, no matter how self-reflexive its figures and self-generated its products. Fiction is never a secure, constituted subject at all. The inevitable necessity to supplement blindness with the insights of figures who know the direction and form of the ideal opens the frame of fiction up to the outside, to problems of history, representation, and form which have from the start informed it and prevented fiction from figuring itself successfully as a totally integral, self-generated, and self-sufficient subject—from becoming the ideal Subject all formalisms have as their project to make it. The subject is still in question in even the most dogmatically formalist of contemporary theories and fictions of fiction; the conflicts and contradictions constituting any formation or figure of the subject are thus not overcome by the ultraformalist program of pure textuality or by any other program at all.

# NOTES

**Chapter One**

1. Paris: Gallimard. Translated by Richard Howard as *For a New Novel: Essays on Fiction* (New York: Grove Press, 1965).

2. See Eugenio Donato, "Language, Vision and Phenomenology: Merleau-Ponty as a Test Case," *MLN* 85, no. 6 (December 1970): 803–14, for an analysis of this problem. Donato argues that after initially modeling language after vision, Merleau-Ponty is forced to oppose them as discontinuous modes "with all the anguish that such a position entails for a philosopher who has only words to describe the world" (p. 811). "In *L'Oeil et l'esprit* the task that originally had been assigned to the philosopher falls to the painter" (p. 813).

3. Jacques Derrida, in "Structure, Sign, and Play in the Discourse of the Human Sciences," analyzes the history of the concept of structure and the particular nature of the 'event' called structuralism: "Perhaps something has occurred in the history of the concept of structure that could be called an 'event' if this loaded word did not entail a meaning which it is precisely the function of structural—or structuralist—thought to reduce or to suspect ... What would this event be then? Its exterior form would be that of a *rupture* and a redoubling." In *Writing and Difference [L'Ecriture et la Différence]*, translated by Alan Bass (Chicago: University of Chicago Press, 1978), p. 278.

4. See Richard Regosin's reading of Montaigne, entitled *The Matter of My Book* (Berkeley: University of California Press, 1977). Regosin meticulously traces the open and conflictual relationship between self and written text (subject and language) in the *Essais* and demonstrates that to give precedence to either term, to make either the absolute origin of the other, is to reduce seriously the complexity of Montaigne's philosophical-literary strategy.

5. Jean Ricardou postulates two stages of the New Novel which would be complementary to the two theoretical phases I am analyzing here: "The one, which has been called the *First New Novel*, operates *a tendentious division in the diegetic Unity* and inaugurates in this way a period of *contestation* ... however, for better or for worse, it manages to safeguard a certain unity. The other phase, which several at the Colloquium on the New Novel at Cerisy called the *New New Novel*, dramatizes the impossible *assembly of a diegetic Plurality* and inaugurates in this way a *subversive* period." *Le Nouveau Roman* (Paris: Seuil, 1973), p. 139.

6. The best example is Léon Roudiez's "La Critique pour ou contre le texte," in *Claude Simon: Colloque de Cerisy* (Paris: 1018, 1975). Roudiez criticizes all "pre-Ricardouian" approaches to Claude Simon's work for supporting the traditional view of the subject and for therefore being "against the text." We shall see that the problem of the "text" cannot be reduced to such a simple schema (for or against), nor can the problem of the subject.

7. See Jonathan Culler, *Structuralist Poetics* (Ithaca: Cornell University Press, 1975), especially chapter 9, "Poetics of the Novel," for a presentation of these advantages.

8. This whole schema resembles Jacques Lacan's "situating of the subject," "where it is the symbolic order which is constitutive for the subject"—"Seminar on the 'Purloined Letter,'" translated by Jeffrey Mehlman, *Yale French Studies*, no. 48 (1972), p. 40. I shall argue that Lacan's logical-formalism, no matter how much more complex, has ultimately the same limitations as the literary-formalist position in question here (see chapter 2). See Philippe Lacoue-Labarthe and Jean-Luc Nancy, *Le Titre de la lettre* (Paris: Galilée, 1973) for a discussion of Lacan's use of linguistics and an analysis of the status of the subject and the truth in his system.

9. Derrida, in "Form and Meaning: A Note on the Phenomenology of Language," translated by David B. Allison, in *Speech and Phenomena and Other Essays on Husserl's Theory of Signs* (Evanston: Northwestern University Press, 1973), argues that the concept of form "is, and always has been, indissociable from the concepts of appearance, sense or essence. Only a form is *evident*, only a form has or is an essence, only a form *presents itself* as such ... The metaphysical domination of the concept of form cannot fail to effectuate a certain subjection of *sense* to seeing, of sense to the sense of sight" (p. 108). In an earlier essay, "Force and Signification," in *Writing and Difference*, Derrida called structuralism an "adventure of vision" (p. 3).

10. See especially *Communications*, no. 8, "Recherches sémiologiques: L'Analyse structurale du récit" (1966).

11. The shifter is also an especially important concept for Lacan: "Once the structure of language has been recognized in the unconscious, what sort of subject can we conceive for it? We can try, with methodological rigor, to set out from the strictly linguistic definition of the *I* as signifier, where it is nothing but the *shifter* or indicative, which, in the subject of the statement *(énoncé)*, designates the subject in the sense that he is now speaking. That is to say, it designates the subject of the enunciation *(énonciation)*, but it does not signify it." "The Subversion of the Subject and the Dialectic of Desire in the Freudian Unconscious," in *Ecrits: A Selection*, translated by Alan Sheridan (London: Tavistock, 1977), p. 298.

12. Jean-François Lyotard, in *Des Dispositifs pulsionnels* (Paris: 1018, 1973), also criticizes Genette, whom he calls the "surgeon of the *récit* whom it is absolutely necessary to take as master" (p. 191), for simplifying the concept of *histoire* in order to contrast the *récit* with it. Lyotard does not accept "what is assumed in Genette as much as in Plato, that there is one reality, here called *histoire*, in terms of which one could measure the deformation which the *récit* forces it to undergo" (p. 206).

13. I am referring to Jacques Derrida's "theory" and practice of *écriture*.

## Chapter Two

1. Neither generation of Freudians, however, questions the assumption that the father or a law acting in his name has the dominant role in generation. For an analysis and critique of the dominance of the function of the father not only in psychoanalysis but also in the entire history of philosophy, see the work of Jacques Derrida, especially "Freud and the Scene of Writing," in *Writing and Difference;* "Plato's Pharmacy," in *Dissemination*, translated by Barbara Johnson (Chicago: University of Chicago Press, 1981); and "The Purveyor of Truth" ("Le Facteur de la vérité"), *Yale French Studies*, no. 52 (1975). See also *La Carte Postale: de Socrate à Freud* (Paris: Flammarion, 1980), which includes "Legs de Freud."

2. There are of course other readings of psychoanalysis than those of either of the "generations" discussed here. The most interesting of the recent ones are Sarah Kofman's *L'Enfance de l'art: une interprétation de l'esthétique freudienne* (Paris: Payot, 1970), in which she gives a double reading of Freud. First she analyzes his idealization of the poet-artist as father-generator, and then she attempts to undermine this aspect of Freud's theory of art by finding within it a concept of the text which, "signifying in the absence of its author, deconstructs the theological conception of art; it proclaims the death of the author, that is to say of the father, as self-sufficient creator" (p. 140). See also Luce Irigaray, *Speculum: de l'autre femme* (Paris: Minuit, 1974), and Kofman's most recent book on Freud, *L'Enigme de la femme: la femme dans les textes de Freud* (Paris: Galilée, 1980), which includes a critique of Irigaray's reading of Freud.

3. Sigmund Freud, "The Interpretation of Dreams," *The Standard Edition of the Complete Works of Sigmund*, translated by James Strachey (London: 1962), 4: 261–62. All references to Freud will be to the *Standard Edition (SE)*.

4. *The American Heritage Dictionary of the English Language* (New York, 1970) gives the following definitions of *example*: "1. One representative of a group; a sample. 2. Something worthy of imitation; a model. 3. Something that serves as a warning. 4. Something that

illustrates a principle." It can be seen already that all of Oedipus is contained within the contradictory definitions of the word itself, that Oedipus is *the example* par excellence. Oedipus contains the following propositions: (1) that is describes a universal situation, that it is representative; (2) that the role of the father is predominant, that he is worthy of imitation ("Be *like* me"); (3) that there are dangers in this imitation if carried too far ("Do not *be me*"); (4) that Oedipus illustrates a law, in fact *the law* in general: that of the father.

5. All references to "The Seminar on 'The Purloined Letter'" will be to Jeffrey Mehlman's translation in *Yale French Studies*, no. 48 (1972). References to Lacan's other texts will be to *Ecrits: A Selection* (trans.: Sheridan) or to the two French editions of the *Ecrits:* (1) Paris: Seuil, 1966, and (2) the "Points" edition in two volumes.

6. Derrida, at the beginning of "The Purveyor of Truth," points to the contradictory relationship between Lacan's version of psychoanalytical truth and the literary example it chooses (which chooses it) to *illustrate* itself: "For example: what happens in the psychoanalytical deciphering of a text when the deciphered (text) already explains itself? When it reveals a great deal more (a debt acknowledged more than once by Freud) than the deciphering text? And above all when it inscribes in itself *in addition (de surcroît)* the scene of deciphering. When it deploys more force in its staging and derives [diverts] the analytical process down to its last word, for example, truth.

"For example, truth. But is truth an example? What happens—and about what [what is dispensed with?]—when a text, for example a so-called literary fiction—but is it still an example—stages truth? When it defines (delimits) analytical reading, assigns the analyst his place, shows him looking for truth and finding it even … then pronouncing in general terms the discourse of truth, the truth of truth? What happens then to a text capable of such a scene, and excelling in its program of situating the analytical bustle *(affairement)* which is grappling with the truth?" (p. 32, translation modified).

7. The title Jeffrey Mehlman gives to *Yale French Studies*, no. 48, is "French Freud: Structural Studies in Psychoanalysis." The title is misleading in many ways for it implies that there is (was) *a* Freud in France and that the reading given to Freud by the French is universally structural, i.e. Lacanian. I would argue that such a consensus never existed and that the readings given to Freud in France are not only in conflict over several crucial issues, but that they are also not specifically French (i.e. the importance of Hegel and Heidegger in Lacan's reading). Already in "Freud and the Scene of Writing," which Mehlman includes in this issue, Derrida formulates a position which is in conflict with Lacan's and which he will develop in "The Purveyor of Truth." Derrida says in the very first paragraph, criticizing the use of a Saussurian linguistic model to read Freud: "Our aim is limited: to locate in Freud's text … those elements of psychoanalysis which can only uneasily be contained within logocentric closure, as this closure limits not only the history of philosophy, but also the orientation of the human sciences, notably of a certain linguistics. If the Freudian breakthrough has an historical originality, this originality is not due to its peaceful coexistence or theoretical complicity with this linguistics, at least in its congenital phonologism" (pp. 198–99).

8. Lacan's reading of "The Purloined Letter" concentrates for the most part on two scenes: the "original" theft of the letter from the queen by the minister and the repetition of this theft when Dupin finds and then steals the letter in turn from the minister in order to return it to the queen. Lacan situates his reading and the theoretical "lesson" he extracts from it in terms of the place of repetition in Freudian theory (especially in "Beyond the Pleasure Principle").

9. Jacques Leenhardt, "L'Ecriture de la Ressemblance," in *Claude Simon: Colloque de Cerisy*, p. 135. See chapter 4 for a further analysis of the problem of historical representation.

10. Dupin of course is the "hero" of Poe's story who returns the purloined letter to the queen (to its "rightful place," as Lacan says). He is equally the "hero" of Lacan's analysis and intermittently equated with the "good analyst" (with Lacan)—that is, insomuch as he maintains the precarious third position of transcendence which Lacan defines as the Symbolic.

11. Marie Bonaparte's description of castration is a *good example* of the traditional Freudian position (in Lacan's terms a *bad example*): "But it is the discovery that a whole

class of beings—namely girls and women—are in fact and forever deprived of the phallus that gives the castration threat its actuality and full horror ... When ... his mother herself appears to him as castrated, when womankind, as personified by the mother, has from this point of view, definitively deceived him, then he takes revenge through hatred or scorn. Despite sexual attraction which comes later and covers over and even submerges such sentiments, every man, in the depths of his psyche to a greater or lesser degree hates or scorns in women the castrated creature." *The Life and Works of Edgar Allan Poe: A Psycho-Analytic Interpretation*, translated by John Rodker (London: Hogarth Press, 1949), p. 467, translation modified.

12. Luce Irigaray's thesis in *Speculum* (especially pp. 165–82) is exactly this: "Every theory of the 'subject' has always been appropriated by 'the masculine'" (p. 165).

13. In Sophocles' *Oedipus the King*, Oedipus too claims (wishes) to be a child of Fortune:

Break out what will! I shall at least be
Willing to see my ancestors, though humble ...
But I account myself a child of Fortune,
beneficient Fortune, and I shall not be
dishonored. She's the mother from whom I spring.
(Translated by David Grene, 11. 1077–82).

14. Jean-Paul Sartre's or André Malraux's version of existentialism, for instance. Malraux's version of Spain is in fact very different from Simon's, and Simon has caricatured Malraux's novel on the Civil War, *L'Espoir (Man's Hope)*, as "Fanfin making war."

15. Evident in the central role he assigns to lack in his vocabulary, Lacan's relation to existentialism is far more significant than is usually thought. For example, Lacan characterizes Freud's "death instinct" as "the assumption by man of his original splitting *(déchirement)"—Ecrits: A Selection*, p. 28.

16. Lacan, "L'Instance de la lettre dans l'inconscient ou la raison dupuis Freud," translated in *Yale French Studies*, nos. 36–37 (1966), and in *Ecrits: A Selection*. For a critical reading of Lacan and of this essay in particular, see Jean-Luc Nancy and Philippe Lacoue-Labarthe, *Le Titre de la lettre* (Paris: Galilée, 1973).

17. In a footnote to his translation of "The Seminar," Jeffrey Mehlman accepts without question the thesis that an absolute difference exists between these two types of identification: "Lacan's analysis of the guessing game in Poe's tale entails demonstrating the insufficiency of an *imaginary* identification with the opponent as opposed to the *Symbolic* process of an identification with his 'reasoning'" (p. 40). This distinction, I hope to have shown, is highly arbitrary; *identification* in general, in whatever form it takes, is the problem.

18. The breaking of a pact ("The Law"), that between the king and the queen, also opens "The Purloined Letter," and this challenge to the king's law is the "sense" of the letter that the queen cannot show the king. For Lacan there is *one Law*, and therefore the letter *must* return to its place: "A letter always arrives at its destination" (p. 41). He chooses to ignore the fact that the very existence of the letter indicates that the pact has already been broken and that there are pacts or laws possible other than the king's and in conflict with his. For Derrida it is the break with the law that is "original" and that initiates the circuit; and thus the circuit is potentially interminable, open rather than circular and closed. For Derrida, "a letter can always not arrive at its destination" ("The Purveyor of Truth," p. 65). To determine *the place* of the letter is what Derrida calls an "ideality of the signifier." His preface to *La Carte postale*, entitled "Envois," is a fictional-theoretical demonstration of the difficulties and contradictions involved in determining the destination, origin, and circuit of a postcard (or letter) in an open communications network.

19. Philippe Lacoue-Labarthe, in "Typographie," *Mimesis: Desarticulations* (Paris: Flammarion, 1975), argues that the role of money is never neutral, that money always has excessive effects in (on) any system, theory, or "economy:" "Mimesis has always been a problem of economy. From the moment money intervenes, a generalized disappropriation *(dépropriation)* occurs, the risk of an uncontrollable polytechnics or polyvalence, the exasperation of desire, the appetite of possession, the setting off of rivalry and hatred" (p. 255).

20. See Barbara Johnson, "The Frame of Reference: Poe, Lacan, Derrida," *Yale French Studies*, nos. 55–56 (1977), pp. 457–505, for a detailed and ingenious analysis of what she calls the "effects of power" in the readings Lacan and Derrida give to the example ("The Purloined Letter") and to psychoanalytical truth. She at first seems to argue the point I have been making here: that the rivalry between theoretical positions—both within fiction and applied to fiction—is endless and ultimately unresolvable, that no transcendent position can ever be effectively occupied. And yet she seems "confused" (although her confusion is certainly motivated) as to who really argues this point in his reading of Poe's story, Derrida or Lacan? In order to rescue and rehabilitate Lacan's text from Derrida's analysis of its limitations and contradictions, she resorts to a technique previously used by Paul de Man in *Blindness and Insight: Essays in the Rhetoric of Contemporary Criticism* (New York: Oxford University Press, 1971) to rescue "the real Rousseau" from Derrida's analysis—she attributes to Lacan's text all of the "insights" (are they really insights?) which "Derrida's seemingly 'blind' reading" (p. 477) criticizes it for lacking (is that really the point of Derrida's critique?) and thus makes Lacan's text into something Derrida could have written. To do this she remains "blind" to the important differences between the two positions ("the pattern is too interesting not to be deliberate," as she says of Derrida, quoting de Man), and especially blind to the explicit arguments in Lacan that language constitutes a closed system, that the third position on the Oedipal triangle (that of the "good analyst") is a transcendent position, and that psychoanalysis is a form *(the form)* of the truth. Even though she accurately describes, at least initially, the "rivalry" between Derrida and Lacan, her analysis implies that there is really a fundamental similarity between them and thus that there exists a position from which their rivalry can be situated and resolved in terms of this similarity, a position from which the common "insights" or truth underlying their rivalry (for which Derrida seems in her mind largely responsible) make their rivalry visible for what it is—a form of blindness. In this way, she is implicitly assuming for herself the transcendent position of truth (the resolution of imaginary, blind conflicts). The question that should be asked of her analysis is what are her interests in resolving such a conflict? Who profits when the differences between Lacan and Derrida are minimized and supposedly overcome? Who is really blind in these conflicts anyway? What if, in fact, these are conflicts that cannot be resolved at all, and certainly not in terms of blindness and insight? Who is framing whom in all this anyway?

## Chapter Three

1. James refers in a letter to Mrs. Humphrey Ward (1899) to the narrative techniques of Tolstoy and Balzac as "the promiscuous shiftings of standpoint and centre." *Theory of Fiction*, edited by James E. Miller (Lincoln: University of Nebraska Press, 1972), p. 157.

2. There is, of course, a third alternative, that of Bruce Morrissette in his *Les Romans de Robbe-Grillet* (1963), translated as *The Novels of Robbe-Grillet* (Ithaca: Cornell University Press, 1975). Morrissette's reading of Robbe-Grillet's novels is basically oriented toward positing and describing the central consciousness or dominant point of view of each novel and thus defending the integrity and unity of their form in traditional Jamesian terms against criticisms that they are random and formless. His work indicates that it is always possible to make an argument in terms of point of view and the unity of form for any novel by subsuming all displacements of point of view and all disruptions in the assumed central consciousness to a unity imposed on such divergencies. Morrissette does this by summarizing (rewriting) the novels in a way that their "unity" is made evident, but this is to reduce seriously the complexity of the novels in the name of an ideal of form imposed on them.

3. See Gérard Genette, *Narrative Discourse*, and Tzvetan Todorov, *Poétique de la Prose* (Paris: Seuil, 1971), especially in the latter as concerns James, "Le Secret du récit," and "Les Hommes-récits."

4. Henry James, "The Art of Fiction," in *The House of Fiction*, edited by Leon Edel (London: Mercury Books, 1962), p. 23.

5. For example, James E. Miller claims that "perhaps the most significant single contribution James made to the theory of fiction was to call attention to the transcendent importance of point of view. It is a mistake to cite 'point of view' as the totality of James' theory (as Percy Lubbock tends to do in *The Craft of Fiction*), so it is also misleading to relegate point of view to a list of fictional techniques which it is nice for novelists to know about. It is not the totality of the theory but it is central and vital." *Theory of Fiction*, p. 15.

6. Percy Lubbock, *The Craft of Fiction* (New York: Viking Press, 1957), p. 39; my emphasis.

7. "Tolstoi and D. [Dostoevski] are fluid puddings, though not tasteless ... But there are all sorts of things to be said of them, and in particular that we see how great a vice is their lack of composition, their defiance of economy and architecture ... He [Tolstoi] doesn't *do* to read over, and that exactly is the answer to those who idiotically proclaim the impunity of such formless shape, such flopping looseness and such a denial of composition, selection and style." From letters to Hugh Walpole (1912, 1913), in *Theory of Fiction*, p. 267.

8. Henry James, *The Art of the Novel* (New York: Charles Scribner's Sons, 1962), p. 15.

9. James defines "genius" as the author's ability to project himself into his opposite. "To project yourself into the consciousness of a person essentially your opposite requires the audacity of great genius." In "Autobiography in Fiction," quoted in *Theory of Fiction*, p. 174.

10. Georges Poulet, *The Metamorphoses of the Circle*, translated by Carly Dawson and Elliot Coleman (Baltimore: Johns Hopkins University Press, 1966), p. 311.

11. Wayne Booth, *The Rhetoric of Fiction* (Chicago: University of Chicago Press, 1961), p. 20; my emphasis.

12. In my mind, E. D. Hirsch's *Validity in Interpretation* (New Haven: Yale University Press, 1967) should be read as a further development of the philosophical issues at stake in the theoretical positions discussed so far. Hirsch defends the status of the author-subject in the determinacy of meaning in literature by sweeping aside all contradictions in the phenomenological tradition in whose name he makes his argument on behalf of the "intrinsic interpretation of a text." For him, "meaning is an affair of consciousness not of words" (p. 4); and his goal is to give back to the author his rightful place which has too often been usurped by the critic. "Thus, when critics deliberately banished the original author, they themselves usurped his place, and this led unerringly to some of our present-day theoretical confusions. Where before there had been but one author, there now arose a multiplicity of them" (p. 5). If Lubbock is the most orthodox (and thus the most reductionary) of the Jamesian critics, Hirsch could be considered the most orthodox and dogmatic phenomenological critic, and what separates the two is probably less important than what they share in common. Hirsch accepts without question the proposition that "verbal meaning is, by definition, *that aspect of a speaker's 'intention' which, under linguistic conventions, may be shared by others.* Anything not sharable in this sense does not belong to the verbal intention or verbal meaning" (p. 218). It is only by eliminating the "nonsharable," inessential aspects of meaning that validity can be determined and the place of the author taken away from its usurpers and given back to its rightful occupant—just as it is only by eliminating the "formless," dispersive elements of form that form is determined and the place of the originating consciousness protected. But the distinction between the sharable and nonsharable (the essential and the inessential) and the resulting suppression of the latter is precisely the problem.

13. Jacques Derrida in his essay on Philippe Sollers, entitled precisely "Dissemination," in *Dissemination*, argues that it is ultimately impossible for the reader or spectator (or author) to find his place in a text and that this is not the result of any failure on the part of the author or any deficiency in form but rather a basic property of textuality in general (p. 240). The usurpation of the author's place denounced by Hirsch is for Derrida inevitable—but it is also the usurpation of the critics's place, of that of any subject attempting to be master of the text by imposing *a* point of view on it.

14. John C. Rowe's essay on James, "The Authority of the Sign in Henry James's 'The Sacred Fount,'" *Criticism* 19, no. 3 (Summer 1977), stresses the ultimate lack of authority

of both the author and narrator in James's fiction. Rowe's reading thus serves to complicate the notion of point of view in much the same way that I am doing here, especially in the following statements: "The narrator sustains his voice only by acknowledging his submission to a language that permits him to exist" (p. 223); "Yet, it is precisely this conception of artistic originality that is questioned by *The Sacred Fount*" (p. 224); and "Jamesian society is fundamentally unauthored, as his novels so clearly demonstrate, even though it is sustained by various 'centers' or 'points of view' struggling to assert their dominance" (pp. 227–28). I would add, however, that the displacement of the subject by submitting it to language is perhaps only a first step in the process—for the "authority of the sign" is itself another form of the "authority of a subject" and equally the resolution of the "struggle of points of view" that Rowe analyzes in his essay. It too needs to be questioned and undermined.

15. Simon himself has advocated this view of his work: "From *Le Tricheur* up to and including *The Wind* ... there is strictly speaking no neat break, but rather a slow evolution by trial and error. With *The Grass*, on the contrary, it seems to me that something fairly different occurred. A turning-point was reached. But it was only in writing *Histoire* that I began to have a clearer consciousness of the powers and internal dynamics of writing and to let myself be guided more by what writing said—or 'discovered'—than by what I wanted to make it say—or 'recover.'" "Réponses de Claude Simon à Quelques Questions Écrites de Ludovic Janvier," *Entretiens*, no. 31 (1972), pp. 16–17. All references to *Le Vent* and to *L'Herbe* will be to Richard Howard's translations: *The Wind* (New York: George Braziller, 1959), and *The Grass* (New York: George Braziller, 1960).

16. Concerning this aspect of Lubbock's reading of James, Robert Scholes and Robert Kellogg, in *The Nature of Narrative* (New York: Oxford University Press, 1966), claim that logically "the Jamesian method leads inevitably to the death of narrative art by a kind of artistic suicide. The narrator is eliminated himself for the good of his art." "The result of the disappearance of the narrator," they go on to say, "is not the refining away of the artist but a continual reminder of his presence—as if God were omnipresent and invisible, yet one could continually hear Him breathing" (p. 270). Their point is well taken as concerns a certain formalist tradition which, through Lubbock, derives itself from James, but they seriously underestimate, as does the Jamesian tradition itself, the complexity of James's own position.

17. Gérard Genette criticizes the showing/telling opposition because for him the concept of showing has a "naively visual character." For Genette, as for Roubichou and other structuralist-formalists, all narration is fundamentally telling *(diegesis)*, and all it can show, therefore, is itself as language. "All it can do is tell it in a manner which is detailed, precise, 'alive,' and in that way give more or less the *illusion of mimesis*—which is the only narrative mimesis, for this simple reason: narrative, oral or written, is a fact of language, and language signifies without imitating." *Narrative Discourse*, p. 164. In order to avoid reinforcing the "naively visual character" of one of the terms of the opposition, Genette prefers the term *focalization* (a term he derives from Brooks and Warren's "focus of narration") to point of view, because it seems "less specifically visual" and "slightly more abstract" (p. 189). But since Genette still asks "Who sees?" one must seriously question how less "naively visual" focalization really is.

18. Maurice Blanchot, in "La Voix Narrative (le 'il,' le neutre)," *L'Entretien Infini* (Paris: Gallimard, 1969), analyzes the problem of narrative voice and discusses this aspect of "realist fiction," the equation of the individual or collective subject with the world. "The novelist is the person who renounces saying 'I,' but delegates this power to others; the novel is populated with small, tormented, ambitious, and unhappy 'egos,' although they remain always satisfied in their unhappiness. The individual is affirmed in all his subjective richness, his interior freedom, his psychology. The novelistic narration is that of individuality; and no matter what its actual content, it is already marked by an ideology to the extent that it assumes that the individual with his particularities and limitations suffices to narrate the world—that is to say, it assumes that the course of the world remains that of individual particularity" (p. 559).

19. "Who describes the world in Balzac's novels? Who is that omniscient, omnipresent narrator appearing everywhere at once, simultaneously seeing the outside and the inside of things, following both the movements of a face and of a consciousness, knowing the present,

the past and the future of every enterprise? It can only be God. It is God alone who claims to be objective" (*For a New Novel*, pp. 138–39; translation modified). This argument against omniscient narration had already been made in almost exactly the same terms by Jean-Paul Sartre in an essay written in 1939, "François Mauriac and Freedom," in *Literary and Philosophical Essays* (New York: Criterion Books, 1955). Sartre asks, "Why hasn't this serious and earnest writer achieved his purpose? ... He has tried to ignore the fact that the theory of relativity applies in full to the universe of fiction, that there is no more place for a privileged observer in a real novel than in the world of Einstein ... He has chosen divine omniscience and omnipotence. But a novel is written by a *man* for *men* ... God is not an artist. Neither is M. Mauriac" (pp. 24–25).

20. Simon in his most recent novels (see chapter 7) will make the formal mechanisms of language the "'engendering principles'" of his fiction—in a certain sense generalizing the formal properties of Montès's "irrational," unstructured consciousness and making them productive of, rather than impediments to, narration and "true" textual consciousness.

21. Henry James also defined "experience" as a complex texture rather than a simple origin: "Experience is never limited, and it is never complete; it is an immense sensibility, a kind of huge spider-web of the finest silken threads suspended in the chamber of consciousness, and catching every airborne particle in its tissue." "The Art of Fiction," in *The House of Fiction*, p. 30.

22. Montès is himself a photographer; and his camera ("that inseparable camera," p. 20), in fixing in place what neither his consciousness nor his discourse could comprehend or recount coherently, serves him as a kind of supplementary organ, a means of overcoming the incoherency and discontinuity of both consciousness and discourse (seeing and telling). As the narrator says of him, "He loves things that don't move" (p. 251).

23. Roubichou follows Genette and other structuralist-formalist critics in assuming that the elimination of all overtly "human traits" from their concept of the subject is, first of all, possible and in the second place, constitutes a radical displacement of the concept itself. This assumption proves faulty on both grounds. Genette, given his self-claimed "strictly analytical point of view" (*Narrative Discourse*, p. 163), attempts to eliminate all attributes of the "living," psychological subject from his categories, but as he himself must admit, with little success. In discussing the categories he will use to analyze the *récit*, categories which he borrows from the grammar of verbs (*tense, mood,* and *person*), he wants to replace *person* with "a term whose psychological connotations are a little less (very little less, alas) pronounced ... This term is voice, whose grammatical meaning Vendryes, for example, defined thus: 'Mode of action of the verb in its relations with the subject.'" *Narrative Discourse*, p. 31. The "alas" should be underlined, for it shows that Genette is aware that he has not cut the "linguistic subject" off from the psychological and philosophical implications of the subject; but nowhere does Genette take account of this failure except to bemoan it.

24. Claude Simon, "La Fiction mot à mot," *Nouveau Roman: Hier, Aujourd'hui*, (Paris: Editions 1018, 1972): 97.

25. For a further discussion of the concept of "self-engenderment," see chapter 7.

26. The placement of the author-subject "within" fiction rather than "outside" is not "new" with the New Novel either. In this century alone, see, for example, Proust's *Contre Sainte-Beuve* (Paris: Gallimard, 1954), and the work of Georges Poulet in general, for such an argument. As I argued in chapter 1, it is highly questionable if the formalist subject within fiction is really substantially different from the phenomenological subject to which it is supposed to be opposed.

27. There is one side of structuralism that looks to uncover the formal laws determining all linguistic artifacts (the work of Greimas and his followers being the most important in this area concerning the *récit*) and thus to diminish, if not eliminate, the "creative" side of literary productivity. But there is another side of structuralism that in fact attributes to linguistic productions the "creativity" Roubichou does here (especially the more recent work of Barthes, Genette, and Ricardou). For example, Genette's analysis of *A la recherche du temps perdu* in *Narrative Discourse* is oriented toward showing not how Proust's novel is a

predictable product of the laws of narration but rather how it exceeds them and is an entirely "new" product. This claim is repeated in each section of the book, and, in terms of each category: this is "enough to prove Proust capable of transgressing the limits of his own narrative 'system'" (p. 208); "the concurrence of theoretically incompatible focalizations, which shakes the whole logic of narrative representation" (p. 211); "the *Recherche* attacks the best established conventions of novelistic narration by cracking not only its traditional 'forms,' but also ... the very logic of discourse" (p. 252), etc., etc. In fact, there is an implicit definition of the "great work of art" in these statements, one which may seem surprisingly romantic in a critic who sees himself and is seen by most as a dry, formalist, "purely analytical" critic. The "great work," even from a "purely analytical point of view," is one that always transcends the categories used to interpret it, precisely one which escapes from simple analytical categorization. The praxis of the "great artist" is always in advance of any theory, even his own: "their genius [that of great artists], that is to say the advance their practice has over any theory—including their own" (p. 158). See Suzanne Gearhart, "L'Intraductibilité Linguistique ou l'Idéalité Littéraire," in *Les Fins de l'homme*, edited by Philippe Lacoue-Labarthe and Jean-Luc Nancy (Paris: Galilée, 1981), for an analysis of this "literary ideality."

28. "The narrative voice is neuter ... On one side, without any particular existence, speaking from nowhere, in suspension in the entire *récit* ... it is radically exterior, it comes from exteriority itself, this outside which is the proper enigma of language in writing ... It is always different from the person who utters it; it is the difference-indifference which taints the personal voice. Let's call it (out of fantasy) spectral, ghostly. Not that it comes from beyond the grave, nor even because it would represent once and for all some essential absence, but because it always tends to be absent in the person who speaks and also to efface itself as center, being thus neuter in this decisive sense that it could not be central, that it does not create a center, speak from a center, but on the contrary would keep the work from having one, withdrawing from it any privileged center of interest, were it even that of focality, and not permitting it either to exist as a completed whole, once and for all times finished" (Blanchot, pp. 565–66).

29. See Derrida, *Speech and Phenomena and Other Essays on Husserl's Theory of Signs*, for an analysis of the problem of voice in Husserl's phenomenology to which my reading of *The Grass* and analysis of voice and point of view are indebted.

30. Derrida argues: "The statement 'I am alive' is accompanied by my dead-being, and its possibility requires the possibility that I be dead; and conversely. This is not an extraordinary tale by Poe but the ordinary story of language. ... Here we understand the 'I am' out of the 'I am dead.' The anonymity of the written *I*, the impropriety of the *I am writing* is ... the 'normal situation.'" *Speech and Phenomena*, pp. 96–97.

## Chapter Four

1. A "theory of the novel" which is not strictly "realist" or overtly mimetic and to which Georg Lukács's *Theory of the Novel* (translated by Anna Bostock; Cambridge, Mass.: MIT Press, 1971) is indebted is that of the German Romantics (esp. Friedrich Schlegel). For a critical analysis of the "theory of literature" of the German Romantics, see Phillippe Lacoue-Labarthe and Jean-Luc Nancy, *L'Absolu littéraire* (Paris: Seuil, 1978), especially the section entitled "Le Poème" (pp. 263–368) which includes Schlegel's "Entretien sur la poésie." The Romantics' theory of the novel should not be seen, however, as a simple alternative to the "rationality" of philosophy, for, as Lacoue-Labarthe and Nancy argue, modeled after the Socratic dialogue, the novel ("the poetic" in general) is nevertheless given a privileged, "ideal" status by the German Romantics as the "ideal" mixture of philosophy and poetry—their "transcendence"—as the Genre of all genres (p. 270).

2. It is true that Eric Auerbach, in what has become one of the most influential works on realism, *Mimesis*, translated by Willard Trask (New York: Anchor, 1957), does not limit his study of the "representation of reality in Western literature" to the novel. But it could be shown that his history of realism is progressive and that the novel in the "modern period" (Joyce, Proust, and Virginia Woolf) realizes for him most completely and adequately the

dictates and objectives of realism. See my analysis of Auerbach's theory of realism, "Mimesis Reconsidered: Literature/History/Ideology" in *Diacritics* 5, no. 2 (Summer 1975).

3. This is basically Auerbach's definition of realism. Ian Watt, in *The Rise of the Novel* (Berkeley: University of California Press, 1957), follows Auerbach's general approach and sees the novel as instituting a break with literary traditionalism and conventional modes of literary discourse, the specificity of the novel for him coming from the fact that it relies largely on the "individual experience" of reality. For instance, he argues that Defoe's "total subordination of the plot to the pattern of the autobiographical memoir is as defiant an assertion of the primacy of individual experience in the novel as Descartes' *cogito ergo sum* was in philosophy" (p. 15). For Watt the novel is the most referential of all literary forms and therefore "the most translatable of the genres" (p. 30). It is the only genre to make realism the "formal principle" of its total structure.

4. An exception is Mikhail Bakhtin, who follows the German Romantics in emphasizing the fundamental heterogeneity of the novel and of the reality with which it is in immediate contact. He considers the novel to be an antihierarchical, antitraditional (and, for him, anti-epic) genre whose "origin" is in popular, carnivalesque (basically oral) literature, in "laughter" and excess rather than "reason" and constraint. See especially "Epic and Novel," in *The Dialogic Imagination*, translated by Caryl Emerson and Michael Holquist (Austin: University of Texas Press, 1981).

5. Friedrich Nietzsche, *The Birth of Tragedy*, translated by Walter Kaufmann (New York: Vintage, 1967).

6. "Novels are the Socratic dialogues of our time. In this liberal form, the wisdom of life fled scholarly wisdom." Friedrich Schlegel, "Fragments Critiques" (26), in *L'Absolu littéraire*. Bakhtin refers to Schlegel when he makes in his turn the Socratic dialogues and other "non-epic" literature the sources of the novel: "the Socratic dialogues, which may be called—to rephrase Friedrich Schlegel—'the novels of their time'" (*The Dialogic Imagination*, p. 22).

7. Paul de Man in *Blindness and Insight*, Peter Demetz in *Marx, Engels, and the Poets*, translated by Jeffrey Sammons (Chicago: University of Chicago Press, 1967), and Fredric Jameson in *Marxism and Form* (Princeton: Princeton University Press, 1971), on the contrary, argue as I do here, that the division between the early and late Lukács is somewhat artificial, even though they argue this from very different ideological-theoretical positions and draw very different conclusions from their respective analyses of Lukács's entire work. De Man sees the early to be more positive than the late but also claims that "the weaknesses of the later work are already present from the beginning, and some of the early strength remains operative throughout" (p. 52). Jameson argues that "the earlier works proved to be comprehensible only in the light of the later ones," that "Lukács's successive positions proved to be a progressive exploration and enlargement of a single complex of problems" (p. 163), and thus sees the late to be an advance over the early. Demetz simply condemns both early and late for being too abstract, and dogmatically philosophical.

8. Lukács, "Es geht um den Realismus," *Essays über Realismus* (Berlin, 1948), p. 157; quoted in Demetz, p. 214. Lukács says at the end of his "Preface" to *The Theory of the Novel*: "As a young writer Arnold Zweig read *The Theory of the Novel* hoping that it would help him to find his way; his healthy instinct led him, rightly, to reject it root and branch (sein gesunder Instinkt führte ihn richtigerweise zur schröffsten Ablehnung)" (p. 23).

9. In 1933 Lukács published an essay entitled "Mein Weg zu Marx," reprinted in *Georg Lukács: Schriften zur Ideologie und Politik*, edited by Peter Ludz (Nevweid: Luchterhand, 1967), pp. 323–29.

10. Louis Althusser, whose reading of Marx is directed against the kind of Marxist-Hegelian humanism represented by Lukács, claims that the difference between the early (Hegelian) "humanist" Marx and the later "materialist" Marx who inaugurates a new science is absolute. See *Pour Marx* (Paris: Maspero, 1965) and *Lire Le Capital* (Paris: Maspero, 1972). For Lukács, Marx's materialism is the *Aufhebung* (negation, conservation, and transcendence) of Hegelian idealism not the absolute break with it; but nevertheless there is at least implicit in his approach a moment when the *Aufhebung* truly and fully occurs instituting a "before"

and "after" a moment when the "way to Marx" reaches its destination in Marx. This view of Marx's relation to Hegel certainly produces a very different reading of Marx than Althusser's, but when the Lukács of the later prefaces and the work on realism speaks with the assurance of someone fully entrenched within "materialism," he takes on the position of a judge who is able to determine where idealism stops and materialism begins, where the latter completely overcomes the former—and in this way the procedure is not as different from Althusser's as might first seem. This would also indicate that Althusser's Bachelardian concept of science as an "epistemological break" owes more to the Hegelian dialectic and to idealism than he admits.

11. Paul de Man characterizes Lukács's terminology in the following way: "Written in a language that uses a pre-Hegelian terminology but a post-Nietzschean rhetoric ... the vocabulary and the historical scheme is that of later eighteenth-century aesthetic speculation; one is indeed constantly reminded of Schiller's philosophical writings ... We are much closer here to Schiller than to Marx." *Blindness and Insight*, pp. 52–54. The general schema followed by Lukács in *The Theory*, making the epic the "original genre" is what Lacoue-Labarthe and Nancy call "the common ground of romanticism ... It is in Schiller's categories the naïve. In those of Schelling, the *Darstellung* of mythology itself, the natural or 'unconscious' epos. It's Homer, that is to say, *Naturpoesie* or the monument at the ahistorical limit which attests to the pure point of origin or emergence of art and unveils the Mystery of the articulation of the subjective and the objective. And if one were to succeed in producing the concept or the idea, it would be in effect this fundamental genre of which the novel—at the end of history, at the moment of the fulfillment of the Subject and the Spirit's return to itself in the 'sentimental' mode—would be the assumption and the sublation *(relève)*" (p. 282).

12. There is one exception to the unique status of "Greece" in *The Theory* (but the conditions for such a repetition are also lost); "Greece" is repeated and the totality again possible, though not in exactly the same form or as completely, in the "Christian era." "In Giotto and Dante, Wolfram von Eschenbach and Pisano, St. Thomas and St. Francis, the world became round once more, a totality capable of being taken in at a glance ... the cry for redemption became a dissonance in the perfect rhythmic system of the world and thereby rendered possible a new equilibrium no less perfect than that of the Greeks; an equilibrium of mutually inadequate, heterogeneous intensities ... A new and paradoxical Greece came into being: aesthetics became metaphysics once more. For the first time but also for the last" (pp. 37–38).

13. For an analysis of the problem of representation (mimesis) in (and between) Plato and Mallarmé see Jacques Derrida, "The Double Session," in *Dissemination*. Derrida gives a "schema" of the contradictory "logic of representation" in Plato—an aspect of which we have seen in Lukács—in note 14, part c, pp. 186–87.

14. Hegel criticizes the "modern irony" of the Romantics in the following terms in his *Aesthetics: Lectures on Fine Art* (translated by T. M. Knox; Oxford: Oxford University Press, 1975): "To these perversities which are opposed to unity and firmness of character we may well annex the more modern principle of irony. This false theory has seduced poets into bringing into characters a variety which does not come together into a unity, so that every character destroys itself as character" (1: 243).

15. Paul de Man argues in a similar vein that *The Theory* is a kind of "Phenomenology of the Novel:" "the book is written from the point of view of a mind that claims to have reached such an advanced degree of generality that it can speak, as it were, for the novelistic consciousness itself; it is the Novel itself that tells us the history of its own development, very much as, in Hegel's *Phenomenology*, it is the Spirit who narrates its own voyage. With this critical difference, however, that since Hegel's Spirit has reached a full understanding of its own being, it can unclaim unchallengeable authority, a point which Lukács's novelistic consciousness, by its own avowal, is never allowed to reach." *Blindness and Insight*, pp. 52–53.

16. The typologies of the novel are the different forms the novel assumes in order to "recognize" its own limitations, even if they do not constitute, strictly speaking, a dialecti-

cal progression as they will in his later work. These forms are (1) "The Novel of Abstract Idealism" (*Don Quixote*, Balzac), (2) "The Romanticism of Disillusionment" *(L'Education sentimentale)*, (3) "The Novel of Apprenticeship" *(Wilhelm Meister)*, and (4) "The Novel of the Social Forms of Life" (Tolstoy). The first two typologies are, of course, the key ones to which Lukács devotes the most attention.

17. For Hegel, the appearance of the novel, and of *Don Quixote* in particular, marks the final dissolution of "Romantic Art," which is itself the dissolution of "Classical Art" (the only "true, accomplished art"), and thus the final dissolution of art in general: "The dissolution of the romantic in the form ... closes, thirdly and finally, with romance in the modern sense of the word." *Aesthetics* 1: 233. Hegel places this "dissolution" within a philosophical-historical dialectic and thus makes it a stage on the way to true philosophical and scientific knowledge. Lukács, on the contrary, in *The Theory* makes the novel the highest form of knowledge possible, the knowledge of the inadequacy of knowledge and representation in general. For an indispensable analysis of "the place" of literature within the Hegelian system, see Philippe Lacoue-Labarthe, "L'Imprésentable," *Poétique*, no. 21 (1975), pp. 53–95.

18. Lacoue-Labarthe, "L'Imprésentable," p. 54. As Lacoue-Labarthe argues, Hegel never raises the "question of literature" as such, because for him it is a question which has already been resolved in and by philosophy: "We are doing nothing else here but raising a question in the Hegelian mode (but not in Hegelian terms), a question which Hegel himself never raised as such. Or that he 'raised' in such a way that it was never really in question and that it was *de facto* 'resolved' before even being properly formulated as a question ... It is certain that Hegel did not simply want, through some movement of retreat or fear, to exorcise its [Romanticism's and thus the novel's] danger in order to 'save' philosophy. He did in this way put the emergence of literature, whose logic, as Blanchot indicates, was a logic of *dissolution*, back in its place" (p. 54).

19. Lukács in his 1962 "Preface" still finds this to be an "unambiguous formulation of the new function of time in the novel," a "discovery" which he made before Proust and Joyce were known in Germany. *The Theory*, p. 14.

20. Lukács's use of memory here is rooted in Hegel's concept of representation as *Erinnerung*. Jacques Derrida, in "Le Puits et le pyramide," analyzes the ideal functioning of representation in Hegel: "Representation *(Vorstellung)* is remembered intuition—interiorized *(erinnerte)* ... Sensible immediacy remaining unilaterally subjective, the movement of intelligence must, through the *Aufhebung*, raise up and conserve this interiority in order 'to be in itself in its own exteriority' (*451)." *Marges de la philosophie*, p. 88.

21. *The Theory of the Novel* ends with an analysis of Tolstoy in which the "new Greece" is sighted from afar: "In Tolstoy, intimations of a breakthrough into a new epoch are visible; but they remain polemical, nostalgic, and abstract. It is in the words of Dostoevsky that this new world, remote from any struggle against what actually exists, is drawn for the first time simply as a seen reality ... Dostoevsky did not write novels ... He belongs to the new world. Only formal analysis of his works can show whether he is already the Homer or the Dante of that world" (pp. 152–53).

22. In a later essay in *Blindness and Insight*, de Man complicates slightly his analysis of the relationship between irony and time—they are no longer seen as simple alternatives, even if de Man still wants to reverse Lukács's schema and make time the "villain" rather than the "hero": "A certain concept, time, is made to function on two irreconcilable levels: on the organic level, where we have origin, continuity, growth, and totalization, the statement of the problematic and self-destructive nature of the novel is explicit and assertive; on the level of ironic awareness, where all is discontinuous, alienated, and fragmentary, it remains so implicit, so deeply hidden behind error and deception, that it is unable to rise to thematic assertion ... The three crucial factors in the problem have been identified and brought into relationship with each other: organic nature, irony, and time ... but ... the plot of the play they are made to perform, is entirely wrong. In Lukács's story, the villain—time—appears as the hero, when he is in fact murdering the heroine—the novel—he is supposed to rescue" (p. 104).

23. In his critique of Derrida's reading of Rousseau, de Man posits a theory of literature

in which the text is assumed to be totally self-conscious of itself at all times, a total presence, and to contain the presence of the "real author" as well: "Rousseau's text has no blind spots; it accounts at all moments for its own rhetorical mode ... There is no need to deconstruct Rousseau; the established tradition of Rousseau interpretation, however, stands in dire need of deconstruction ... instead of having Rousseau deconstruct his critics, we have Derrida deconstructing a pseudo-Rousseau by means of insights that could have been gained from the 'real' Rousseau." "The Rhetoric of Blindness: Jacques Derrida's Reading of Rousseau," in *Blindness and Insight*, pp. 139–40). For an analysis and critique of de Man's metaphysics of textual truth, see Frank Lentricchia, "Paul de Man: The Rhetoric of Authority," in his *After the New Criticism* (Chicago: University of Chicago Press, 1980).

24. Two essays from Lukács's "Marxist" period in which he traces the development of the novel out of the epic and which are thus rewritings and "rectifications" of *The Theory of the Novel* have been included in a French collection of essays from his time in Moscow in the 1930s. They are: "Rapport sur le Roman," and "Le Roman," in *Ecrits de Moscou*, translated by Claude Prévost (Paris: Editions Sociales, 1974).

25. Lukács argues that "the theory of reflection provides the common basis for *all* forms of theoretical and practical mastery of reality through consciousness" in "Art and Objective Truth," in *Writer and Critic*, translated by Arthur D. Kahn (New York: Grosset and Dunlap, 1970), p. 25.

26. "Narrate or Describe?" in *Writer and Critic*, p. 126. For Lukács there is one "poetry" and it is epic: "Without this inner poetry to intensify and maintain its vitality, no real epic is possible and no epic composition can be elaborated that will rouse and hold people's interest. Epic art—and, of course, the art of the novel—consists in discovering the significant and vital aspects of social practice. From epic poetry men expect a clearer, sharper mirror of themselves and of their social activity" (p. 126).

27. Fredric Jameson sees Lukács here effectively standing Hegel on his feet because he refuses to privilege philosophy ("pure thought" in Jameson's terms): "No doubt Hegel had already felt the novel to be a modern replacement of epic, in Lukács's sense. But for him, as is well known, the fulfillment of art lies not in any art form but in its self-transcendence, in the transformation of art into philosophy ... But for Lukács, as we will see again and again in varying contexts, pure thought never has absolute value as a privileged means of access to reality. On the contrary, it is narration which is for him the absolute, and even the preliminary sketch of the stages of Greek art has as its premise the primacy of narration" (*Marxism and Form*, p. 171). Jameson is right as far as he goes, but what he doesn't see is that there is something in Lukács more primary then even narration (and less "historical," less "materialistic"): i.e., "poetry." It is also questionable whether philosophy, even in its most idealist form, is ever really "pure thought."

28. Lacoue-Labarthe analyzes the difficulty the double status of prose and poetry poses for Hegel: "Poetry is in effect the place in Hegel of a double problem ... On the one hand, as Hegel never ceases to repeat, poetry, of all the vocal arts, is the most ancient ... But on the other hand, poetry also comes after prose and is determined against prose. It is as if there were two poetries or, more precisely, as if this double position breaches, in a certain sense, the unity of the historical and systematic process of truth" ("L'Imprésentable," p. 78).

29. The expression *das geistige Tierreich* ("the spiritual animal kingdom"), is of course taken from Hegel's *Phenomenology* and is the first part of the section entitled "Individuality which takes itself to be real in and for itself" (pp. 237–52).

30. For Hegel the ability to overcome contradictions through the *Aufhebung* is the sign of the "greatness and force" of the Spirit: "For greatness and force are truly measured only by the greatness and force of the opposition out of which the spirit brings itself back to unity with itself again. The intensity and depth of subjectivity come all the more to light, the more endlessly and tremendously is it divided against itself, and the more lacerating are the contradictions in which it still has to remain firm in itself. In this development alone is preserved the might of the Idea and the Ideal, for might consists only in maintaining oneself within the negative of oneself." *Aesthetics*, 1: 178.

31. "At the same time we must stress particularly strongly that any utopian anticipation

of the future, any transformation of the future into a supposed reality can very easily cause a slipping-back into the style of the period of decline by blunting the antagonistic contradictions which operate in reality." *The Historical Novel*, translated by Hannah and Stanley Mitchell (London: Merlin Press, 1962), p. 349. In fact, this is exactly what Lukács's own theory of realism does.

32. The type is an ideal/real figure, *the subject* necessary for Lukács's eschatological, ontotheological view of history and realism. Peter Demetz is entirely justified, therefore, in emphasizing this aspect of Lukács's theory in his analysis: "By requiring an anticipation of what is going to happen, Lukács's concept of the type—like that of Engels—rejoins the theological tradition. Lukács, too, reasserts its messianic implications when he quotes Paul Lafargue and speaks of the type as a 'prophetic figure.'" *Marx, Engels, and the Poets*, p. 210. Demetz criticizes Lukács and the whole Hegelian-Marxist tradition for elevating philosophy to the position of a supreme judge of art because philosophy, which may be "a wise judge" elsewhere, is "incompetent in this particular case" (p. 203). Demetz is right to show what Lukács's "Marxism" and idealist approaches have in common: "the objective idealist looks at the individual work of art just as condescendingly from the heights of the absolute spirit as does the Marxist from his standpoint of absolute history" (p. 215). But Demetz's own critique is limited by the assumption that purely aesthetic, nonphilosophical criteria exist with which "to judge art competently" and which can be used to define "the artistic character of the work." His analysis thus degenerates into a diatribe against philosophy and ideology "condescendingly" made "from the heights" of a position which he assumes to be just as absolute and "pure" as Lukács assumes his own to be.

33. See "The Ideal of Harmonious Man in Bourgeois Aesthetics," in *Writer and Critic*.

34. O. K. Werckmeister, taking a decidedly anti-Lukácsian position, argues that Marx's work as a whole totally discredits using Greek art as an ideal: "Marx may have accepted it as an ideal at the moment when he sketched out his preliminary text. But since then it has long become doubtful whether ancient Greek art embodies the brand of human perfection that was projected into it by idealist philosophy ... It has even become more doubtful whether in turn this particular ideal of humanity really expresses the social and political emancipation at which Marx's own political theory was aimed." For Werckmeister, therefore, "the end of art ... if it has any meaning, it means the end of aesthetics. Marx may have anticipated this when he refrained from writing on aesthetic theory." "Marx on Ideology and Art," *New Literary History* 4, no. 3 (1973):518–19. Werckmeister's critique of the idealist core of Lukács's aesthetics (and Marxist aesthetics in general) is well taken, but in his desire to "purify" Marxism of its idealist remnants he moves too quickly and falls back into a fairly restrictive and deterministic form of historical empiricism. Hans Robert Jauss is right to criticize Werckmeister for this, but his own solution to this contradiction within Marxism is even more questionable: to valorize the idealist core of Marxist aesthetics. Jauss argues that Marxist aesthetics not only "contains" but also "needs idealism as an element of both its theory and practice." Jauss goes on to say: "However, my thesis of the work of art as a paradigm of nonalienated labor does not remove the idealist embarrassment of Marx's passage about construction according to the laws of beauty, but elevates it into an indispensable component of a materialist aesthetic, which has no wish to deprive art of the high rank still attributed to it in the concept of the young Marx." "The Idealist Embarrassment: Observations on Marxist Aesthetics," *New Literary History* 7, no. 1 (1975): 195, 200.

35. Jameson argues that when the "golden age or lost Utopia of narration in Greek epic" is projected into the future by Lukács "with such a shift in perspective we are already well within a Marxist theory of history" (pp. 179–80). Jameson is faithful to Lukács in arguing this and thus chooses to ignore the effects that I have analyzed here of such a projection (retention) of the Greek ideal on Lukács's view of history and on Marxism in general when it is defined in these terms.

36. Lukács even goes so far as to explain the "greatness" of Balzac, Stendhal, Dickens, and Tolstoy by mystifying their personal "active lives": "They themselves actively experienced the crises in this development ... In their public activity as well as in their private lives,

they followed the tradition of the writers, artists and scientists of the Renaissance and of the Enlightenment, men who participated variously and actively in the great social struggles of their times, men whose writing was the fruit of such rich, diverse activity. They were not 'specialists' in the sense of the capitalist division of labour." *Writer and Critic*, p. 118. Lukács claims that Marx and Engels before him had discovered what allows writers to overcome ideology: "What is involved is the uncompromising honesty, free of all vanity, of truly great writers and artists" (p. 84).

37. Michel Deguy, "Claude Simon et la Représentation," *Critique*, no. 187 (1962): 1009–32. In spite of this general evaluation, Deguy for the most part follows quite faithfully Simon's theory and practice of representation in *The Palace*, the *reduction*, in the phenomenological sense, of the world to representation: "Everything is transparency to this art...He [man] has reduced the being of what is and what he is to this transparency, to representation, to this 'representability'... [He is] a knowing eye which is only that, which only has to do with representations; while at the same time *being*, emptied of everything except that which is 'representable,' has lost its reality, its substance, and reveals itself to vision as image, as phantom" (p. 1015). Deguy's reading of Simon is limited by the fact that he is only able to conceptualize Simon's theory and practice of representation in Hegelian terms as a negative *Weltanschauung* and thus sees *The Palace* as a novel which "is a good reflection of its era" (p. 1031).

38. See again Jacques Leenhardt, "Claude Simon: L'Ecriture de la ressemblance," in *Claude Simon: Colloque de Cerisy*. Leenhardt attempts to defend a certain form of representation (of realism) against the ever-increasing formalization of literary studies. This essay and the discussion which follows it, however, are limited by the fact that both the concept of representation he defends and the one Ricardou and others reject are fairly reduced versions of representation. See especially the somewhat ridiculous discussion of the status of a photograph of the Hotel Colon, the "model" for the hotel in *The Palace*, which is an excellent illustration of how the problem of representation is caricaturized by formalists and "realists" alike.

39. Lukács defines Marxism as providing the knowledge of the laws of history, of its origin and end: "Marxism has a grasp of the main lines of human development and recognizes its laws. Those who have arrived at such knowledge know, in spite of all temporary darkness, both whence we have come and where we are going...Marxism is not a Baedeker of history, but a signpost pointing the direction in which history moves forward." Preface to *Studies in European Realism*, pp. 2–4. It is precisely this version of Marxism that the "American" satirizes: "The good old uncle! I mean our good old aunt! That dear damn nice old bearded lady who's foreseen everything." *The Palace*, p. 155. Brecht also criticized this aspect of Lukács's Marxism by claiming that he and his colleagues in Moscow, because they acted as if they knew the laws of history and thus were able to determine the "true representation" of the real, were against "production:" "They are to put it bluntly enemies of production. Production makes them uncomfortable. You never know where you are with production; production is the unforeseeable. You never know what's going to come out." "Introduction to Brecht on Lukács," *New Left Review*, no. 84 (March–April, 1974), p. 36.

40. The different figures constituting the narrator's memory represent different political positions: Naive, liberal humanism ("the student"), anarchism ("the Rifle"), bureaucratic Communism ("the schoolmaster"), and cynical, left-wing adventurism (the "American").

41. This would be a perfect example of naturalism for Lukács, of a subjective and arbitrary reflection of reality. "On the other hand, the artistic truth of a detail which corresponds photographically to life is purely accidental, arbitrary and subjective...It is therefore entirely possible that a collage of photographic material provide an incorrect, subjective and arbitrary reflection of reality." To avoid naturalism and "discipline accident...the detail must be so selected and so depicted from the outset that its relationship with the totality may be organic and dynamic." *Writer and Critic*, p. 43. What is missing from *The Palace* is the assumption of a *Historical Subject* that would guarantee the "correctness" of the totality.

42. "What man has become here is such that it can be revealed in an art which conforms

to, is modeled after cinematographic art, which consists in the exhibition of what is as image. The nature of the photographic instrument is such ... that a man in the world (appears) as pure vision fascinated by images ... Our sight has become *aesthetic* ... Industrialized society is the director of the real, organizing every situation in the form of a spectacle ... Everyone finds himself in his own life mediated-alienated by representation" (Deguy, pp. 1015, 1017).

43. Benjamin's analysis of photography as a model for art is of course contained in his essay "The Work of Art in the Age of Mechanical Reproduction," translated by Harry Zohn in *Illuminations* (New York: Schocken, 1969). Benjamin argues: "The uniqueness of a work of art is inseparable from its being imbedded in the fabric of tradition ... In other words, the unique value of the 'authentic' work of art has its basis in ritual, the location of its original use value. This ritualistic basis, however remote, is still recognizable as secularized ritual even in the most profane forms of the cult of beauty ... An analysis of art in the age of mechanical reproduction must do justice to these relationships, for they lead us to an all-important insight: for the first time in world history, mechanical reproduction emancipates the work of art from its parasitical dependence on ritual. To an even greater degree the work of art reproduced becomes the work of art designed for reproductibility. From a photographic negative, for example, one can make any number of prints; to ask for the 'authentic' print makes no sense. But the instant the criterion of authenticity ceases to be applicable to artistic production, the total function of art is reversed. Instead of being based on ritual, it begins to be based on another practice—politics" (pp. 223-24). I would argue following Benjamin that the fact that historical/fictive representations are also in this sense never "original" or "authentic" does not remove them from history and politics but on the contrary inserts them completely within the conflictual realm of ideology.

44. See chapter 6 for a further analysis of "photography" in Simon and its implications in his fiction.

45. Lukács repeatedly criticizes Zola and all other "naturalist" writers for presenting an arbitrary, "photographic" view of reality and thus failing to overcome dialectically their limited, subjective view for a true, objective view.

## Chapter Five

1. In terms of the reformulation of history currently being undertaken in France in connection with the Annales School, see the three-volume *Faire de l'Histoire* (Paris: Gallimard, 1974), eds., Jacques Le Goff and Pierre Nora, as well as the work of Michel de Certeau, esp. *L'Ecriture de l'histoire* (Paris: Gallimard, 1975). For an analysis of the relationship between history and literature in the eighteenth and nineteenth centuries, to which my own work is indebted, see the work of Lionel Gossman, especially "Voltaire's *Charles XII:* History into Art," *Studies in Voltaire and the Eighteenth Century* 25 (1963); *Augustin Thierry and Liberal Historiography* (Middletown: Wesleyan University Press, 1976); and "History and Literature: Reproduction or Signification," in *The Writing of History: Literary Form and Historical Understanding,* edited by Robert H. Canary and Henry Kozicki (Madison: University of Wisconsin Press, 1978). See also *Yale French Studies,* no. 59 (1980), entitled "Rethinking History: Time, Myth, and Writing."

2. The position of direct opposition to the subject which Foucault has articulated throughout his work is ultimately a reaffirmation of the subject in its "archeological form." See my analysis of the limitations of Foucault's position on the subject (especially as it is formulated in *The Order of Things*), entitled "The Subject of Archeology or the Sovereignty of the Epistémè," *Modern Language Notes* 93, no. 4 (1978).

3. Along with *commentary* and the *principle of the author* Foucault considers the division of the discursive field into fixed disciplines to be one of the "principles of limitation" of discourse. *The Discourse on Language,* p. 222.

4. This is basically the position of Jean Ricardou in his influential essay on *The Flanders Road,* entitled "Un Ordre dans la Débâcle" ("An Order in the Debacle"), in *Problèmes du Nouveau Roman* (Paris: Seuil, 1967). Ricardou, like other structuralist-formalist critics,

argues that there is a fundamental and totalized order underlying all disorder: the structure or order of language, what Ricardou calls here "the undersides of a language" (p. 52). In terms of this structural order, history, reality, meaning, etc. are all illusions or secondary effects—it alone is determining, the "true order."

5. Serge Doubrovsky, "Notes sur la Genèse d'une Ecriture, in *Entretiens*, no. 31, p. 54. Here Doubrovsky uses the term *fiction* to refer to what Benveniste calls *histoire*. See chapter I for a discussion of this problem. After criticizing the "order of language" or the "scripturalism" defended by Ricardou, Doubrovsky claims that there is, however, one element of language which escapes from the general debacle: the word. "Contrary to what Ricardou says concerning this point, the word in Simon's work is respected; it escapes from the debacle" (p. 56). Without realizing it, in defending the integrity of the word, Doubrovsky is reintroducing in his own turn an order of language based on such integrity (of the word and of meaning). Here Ricardou is closer to Simon's text than Doubrovsky, even if the disintegration of the word for Ricardou is only part of a process of destruction/reconstruction which will reveal a more fundamental level on which the order of language does effectively work. As Ricardou argues: "The word, which is primarily the indivisible atom of the organism of language, bursts into pieces here in a very overt way through a very curious use of puns"— Postface, *La Routes des Flandres* (Paris: 1018), p. 285. The debate between Doubrovsky and Ricardou is in fact really over what level to locate the order of language: on the level of meaning (Doubrovsky) or structure (Ricardou), of signified or signifier.

6. Hayden White in *Metahistory* (Baltimore: The Johns Hopkins University Press, 1974) argues that all historical discourse is ultimately (metahistorically) ordered in terms of four dominant tropes: metaphor, metonymy, synecdoche, and irony. No matter how interesting and necessary White's critique of the limitations and naiveté of traditional historiography is, his alternative, a rigid formalist system of tropes, establishes an order just as naive and restrictive as the historical orders he criticizes. See my analysis of *Metahistory* called "On Tropology: The Forms of History," in *Diacritics* 6, no. 3 (1976). See also Roland Barthes's short essay "Le Discours de l'histoire," *Information sur les Sciences Humaines* 4, no. 4 (1967), translated in Michael Lane, *Introduction to Structuralism* (New York: Basic Books, 1970). In this essay Barthes attempts to analyze and classify historical narrative according to "purely linguistic" categories. Barthes's goal, like White's, is to refute the claim that history and fiction are *by nature* opposed. As in the case of White, it is the assumptions behind the linguistic categories Barthes uses (the binary opposition between metaphor and metonymy being the central one) and the linguistic order they imply which raise problems, not the critique of traditional history per se.

7. Doubrovsky and Ricardou agree on this general point. Doubrovsky states: "The basic situation, the fundamental dilemma of Simon's work is formulated well before *The Flanders Road:* to reconcile, to connect an *order* and a *disorder,* the irremediable disorder of lived experience and the artificial order of language." "Notes," p. 52. Ricardou's formulation of basically the same problem is the following: "in the midst of extreme disorder, a new order is established ... From this perspective, dechronology plays a central role. Freed from pure, chronological succession which would have linked them together by only one of their sides, events are brought together in all ways possible, brought into each other's presence in terms of a kind of eternal present, where chronological order gives way to a *morphological order*" (*Problèmes du Nouveau Roman,* p. 50). Simon himself sees the problem in exactly the same way. "In what order shall I say all these things that in reality are simultaneous and don't have any order?" In Bettina Knapp, "Interview avec Claude Simon," *Kentucky Romance Quarterly* 16, no. 3 (1969): 185.

8. See Léon S. Roudiez, "La Critique pour ou Contre le texte," *Claude Simon: Colloque de Cerisy,* for a critique of Doubrovsky's use of the opposition insomuch as it implies an individual subject who suffers the "tragic" consequences of not being able to overcome disorder—especially pp. 40–44.

9. It is difficult to see how Doubrovsky can argue the contrary, that the photograph and the portrait (like the word) are in Simon's novels the "ultimate elements" of the real. "Notes,"

p. 56. They are in fact as divided or fragmented by the contradictions of history and discourse as everything else. They can in no sense, therefore, be considered "ultimate" or original.

10. Lucien Dällenbach, in "Mise en abyme et redoublement spéculaire chez Claude Simon," *Claude Simon: Colloque de Cerisy*, is right to compare the *condensation* of the ancestor and de Reixach to the Galton composite portraits discussed by Freud in *The Interpretation of Dreams*. "What it [the novel] wants to do here, like Galton, is to make the parts of one ancestor or another indiscernable so that de Reixach himself, after having undergone the same treatment, can be *superimposed* in turn onto his ancestors" (p. 159).

11. See also *The Grass* for the continual and repetitive conflict between the land and the word within the family history, a conflict inherent in its structure and in the social order it supports. This is another example of how history is never simply evolutionary, the past never simply transcended.

12. As I have argued in chapter 1, to characterize the narrator as a *shifter*, thus emphasizing his function—or place—in the narration, is not necessarily to avoid all implications of the subject. Shifters are supposedly indications of the "present" of discourse, of *the moment* of narration; but since the moment of narration is never simple in *The Flanders Road*, never totally or simply *present*, the category of the shifter is not completely pertinent. The narrator (the narrative function as well) is no "anchor" but is dispersed or adrift in the text; narrative voice is plural and conflictual rather than singular.

13. See *Of Grammatology*, translated by Gayatri Spivak (Baltimore: Johns Hopkins University Press, 1974), for Jacques Derrida's analysis of Rousseau's place in the theological-metaphysical tradition of the book, as well as Derrida's deconstruction of this tradition in terms of a concept of writing different from that proposed by the tradition. Chapter 1 of *Of Grammatology* is entitled "The End of the Book and the Beginning of Writing." For Derrida, structuralism is not outside this tradition but is rooted in it.

14. This position recalls that of Jean-Paul Sartre, when in an interview in *Le Monde* (18 April 1964) he said of his own novel, "Confronted with a dying child, *Nausea* has no importance"—a statement that was taken as a total condemnation of all literature which was not directly "engagé." See Simon's reply to Sartre, "Pour qui écrit Sartre?" *L'Express*, no. 675 (28 May 1964).

### Chapter Six

1. Probably no philosopher was more critical of reductionary "historical thinking" than Maurice Merleau-Ponty. In part the idea for this chapter grew out of a rereading of his "Indirect Language and the Voices of Silence," in *Signs*, translated by Richard C. McCleary (Evanston: Northwestern University Press, 1964). What Merleau-Ponty wrote about the "theological" aspects of much of the historical thinking of his day certainly still holds true today: "Whether it be to worship it or to hate it, we conceive of history and the historical dialectic today as an external Power ... For the sake of that future [assumed to be the end of the historical process], we are asked to renounce all judgment upon the means of attaining it ... This history-idol secularizes a rudimentary conception of God, and it is not by accident that contemporary discussions return so willingly to a parallel between what is called the 'horizontal transcendence' of history and the 'vertical transcendence' of God" (p. 70). Merleau-Ponty's interest in the work of Claude Simon is well known: see especially "Cinq Notes sur Claude Simon," *Médiations*, Winter, 1961–62, reprinted in *Entretiens*, no. 31.

2. Fredric Jameson's critique of formalism and structuralism takes its title from this Nietzschean metaphor: *The Prison-House of Language: a Critical Account of Structuralism and Russian Formalism* (Princeton: Princeton University Press, 1972). As we shall see, "prison-houses" take on many forms; for Lévi-Strauss it is the Cogito that is the prison: "Sartre in fact becomes prisoner of his Cogito: the Cogito of Descartes made it possible to attain universality, but on the condition of remaining psychological and individual; by sociologizing the Cogito, Sartre merely exchanges one prison for another." "History and Dialectic," in *The Savage Mind* (Chicago: University of Chicago Press, 1966), p. 249. The real problem, as we shall see, is to uncover and undermine the premises and processes behind

the formulation of the various forms of "prison-houses" and not just to exchange one form for another.

3. "And indeed what can one make of peoples 'without history' when man has been defined in terms of the dialectic and the dialectic in terms of history?" (p. 248). "By reducing the latter [all cultural others] to the state of means, barely sufficient to satisfy its philosophical appetite, historical reason indulges in a kind of intellectual cannibalism which is much more revolting to the anthropologist than the other kind" (p. 258).

4. See Jacques Derrida's deconstruction of the logocentric, metaphysical enclosure of which Lévi-Strauss's concept of "Man" is equally supportive: "The Violence of the Letter: From Lévi-Strauss to Rousseau," in *Of Grammatology*, pp. 101–40.

5. For the common "origin" of time and space and their complicity, see Jacques Derrida, "Ousia et Grammē," in *Marges de la philosophie*, pp. 31–78. *Différance, trace, espacement*, and the other strategic "concepts" Derrida uses to undermine the synchronic/diachronic opposition at the heart of metaphysics cannot be thought uniquely or ultimately in terms of either time or space: "differance, as it is written here, is no more static than genetic, nor more structural than historical. Nor is it any less so. And it is not to read, and especially not to read what here does not obey the ethic of orthography, to want to object to it on the basis of the oldest of metaphysical oppositions—for example, by opposing some generative point of view to a structuralist-taxonomic point of view, or conversely. As for differance, these oppositions don't pertain to it in the least; and this, no doubt, is what makes thinking about it uncomfortable and uncertain." "Differance," in *Speech and Phenomena and Other Essays on Husserl's Theory of Signs*, p. 142.

6. Roland Barthes, "Introduction à l'analyse structurale des récits," *Communications*, no. 8 (1966); translated in *New Literary History* 6, no. 2 (1975): pp. 251–52. See also Barthes's "Historical Discourse," in *Introduction to Structuralism*, edited by Michael Lane.

7. Sylvère Lotringer, in "Le Dernier Mot de Saussure," *L'Arc*, no. 54 (issue devoted to Derrida), pp. 71–80, analyzes the hesitancy of Saussure to make the "word" the basic unity of language and the necessity that he do so in order to affirm that language constitutes a closed system. "He chooses then in this instance the approximation, that he himself has admitted is imperfect, in order to root the elusive entity in the sensible presence of a material signifier that is equally irreducible to conceptualization" (p. 73).

8. "Réponses de Claude Simon à quelques questions écrites de Ludovic Janvier," *Entretiens*, no. 31, p. 23. Other recent instances in which Simon has expressed his theoretical position on the questions of diachrony and synchrony are the following, to be referred to in the text: "La Fiction mot à mot," *Nouveau Roman: hier, aujourd'hui*, 2 (Paris: 1018, 1972), pp. 73–97; Bettina L. Knapp, "Interview avec Claude Simon," *Kentucky Romance Quarterly* 16, no. 3 (1969): 179–90; Claude Du Verlie, "Interview with Claude Simon," *Sub-Stance*, no. 8 (Winter, 1974), pp. 3–20; "Claude Simon, à la question," *Claude Simon: Colloque de Cerisy* pp. 403–31.

9. Michel Deguy, "Claude Simon et la Représentation." "But vision itself has lost its measure, the sense of its own measure, and never can the *visible* fill it. It is an insatiable vision that has lost the world and desires to be crushed by it but is unable to fix itself there, deprived of the invisible where it could anchor itself, vision without pause because without pose, for everything is spread out in the unfathomable, conflictual multiplicity of the appearance" (p. 1010). See chapter 4 for a discussion of other aspects of the problems of perception and representation in Simon's novels (especially in *The Palace*).

10. Thus, given his spatial, structural definition of the novel, Simon is able to draw sketches of his novels which account for their formal unity and thus their "essential" formal characteristics. See *Nouveau Roman: hier, aujourd'hui*, 2:89, 93–96. For Simon equivalences between text and painting do exist: "Concerning *The Flanders Road*, I would say to you that I was literally astounded when I saw at Amsterdam, on the occasion of an important exhibition of the work of Dubuffet, the series of paintings called "Roads and Paths," which gave *the exact pictorial equivalence of what I had tried to do with words*" ("Claude Simon à la question," pp. 410–11; my emphasis).

11. Michel Serres, in his *Esthétiques sur Carpaccio* (Paris: Editions Hermann, 1975), argues for the complexity of space which is complicit with neither "the pathetic linearity of discourse" (p. 83) nor the closed, hierarchical structure of sense. "Space is strung together with voyages from space to space. They thought they had found the concept [for the totality of space], those who made one of the spaces, the space of all spaces, who acclimatized the inevitable contradiction of the enterprise by integrating it into their own logos. The truth, resonating here, is that there is no dominant space" (p. 98).

12. Sylvère Lotringer calls attention to the moment when Saussure in his analysis of the structural aspects of language uses the metaphor of the home, which Lotringer argues is an assertion of property, of the *sens propre*, of the identity of the self to itself: "Upsetting the most severe of his proscriptions, the linguist uses a metaphor...a privileged figure, a metaphor of metaphor—that of the residence: 'The word is like a house whose interior arrangement and function have been changed several times. Objective analysis totalizes and superimposes these successive distributions, but for those who live in the house there is always only one' (*Course in General Linguistics*, pp. 183–84). The word, in the metaphor, is diverted from its proper sense and assigned a residence different from its own but which it nevertheless appropriates for itself, recapturing itself in itself outside of itself (cf. *Marges de la philosophie*, p. 302). The Saussurian metaphor is, more simply, the celebration of the circumference *(du tour)*; the property is kept intact irrespective of exterior attacks against its inner resource." "Le Dernier Mot de Saussure," p. 74).

13. Gregory Bateson defines noise as "everything that is neither information nor redundancy, nor form, nor constraint...the only possible source for new patterns." Henri Atlan, elaborating Bateson's definition, argues that noise consists of "all aleatory, parasitical phenomena which disturb the correct transmission of messages and which one usually tries to eliminate as much as possible. As we shall see, there are cases where, in spite of a paradox which is only apparent, a 'beneficial' role can be recognized for it." "Du Bruit comme principe d'auto-organisation," *Communications*, no. 18 (1972), p. 21. Anthony Wilden, in "Order from Disorder: Noise, Trace, and Event in Evolution and in History," connects Derrida's concepts of *trace* and *differance* to that of noise: "What breaks this circuit in nature, whether at the level of the genetic code or at higher levels...is not so much the 'internal contradiction' alone in the classically bioenergetic, materialist sense, but rather random variation or noise. Noise triggers and escalates pre-existing 'oscillatory' or 'contradictory' potentialities"—*System and Structure: Essays in Communication and Exchange* (London: Tavistock, 1972), p. 400.

14. This model is certainly used by Saussure (*Course*, pp. 11–12) and by Roman Jakobson and it has as its goal the elimination of all noise through the institution of a closed system of sense.

15. Michel Serres also proposes another use of the dictionary than the imposition of a final sense: "The basic condition for reading, or the contract tacitly agreed to in the writing of any sentence, is that *there exists a biunivocal relation between the symbol and its sense* ...The dominant method of deciphering assumes this simple relation. But it is not necessary to travel very far to see it evaporate: it suffices to open any dictionary. Through the expansion of relations, the elementary condition of writing or reading disappears, everything appears to disseminate. Meaning explodes into divergent lines." *Esthétiques sur Carpaccio*, p. 120.

16. The repetition of fragments of the newspaper headline of a woman's suicide, "She Throws Herself from the Fourth-Floor Window," is the constant reminder of what has been repressed—everything that cannot be remembered without cost to the integrity of the family.

17. In the sense that Derrida argues that differences are historical: "If the word 'history' did not carry with it the motif of a final repression of difference, one could say that only differences could be from the beginning and throughout 'historical.'" "Differance," p. 141.

## Chapter Seven

1. In an interview with Claude Duverlie, Claude Simon indicates what for him links together certain painters he admires (Miro, Dubuffet, Novelli, and especially Rauschenberg),

whose work serves as a kind of model for his own program of (bri)collage: "What strikes me in their work is the common desire to return to the source, to the basic, to the concrete... Or Rauschenberg, who seeks no longer to 'copy' or to 'reproduce' an object (preferably scrap) but to integrate it indirectly in the composition. Not the deceptiveness of *trompe l'oeil* but collages and constructions—the concrete, *the work of art which exists only to show its constituent parts.*" "The Crossing of the Image," *Diacritics*, December 1977, p. 48; my emphasis.

2. The formalism in question in this chapter is predominantly the mechanistic, (post) structuralist, linguistically based formalism dominant in France today. And yet I would argue that my analysis and critique also apply to the less mechanistic strategy but equally formalist and "absolutist" theory of the so-called "Yale School" of deconstruction. The ends and effects of the two kinds of formalisms are practically identical—each could be said to constitute in its own right an ultratextualism. The goal in each case is to argue for a concept of the text as a closed, autonomous, self-generating, self-conscious (and self-deconstructive) entity, origin and end of itself: in other words, the text as an *Absolute Subject.*

3. "There still exists in our civilization an activity which on the technical plane allows us to conceive fairly well what on the speculative plane could be a science that we prefer to call 'primary' rather than primitive: this activity is commonly designated by the term 'bricolage'" (*The Savage Mind*, p. 16; translation modified).

4. Where Lévi-Strauss himself places literature is a more difficult question. In *The Savage Mind* he places art "half-way between scientific knowledge and mythical or magical thought. It is common knowledge that the artist is both something of a scientist and of a *bricoleur.* By his craftsmanship he constructs a material object which is also an object of knowledge" (p. 22). In an interview with Georges Charbonnier he speaks of the poet in much the same terms as he speaks of the abstract artist, for whom the work on the matter of their art is their art. "The poet stands in the same relation to language as the painter to the object. Language is his raw material and it is this raw material that he sets out to signify—not exactly the ideas or concepts that we may try to transmit in speech, but those more massive linguistic objects that are constituted by pieces or units of discourse" (pp. 110–11). Abstract art is for him "a system of signs, a system which has an intentionally arbitrary relationship with the object" (p. 115). *Conservations with Claude Lévi-Strauss*, edited by G. Charbonnier (London: Jonathan Cape, 1969).

5. This is hardly a new idea or one specific to structuralism, for the thesis that art is essentially *technique* has a history as long as philosophy itself and should be traced at least back to Plato and Aristotle. If structuralism has a specific or new role to play within this history, it is not in its emphasis on technique itself but rather in what, if anything, makes the structuralist definition of technique different from previous definitions.

6. Lévi-Strauss's approach to the study of myth implies that what myths are really about is themselves, how they operate. Fredric Jameson is right to argue then in *The Prison-House of Language* that "the 'content' is precisely the form itself, myths are *about* the mythological process, just like poems about poetry or novels about novelists [Jameson probably means to say novels about novels]. Only in this way can Lévi-Strauss avoid introducing extraneous content, a foreign body of imported and external 'meaning' into these pure relational equations which are his structural analyses of myths: only thus can he avoid interpreting, but the way he does so ultimately has the result of turning the form of Structuralism (the linguistic model) into a new type of content (language as the ultimate signified)" (p. 198). The lack of explicit self-consciousness on the part of the myth is ultimately not important if its essence *is* the way it functions—in fact, in later works, Lévi-Strauss will interpret myths that are explicitly self-reflexive.

7. Roland Barthes, in "The Structuralist Activity," announces the structuralist program, which is, as we shall see, exactly that of recent fiction. "The goal of all structuralist activity, whether reflexive or poetic, is to reconstruct an 'object' in such a way as to manifest thereby the rules of functioning (the 'functions') of this object. Structure is therefore actually a *simulacrum* of the object, but a directed, interested simulacrum, since the imitated object makes something appear which remains invisible or, if you prefer, unintelligible in the natural object" (pp. 214–15).

8. Lévi-Strauss also seems to indicate this when he talks about the representational or figurative effects of "non-figurative" painting: "Non-representational painting adopts 'styles' as 'subjects.' It claims to give a concrete representation of the formal conditions, of all painting. Paradoxically the result is that non-representational painting does not, as it thinks, create works which are as real as, if not more real than, the objects of the physical world, but rather realistic imitations of non-existent models. It is a school of academic painting in which each artist strives to represent the manner in which he would execute his paintings if by chance he were to paint any" (*The Savage Mind*, pp. 29-30).

9. For Lévi-Strauss, as for the structuralist critics of the New Novel, the work of art (the text) remains a form of knowledge, even if more and more this knowledge is claimed to be only the knowledge of self—in making manifest or visible this "knowledge" the work of art and the text remain fundamentally mimetic. "Insofar as the work of art is a sign of the object and not a literary reproduction, it reveals something that was not immediately present in our perception of the object, and that is its structure" (*Conversations*, p. 89).

10. Ricardou was a member of the editorial staff of *Tel Quel* during its most important periods—i.e. before its "Maoist," and now religious, "New Philosophy" periods. Since leaving *Tel Quel*, he has had a major role in the planning and running of the various colloquia at Cerisy on the New Novel (published by 1018). The publication of these colloquia reflect the status given to his position, his person, and his image—invariably photographs of him will appear on the cover or in the volumes.

11. Lévi-Strauss also claims that there are two positions that threaten art: art becoming pure signifier or pure signified. "The great danger threatening art seems to me to be twofold. First, instead of being a language, it may become a pseudo-language, a caricature of language, a sham, a kind of childish game on the theme of language, which does not succeed in achieving signification. Secondly, it may become a total language, of the same type as articulated language except for the material it uses, and in this case, it may in all probability signify, but it cannot at the same time be accompanied by any real aesthetic emotion." *Conversations*, pp. 122-23.

12. See Ricardou's discussion of the *mise en abyme* in *Le Nouveau Roman*, pp. 47-75. See also Lucien Dällenbach, *Le Récit spéculaire* (Paris: Seuil, 1977). Dällenbach describes in his book the various forms of the *mise en abyme*, but for him they all have one function: to affirm the fundamental "literariness" of literature. "Insomuch as it is a *second-level* sign, the *mise en abyme* does not only highlight the signifying intentions of the *first-level* sign (the *récit* that contains it), but it also manifests that the *récit* itself is also (only) a sign and proclaims the following of any trope whatsoever...: '*I am literature, I and the récit that frames me*'" (pp. 78-79; Dällenbach's emphasis). As we shall also see in the case of Ricardou, the *mise en abyme* is the technique which supposedly guarantees that the *récit* is speaking for itself as an "I" and demonstrates time and time again that the *récit* is only language. It is the technique that constitutes the *récit* as *a subject* in its own right. Is it any different for Paul de Man, who argues: "The self-reflecting mirror-effect by means of which a work of fiction asserts, by its very existence, its separation from empirical reality, its divergence, as a sign, from a meaning that depends for its existence on the constitutive activity of this sign, characterizes the work of literature in its essense." "Criticism and Crisis," in *Blindness and Insight*, p. 17.

13. Dällenbach refers to the "victory of language" just as Ricardou will speak of the "battle of the sentence" *(la bataille de la phrase)*: "This victory of language, we know that it was not only announced but also prepared from the beginning by the *mise en abyme*. To the extent that the *mise en abyme* never ceased short-circuiting the representational function and showing that the text does not emanate from an author through expressive means, it freed the novel from every exterior attachment." *Le Récit spéculaire*, p. 187. In a similar vein, Geoffrey Hartman describes "the force of literature" as the "priority of language to meaning," the "excess [of figurative language] over any assigned meaning," the "strength of the signifier vis-à-vis a signified (the 'meaning') that tries to enclose it" (*Deconstruction and Criticism* [New York: Seabury Press, 1979], p. vii). (Hartman claims in fact that all

those contributing to this volume share with him this position—a highly questionable statement when it comes to Derrida at least.) Once the formalist, theoretical machinery underlying the concept of the *mise en abyme* is in place, the "victory of language," of the text, is assured before the "battle" of interpretation or reading even begins.

14. Lacoue-Labarthe and Nancy, in *L'Absolu littéraire*, argue that the project of "literary absolutism" is not original to the contemporary period, but that it has a history that can be traced back at least to German Romanticism—which they call not only "our birthplace" (p. 17) but also "our naiveté" (p. 27). "The absolute of literature is not so much poetry ... as *poiesie* ... that is to say, production ... Romantic poetry was understood as penetrating the essence of poetry, the literary object producing in it the truth of production in itself and thus ... of the production *of self*, of the autopoïsie. And if it is true ... that autoproduction forms the ultimate instance and the closure of the speculative absolute, it is necessary to recognize in Romantic thought not only the absolute of literature, but literature as the absolute. Romanticism is the inauguration of the *literary absolute*" (p. 21). Lacoue-Labarthe and Nancy argue further that this is a form of "speculative idealism," if this means "the possibility of the autorecognition of the Idea as the proper form of the subject" (p. 47).

15. J. Hillis Miller's definition of the text is very close to Ricardou's in such statements as the following: "Deconstruction is not a dismantling of the structure of the text but a demonstration that it already has dismantled itself. It's apparent solid ground is no rock but thin air." "Steven's Rock and Criticism as Cure," *Georgia Review* 30, no. 2 (1976): 341. For Miller the text is nothing and rests on nothing—nothing but his version of the process of (self-)deconstruction, that is. This is not nihilism, as some have argued, but metaphysics. The privileging of one set of operations, either self-engenderment or self-deconstruction, indicates that in each case *an essence* is being assigned to literature.

16. Namely, *The Battle of Pharsalus*, translated by Richard Howard (New York: George Braziller, 1971); *Conducting Bodies*, translated by Helen R. Lane (New York: Viking Press 1974); *Triptych*, translated by Helen R. Lane (New York: Viking Press, 1976); and *Leçon de choses* (Paris: Minuit, 1975), not yet translated.

17. "Réponse de Claude Simon à quelques questions écrites de Ludovic Janvier," *Entretiens*, no. 31, p. 28.

18. "L'Opinion des Nouveaux Romanciers," *La Quinzaine Littéraire*, no. 121 (1–15 July 1971), p. 10.

19. For fiction "to be even more what it already is" is a formula that is often repeated in some form or another by critics (and by Simon himself) following Ricardou's lead—however, the contradiction at the heart of such a formula is totally ignored by the critics using it. For example, Tom Bishop argues: "The works of Claude Simon are made as he writes them, and *Conducting Bodies* even more than the others." "L'Image de la création chez Claude Simon," *Nouveau Roman: Hier, Aujourd'hui*, 2: 71.

20. "Interview avec Claude Simon," *Kentucky Romance Quarterly*, no. 2 (1970), p. 189.

21. The epigraph is the following:
> ACHILLE IMMOBILE A GRANDS PAS
> Zénon! Cruel Zénon! Zénon d'Elée!
> M'as-tu percé de cette flèche ailée
> Qui vibre, vole, et qui ne vole pas!
> Le son m'enfante et la flèche me tue!
> Ah! le soleil ... Quelle ombre de torture
> Pour l'âme, Achille immobile à grands pas!
> Paul Valéry

22. This is precisely the "contradictory coherence" Derrida finds in the classical concept of structure: "Thus it has always been thought that the center, which is by definition unique, constituted that very thing within a structure which while governing the structure, escapes structurality. This is why classical thought concerning structure could say that the center is, paradoxically, *within* the structure and *outside* it. The center is at the center of the totality, and yet, since the center does not belong to the totality (is not part of the totality), the

totality *has its center elsewhere.* The center is not the center. The concept of centered struc-ture—although it represents coherence itself, the condition of the *epistēmē*—as philosophy or science—is contradictorily coherent" ("Structure, Sign and Play," in *Writing and Differ-ence*, p. 279).

23. Ricardou argues: "The epigraph from Valéry is generative because the first paragraph of the book in a certain way reflects back on it; the word *jaune* [yellow] is because it is many times repeated as such, as synonym or anagram, by the passages it authorizes" (Pour une théorie du Nouveau Roman, p. 146).

24. The apparent circularity of the novel, which will be discussed shortly, is modeled after the circularity of the sun and is also to be found in *Le Cimetière marin* of Valéry: "just like *Le Cimetière marin, The Battle of Pharsalus* repeats, in its last lines, its inaugural lines" (Ricardou, *Pour Une Théorie*, p. 153).

25. See Jacques Derrida, "La Mythologie blanche," in *Marges*—translated by F. C. T. Moore, *New Literary History* 6, no. 1 (1974)—for a study of the "use" or *usure* (wearing away) of metaphor in philosophical (and literary) texts: "And first of all we shall be inter-ested in a certain wearing away *(usure)* of metaphorical force in philosophical intercourse. Wear does not happen to a tropic energy otherwise destined to remain intact: on the con-trary it constitutes the very history of the structure of the philosophical metaphor" (p. 6; translation modified).

26. Claudia Hoffer Gosselin, in her article "Voices of the Past in Claude Simon's *La Bataille de Pharsale*," criticizes Ricardou's concept of intertextuality for being reductionary in terms similar to the ones I am using here: "If we unquestionably accept Ricardou's argu-ments, then, it is the language of one text that becomes the sole source of another text, its unique origin. In this case, intertextuality, rather than being used to assert the presence within and without the text of multiple generators, becomes the instrument of ideologies as reac-tionary as those attacked." *New York Literary Forum* 2, "Intertextuality" (1978), pp. 28–29. This is one of the very few studies to challenge Ricardou's ultra-formalist position on the New Novel in any serious way.

27. See Françoise Van Rossum-Guyon, "De Claude Simon à Proust: Un exemple d'inter-textualité," *Les Lettres Nouvelles*, September, 1972, pp. 107–33, for a close, textual analysis of these fragments from Proust in *La Bataille.* Her position is basically that of Ricardou, but she is just less dogmatic in the way she argues it.

28. Not only is this figure implied in Ricardou's emphasis on the operations or "machin-ery" of the text at the expense of all other elements, but he often refers to the text directly as a machine. For example: "In short, the *récit* resembles a machine, or a body." *Le Nouveau Roman*, p. 31. "Fiction is a machine whose function is to suppress the safeguards of estab-lished meaning." *Claude Simon: Colloque de Cerisy*, p. 38.

29. "In speaking of the feeling of failure that accompanies the completion of a work, I had in mind...that every time, one sees that one could have done better and that errors had been committed. For example, thanks to those committed in *Conducting Bodies*, I wrote *Triptych.* You ask if after my last novel the feeling of failure surfaced nevertheless. I shall answer you: no, at least not in the same way as after the other novels. That is to say that in the path I chose, I do not think that I could have done better. This does not mean, though, that I think that I wrote the perfect novel" (*Claude Simon: Colloque de Cerisy*, p. 424).

30. Ricardou, like Simon, feels that *Triptych* avoids the shortcomings of *Conducting Bodies:* "Indeed, in this novel breaks and connections are produced obeying the same rules as in *Conducting Bodies* ...Only this time the junctions of sequences, instead of tending towards a supersequence issued from a unitary theme, distribute three irremediably autono-mous and adversative sequences" (*Nouveaux Problèmes du Roman*, p. 232).

31. Simon describes the formal program for *Triptych* in terms of the reduction of all relations established in the novel to those determined by "language itself": "To accomplish this, it was necessary that among the three series no other relations be established than those correspondences or, if you prefer, those echoes, those interferences, those short-circuits,

those 'convocations' (more credible than the relations emerging from some psychological or sociological theory or system, which are always debatable) which permit (and even suggest) what we call 'figures,' by which, as Michel Deguy has said, 'language speaks before us.'" *Claude Simon: Colloque de Cerisy*, p. 425. One of the principal goals of my analysis is to challenge the assumption that formal, linguistic models, theories, or systems are any more "credible" than any others.

32. Lotringer argues convincingly that no construction of a puzzle (no *bricolage*) is ever entirely free or unmotivated. It is always determined by a series of choices and a logic which governs how the pieces fit together, for they are designed to fit together: "The selection of formative elements is not brought about by chance: it is their capacity to be grouped together in a unique configuration which motivates their choice. The process of homogenization is thus determined from the outset by the inventory of pieces in the storagehouse of the narrative. The field thus delineated and protected by *an exclusion* of every external interference, every insoluable contradiction, offers itself from then on to be classified." *Claude Simon: Colloque de Cerisy*, pp. 316–17.

33. M. M. Bakhtin (P. N. Medvedev), in *The Formal Method in Literary Scholarship*, translated by Albert Wehrle (Baltimore: Johns Hopkins University Press, 1978), criticizes the Russian Formalists for subordinating art "to one purpose which is best defined in the words of Shklovski: 'to make the construction of language perceptible ... the goal of its [artistic] creation is that it be seen'" (p. 89). Bakhtin (Medvedev) further argues—and his argument could easily be applied to the "ultratextualism" in question here—that "the orientation of the work towards perceptibility is the worst kind of psychologism, since it makes the psychophysiological process into something self-sufficient and empty of all content ... While ridiculing those who seek 'soul' and 'temperament' in the artistic work, the formalists search it for psychophysiological stimuli at the same time" (p. 150). Thus, by depending on a naive, unquestioned concept of visibility, the Russian Formalists according to Bakhtin (Medvedev), like their heritor, Ricardou, force the work into the narrow frame of a visible present: "The formalists in essence know only some 'permanent present,' some 'permanent contemporaneity' ... Everything that takes place in formalist literary history takes place in some eternal contemporaneity" (p. 171).

34. For an indispensable analysis of the problematic of the frame in the history of aesthetics, see Jacques Derrida, *La Vérité en peinture* (Paris: Flammarion, 1978). In his essay entitled "Parergon," Derrida analyzes how Kant attempted (and failed)—as do all philosophies of art and all aesthetic strategies—to put the whole question of art within a closed frame, to delimit the inside from the outside, the *para* from the *ergon*: "Every analytic of aesthetic judgment supposes up to the end that it is rigorously possible to distinguish between the intrinsic and the extrinsic. Aesthetic judgment *must* concern itself rightly with intrinsic beauty, not with ornaments and surroundings. It is necessary therefore to know—a fundamental presupposition, a presupposition of the fundamental—how to determine the intrinsic—the framed—and to know what is being excluded as frame *and* as outside-the-frame" (p. 74).

35. Simon beings his presentation for the colloquium on the New Novel at Cerisy with this quotation from Jacques Lacan: "The word is not only sign but knot of significations ... If I say the word curtain [*rideau*], for example, it is not only through convention to designate the use of an object which the different ways it is perceived can change in a thousand ways—that is, depending on whether it is perceived by the worker, the merchant, the painter, or the gestalt psychologist as work, exchange value, colored physionomy, or spatial structure. It is, through metaphor, a curtain of trees; through punning, the ripple and the reefs of water [*les rides et les ris de l'eau*] ... It is, through interjection, at the intermission of a play, the cry of my impatience or the word of my weariness. Curtain! *It is in short an image of sense as sense, which in order to become perceptible must unveil itself*" (*Nouveau Roman: hier et aujourd'hui*, p. 73; my emphasis).

36. I am indebted here to Dennis G. Sullivan's analysis of the problems of perception and form in Proust, entitled "On Vision in Proust: The Icon and the *Voyeur*," *Modern Language Notes* 84, no. 4 (1969): 646–61. Sullivan argues: "The hidden spectator, the solitary specta-

tor, will see the other as figure upon ground. The *voyeur* and the icon are inseparable. Proust juxtaposes them consistently throughout the novel as components of a unit which is imaginary. The *voyeur* is one moment of desire, that moment in which the object seems accessible. A subject defined by immediacy, meets an object transparent to his glance. The object is exterior to the subject, but not irretrievably so. For the object appears immutable; as an icon its existence is spatial and it manifests pure intelligibility" (p. 658).

37. Maurice Blanchot, in "La Voix narrative (le 'il,' le neutre)," *L'Entretien Infini*, discusses how the "impersonal novel" rests on the assumption that a neutral, disinterested, "aesthetic distance" can be established, and thus strives to make formalist voyeurs of us all: "The impersonality of the impersonal novel is that of aesthetic distance. The command is imperious: the novelist must not intervene ... Why? For two reasons which are different though often confused. The first: what is recounted has aesthetic value to the extent that the interest one has in it is an interest at a distance; disinterestedness—the essential category in the judgment of taste since Kant and even Aristotle—means that the aesthetic act should not be founded in any interest if it wants to produce one that is legitimate. Disinterested interest ... The ideal remains the representation of the classical theater: the narrator is there only for the raising of the curtain; the play is performed, at the bottom, from all eternity and as if without him; he does not recount, he shows, and the reader doesn't read, he looks, assisting, taking part without participating. The other reason is almost the same, although completely different: the author should not intervene because the novel is a work of art and the work of art exists all by itself, an unreal thing in the world and outside the world. It is necessary to let it be free, to suppress its stays, to cut it adrift, in order to maintain it in its status as an imaginary object" (p. 560). The new, aesthetic "impersonalism" proposed by Ricardou resembles point for point the "impersonalism" analyzed and criticized here by Blanchot (see also chapter 3).

38. Voyeurism in the novel is a masculine activity. From the boys' perspective (and in terms of their own self-interest), the most visible of all the elements of the lovemaking scene they spy on is the erect male penis. The visibility and thus the value they assign to all sexuality is measured against it. In fact, the measure of visibility in terms of elements which stand forth to be represented is never a neutral activity but always works in the interests of those (hidden outside the scene or "fully visible" within) who have visibility and representation on their side. The visible, no matter how it is defined, is never a neutral field.

39. Lotringer's telling critique of the kind of ultraformalist, technical, puzzle-solving approach best represented by Ricardou is itself unfortunately limited by his belief in a free, unformed *sujet-désirant* which for him, following Gilles Deleuze and Félix Guattari in *L'Anti-Oedipe* (Paris: Minuit, 1972), is original and constitutive: "the liberating-delirious [*déliante-délirante*] constituent intervention of the subject" (p. 325). In response to Lotringer's critique, Ricardou suggests that "there is in the discourse of Lotringer a sporadic depreciation of science that should be watched with great care" (p. 335). Lotringer's answer to Ricardou is again made in the name of a mystified view of madness: "that is why it is necessary that the science of the text (and besides this is true in your case) be doubled by a mad, delirious practice" (p. 336). The debate in these terms—one defending an original, unstructured subject, the other the structure of a linguistic science—is questionable, the alternatives presented not real alternatives at all.

40. The title of this section is an obvious reference to Paul de Man's *Blindness and Insight.* De Man's position, even though it is formulated in this collection for the most part in phenomenological terms, and even though it is infinitely more subtle in its argumentation and critical strategy than Ricardou's, is nevertheless in the end as formalist as Ricardou's position. It most definitely has the same ends: to make visible the text's consciousness or vision of itself, to ensure that the text be allowed to speak in "its own voice" without interference from other, "exterior voices"—in other words, to ensure that the "insights" of the text (its view of itself) will overcome the "blindness" of any theory that challenges or questions these "insights" or the notion of self-reflexivity in general. De Man's *Allegories of*

*Reading* (New Haven: Yale University Press, 1979) substitutes a "deconstructive" vocabulary and strategy for the earlier, phenomenological approach, but in privileging "figural language," it has the same ends as the earlier collection: it is still intent on safeguarding the integrity of the text, on closing it back in on itself and protecting it from all "exterior," non-literary relations and forces. Both Ricardou and de Man defend the integrity of the text as an autonomous, self-reflexive, "original" Subject; each in his own way claims to speak for/as this Subject. To transpose the title of Frank Lentricchia's chapter on de Man in *After the New Criticism,* this is the supreme authority they claim for their rhetoric and textual theories and strategies.

# INDEX